# Windows onto Jewish Legal Culture

## Fourteen Exploratory Essays



This book opens windows onto various aspects of Jewish legal culture. Rather than taking a structural approach, and attempting to circumscribe and define 'every' element of Jewish law, *Windows onto Jewish Legal Culture* takes a dynamic and holistic approach, describing diverse manifestations of Jewish legal culture, and its general mind-set, without seeking to fit them into a single structure.

Jewish legal culture spans two millennia, and evolved in geographic centers that were often very distant from one another both geographically and socio-culturally. It encompasses the Talmud and talmudic literature, the law codes, the rulings of rabbinical courts, the responsa literature, decisions taken by communal leaders, and study of the law in talmudic academies, the local study hall, and the home. But Jewish legal culture reaches well beyond legal and quasi-legal institutions; it addresses, and is reflected in, every aspect of daily life, from meals and attire to interpersonal and communal relations. *Windows onto Jewish Legal Culture* gives the reader a taste of the tremendous weight of Jewish legal culture within Jewish life.

Among the facets of Jewish legal culture explored are two of its most salient distinguishing features, namely, toleration and even encouragement of controversy, and a preference for formalistic formulations. These features are widely misunderstood, and Jewish legal culture is often parodied as hair-splitting argument for the sake of argument. In explaining the epistemic imperatives that motivate Jewish legal culture, however, this book paints a very different picture. Situational constraints and empirical considerations are shown to provide vital input into legal determinations at every level, and the legal process is revealed to be attentive to context and sensitive to cultural concerns.

The Institute of Jewish Law
Boston University School of Law
765 Commonwealth Avenue
Boston MA 02215

Publication No. 35

# Windows onto Jewish Legal Culture

## Fourteen Exploratory Essays

**Hanina Ben-Menahem**
**Arye Edrei**
**Neil S. Hecht**

Editors

# VOLUME ONE

Routledge
Taylor & Francis Group
LONDON AND NEW YORK

First published in paperback 2024

First published 2011
by Routledge
4 Park Square, Milton Park, Abingdon, Oxon OX14 4RN

and by Routledge
605 Third Avenue, New York, NY 10158

*Routledge is an imprint of the Taylor & Francis Group, an informa business*



Publisher's Note
The publisher has gone to great lengths to ensure the quality of this reprint but points out that some imperfections in the original copies may be apparent.

*British Library Cataloguing in Publication Data*
A catalogue record for this book is available from the British Library

*Library of Congress Cataloging in Publication Data*
A catalog record for this book has been requested

ISBN: 978-0-415-50049-4 (set)
ISBN: 978-0-415-35978-8 (hbk)
ISBN: 978-1-03-292202-7 (pbk)
ISBN: 978-0-203-00775-4 (ebk)

DOI:10.4324/9780203007754

Typeset in Palatino
by RefineCatch Limited, Bungay, Suffolk

For Elly Leary, Richard Pearlstone,
and the Pearlstone Foundation,
whose support made possible
the publication of these volumes

# Table of Contents

## VOLUME ONE

# VOLUME TWO

# Acknowledgments

Chapters 1, 2, 3, 6, 8, 10 and 13 are based on material first published in Hebrew by the Open University of Israel, in *Selected Topics in Jewish Law* (Hebrew), edited by Hanina Ben-Menahem. Chapters 2, 3, 6, 8, 10 and 13 were published in English, by the Open University of Israel and Boston University's Institute of Jewish Law, as *Selected Topics in Jewish Law*, edited by Hanina Ben-Menahem and Neil S. Hecht. They have been reworked for the present volume. An English version of chapter 1 originally appeared, under the title "Controversy in Jewish law: The Talmud's attitude to controversy," in Marcelo Dascal and Han-Liang Chang (eds.), *Traditions of Controversy* (Amsterdam: John Benjamins, 2007), 17–62; it is published here, with minor revisions, with the permission of the John Benjamins Publishing Company.

Chapters, 5, 7, 11, and 14 were first written in the framework of a project headed by Ben-Zion Eliash. They have been significantly elaborated on and extensively revised for the present volume by Arye Edrei. Chapters 4, 9, and 12 are newly written. The work was made possible by a generous grant from the Ritz Foundation. The editors are grateful to Benjamin Porat for his contribution to the editing of these chapters.

All the chapters in *Windows onto Jewish Legal Culture: Fourteen Exploratory Essays* have been edited for publication by Nessa Olshansky-Ashtar, and the editors wish to express their gratitude and appreciation for her painstaking work.

# Contributors

| | | |
|---|---|---|
| 1. | Controversy | Hanina Ben-Menahem |
| 2. | Legal formalism | Hanina Ben-Menahem |
| 3. | Exigency authority | Hanina Ben-Menahem |
| 4. | Erroneous rulings | Arye Edrei |
| 5. | Finality of judgment | Eliav Shochetman |
| 6. | Self-help | Shimshon Ettinger |
| 7. | Law of the pursuer | Arnold Enker |
| 8. | Equity | Hanina Ben-Menahem |
| 9. | Charity and distributive justice | Benjamin Porat |
| 10. | Euthanasia | Daniel Sinclair |
| 11. | Agency | Shimshon Ettinger |
| 12. | Employee and independent contractor | Berachyahu Lifshitz |
| 13. | Unjust enrichment | Itamar Warhaftig |
| 14. | Free market competition in Jewish law | Sinai Deutch |

# Note to the reader

The chapters of *Windows onto Jewish Legal Culture: Fourteen Exploratory Essays* are replete with references to halakhic authorities and their writings. Many of these authorities are customarily referred to by acronyms of their names (e.g., Rashi, the Hida) or of the titles of their best-known works (e.g., the Shela, the Shakh); or by the titles of these works themselves (the Tur, the Arukh Hashulhan). To assist the reader in identifying these individuals, a list of the rabbinical authorities cited or referred to is provided at the end of each volume, along with a brief bio-bibliographic description. The authorities and scholars are listed alphabetically by their first name in English; in some cases they are also listed by their acronym (Rashi, the Rabad) or other commonly-used appellation (Maimonides, Gerondi). When a book title is used to refer to an individual, it is not italicized.

In references to the Talmud, m, b, j, or t prefixed to the tractate name indicates whether the Mishnah, the Babylonian Talmud, Jerusalem Talmud, or Tosefta is being referred to.

# Introduction

This book is not an introduction to Jewish law. Rather, it takes the reader on a journey through largely unmarked territory, seeking to provide an idea of the complexity, multi-dimensionality, and unevenness of the area being explored. It assumes that the traveler has a general idea of the terrain she is exploring. It does not seek to present the 'received' view, that is, the generally accepted view, but rather to present an analysis of the subject from the author's perspective.

Accordingly, the target audience of this volume is made up of those to whom the basic elements of Jewish legal culture are somewhat familiar, for though the book does provide background information on the principal concepts and legal sources, it does not present a comprehensive overview of the structure, history, and sources of Jewish law.

The Jewish legal heritage, in the broad sense, is best thought of as a legal culture rather than a legal system. The term 'legal system' assumes an organized institutional hierarchical order, an order that can hardly be said to have existed throughout Jewish history. Jewish legal culture is generated by various constituencies, between which there is often tension: the rabbinical establishment; the teachers and students of the law at the rabbinical academies (*yeshivot*), where they study the canonical texts of Jewish law, engaging in debate and dialogue as questions arise; the lay leadership, which conducts the civic affairs of Jewish communities; members of the community, who, by adopting certain customs and comportments on their own, force the establishment to acknowledge these behaviors, either condoning them or seeking to repress them; and the Gentile societies within which Jews live. As to the latter, it is important to keep in mind that there has always been a certain trickle-down effect by which Gentile mores penetrated and were unconsciously absorbed by Jewish communities.

The term 'Jewish law,' the usual English epithet for halakha, covers legal arrangements in a wide range of geographic areas and historical eras, from biblical times to the present. Jewish law, the foundational texts of which are the Torah (the Pentateuch) and the Talmud, is a normative system regulating all aspects of daily life, private and public, including ritual, property, family, commercial, tort, and penal law. In the public domain, it encompasses the judiciary, communal regulations, taxation and constitutional law.

Since the destruction of the Second Temple almost 2,000 years ago, Jewish law has not been the positive law of any state, and its central institution, the Great Sanhedrin—the high court—has been defunct. Moreover, since that time, certain parts of Jewish law, especially those corresponding to modern criminal law, have not been in force. A tension between this anomalous reality and the ideal of a sovereign Jewish regime in its own territory with its own institutions, reflected in the frequently-encountered term "in our day," which connotes the inferiority of our times, pervades Jewish law.

Although some segments of the halakha are valid only in the land of Israel, the jurisdiction of Jewish law is personal, not territorial, and applies to Jews everywhere.

The role of Jewish legal culture in post-biblical Jewish civilization cannot be overestimated. The law is not only the force that held Jews together, both in the land of Israel and throughout the Diaspora, but its study and interpretation are also the primary focus of Jewish intellectual endeavor, by far overshadowing philosophy, homiletics and Kabbala. Study of the law is a paramount religious duty, to be carried out daily by laymen as well as scholars. Social and personal success are measured by achievement in studying the law. Furthermore, students are encouraged to speak their mind, even if their opinions diverge from the received view, empowering individuals to participate in the evolution of the law. Though limited to those actually engaged in Torah study, this participation has a ripple effect, generating a sense in the community that the law, being an ongoing enterprise rather than dictated from above, is democratic, so to speak. Another element that reflects the participatory dimension of Jewish legal culture is the cardinal, all-embracing decision-making principle that the law is decided in accordance with the majority view.

The formative era of Jewish law is the talmudic period, during which the foundational texts of Jewish law–the Mishnah and the Talmud–were composed. The Mishnah is the preeminent compilation of the teachings of the Tannaim, sages who lived in Palestine in the first two centuries CE. Arranged thematically, it covers the entire legal spectrum: family law, civil law, agricultural law, ritual law, criminal law, etc. The Mishnah itself became a focus of interpretative analysis by later sages, the Amoraim, whose work was not limited to commentary on the law, but also addressed the general culture of the time. Palestinian Amoraic academies produced the Jerusalem Talmud, compiled around 400 CE; Babylonian Amoraic academies produced the Babylonian Talmud about a century later. Redaction is far more evident in the latter than the former.

The evolution and philosophy of Jewish legal culture cannot be understood without a firm grasp of talmudic law. The unique position of the Babylonian Talmud vis-à-vis later works is grounded in the fact that it is the latest text universally accepted by Jewish legal culture as halakhically authoritative. Its authority was established by the Geonim, heads of Babylonian talmudic academies after the Muslim conquest of Babylonia. From then on, every legal discussion takes as its starting point the Babylonian Talmud's position on the question at hand, though it is not necessarily upheld as law. Most of the halakhic literature is essentially elaboration of and commentary on the Talmud. Due to its interpretative nature, halakhic creativity emerges in successive layers, in tree-ring fashion. As earlier contributions are always retained, the evolution of Jewish legal culture can be traced relatively easily.

A potentially misleading duality between the exposition of the law and its implementation in practice has always existed in Jewish law. The use of exact measurements and precise, detailed formulations (*midot veshiurim*), and the avoidance of such abstract formulations as 'reasonable behavior' and 'bona fide conduct,' could create the impression that talmudic law is a dry legalistic system within which rights and obligations are rigid and decisions pedantic. But this impression is fundamentally incorrect. Talmudic law as applied in practice (*halakha lemaase*) cannot be inferred from its theoretical exposition (*halakha*). This distinction is not imposed upon the sources, but found in the sources themselves. Thus, for example, the Talmud explains a misunderstanding as follows: "He was talking in terms of theoretical law, and they understood him as if he were talking about implementation of the law" (jBeitza 2:1[61b]); and states: "One who inquires about practical law must state that he is inquiring for practical purposes.... [given] a practical inquiry and a theoretical inquiry, the practical takes precedence" (tSanhedrin 7:7).

Any attempt to describe Jewish law must therefore carefully distinguish between theoretical law and law intended for implementation. With respect to the talmudic period, an account of the latter can be provided on the basis of episodes, precedents, and rulings reported in the Talmud itself; for the post-talmudic period, the responsa literature is a more reliable source for ascertaining the law intended for implementation than the other genres of halakhic writing. The responsa literature, which originated in the Geonic period, and has flourished ever since, consists mainly of legal opinions issued in response to queries submitted by courts regarding cases before them. Over the years, a corpus of some 250,000 responsa has accumulated; part has been electronically indexed by the Bar Ilan Responsa Project. Another source of information about actual application of the law is extant records of the legal activity, judicial and legislative, of various communities (*pinkasei hakehilot*) from centuries past, as well as collections of extant legal instruments.

This wealth of legal material, virtually every layer of which refers to, comments on, or takes issue with earlier views, is adduced frequently in the chapters of this book. Invoking this literature underscores its vitality, and gives readers a sense of the ongoing halakhic conversation, to which scholars from all periods and from around the world have contributed. Readers are invited to work through and participate, in their own ways, in this continuing discussion.

# Distinguishing features

# 1 Controversy



## 1 Introduction

Controversy pervades Jewish law. Not only is it the case that, with regard to almost every legal issue, opposed opinions have been voiced, but the halakhic literature is also replete with discussions about controversy and its ramifications.[1] The self-awareness of the rabbinical authorities with regard to the pervasiveness of legal controversies is reflected in the adage "controversy is an inherent characteristic of the Torah."[2] "Controversy" is sometimes used to denote real-time debate and dialogue over a contentious question among those engaged in Torah study, during which the disputants attempt to persuade each other of the correctness of their respective views. This real-time debate is sometimes referred to as "the war of the Torah."[3] However, another sense of "controversy," which will be our primary interest, refers to holding contradictory opinions after all such attempts to persuade the opposite side of the correctness of one's view have failed.

This chapter will focus on rabbinical attitudes to controversy. It seeks to open a window onto the nature and centrality of controversy in the talmudic literature by presenting the sources and inviting the reader to be actively engaged in interpreting them and perhaps formulating his own readings, however novel. The material will be presented according to the logic of the sources themselves, and not in a linearly thematic fashion. The connections will become clear in due course, when all the pieces are in place.

As our discussion of controversy unfolds, we will move between two different planes of halakhic discourse. The first is that of the conceptual issues that arise from the phenomenon of controversy; the second that of the practical questions that arise in the wake of controversy. How is a ruling to be reached in case of a dispute? How should the individual conduct himself? How is the obligation to study the law to be fulfilled? How is legal uniformity to be achieved?

Although discussion about controversy occupies the halakhic mind, it is a cross-cultural concept, and thus, it is possible—and perhaps, recommended—to analyze controversy in universal rather than exclusively Jewish terms. Readers should bear this in mind, and are invited to relate the concepts that appear in the halakhic sources to more general philosophical categories.

1 See H. Ben-Menahem, N.S. Hecht, and S. Wosner (eds). *Controversy and Dialogue in the Jewish Tradition: A Reader*, with an interpretive essay by H. Ben-Menahem (London: 2005).

2 See R. Israel Isserlein, *Trumat Hadeshen*, Pesakim Ukhtavim #238.

3 See, e.g., Sifre Deuteronomy, Haazinu (Finkelstein edition, p. 370): "And Scripture states, "All of them valiant, wagers of war" (II Kings 24:16). Now what valor can people who are going into exile display? And what war can people wage when they are fettered in shackles and bound by chains? Rather, "valiant" refers to those who are valiant in Torah study. This is like the thrust of the verse, "Bless the Lord, O you His angels, valiant and mighty, who do His word … " (Ps. 103: 20); "wagers of war"—who engaged in dialogue and debate [lit., give and take] in the war of the Torah, as it is said, "Wherefore it is said in the book of the Wars of the Lord" (Num. 21:14)."

## 2 Sources evincing a positive attitude to controversy

The talmudic sources manifest two distinct attitudes to controversy, one of which is clearly favored over the other. The preferred attitude views controversy in a positive light. Below, we will explore what this positive evaluation entails. For now, however, we will simply characterize it as a non-critical attitude. The other attitude is hostile to controversy, seeking to minimize it. On this approach, controversy is at best tolerated as a necessary evil, and not seen as a phenomenon to be encouraged and fostered. We will begin our examination with a discussion of sources that reflect the former attitude.

The first text we will consider is one of the seminal *sugyot* on controversy in the talmudic corpus. Though it is not presented as an introduction to talmudic legal thinking, it nonetheless serves, philosophically, to fulfill that role, by providing the background against which the phenomenon of controversy should be understood. Referred to endlessly in the post-talmudic literature, almost every aspect of the *sugya* has generated numerous interpretations. Our analysis will present a deconstruction of the text, revealing the internal tensions and oppositions it harbors.

### 2.1 bEruvin 13b

> R. Abba stated in the name of Samuel: For three years there was a dispute between the house of Shammai and the house of Hillel, the former asserting, The law is in accordance with our views, and the latter contending, The law is in accordance with our views. A heavenly voice (*bat kol*) went forth, announcing, Both [lit., these and those] are the words of the living God, but the law is in accordance with the view of the house of Hillel. Since, however, both are the words of the living God, what was it that entitled the house of Hillel to have the law fixed in accordance with its view? Because they were kindly and modest, they studied their own views and those of the house of Shammai, and were even so humble as to mention the words of the house of Shammai before their own.
>
> As may be seen from what we have learned: If a man had his head and the greater part of his body within the booth (*suka*) but his table in the house, the house of Shammai ruled it invalid but the house of Hillel ruled that it was valid. Said the house of Hillel to the house of Shammai, Did it not happen that the elders of the house of Shammai and the house of Hillel went on a visit to R. Johanan b. Hahoranit and found him sitting with his head and greater part of his body within the booth while his table was in the house? The house of Shammai replied, That constitutes proof?! [lit., from there proof?] They indeed told him, If you have always acted in this manner you have never fulfilled the

> precept of *suka*.[4] This teaches you that he who humbles himself, the Holy One, blessed be He, raises up, and he who exalts himself, the Holy One, blessed be He, humbles; from him who seeks greatness, greatness flees, but he who flees from greatness, greatness follows; he who forces time is forced back by time, but he who yields to time finds time standing at his side.

The style of the Hebrew in this *sugya* suggests to the trained eye that its origin is Tannaitic,[5] despite the fact that the discussion is attributed to the Amoraim R. Abba and Samuel. And indeed, the kernel of the passage appears in the Jerusalem Talmud as a baraita:

> It was taught: A heavenly voice went forth and announced: Both are the words of the living God, but the law is in accordance with the view of the house of Hillel.
>
> jBerakhot 1:4 (3b)

Thus, the passage from bEruvin 13b is, at the very least, an Amoraic elaboration of this baraita.

The *sugya* describes a controversy between the house of Hillel and the house of Shammai, the only two distinct schools of thought in the long formative period of the Talmud. The life-span of these schools of thought was relatively short, just 80–90 years, but while they existed, the schools were a vital creative force, and had a tremendous impact on the subsequent development of the Talmud. The relations between the schools are sometimes described as violent to the point of bloodshed, but elsewhere are said to constitute a model of peaceful coexistence between sides to a dispute. More than 300 different controversies between the two schools, over questions pertaining to all aspects of daily life, are set out in the Talmud. The controversy described in our *sugya* is exceptional in that it does not identify the contested issue: no substantive dispute is mentioned, as would normally be the case. It seems, however, that the controversy had to do with the method by which controversies are to be resolved. (Philosophers would thus describe it as a 2nd-order controversy). There was, indeed, an accepted procedure for resolving controversies—the

4 I.e., "dwelling" in a booth on the festival of Sukkot; see Leviticus 23:42–43. The story of R. Johanan b. Hahoranit quoted here by the Talmud appears in mSuka 2:7 (bSuka 28a); it is also found in bBerakhot 11a. The version that appears in these two sources includes the words "and they said nothing to him" within the house of Hillel's report on the visit. On this account, the controversy between the house of Shammai and the house of Hillel is not simply about assessing the permissibility of R. Johanan b. Hahoranit's behavior, but also about the actual facts of the incident—what was said at the time. Textual analysis favors the version in bEruvin 13b, which is supported by the text of the Mishnah as it appears in the Jerusalem Talmud.

5 Hence, it is an early source.

majoritarian principle ("follow the majority"), but the question was how to define "majority": was the majority the camp that was greater in wisdom, or that which was greater in numbers? (The school of Hillel is said, in the Talmud, to have been greater in numbers, while the school of Shammai is said to have been greater in wisdom; each school apparently adopted the position beneficial to itself). In the absence of an agreed-upon mechanism for deciding controversies, the question remained open, and constituted a kind of vicious circle.

The significance of the duration of the controversy, which is not particularly exceptional, is not made clear. What is to be assumed, however, is that during this period there was not simply a stalemate, but new arguments were put forward by the sides, though to no avail—the question could not be resolved rationally. The resort to the heavenly voice in this *sugya* suggests a certain resignation, a rejection of the possibility of arriving at an ultimate resolution of the impasse by means of human reason.

On the surface, it appears that the intervention of the heavenly voice is accepted without opposition. On this point, the *sugya* in bEruvin 13b conflicts with the picture painted in another classic talmudic *sugya*, 'the oven of *akhnai*,'[6] where a similar halakhic pronouncement by a heavenly voice is rejected out of hand:

> It has been taught: On that day R. Eliezer brought forward every imaginable argument, but they did not accept them. Said he to them: If the law is in accordance with my view, let this carob-tree prove it! Thereupon the carob-tree was torn a hundred cubits from its place—others affirm, four hundred cubits. No proof can be brought from a carob-tree, they retorted. Again he said to them: If the law is in accordance with my view, let the stream of water prove it! Whereupon the stream of water flowed backwards. No proof can be brought from a stream of water, they rejoined. Again he urged: If the law is in accordance with my view, let the walls of the house of study prove it, whereupon the walls started to tilt. But R. Joshua rebuked them, saying: When scholars are engaged in a halakhic dispute, what have ye to interfere? Hence they did not fall, in honor of R. Joshua, nor did they resume the upright, in honor of R. Eliezer; and they are still standing thus inclined. Again he said to them: If the law is in accordance with my view, let it be proved from heaven! Whereupon a heavenly voice called out, saying: Why do you debate with R. Eliezer, seeing that on all matters the law is in accordance with his view?! But R. Joshua rose to his feet and exclaimed: It is not in heaven (Deut. 30:12).

6 The discussion focuses on a dispute over a question of purity and impurity. The precise issue had to do with a specific kind of oven, hence, the *sugya* is known as the "oven of *akhnai*"; see mKelim 5:10 and mEduyot 7:7. R. Eliezer's view regarding the purity of the oven is disputed by the Sages.

> What did he mean by this? Said R. Jeremiah: [it means that] the Torah had already been given at Mount Sinai; we pay no attention to a heavenly voice, because Thou hast long ago written in the Torah at Mount Sinai, "Follow the majority" (Exod. 23:2). R. Nathan met Elijah and asked him: What did the Holy One, blessed be He, do in that hour? He replied: He smiled, saying, My sons have triumphed over Me, My sons have triumphed over Me.
>
> bBaba Metzia 59b

The original Tannaitic tradition ends without taking a position on the question of who was right, R. Joshua, who rejects the heavenly voice, or R. Eliezer, who relies on it. It is only the later Amoraic insertion, "What did he mean by this? ... over Me," that makes it clear, by arguing that the Almighty Himself supports it, that the rejectionist view of R. Joshua takes precedence. A hint of irony is perceptible in R. Nathan's remark here to the effect that there is heavenly support for a position that rejects divine intervention.

### i Implicit critique of reliance on the heavenly voice

Returning to the *sugya* from bEruvin, note that after the heavenly voice has issued its decree, which will be discussed shortly, a question is raised:

> Since, however, both are the words of the living God, what was it that entitled the house of Hillel to have the law fixed in accordance with its view?

This question seeks a rational explanation for the fact that the law follows the house of Hillel, pointing to dissatisfaction with the concept of heavenly intervention in halakhic decision-making. The answer given in the text, "because they were kindly and modest, they studied their own views and those of the house of Shammai, and were even so humble as to mention the words of the house of Shammai before their own," appears to be straightforward: the members of the house of Hillel were morally superior.

But as R. Joseph Caro asked, "I am perplexed. Suppose the law was not [really] in accordance with their view. Would it have been the case that the law was nonetheless decided in accordance with their view due to the preponderance of their moral virtues?"[7] While it seems that the moral dimension is indeed being highlighted here, and in the continuation of the *sugya*, a more penetrating insight is also expressed. Epistemic advantages resulted from the house of Hillel's elevated moral standing: because they were humble, they were willing to listen to and reflect on the arguments put forward by their opponents; having withstood the encounter with these contrary views, their own arguments are stronger.

7 *Halikhot Olam*, gate 5, p. 101.

This interpretation is supported by the Jerusalem Talmud, which brings an unequivocally epistemic answer to the question:

> Why did the house of Hillel merit having the law decided in accordance with their view? Said R. Judah b. Pazi: They quoted the opinions of the house of Shammai before their own. Furthermore, when they saw merit in the opinions of the house of Shammai, they retracted their own.
>
> jSuka 2:8 (53b)

Thus, a rational explanation is put forward for the fact that the view of the house of Hillel is preferred. We see, then, that there appears to be a certain gap between the external appearance of the text of bEruvin 13b, which accepts the intervention of the heavenly voice without protest, and the subtle criticism implied by its undertaking to provide a rationalization of the "but the law is in accordance with the view of the house of Hillel" ruling.

### ii The precedent

To illustrate the moral and epistemic qualities attributed to the house of Hillel, the text in bEruvin cites a mishnaic passage:

> As may be seen from what we have learned: If a man had his head and the greater part of his body within the booth (*suka*) but his table in the house, the house of Shammai ruled it invalid but the house of Hillel ruled that it was valid. Said the house of Hillel to the house of Shammai, Did it not happen that the elders of the house of Shammai and the house of Hillel went on a visit to R. Johanan b. Hahoranit and found him sitting with his head and greater part of his body within the booth while his table was in the house? The house of Shammai replied, That constitutes proof?! [lit., from there proof?] They indeed told him, If you have always acted in this manner you have never fulfilled the precept of *suka*.

The illustration is relevant to the third virtue mentioned in explanation of the fact that the house of Hillel is favored, namely, that they mentioned the words of the house of Shammai before their own. But what precisely is the connection? It might be thought that the mishnaic passage is adduced here because of the conversation between the house of Hillel and the house of Shammai: in the question posed by the former, the phrase "house of Shammai" is used before the house of Hillel mentions itself: "Did it not happen that the elders of the house of Shammai ...?"

But with all due respect, this explanation, put forward by Rashi and other commentators, is not fully satisfactory, since the commended quality is that the house of Hillel mentioned the opinions [lit., the words] of the house of Shammai prior to their own. The sentence in question, however, merely constitutes an instance where the phrase "house of Shammai" appears first.

A better explanation, then, might be that, on the assumption that the mishnaic passage originates in the house of Hillel, the connection seems related to the fact that the view of the house of Shammai is reported before that of the house of Hillel: "the house of Shammai ruled it invalid but the house of Hillel ruled that it was valid." But the question arises, why is this particular mishnaic passage, out of hundreds of possibilities, used to illustrate the point? After all, the norm in the Mishnah is that the view of the house of Shammai is mentioned first.

One possible answer is that the choice of this passage as an illustration is quite deliberate. R. Abba,[8] who presents the passage declaring that the law is decided in accordance with the house of Hillel, remarks elsewhere in the Talmud (bSuka 28a) that in the case of the *suka* dispute adduced in discussing the virtues of the house of Hillel, the law is decided in accordance with the view of the house of Shammai. Thus, it would appear that in choosing this example, a veiled qualification to what is presented as a universal principle—the principle that the law is in accordance with the view of the house of Hillel—is in fact being articulated, namely, that it is subject to exceptions.

### iii "Both are the words of the living God"

Having given the reader a taste of the subtle differences of opinion that are hidden beneath the apparently calm waters of the text, we now turn to the primary focus of the *sugya*, the ruling issued by the heavenly voice.

> A heavenly voice (*bat kol*) went forth, announcing, Both [lit., these and those] are the words of the living God, but the law is in accordance with the view of the house of Hillel.

The dictum "both are the words of the living God" is derived from a verse in Jeremiah. There, the verse appears in the context of a polemic against false prophets. Jeremiah emphasizes that the true God has but one voice, and that false prophets "pervert the words of the living God" (Jer. 23:26). The author of the *sugya* thus takes the biblical phrase out of its context and clothes it with a new—and incompatible—meaning. In bEruvin, the Sages present God pluralistically, as speaking with a variety of voices, despite the fact that in the Bible, the position of the prophet is the very opposite.

Note the determination on the part of the Sages to reframe the biblical attitude pluralistically: the sage seeks to establish his authority by

8 In variant texts a different name is given.

repudiating the view that God's voice is monolithic—a view welcomed by the prophet—attesting to an ongoing polemic against the prophet's attempt to monopolize the role of conduit of God's word.

This impression is reinforced if we consider another passage from the Talmud pertaining to controversy, where the same stratagem is employed.

> The school of R. Ishmael taught: "And like a hammer that breaketh the rock in pieces" (Jer. 23:29): just as a hammer breaks forth many sparks, so every single word that went forth from the Holy One, blessed be He, split into seventy languages.[9]
>
> bShabat 88b

Here, the allusion is to the same chapter of Jeremiah, where false prophecy is assailed, and here too, it is taken out of context and given an entirely new meaning, a meaning quite different from the biblical meaning. In Jeremiah 23:29, after the false prophet is contrasted with the prophet who reports God's word faithfully, God declares: "Behold, My word is like fire, and like a hammer that shatters rock!" Jeremiah is again asserting that God's word is monolithic and unfragmented. The exegete, however, uses this passage to support a contrary vision, one that endorses controversy and pluralism.

Even without regard to the innovative use of the biblical passage in this particular context, and its ramifications, the dictum of R. Ishmael is another classic expression of the pluralistic principle in Tannaitic thought, and is much referred to in the post-talmudic literature. It also closely resembles a phrase not found in the Talmud—"the Torah has seventy facets"[10]—which became a maxim of the pluralistic approach.

The idea that the choice of the verses from Jeremiah in both instances reflects a hidden polemic between the sage and the prophet, merits further discussion. The distinction between the two is quite straightforward: the prophet, but not the sage, has direct access to the word of God. It would seem, on the surface, that as a result of this disparity, the position of the sage is inferior. The contrast between the univocal voice of the prophet, and the incessant controversies of the Sages, could be taken to demonstrate such an inferiority. The alleged prophetic advantage is so pronounced that R. Menahem Hameiri, the Meiri, sees the emergence of controversy as caused by the cessation of prophecy.[11] The resolve of the Sages to discredit their alleged inferiority vis-à-vis prophets is thus understandable. The

9 The teaching of R. Ishmael here is far from clear. While the biblical verse speaks of a hammer that breaks up rock, the exegete focuses on a different aspect of the blow—the sparks it generates.

10 On the adage, "The Torah has seventy facets," see Hananel Mack, "'The Torah has seventy facets'—the history of this expression" (Hebrew), *Jubilee Volume for R. Breuer*, (Jerusalem: 1992), 449–62.

11 *Beit Habehira*, mAvot, introduction.

most succinct formulation of this program is the dictum, "A sage is superior to a prophet" (bBaba Batra 12a).

The same idea is also found in the Jerusalem Talmud, in the very discussion which quotes the baraita that has been identified as the source of the "both are the words of the living God" dictum.

> The prophet and the sage–whom do they resemble? A king sends supervisors (*mefakhim*) to one of his domains. Of one he wrote to the subjects in that domain: if he does not show you my seal, and my insignia, do not trust him; of the other he wrote: even if he does not show you my seal and my insignia, trust him. So with regard to prophets, He wrote, "and he give thee a sign or a wonder" (Deut. 13:2); but with regard to sages, "According to the law which they shall teach thee" (Deut. 17:11).
>
> jBerakhot 1:4 (3b)

### iv Meaning of the pluralism principle

The reader may be wondering how the principle can be understood, if taken literally—how can contradictory statements both be true? Addressing this concern, at least four meanings have been proposed for the principle, which we will call the pluralism principle:

#### a The law of contradiction does not apply to God

On this approach, the criterion of truth, that is, the concept of what truth is, is not uniform, but differs for God and for mankind. God is not subject to the law of contradiction. From the point of view of God, both a statement and its negation can be true. Thus each side to a halakhic dispute is indeed expressing the word of God.

This interpretation is reflected in the following commentary by the great medieval Spanish halakhist, R. Yomtov of Seville (Ritba):

> Both are the words of the living God. The scholars of France, of blessed memory,[12] asked, how is it possible that both are the words of the living God, when one forbids and another permits? They answered: When Moses ascended to heaven to receive the Torah, on every issue he was shown forty-nine aspects to forbid and forty-nine aspects to permit. He asked the Holy One, blessed be He, about this, and He said that the decision is delegated to the scholars of each generation, and the ruling will be made according to their view. This is so in terms of exegesis, but with respect to truth, there is an esoteric reason for all this.
>
> *Hidushei Haritba*, bEruvin 13b

12 The reference is to R. Yehiel of Paris, died c. 1265.

Although, by virtue of this divine freedom from the law of contradiction, whatever decision a court renders is true, for the halakhic ruling of a court to be valid, it must be based on the assent of all the authorities of a given generation. While the truth of halakhic decisions is grounded in the premise that "both are the words of the living God," the validity of human decision-making is not. Validity calls for consensual determination of the law by scholars. In this sense, the fact that the law of contradiction does not apply to God allows for a conception of 'validity by convention' in the human sphere, a recurrent theme in the halakhic sources.

There are a number of variants of this basic interpretation. Later on, we will explore a few of them, and the reader is advised to be alert to the subtle differences of nuance in the different variants.

### b Human rulings constitute partial perspectives on the divine truth

On this approach, the dictum "both are the words of the living God," does not allow contradiction from God's perspective, as the first approach suggests. On the contrary, from God's perspective there are no contradictions, only imperatives and truths that apply universally. The perspective of the human attempting to determine the law, however, will necessarily be partial, as circumstances vary in space and time. Reality is so rich and complicated that more than one view is required if all the human perspectives are to be covered. From a given perspective, one view will be correct, while from a different vantage point, its negation may be correct. The correctness of a halakhic ruling will thus be relative to its author's perspective.

This interpretation of "both are the words" can be found in Rashi's comments on bKetubot 57a, where he distinguishes between controversies over historical facts about the tradition (Rabbi A said p vs. Rabbi A said not-p) and controversies regarding halakhic positions (p is correct vs. p is incorrect).

> When two Sages disagree concerning the view of a third, one saying, he said thus, and the other saying, he said so, one of the two must be uttering a falsehood; but when two Amoraim have a legal disagreement concerning monetary or ritual law, each adducing his own reasoning, there is no falsehood involved. Each of the two is putting forward his own argument, one providing reasons for permitting, and one reasons for prohibiting; one makes such an analogy, and the other makes a different analogy, and the principle of "both are the words of the living God" applies. Sometimes one argument is pertinent, and sometimes the other argument is pertinent, since the law's rationale changes according to variations in the circumstances, however minute.
>
> *Rashi*, bKetubot 57a

### c The motivational account

#### Weak version

The third interpretation refers to the motivation of the halakhic authority in question. There are two versions of this account: a weak version, and a strong version. On the weak version, only one of the opinions is correct; the formula "both are the words of the living God" signifies only that both views are sincere attempts to ascertain the truth. Accordingly, this view, like the 'partial perspectives' account, rejects the possibility that both views are true, and makes a claim regarding the motivations and methods of the proponents of the opposed views, namely, that they are legitimate. The correctness of the views themselves, however, is a separate question.

To illustrate this version of the third interpretation, we will examine the only other talmudic source for the expression "both are the words of the living God."

> Said R. Joseph: Can it be maintained that R. Eviatar is an authority who can be relied upon? Have we not, moreover, evidence to the contrary? [An instance where R. Eviatar is allegedly to have conducted himself not in accordance with a certain legal ruling is cited] .... Said Abbaye to him: Because a man does not know this rule of R. Isaac, is he therefore not to be counted a great scholar? If it were a rule established by logical deduction, we might think so. But it is purely a tradition, and it is a tradition that R. Eviatar had not heard.
>
> Moreover, R. Eviatar is the authority whose view was recognized by his Master [in the following way]: Commenting on the text, "And his concubine played the harlot against him," R. Eviatar said that the Levite found a fly [in food she prepared], and R. Jonathan said that he found a hair on her. Soon afterward R. Eviatar encountered Elijah and said to him: What is the Holy One, blessed be He, doing? and he answered, He is discussing the question of the concubine in Gibeah. What does He say? He said to him, My son Eviatar says this, and My son Jonathan says that. He [R. Eviatar] said to him: Can there possibly be uncertainty in the mind of the Heavenly One? He replied, Both are the words of the living God. He [the Levite] found a fly and excused it, he found a hair and did not excuse it.
>
> bGitin 6b

R. Eviatar, a certain not particularly prominent Sage, issued a legal ruling. This *sugya* addresses the question of his authority. To establish R. Eviatar's authority, one of the Sages discussing the matter introduces an episode in which R. Eviatar figures. The episode relates a controversy between R. Eviatar and one of his colleagues, R. Jonathan, concerning the historical facts pertaining to the biblical story of the concubine at Gibeah

(Judges 19). Her master's wrath having been incited, the concubine, described as having "played the harlot," fled, whereupon he went after her to bring her home. Since it is not permissible for a man to remain with his adulterous wife or concubine (a Rabbinic proscription, which the Sages, projecting backwards, apply to the concubine of Gibeah), the Sages attempt to interpret the story in a non-literal manner.

R. Eviatar argues that he must have found a fly in food she had prepared for him, while his colleague postulates that the husband must have objected to a hair, that is, found her sexually unattractive.[13] At this point in the narrative, R. Eviatar encounters Elijah the Prophet, the traditional divine messenger, and seizes upon this opportunity to ask for a report on God's doings. To his astonishment, Elijah tells him that God is engaged in studying the biblical story of the concubine at Gibeah.

The Midrash dramatically conveys R. Eviatar's great suspense over whether God takes his view or that of his colleague. At last Elijah states, "both are the words of the living God": while R. Eviatar was right about the fly, he was wrong about the causal question of what had incited the master's wrath.[14] Yet what is significant is that although his view is rejected, it is nonetheless considered to be "the words of the living God," attesting to the intentions and reliability of R. Eviatar. This thus constitutes evidence that he is recognized as an authority on halakhic questions.

### Strong version

The strong version of the motivational account rejects the idea that there is a fact of the matter, that God gave explicit pronouncements regarding halakhic issues. On this view, in addition to the Torah, what was given at Sinai were the thirteen exegetical principles for expounding the law:

> Therefore, it appears that the God, blessed be He, gave the Torah and the thirteen exegetical principles for its interpretation, [for the use of] every single sage, according to his intellectual capacity, provided that he occupies himself with it and studies it with all his might, without dereliction. And if it appears to the Sanhedrin, on the basis of the Torah and the exegetical principles, that a thing is pure, it is pure. And should a future Sanhedrin arise, to whom it appears that according to the Torah and the exegetical principles that very thing is impure, it will be impure. Because God, blessed be He, who gave us the Torah, made it dependent on the sages' views, based on their perceptions. And

13 The Hebrew word for "play the harlot" (*tizne*) is derived from the word for food (*mazon*). This discussion alludes to a controversy found in mGitin 9:10.

14 Some of the commentators maintain that R. Eviatar is nonetheless correct in maintaining that her culinary sloth was causally related to the master's wrath, arguing that his anger was cumulative, being initially precipitated by the fly, then compounded by the hair.

> concerning this it is said, "And from Zion shall go forth the Law" (Isa. 2:3), meaning, an understanding of the Torah will go forth today that did not go forth yesterday.
>
> R. Yomtov Lipmann Muhlhausen, *Sefer Hanitzahon*, sec. 321

This strong motivational account of "both are the words of the living God" claims that if one works diligently within the correct methodological framework, whatever decision is reached is valid.

### d The instrumental account

A fourth interpretation, like the second and third, rejects the notion that two opposed views can both be true. On this view, both can, however, nonetheless be described as "the words of the living God," because even the incorrect view makes an essential contribution to determining the truth. Analysis of the incorrect view, and its ultimate elimination, is a necessary stage in the process of arriving at the truth.

This view is expressed in several post-talmudic sources.

> They were all spoken by one shepherd, meaning that most times we gain a good understanding of something by considering its negation, and we cannot understand the matter on its own so well as by considering its negation. Therefore the Holy One, blessed be He, sought to endow us with dissenting opinions, in order that when we arrive at the true opinion, we will understand it thoroughly.
>
> R. Abraham Akra, *Meharerei Nemeirim* 17a, bHagiga 3b

The idea of arriving at the truth by means of a process of working through a number of conflicting opinions is dramatically illustrated by a *sugya*, perhaps the most tragic in the Talmud, relating the end of the relationship between R. Johanan and Resh Lakish.

> One day there was a dispute in the study hall [between Resh Lakish and R. Johanan] regarding a sword, knife, dagger, spear, hand-saw and scythe—at what stage of their manufacture do they become susceptible to impurity? When their manufacture is finished. And when is their manufacture finished? R. Johanan ruled, when they are tempered in a furnace. Resh Lakish maintained, when they have been polished in water. Said he to him, A robber understands his trade. [R. Johanan is alluding to Resh Lakish's impious past.] Said he to him, And in what have you benefited me? There [as a robber] I was called Master, and here I am called Master. By bringing you under the wings of the Divine Presence, he retorted. R. Johanan therefore felt himself deeply hurt, [as a result of which] Resh Lakish fell ill. His sister [R. Johanan's sister, married to Resh Lakish] came and wept before

> him: Forgive him for the sake of my son, she pleaded. He replied, "Leave thy fatherless children and I will preserve them alive" (Jer. 49:11). For the sake of my widowhood then. "And let thy widows trust in Me" (ibid.), he assured her. Resh Lakish died and R. Johanan was plunged into deep grief. Said the Sages, Who will go to ease his mind? Let R. Eleazar b. Pedat, whose legal teachings are very subtle, go. So he went and sat before him; and on every dictum uttered by R. Johanan, he remarked: There is a baraita that supports you. "[Do you think] you are, then, like the son of Lakisha? When I stated the law, the son of Lakisha would raise twenty-four separate objections, to which I gave twenty-four answers, which led to a fuller understanding of the law. All you say is, There is a baraita that supports you. Do I not know myself that my opinions are well-grounded?" He went on rending his garments and weeping, saying, Where are you, O son of Lakisha, where are you, O son of Lakisha? And he cried thus until his mind broke down. Thereupon the Sages prayed for him and he died.
>
> bBaba Metzia 84a

Although other personal issues and emotions contributed to R. Johanan's tremendous sorrow, this moving passage clearly conveys the deep distress caused by his loss of the study partner who had enabled him to gain a deeper understanding of the law. Critical feedback is presented as an essential element in arriving at the truth. More generally, forthright confrontation of contentious issues is not seen as a negative practice, but viewed favorably as having great epistemic benefit. This interpretation of "both are the words"—the idea that controversy is instrumental to arriving at the truth—is also expressed in numerous other halakhic sources.

## v Scope of the pluralism principle

As we noted, the dictum "both are the words of the living God" appears only twice in the entire Talmud—once regarding the most central controversies in the Talmud, those between the schools of Hillel and Shammai, and once with regard to a minor controversy between peripheral Sages. From the overall perspective of the talmudic literature, all kinds of inferences can be drawn from the stark contrast between these two contexts. They can be seen as designating the poles of a continuum, implying that the dictum applies to all controversies in between, that is, to the entire spectrum of halakhic controversy. On the other hand, the second occurrence of the dictum can be construed as a comic parody, intended to critique the engagement of scholars in speculative fantasies about the minutiae of past events. On this reading, the *sugya* from Gitin is not to be regarded as legitimizing the application of the "both are the words" dictum to every halakhic controversy.

Indeed, on the question of the scope of the "both are the words" dictum, post-Rabbinic scholars express a wide range of opinions, one of which we will now consider.

> And you should know that it is only within the sphere of controversy between the houses of Hillel and Shammai that the dictum "both are the words of the living God" applies. Because they were the first to engage in halakhic controversy, since prior to them there were no disputes about the Torah at all. And when the houses of Hillel and Shammai arose, their controversies were such that both views were "the words of the living God."... And it is inappropriate that Israel should descend [directly] from the lofty level of absence of controversy to a level where controversy occurs and one view is invalidated. And therefore the controversy between the house of Hillel and the house of Shammai was such that "both are the words of the living God." And after this, common controversy began to occur.
>
> Maharal, *Beer Hagola*, 1, p. 19

Note the singular status accorded controversy between the house of Hillel and the house of Shammai, and its role as a transitional stage in the historical evolution of the halakha, according to the Maharal. On this view, controversy between the house of Hillel and the house of Shammai reflects an element of the original idyllic situation in which there was no controversy, and all views put forward were correct, yet also reflects the unpleasant later reality of dissent. This view construes history as the unfolding of a divine plan, on which all events have a purpose. The controversy between the house of Hillel and the house of Shammai, with its unique logical status, serves to prepare future generations for the coming decline.

From this passage, it would seem that the Maharal's assessment of controversy is unfavorable. However, elsewhere he expresses views more sympathetic to controversy, arguing that it enriches the halakha.

## vi Theory and practice

We have seen that the function of the heavenly voice is to resolve the dispute, thereby serving as arbiter of how the individual is to conduct himself in practice. Yet if "both are the words of the living God," why is it necessary to decide between the two opinions? Whichever is chosen, the individual will be acting in accordance with the divine command. And in fact, there are a number of traditions that allow individuals freedom of choice regarding which opinion they prefer to follow, provided they remain consistent. Most of the following *sugya* reflects this approach, thus disputing bEruvin 13b:

> The law is always in accordance with the view of the house of Hillel, but he who wishes to act in accordance with the view of the house of Shammai may do so, and he who wishes to act in accordance with the view of the house of Hillel may do so. He who adopts the more lenient rulings of the house of Shammai and the more lenient rulings of the house of Hillel is a wicked man, while of one who adopts the restrictions of the house of Shammai and the restrictions of the house of Hillel, Scripture said: "But the fool walketh in darkness" (Eccles. 2:14). One should, rather, act either in accordance with the house of Shammai with respect to both their lenient and their restrictive rulings, or in accordance with the house of Hillel with respect to both their lenient and their restrictive rulings.
>
> bEruvin 6b

We can easily detect a contradiction between the first statement, viz., that the law is always in accordance with the house of Hillel, and the statement that follows it, viz., that he who wishes to act in accordance with the view of the house of Shammai may do so, while he who wishes to act in accordance with the view of the house of Hillel may do so as well. The contradiction here is between two practical directives. In bEruvin 13b, by contrast, there is a tension between theory and practice: the heavenly voice preserves the conflicting views at the level of theoretical law, while providing a uniform norm governing practice.

The Talmud itself is conscious of this inconsistency in the directives of bEruvin 6b, and one of the solutions it proposes as a means of resolving it is to argue that the first reflects the situation after the intervention of the heavenly voice, while the second describes the situation prior to this intervention. Shortly, we will consider another solution to this difficulty.

Seeing as there are standard halakhic decision-making rules—the law follows the majority; regarding biblical controversies, the stricter view is followed, while regarding Rabbinic controversies, the lenient view is followed; and so on—why is it that these rules are not invoked to resolve controversies between the houses of Hillel and Shammai? One possible answer is suggested by Nahmanides:

> And it can be said that . . . the controversy between the students of the house of Shammai and the house of Hillel is broad, and all the scholars of Israel are encompassed by it, and for them the Torah becomes like two sets of laws [lit., like two Torahs].[15]
>
> *Hidushei Haramban*, bHulin 43b

15 As members of the scholarly community cannot be indifferent to the controversy, but must take a position, and, given the either-or nature of the controversy, no alternative position is possible, the community is in essence bifurcated—split into two legitimate camps. Hence, every individual can choose for himself which of the two he sides with. In that it divides the scholarly community so completely, the house of Shammi/house of Hillel controversy is a unique phenomenon in the history of Jewish law.

Nahmanides' answer is that the standard decision-making rules apply to isolated controversies, whereas the controversies between the houses of Hillel and Shammai generated two autonomous orientations. However, this answer, as Nahmanides himself notes, is problematic, in that the Gemara in bEruvin 7a suggests that the either-or solution is applied to all controversies, not only to those between the house of Hillel and the house of Shammai.

If we take the idea of halakhic pluralism as reflecting an ontological state (interpretation 1 above), the law can be decided in more than one way because there is no one uniquely-correct answer to the legal question at hand. In this case, we have a tension between a theological consideration, namely, that the divine will, the halakha, can be carried out in a variety of ways equally acceptable to God, and the social desideratum of maintaining uniformity of practice.

In contrast, if we adopt one of the other three interpretations, on which halakhic pluralism does not reflect a true multiplicity of truths, but only a multiplicity of well-intentioned views, the dilemma does not arise, and the heavenly voice serves as a decision-making device, a device for identifying the opinion that reflects the one unique truth regarding the issue at hand, thereby both identifying the divine will and ensuring uniformity of practice.

In the next section, we will further examine sources that deal with the tension between theory and practice.

## 2.2 Four sources on the legal ramifications of controversy

Let us now survey four passages from the halakhic literature—mEduyot 1:5; jSanhedrin 4:2 (22a); Masekhtot Ketanot, Soferim 16, 5–6; and *Hidushei Haritba*, bEruvin 13b—that discuss the legal ramifications of controversy. Only the first, mEduyot 1:5, will be analyzed in detail, as it is the most direct and explicit reference to the legal ramifications of controversy.

### i mEduyot 1:5

We now turn to the examination of a statement in which the Mishnah discusses its own methodology, one of the very few self-reflective statements found in the Mishnah. It is also one of the few mishnaic passages that discuss the issue of controversy directly.

> And why do they record the opinion of the individual against that of the majority, since the law may only be decided in accordance with the opinion of the majority? So that if a court approves of the opinion of the individual it may rely on him.
>
> mEduyot 1:5

Above, we concluded our discussion of bEruvin 13b by juxtaposing it to bEruvin 6b, and noting that two different strategies are proposed for addressing controversy in the practical realm: the disjunctive, either-or, solution, found in the latter part of 6b, and the heavenly voice solution, which sanctions one particular course of behavior, eliminating all others, found in 13b. The Mishnah we have just quoted puts forward an intermediate strategy. On the one hand, as in the case of bEruvin 13b, there is indeed a single acceptable opinion, that of the majority. However, the repudiated opinion, that of the minority, is not completely effaced, but rather preserved for future reference, allowing for its eventual adoption. Thus this intermediate strategy sanctions possible implementation of dissenting views, but unlike bEruvin 6b, does not legitimate them unequivocally.

tEduyot, which parallels mEduyot, contains an important qualification of the mishnaic ruling that minority views can be relied upon.

> The law is always in accordance with the opinion of the majority. The opinion of the individual is recorded against that of the majority only to render it invalid. R. Judah says: The opinion of the individual is recorded against that of the majority only because the times may require it, and they may rely on it. And the Sages say: The opinion of the individual is recorded against that of the majority only because it might be that one declares something impure, and another, pure; one might declare it impure according to R. Eliezer. They will be able to say to him, you heard this according to R. Eliezer.
>
> tEduyot 1:4

R. Judah stresses that reliance on a minority view is to be resorted to only because "the times may require it." This qualification, though not explicitly articulated as an element of the Sages' view in the Mishnah (which parallels that of R. Judah in the Tosefta) is read into mEduyot, to the effect that the Sages too hold that a minority view may be relied upon only if the times requires it. There are, indeed, several instances in the Talmud where judges rely on minority views on the basis of mEduyot 1:5, understood in this qualified manner. The common formula introducing such cases is, "So-and-so deserves to be relied in times of exigency." However, given that the definition of when an exigency exists is left to the judge who will be citing it as a justification, it is difficult to characterize the precise scope of the qualification.

However, if we consider the passages in question from another perspective, their relationship appears to be different. The three passages, bEruvin 13b, bEruvin 6b, and mEduyot 1:5, can be seen, not as two polar positions and a synthesis between them, but rather, simply as variants of the same position. bEruvin 6b can be read, not as an alternative strategy for addressing intractable controversies, but rather, as an interpretation of bEruvin 13b. Like bEruvin 13b, it determines that the law is decided in accordance with the view of the house of Hillel (the first part of 6b), and interprets the "both are the words" dictum of 13b as sanctioning the disjunctive, either-or solution. On this reading, mEduyot 1:5 presents a means of implementing this paradoxical affirmation of the two approaches, the heavenly voice approach, on the one hand, and the either-or approach, on the other. But rather than presenting the solution as leaving the choice to the individual, as proposed in bEruvin 6b, it mandates that the rejected opinion be preserved for future judicial reference. Thus interpreted, mEduyot, too, sanctions the "both are the words" dictum.

The following Mishnah, which is, perhaps, the most renowned mishnaic discussion of controversy, and has generated a huge sea of commentary, can also be interpreted as in line with the view that the various *sugyot* should be regarded as complementary.

> Every controversy that is for the sake of heaven, its end is to be sustained. And every controversy that is not for the sake of heaven, its end is not to be sustained. What controversy is for the sake of heaven?—the controversy between Hillel and Shammai. And that which is not for the sake of heaven?—the controversy of Korah and all his congregation.
>
> mAvot 5:17

Although rather than referring only to the dissenting side, this Mishnah uses the more inclusive term "controversy," it nonetheless presumably seeks to encourage the losing party, and not both sides to the dispute. The Meiri was also sensitive to the peculiar language of mAvot, in referring to "controversy" as being sustained in the end.

> It is puzzling: in what way is it apt to say of a controversy that it will be sustained? After all, only one of the two opposing views will ultimately be sustained. And the term "controversy" covers two sides, and how can both be sustained? It seems to me that the term "controversy" [here] refers only to the side challenging an existing view.... Therefore, "controversy" does not encompass both sides, but only one, namely, that which challenges an existing view.
>
> *Beit Habehira*, mAvot 5:19[16]

In the Meiri's view, the Mishnah envisages that eventually, only one view will be sustained, namely, the view of the challenger. However, contra the Meiri, in the spirit of mEduyot 1:5, which states that dissenting views might be relied upon by a court, under specified conditions, at some future

16 The reference here to 5:19 rather than 5:17 is due to the fact that there are several different arrangements of the verses and chapters of mAvot.

time, we can suggest that the mAvot is likewise envisaging a point in the future when the challenging view will—alongside the majority view—be relied upon.

The claim that the Mishnah refers only to the losing party, assuring him that if he disagrees for the sake of heaven, his opinion will eventually be relied upon, is supported by the fact that the latter part of the Mishnah refers explicitly only to one side, the dissenting side, namely, to Korah and all his congregation. It might be asked why, if this is so, the penultimate sentence mentions both the house of Hillel and the house of Shammai. The answer is that with respect to certain issues, however few, the former are on the dissenting side, and with respect to the others, the latter.

The Mishnah we have just examined points to a problem also found elsewhere, the ambiguity of the very term "controversy." It is sometimes used to denote a halakhic controversy, that is, a dispute over how to decide the law. This is the sense in which we have been using it. In other contexts, however, it can refer to social strife. Since, in this latter sense, controversy is unquestionably a deplored phenomenon, the fact that the same term is used for both is not without consequences, as the pejorative connotations of this sense of the term are sometimes carried over into contexts where the former, neutral sense is intended.

At times, it is unclear which of the two senses is intended. mAvot 5:17 is an example of such a context.

### ii jSanhedrin 4:2 (22a)

Said R. Yanai, Were the Torah to have been handed down in a clear-cut form, one would have had no solid ground to stand on. What is the basis for this statement? Scripture says, "And the Lord spoke to Moses ...." Moses said to Him, Master of the Universe, tell me how the law is decided. He said to him, "follow the majority" (Exod. 23:2). If those who declare [the accused] innocent are in the majority, declare him innocent. If those who declare [the accused] guilty are in the majority, declare him guilty. This is so that the Torah may be expounded in forty-nine ways for a decision that something is impure and in forty-nine ways for a decision that it is pure. And forty-nine is the numerical equivalent of "and his banner" (*vediglo*) (Song of Songs 2:4).[17]

### iii Masekhtot Ketanot, Soferim 16, 5–6

R. Tanhum b. Hanilai said: Were the Torah to have been handed down in a clear-cut form, no judge would have had solid grounds for his ruling. But now, if he renders a thing impure, there are others who rendered it impure under similar circumstances. And if he

17 By adding the numerical values of the letters (6 + 4 + 3 + 30 + 6).

renders it pure, there are others who rendered it pure under similar circumstances.

### iv *Hidushei Haritba,* bEruvin 13b

Both are the words of the living God. The scholars of France, of blessed memory, asked, how is it possible that both are the words of the living God, when one forbids and another permits? They answered: When Moses ascended to heaven to receive the Torah, on every issue he was shown forty-nine aspects to forbid and forty nine aspects to permit. He asked the Holy One, blessed be He, about this, and He said that the decision is delegated to the scholars of each generation, and the ruling will be made according to their view. This is so in terms of exegesis, but with respect to truth, there is an esoteric reason for all this.

We have considered four sources that address the practical implications of controversy for halakhic decision-making: mEduyot, jSanhedrin, Soferim, and *Hidushei Haritba*. Despite some similarities of theme, there are also important differences. According to the pluralism principle, both sides of every dispute were given to Moses at Sinai. The sources in question all draw different conclusions from the pluralism principle. mEduyot deals with the conscious employment of a minority view by a judge. The Jerusalem Talmud, in jSanhedrin, sanctions any decision of an assembly of sages. The passage from Soferim justifies any decision made by a judge, and the Ritba goes one step further than the Jerusalem Talmud, saying that each generation can make decisions anew.

## 2.3 bHagiga 3b

And he too began to expound: "The words of the wise are as goads, and as nails well planted are those of masters of assemblies; they were given from one shepherd" (Eccles. 12:11). Why are the words of the Torah likened to a goad? To teach that just as a goad directs the cow along the furrow in order to bring life to the world, so the words of the Torah direct those who study them from the paths of death to the paths of life. But [should you think] that just as a goad is movable, so the words of the Torah are movable, therefore Scripture says: "nails." But [should you think] that just as a nail diminishes by being driven in, and does not increase, so too the words of the Torah diminish, and do not increase, therefore Scripture says: "well planted"; just as a plant grows and increases, so the words of the Torah grow and increase.

"Masters of assemblies" refers to the scholars (*talmidei hakhamim*) who sit in various assemblies and apply themselves to the Torah; some deem a matter impure, others deem it pure, some prohibit, others permit, some disqualify, others declare fit. Lest someone say, Under

> these circumstances, how can I learn the Torah?, therefore Scripture says: All were given from one shepherd. One God gave them, one leader uttered them from the mouth of the Master of all deeds, blessed be He, as it is written, "And God spake all these words" (Exod. 20:1). So let your ears be as funnels [lit., hoppers], and cultivate an understanding heart, to hear the words of those who deem a matter impure and those who deem it pure, those who prohibit and those who permit, those who disqualify and those who declare fit.

Based on a verse from Ecclesiastes, this exegesis, also referred to in the passage we considered above from *Meharerei Nemeirim*, which has many parallels and variants in the Rabbinic literature, is attributed to R. Eleazar b. Azariah, to whom the pronoun "he" at the beginning of the passage refers. We know that R. Eleazar b. Azariah was involved in the decision to declare the book of Ecclesiastes part of the biblical canon (mYadayim 3:5). Given that it justifies dissenting opinions, it is possible that the exegesis before us was delivered in connection with the deliberations on this matter, despite the fact that in the present *sugya*, bHagiga 3b, it is invoked in a different context.

The exegesis has two sections, the first dealing with the tension between the static and dynamic dimensions of the Torah, and the second dealing with controversy. We will be most concerned with understanding the latter section.

Let us begin our consideration of the treatment of controversy in this *sugya* by noting a variant in the Jerusalem Talmud that distinctly changes its meaning:

> The term "assemblies" (*asufot*) refers only to the Sanhedrin, as it is stated in Numbers 11:16—"Gather (*esfa*)[18] unto Me seventy men of the elders of Israel." Another interpretation: "masters of assemblies"—that which is spoken at assemblies.
>
> jSanhedrin 10:1 (28a)

This change allows the Jerusalem Talmud to avoid interpreting the verse in a manner that underlines the connection with controversy, and instead, to reframe the matter as pertaining to the activity of the Sanhedrin in general, and not necessarily to controversy.[19]

Despite the Jerusalem Talmud's preference for recasting the biblical term as referring to a specific forum, namely, the Sanhedrin, if we return to the text of bHagiga 3b, it is quite clear that the subject addressed is

18 "Assemblies" and "gather" share the same lexical root, *as"f*.

19 This attitude may be related to the Jerusalem Talmud's overall policy of minimizing pluralism and presenting a unified front; see H. Ben-Menahem, *Judicial Deviation in Talmudic Law* (Chur, Switzerland: 1991), ch. 4.

indeed controversy in general, as is evident, for one thing, from the term "assemblies," emphasizing that many different forums for deciding the law are being referred to.

An observer of the activity taking place at these different gatherings would readily have discerned that "some deem a matter impure, others pure, some prohibit, others permit, some disqualify, others declare fit." From the continuation of the *sugya*, it is evident that the opposed pronouncements relate to the same legal question, and not to different issues. It is not surprising, therefore, that the observer's response to this bewildering profusion of controversy and discussion is to inquire, "Under these circumstances, how can I learn the Torah?" In variants of this passage, the query is sometimes posed differently—"Under these circumstances, whom shall we listen to?" (Midrash Tanhuma, Behaalotkha 15); "Why should we bother to learn the Torah?" (tSota 7:11–12).

The answer provided in the various parallels: "All were given from one shepherd. One God gave them, one leader uttered them from the mouth of the Master of all deeds, blessed be He," is based on the verse from Ecclesiastes. Note that these parallels, when quoting the verse, add the word "all," which does not appear in the biblical text. The verse in the Torah that serves as the proof-text for the entire passage reads: "for it is written, And God spoke all these words" (Exod. 20:1), and it would appear that this is the basis for the emphasis on "all." The exegete does not directly address the observer's perplexity, but instead reassures the observer by announcing that all the different views were spoken to Moses at Sinai. In so doing, this source invokes an idea very similar to the pluralism principle put forward in bEruvin 13b, "both are the words of the living God." And indeed, many of the later commentators who quote the *sugya* from bHagiga interpolate this dictum into it, as if it were an integral part of the *sugya*. The *sugya* also calls to mind the "forty-nine aspects" idea expressed in jSanhedrin 4:2(22a), which we discussed above.

### i Interpretations of the *sugya*

A noted late medieval commentator, R. Nissim Gerondi, the Ran, interprets this fascinating *sugya* as follows:

> It is also said, "masters of assemblies" (bHagiga 3b). This refers to the scholars (*talmidei hakhamim*) who sit in various assemblies and apply themselves to the Torah. Some deem a matter impure, others deem it pure, some prohibit, others permit, some disqualify and others declare fit. Lest one say, under these circumstances, since some deem it impure and others pure, and so on, how can I learn the Torah?, Scripture teaches, "given from one shepherd" (Eccles. 12:11). One leader uttered them from the mouth of the Master of all, and so on. For it is said, "And God spoke all these words" (Exod. 20:1). And they interpreted

the word "all" as including even the opinions of those who did not arrive at the truth—all opinions were given at Sinai.

Now this matter needs some study. How can we say that both sides of a controversy were spoken to Moses by the Almighty? For example, Shammai and Hillel had a disagreement. Shammai says that the priestly portion must be donated from one *kab* of dough and Hillel says from *two kab* (mEduyot 1:2). Verily, one of these two opinions is true and the opposed view is not, yet how can it be maintained that an untruth was spoken by God?

But the matter is as follows: It is known that the entire written and oral law was transmitted to Moses, as it is stated in tractate Megila: R. Hiya bar Abba said in the name of R. Johanan: What is the meaning of the verse "and on them was written according to all the words" (Deut. 9:10)? It teaches us that the Holy One, blessed be He, showed Moses the "finer points of the Torah and the finer points of the Sages" and all the new points that scholars would formulate in the future. And what are they? Reading the Book of Esther. "Finer points of the Sages" denotes the controversies and dissenting opinions among the scholars of Israel. And Moses learned all of them from the Almighty, though without a decision on every particular point of contention. But He gave him a rule for recognizing the truth, and it is "*aharei rabim lehatot*"—follow the majority (Exod. 23:2), and "do not deviate from the words which they shall declare unto thee" (Deut. 17:11).[20]

When dissent proliferated among the Sages, if it was one against many, the law was determined according to the majority. If many against many, or one person against another, the law was decided according to what seemed proper to the scholars of that generation, since the power to decide had been delegated to them. As it is said: "And thou shalt come unto the priests the Levites, and unto the judge that shall be in those days" (Deut. 17:9). Furthermore, there is the injunction, "do not deviate." For authorization was given to the scholars of every generation to decide between dissenting opinions as they saw fit, even if their predecessors were greater and more numerous than they. For we were commanded to follow their wisdom, whether what they agree on is the truth or its converse.

And this is so in the controversy involving R. Eliezer the Great. As it is said in the discussion in tractate bBaba Metzia: R. Joshua rose to his feet and said, "It is not in heaven" (Deut. 30:12).[21] What does "it is not in heaven" mean? It means that the Torah had already been given to Moses on Mount Sinai, and in it is written "follow the majority" (*aharei rabim lehatot*) (Exod. 23:2). To be sure, they were all aware that R. Eliezer's view agreed with the truth more closely than did their

20 bMegila 19b.
21 bBaba Metzia 59b.

> own, that its signs were all genuine and correct, and that the heavenly decision had been as he said. Nevertheless, they decided the law in line with their own consensus. Since their reasoning inclined them to deem the matter impure, even though they knew that this consensus was the opposite of the truth, they did not want to render it pure, and would have transgressed the words of the Torah had they done so, since their reasoning inclined them to render it impure. For the power to decide has been delegated to the scholars of the given generation, and whatever they agree upon is what God commanded.
>
> *Derashot Haran*, #7

The Ran uses the concept "truth" in two distinct senses. The first is that of objective truth, which reflects the divine determination of the law; the second is that of validity, reflecting human decisions about the law, which do not necessarily coincide with the objective truth. The validity of a human decision rests on human understanding of the law taken in conjunction with the divine desire that human conduct be in accordance with human understanding.

But the Ran also emphasizes that every human understanding of the law was actually revealed to Moses at Sinai:

> It teaches us that the Holy One, blessed be He, showed Moses the finer points of the Torah and the finer points of the Sages and all the new points that scholars would formulate in the future. And what are they? Reading the Book of Esther. "Finer points of the Sages" denotes the controversies and dissenting opinions among the scholars of Israel.

That is, conceptually speaking, the function of human decisions as to the law, decisions made on the basis of the principle of majority rule, is to determine which of the existing views will be adopted in practice.

It is interesting to compare the Ran's interpretation to an interpretation put forward by R. Menahem Mendel Haim Landau, a distinguished pre-war Polish halakhic authority.[22]

> And it is in this spirit that we are to understand the passage in tractate bEruvin about the house of Shammai/house of Hillel controversy: "a heavenly voice (*bat kol*) went forth, announcing, Both are the words of the living God, but the law is in accordance with the view of the house of Hillel." It is important to understand how two contrary opinions, one forbidding and the other permitting, can, with respect to the same matter, both be the words of the living God. And on this point see the comments in R. Yomtov of Seville's novellae (*Hidushei Haritba*) ad loc.

22 His responsa, *Kuntres Pri Haaretz*, appear at the end of a work by his grandfather, R. Abraham of Ciechanow, *Vayaas Avraham*.

In the said passage, the Talmud raises a problem. "Since, however, both are the words of the living God, why was the house of Hillel entitled to have the law fixed in accordance with its view?" Note that the Talmud does not question the possibility of two contrary opinions both being the words of the living God....

But you must know and understand that halakhic truth is unlike the truth of arithmetic and geometry, wherein there is but a single correct solution. Rather, it is based on intelligence and reasoning, that is, it is as people understand it through their own cognition. And the Holy One, blessed be He, commanded in His Torah that when a matter in the laws of the Torah is too perplexing, we obey the decision of the court of that generation, which will inform us of the solution to which its understanding points. And, as no two individuals have identical intellects, and opinions of necessity will differ, even within the court itself, God, may He be blessed, commanded that we accept the opinion of the majority. If the majority view asserts that something is forbidden, it is the will of God, may He be blessed, that it be forbidden. However, should the majority of a court in a future generation be inclined to accept the previous minority opinion, and permit the matter, this would also be the will of God, may He be blessed, for Scripture says, "unto the judge that shall be in those days" (Deut. 17:9). And as Maimonides, of blessed memory, wrote, "If the high court arrived at a conclusion on the basis of the accepted exegetical principles as it saw fit, determining that the law was thus and rendering its legal decision accordingly, and then a later court contradicts it, the second court may contradict it and rule as it sees fit, for Scripture says, 'and unto the judge that shall be in those days' (Deut. 17:9). The sole authority is the judge of the present generation."[23]

And it is all for the same reason: the Torah chose a solution that is dependent on intelligible truth and variable opinion. For every point of view has some hold on human opinion, and even within an individual, opinions may vary. The Talmud relates, for example, that R. Meir was able to argue that an impure matter was pure, and could support his claim logically (bEruvin 13b). That is, he explained it so as to show that it was plausible. Hence, the arguments for purity and for impurity can both be grounded in reason. And everything that can be so grounded is the word of the living God, since He commanded us to listen to the arguments and reasoning of the court, to its understanding of the solutions to doubtful points concerning the precepts of the Torah.

*Kuntres Pri Haaretz*, p. 506 in *Vayaas Avraham*

23 Maimonides, *Code*, Laws concerning Rebels 2:1.

The conception expressed in this passage is similar to that suggested by the Ran, but with one crucial difference. On both views, the halakhic decision made by the Sages on the basis of majority rule does not necessarily mirror the divine truth regarding the matter. And on both views, the divine will is that the Sages be the arbiters of the law. Thus the decision-making methods these thinkers champion are what we would today describe as process-oriented. The crucial distinction, however, is that according to *Kuntres Pri Haaretz*, there is no presumption that the different views were given to Moses at Sinai, and hence human intellectual creativity has, theoretically speaking, far greater importance. Logic and human reasoning alone suffice to guarantee the admissibility of a halakhic opinion that has the sanction of the majority.

### ii Other commentators on bHagiga 3b

This problem was also taken up in a responsum by an eminent nineteenth century Iraqi halakhic authority, R. Abdallah Abraham Joseph Somekh:

> Question: You asked about controversy between Sages, one forbidding, the other permitting—how could both views have been given to Moses at Sinai?
>
> Answer: This is a very profound question, and we cannot get to the bottom of it, for even the early scholars, of blessed memory, could not master it. This question was asked by the scholars of France, of blessed memory, about the passage in tractate bEruvin 13b:
>
>> R. Abba stated in the name of Samuel: For three years there was a dispute between the house of Shammai and the house of Hillel, the former asserting, The law is in accordance with our views, and the latter contending, The law is in accordance with our views. A heavenly voice (*bat kol*) went forth, announcing, Both are the words of the living God, but the law is in accordance with the view of the house of Hillel. Since, however, both are the words of the living God, what was it that entitled the house of Hillel to have the law fixed in accordance with its view? Because they were kindly and modest.
>
> R. Yomtov of Seville [Ritba], in his commentary on Eruvin, wrote as follows:
>
>> The scholars of France, of blessed memory, asked, how is it possible that both are the words of the living God, when one forbids and another permits? They answered: When Moses ascended to heaven to receive the Torah, on every issue he was shown forty-nine aspects to forbid and forty-nine aspects to permit. He asked the Holy One, blessed be He, about this, and He said that the decision is delegated

> to the scholars of each generation, and the ruling will be made according to their view. This is so in terms of exegesis, but with respect to truth, there is an esoteric reason for all this.

That is what the Ritba, of blessed memory, wrote. A similar approach is taken by R. Nissim Solomon Algazi in *Yavin Shmua* (p. 81b), quoting [R. Samuel b. Moses Kalai's] *Responsa Mishpetei Shmuel*, which brings an interpretation in the name of Rabbenu Hananel, of blessed memory:

> Concerning "both are the words of the living God"—the interpretation is that the Holy One, blessed be He, related to Moses at Sinai forty-nine ways to render a thing pure and forty-nine ways to render the same thing impure, and did not decide, but left the decision to the majority, as it is written, "follow the majority" (Exod. 23:2).

And so it appears from the Gemara in tractate bHagiga 3b:

> "Masters of assemblies" refers to the scholars (*talmidei hakhamim*) who sit in various assemblies and apply themselves to the Torah; some deem a matter impure, others pure, some prohibit, and others permit, some disqualify and others declare fit. Should one say: Under these circumstances, how can I learn the Torah? Therefore Scripture says: All "were given from one shepherd." One God gave them, one leader uttered them from the mouth of the Master of all deeds, blessed be He.

There is thus clear proof in the Talmud supporting the assertion of the scholars of France and Rabbenu Hananel, of blessed memory, that the two opposed opinions were given to Moses at Sinai. As was also explained by the Shela [R. Isaiah Horowitz], of blessed memory, who begins by quoting R. Yomtov of Seville, then quotes the scholars of France, cites the said talmudic passage, and then states: "These authorities, of blessed memory, attested that all the disputes and contradictory opinions were given by one God, uttered by one leader" (*Shnei Luhot Habrit*, 25b). And consult the text. And the Hida, of blessed memory, offers three explanations:

> About the saying, "both are the words of the living God," the early scholars pondered the question, how is it possible that both are the words of the living God, since the one whose opinion is not affirmed as law did not speak correctly? The early scholars said that just as light cannot be discerned without darkness, and truth cannot be discerned without falsehood, so too in this matter the one cannot be understood unless it is juxtaposed to its opposite. Therefore God told Moses the opinions of those who acquit and those who find liable, and so on, for from the rejected opinion, the true opinion can be formulated and upheld. That is one answer.
>
> And another one we learn from Rashi: sometimes one thesis is right and sometimes another, and it turns out that in any event a

> rejected opinion might be correct under slightly different circumstances.[24]
>
> The third explanation is according to the scholars of France, namely, that the Holy One, blessed be He, gave Moses forty-nine reasons that it be pronounced pure, and forty-nine aspects for pronouncing it impure, and so forth, and told him that the law would be according to the agreement of the scholars of the given generation. Thus, all opinions are indeed the words of the living God.[25]

And consult the text.

And what the Hida, of blessed memory, wrote in his second explanation, is based on what Rashi, of blessed memory, wrote in Ketubot, at the end of his comments:

> But when two Amoraim have a legal disagreement concerning monetary or ritual law, each adducing his own reasoning, there is no falsehood involved. Each of the two is putting forward his own argument, one providing reasons for permitting, and one reasons for prohibiting; one makes such and such an analogy, and the other makes a different analogy, and the principle of "both are the words of the living God" applies. Sometimes one argument is pertinent, and sometimes the other argument is pertinent, since the law's rationale changes according to variations in the circumstances, however minute.

That is what Rashi, of blessed memory, wrote. From this we learn that the Sages, of blessed memory, were right in saying, "Both are the words of the living God," for even if one scholar rules to forbid or permit a matter, and the law is not so, nevertheless, the ruling is true and exists in the world, and was received by Moses at Sinai regarding a different situation. And it is correct to say that this opinion too is the word of the living God.

There are more explanations by later scholars, of blessed memory, but nevertheless this inquiry has not proven very satisfactory, and we do not possess the understanding to pursue it to its ultimate conclusion, because even regarding the explanation of the scholars of France, of blessed memory, the great scholar, the Shela, remarks: "This is remote from human cognition, and cannot be grasped by man unless accompanied by divine guidance and His true light." He also says: "The explanations of the scholars of France, of blessed memory, do not give peace of mind, because they are not adequate. The mind will have rest only through the reasoning and secrets alluded to by the master [the Ritba]." Therefore we cannot delve any deeper into this question, or elaborate on it further. On a literal level, to bring some peace of

24 *Rashi*, bKetubot 57a s.v. *ha ka mashma lan*.

25 *Petah Einayim*, bBaba Metzia 59b s.v. *im halakha kamoti*.

> mind, and in particular, in order to answer the queries of ordinary people, we have brought the three explanations, and they more than suffice for the purpose of this investigation. Let the wise man answer the queries of the curious, and in particular, cite the explanation of the scholars of France, which is the most satisfying of the three. But the essential explanation is arrived at by way of secrets, and none of us have any business delving into it.
>
> *Responsa Zivhei Tzedek*, YD #26

This responsum displays a virtuosic grasp of the halakhic literature as well as a sophisticated sense of the complexity of the philosophical problems raised by the multiplicity principle. At the same time, it evidences unquestionable ambivalence, disquiet and even confusion regarding the best way of dealing with these issues. The responsum reflects a tension between the desire to find a satisfactory resolution for the dilemma, and awareness of the problematics attendant on such an endeavor. Particularly noteworthy is the responsum's concluding sentence, which explicitly associates the principle that "both are the words of the living God" with the mystical realm, and advises ordinary people to keep their distance.

### 2.4 Aggadic materials on celestial controversy

We will conclude our analysis of the sources that manifest a positive attitude to controversy by considering a number of Aggadic passages that allude to controversy on high—that is, controversy between God and the "heavenly academy." However we interpret this celestial metaphor, attribution of controversy to the heavenly sphere is indicative of the fact that controversy is not regarded as the result of human weaknesses and limitations, but rather, as an integral dimension of Torah study.

First of all, let us consider a fascinating Aggada about the death of Rabbah, after which we will look at some remarks on the story made by the Ran, R. Nissim Gerondi.

> R. Kahana said: R. Hama, the son of the daughter of Hasa, related to me that Rabbah bar Nahmani died of persecution, information against him having been leaked to the state. Said they [the informers]: There is an Israelite who keeps twelve thousand Israelites from paying the royal poll-tax one month in summer and one in winter. A royal officer was sent for him, but did not find him ... and he fled to Agama; there he sat upon the trunk of a [fallen] palm and studied. Now they were debating in the heavenly academy thus: If the spot preceded the white hair, he is impure; if the reverse, he is pure.[26] If [the order is] in doubt,

26 The reference is to the laws of leprosy, see Leviticus 13:10.

> the Holy One, blessed be He, ruled, he is pure; while the entire heavenly academy maintained, he is impure. Who shall decide it?, they asked. Rabbah bar Nahmani will decide, for he has declared, I am pre-eminent in the laws of leprosy and tents. A messenger was sent for him, but the Angel of Death could not approach him, because he did not interrupt his study. In the meantime, a wind blew and caused a rustling in the bushes, which he imagined to be a troop of soldiers. Let this person [referring to himself] die, he said, rather than be delivered into the hands of the state. As he was dying, he uttered, Pure, pure! A heavenly voice cried out, Happy art thou, O Rabbah bar Nahmani, whose body is pure and whose soul hath departed in purity.
>
> bBaba Metzia 86a

R. Nissim Gerondi comments as follows:

> This narrative requires explanation. To be sure, no one doubted what had been imparted by God himself: He had declared it pure. They knew with certainty that this was the sole truth. If so, how could they argue that it was impure until they had no recourse but to seek the decision of Rabbah bar Nahmani? This narrative should be interpreted in accordance with what we have written. Although they knew that "a doubtful spot is pure," they declared it impure, since the determination of the law, having been granted them when they were alive, was within their jurisdiction. And since their reasoning impelled them to declare it impure, it was fitting that it be declared impure, even though this contradicted the truth, because this position is dictated by human cognition. Even if the other position constitutes the objective truth, it is unseemly to act in accordance with it.
>
> Similarly, the opponents of R. Eliezer did not declare the oven pure (bBaba Metzia 59b), despite the fact that a heavenly voice had been sent to them proclaiming the law to be in accordance with the view of R. Eliezer. And as in this case, they did not doubt the veracity of the heavenly voice, yet they nonetheless declared: the law is not from heaven.
>
> *Derashot Haran* #5, version 2

The Ran alerts us to the connection between this Aggadic passage and the story we discussed above regarding the "oven of *akhnai*" controversy between R. Eliezer and the Sages (bBaba Metzia 59b). There, the controversy was decided against God, and in favor of the view of the Sages. Here too, ultimately, God's view is rejected,[27] and that of his opponents affirmed, although in this case He is opposed by a heavenly assembly, rather than by the Sages.

27 Maimonides, *Code*, Laws concerning the Uncleanness of Leprosy 2:9.

The story also serves to ground the claim that one who writes a document has no preferred status vis-à-vis its interpretation, and must defend his views along with all other opinions put forward.

The Maharam Mintz was asked whether the interpretation of those who had issued a writ of mediation was privileged.[28] Distinguishing between a document and the intentions of its authors, he answered that their interpretation of the writ is not necessarily to be preferred. Were authors to have such a special status, he noted, this would certainly apply in the case of the Torah, yet we see from the story of Rabbah bar Nahmani that God Himself has no privileged status in interpreting the Torah, which he authored.

The Maharam Mintz's invoking of the story of Rabbah bar Nahmani is a good example of how non-legal Aggadic material is adduced to draw conclusions regarding specific points of law. However, it should be also noted that not all the commentators accept the Maharam Mintz's analogy between the Torah and human documents.

Let us now look at another Aggadic passage describing a heavenly controversy.

> "And I will make thy spires of *kadkhod*" (Isa. 54:12)—R. Samuel b. Nahmani said: There is a controversy [over the meaning of *kadkhod*] between two angels in heaven, Gabriel and Michael. Others say, The dispute is between two Amoraim in the West [the land of Israel]. And who are they? Judah and Hezekiah, the sons of R. Hiya. One says it means onyx, and the other says, jasper. The Holy One, blessed be He, said unto them, Let it be as this one says, and as that one says.
>
> bBaba Batra 75a

The Gemara reads the prophecy as referring to the rebuilding of Jerusalem: Isaiah is describing the precious stones out of which its walls will be constructed. The controversy is over precisely what kind of stone it is that will be used. This passage is relevant to our discussion because it recounts the story of a heavenly controversy, at least according to the first opinion quoted. But in addition, it is also relevant due to its presentation of the divine response to the controversy: God decides that the walls will be built of both types of stones (here *kadkhod* is interpreted, by a play on words, as meaning "this and that"). Note that the book of Isaiah pre-dates the Talmud, wherein the controversy is described, by many centuries. It is, then, highly significant that the outcome of the later controversy establishes the meaning of the much earlier biblical text. Resolution of the controversy here does not merely settle the question by making a choice between various possible interpretations, but actually generates the meaning.

28 *Responsa Maharam Mintz*, #100.

This prompts the question, what is the role played by controversy in the talmudic literature? On the one hand, controversy can be seen as an attempt to uncover the meaning of a given term, text or teaching; on the other, it can be construed as assigning meaning to these elements. Now literary theory distinguishes between two positions: the view that the text has a fixed meaning, to be uncovered by the reader; and the view that the text has no meaning prior to its interpretation. It is possible to detect echoes of these positions in the various passages we have considered thus far. For instance, recall the passage from the Jerusalem Talmud that recounts how Moses was given all the possible interpretations of the law—forty-nine aspects in favor and forty-nine against—at Sinai (jSanhedrin 4:2). Upon comparing it with the Aggadic passage we have just looked at, the contrast between these two positions vis-à-vis the assignment of meaning is quite pronounced.

Let us consider one more *sugya* that takes a stand on the meaning issue:

> R. Judah said in the name of Rav, When Moses ascended on high he found the Holy One, blessed be He, engaged in affixing coronets to the letters. Said Moses, Master of the universe, who stays Thy hand?[29] He answered, There will arise a man, at the end of many generations, Akiva b. Joseph by name, who will expound upon each tittle heaps and heaps of laws.
>
> Master of the universe, said Moses; permit me to see him. He replied, Turn thee round. Moses went and sat down behind eight rows [of R. Akiva's students] and listened to the discourses on the law. Not being able to follow their arguments, he was ill at ease; but when, upon coming to a certain subject, the students said to the master, Whence do you know it? and the latter replied, It is a law given unto Moses at Sinai, he regained his composure. Thereupon he returned to the Holy One, blessed be He, and said, Master of the universe, Thou hast such a man and Thou givest the Torah through me! He replied, Be silent, for that is what occurred to Me. Then said Moses, Master of the universe, Thou hast shown me his Torah, show me his reward. Turn thee round, said He, and Moses turned round and saw them weighing out his flesh at the market-stalls.[30] Master of the universe, cried Moses, such Torah, and such a reward! He replied, Be silent, for that is what occurred to Me.
>
> bMenahot 29b

29 According to Rashi, this is a description of Moses' perplexity upon observing God affixing coronets to the letters of the completed Torah, that is, adding the small strokes (*tagin*) that serve as flourishes on certain letters. He questioned why the flourishes were needed, when all of mankind awaited the Torah.

30 R. Akiva died a martyr's death at the hands of the Romans during the Hadrianic persecution; see bBerakhot 61b.

Having distinguished between uncovering and assigning meaning, we can distinguish between two conceptions of the relationship between the Torah and the sages. On one conception, the Torah, with all its detailed ordinances, was given to Moses, leaving the nation the humble task of discovering and applying it, whereas on the other conception, the Torah is continually being completed by human creativity and ingenuity.

Our final example of a celestial controversy comes from the post-talmudic literature. The fact that the post-talmudic literature uses the device of heavenly controversy, which is relatively rarely used in the Talmud itself, demonstrates that it is nonetheless viewed as a legitimate metaphor.

> I also asked about the order of the passages in phylactery scrolls. My question was thus: I pray to You, great, mighty and awesome King, discerner of secrets, expounder of the recondite, guardian of the covenant and of loving-kindness, to increase Your loving-kindness toward us this day, and command Your holy angels to advise me regarding an uncertainty that has bewildered us with respect to the order of the passages in phylacteries. For some scholars say that the existential verses[31] must be in the middle, and that if this order is changed, the phylacteries are invalid. Other scholars say that the passages should be in the order of their appearance in the Torah, and that if this order is changed, the phylacteries are invalid. Now, King of Kings, command Your holy angels to advise me in accordance with which view the law is decided, and whose opinion you favor.
>
> And they replied: Both are the words of the living God, and as there is controversy below, so there is above. The Holy One, blessed be He, says that the existential passages should be in the middle, while the entire heavenly entourage says that they should be in the order of their appearance in the Torah. This is the meaning of the verse, "Through them that are nigh unto me I will be sanctified, and before all the people I will be glorified" (Lev. 10:3). This is His glory, to mention first the passage that attests to divine sovereignty.
>
> R. Jacob of Marvège, *Responsa Min Hashamayim*, #3

Without getting into the halakhic details pertaining to the issue described here, let us attend to the use of the expression "both are the words of the living God." Though this expression is frequently used in the halakhic sources, here it has a special salience. Usually, the expression denotes, as we saw, the fact that equal merit is ascribed to both sides to a controversy. In bGitin 6b, the expression was intended almost literally, describing an episode where the views of both sides were uttered by God. Here, it is

31 That is, Exodus 13:11 and Deuteronomy 11:13, the verses traditionally known as existential (*havaiot*), from the words "and it shall be" (*vehaya*) with which they open.

intended more literally still, describing a heavenly controversy in which one of the sides to the dispute is God Himself.

## 3 Sources evincing a negative attitude to controversy

Before turning to sources evincing a negative attitude to controversy, let us consider an ambivalent source.

The incredibly erudite eighteenth century authority R. Haim Joseph David Azoulay (Hida) was asked about the enactment of the Sages mandating recitation of Abbaye's account of Abba Saul's order of the Temple service (bYoma 33a) in the morning prayers. The question arises because the view of Abba Saul on the matter is not accepted as the law. His answer evinces a certain ambivalence as to the value of controversy:

> Thus I reply to you, my dearest friend, apple of my eye, to inform you that the main reason for the enactment of our predecessors mandating recitation of Abbaye's recounting of the Temple service in the morning prayers, is to gain merit for the whole nation by reciting a passage from the Mishnah and Gemara. They chose this passage, which deals with the Temple sacrifices. And it is known from what is stated in the discussion in bEruvin 13b that all are "the words of the living God." Relying on the scholars of France, R. Yomtov of Seville writes in his novellae [*Hidushei Haritba*] that the two contrary opinions are true. And Moses our teacher, may he rest in peace, asked the Holy One, blessed be He, But in accordance with whom is the law decided? and He answered that the decision is entrusted to the scholars of the given generation. Therefore, since such halakhic opinions are true, their recitation is tantamount to studying the Talmud. Even if they entail something not accepted as law, it does not matter, because this opinion is also true, and "both are the words of the living God."
>
> As an example, I mention the enactment to recite a chapter of the Mishnah, the fifth chapter of Zevahim, in the morning prayer. R. Joseph Caro writes in the name of R. Aaron Halevi that this chapter was chosen because it contains no controversy.[32] And the pre-eminent scholar of the generation, R. Haim [b. Isaac] Alfandari, of blessed memory, in his glosses on [R. Haim b. Menahem Algazi's] *Bnei Hayai*, notes that indeed, the chapter does not contain any controversy, but some of the laws mentioned there are disputed elsewhere by Sages of the Mishnah. R. Yomtov of Seville, of blessed memory, goes even further: "My teacher,[33] may God protect and deliver him, said that the choice of this chapter rests on the fact that it contains no controversy, though not all of it is accepted as law. For example, it is said there that

32 *Beit Yosef*, *Tur*, OH 50.
33 R. Aaron Halevi.

the Passover sacrifice may be eaten until midnight, but we have a tradition from our teacher Nahmanides that the law is according to R. Akiva, who opines that it may be eaten all night, since his view is supported by an anonymous Mishnah.[34] Nevertheless, since the whole chapter is presented without a dissenting view, it is more appropriate for recitation than any other."[35]

So this chapter contains controversial material and not all of it is considered law.

Similarly, I saw the comments[36] of R. Shimon b. Tzemah Duran, of blessed memory, who says that some Sages of the Mishnah disagree with R. Ishmael regarding some of his rules. Nevertheless, since we have the tradition that all are the words of the living God, it is all true Torah, and a person discharges his duty to study Scripture, Mishnah and Gemara by reciting it. Although in the opinion of R. Jacob b. Asher (Tur) and R. Yomtov of Seville and their followers, the baraita of R. Ishmael is recited in place of Gemara, in any event, it is likely that the passage with Abbaye's account is for the same purpose, for which it is suitable even if not all of it represents the law, because his reasoning is also true, since "both are the words of the living God," as explained.

*Responsa Yosef Ometz*, #51

The question under consideration in this responsum is why a Tannaitic passage that does not reflect the law is included in the prayerbook. The question is particularly acute given that the prayerbook is the quintessential philosophical work in the Jewish tradition, and the passages chosen to be included in it are by no means arbitrary selections. The Hida's answer to this question reveals a certain ambivalence about controversy. He begins by asserting that the principle "Both are the words of the living God" is best exemplified by choosing a passage that does not reflect the law. This remark implies that he views controversy and differences of opinion as a positive phenomenon. However, the Hida goes on to mention yet another mishnaic passage that is part of the prayerbook, one which also contains paragraphs that do not reflect the law, and asserts that it was chosen precisely because it does not record any controversy between the Sages, and thus, is most appropriate for recitation: "Nevertheless, since the whole chapter is presented without a dissenting view, it is more appropriate for recitation than any other." We see, then, that the responsum reflects a complex position which cannot be characterized as either positive or negative. On the one hand, the Hida understands the value of embracing a range of views, but on the other, he recognizes the potential social

34 Namely, mMegila, ch. 2.
35 *Hidushei Haritba*, Avoda Zara 18.
36 On Zevahim 5 (Maamar Hametz) and on the baraita of R. Ishmael.

dangers inherent in endorsing controversy. This ambivalence is itself a reflection of talmudic ambivalence about controversy. We will now turn to four Rabbinic sources—tSanhedrin 7:1; Sifre Deuteronomy 9:6; mEduyot 1:6; and mEduyot 8:7—evincing a clearly negative attitude to controversy.

### 3.1 tSanhedrin 7:1

> Said R. Jose: Initially there was no controversy in Israel; but there was the court of seventy in the Hall of Hewn Stone, and the other courts of twenty three were in the towns of the land of Israel ... if one needs a court, he turns to the court in his town; if there is no court in his town, he goes to a court near his town. If they [the court] had heard [a tradition], they told it to them [the litigants]; and if not, [the initiator of the action] and the most eminent member of the court go to the court on the Temple Mount. If they had heard, they told it to them; and if not, he and the most eminent of them go to the court on the Rampart. If they had heard, they told it to them; and if not, these and the others go to the court in the Hall of Hewn Stone.... If they had heard, they told it to them; and if not, they stand up for a vote; if the majority is for impurity, they declare it impure, if the majority is for purity, they declare it pure. From there the law originates and is disseminated in Israel. When there multiplied students of Shammai and Hillel who did not attend their teachers sufficiently, controversies multiplied in Israel, and the law became like two sets of laws [lit., two Torahs].
>
> tSanhedrin 7:1[37]

#### i The emergence of controversy

The Tosefta describes the judicial hierarchy and the process of recourse to the courts at the time of the Temple. It relates how an individual with a legal grievance could take his adversary to court for resolution of his complaint. The court resolved the dispute by seeking to apply a known tradition to the case before it. If there was no relevant tradition known to the court, the case was heard before a higher court. The culmination of the process was appearance before the court in the Hall of Hewn Stone, which, if no relevant tradition was at hand, decided on the basis of a majority vote.

The Tosefta contrasts an ideal situation with an existent situation, the ideal situation being that in which there is no controversy, and the existent situation that in which controversy is endemic. We are not concerned, here, with the question of the historical veracity of this portrayal, but will take it at face value.

37 There are a number of variants of this Tosefta: tHagiga 2:9, jSanhedrin 1:4 (19c), bSanhedrin 88b.

What brought about the transition from the ideal situation to the non-ideal situation? The Tosefta suggests two different answers to this question, hinting that the passage may, in fact, be compiled from two separate texts.[38] One answer is explicitly formulated at the very end of the passage: "When there multiplied students of Shammai and Hillel who did not attend their teachers sufficiently, controversies multiplied in Israel, and the law became like two sets of laws." We will discuss this answer shortly; now we need only point out that it is also found as an independent baraita in bSota 47b. The second answer, which is only implied, attributes the emergence of controversy to the destruction of the Temple and the elimination of the high court in the Hall of Hewn Stone. On this explanation, the emergence of controversy is linked to the absence of a decisive high court capable of resolving all cases that came before it, thereby precluding controversy.

On either explanation, however, tSanhedrin provides a historical account of the emergence of controversy. That is, it regards controversy as a historical contingency rather than as inherent in the nature of the Torah. This type of attempt to explain controversy as a contingency, a historical accident, implies a critical attitude. This contrasts markedly with the accounts of controversy we saw above, in which controversy is presented as so inherently a part of Torah that it even occurs on high.

However, although the relationship between the two states, the ideal state and the later reality, is presented as straightforward, in another talmudic account of the same judicial process we can find evidence that some sort of controversy was not entirely unheard of even in the ideal state. Although its description of the early phases of the judicial process is indeed identical to that in tSanhedrin, when the stage is reached where the case is heard before the court on the Rampart, there is a marked discrepancy:

> And he [the most eminent member of the court] declared: Thus have I expounded, and thus have my colleagues expounded; thus have I taught, and thus have they taught.
>
> bSanhedrin 88b

Whether or not this passage leaves open the possibility that this phenomenon also existed at the earlier stages in the judicial process, these lines clearly depict a situation where contending analyses of a legal situation are being put forward.

### ii Moral degeneration

Let us now take a closer look at the first explanation offered for the emergence of controversy, which, as we said, also appears elsewhere, as an independent baraita, prefaced by another remark:

38 See David Z. Hoffman, *The First Mishna and the Controversies of the Tannaim*, trans. P. Forchheimer (New York: 1977).

> When the haughty of heart multiplied, controversy multiplied in Israel.[39] When there multiplied students of Shammai and Hillel who did not attend their teachers sufficiently, controversies multiplied in Israel, and the law became like two sets of laws.
>
> bSota 47b

The context in which this passage appears is a *sugya* that lists different types of decline in moral character.

It is clear here that controversy is perceived as an evil. What is not clear, however, is whether the emergence of controversy is being presented as a punishment for moral decline. Much depends on how we interpret the behavior of the students of Shammai and Hillel, who "did not attend their teachers sufficiently." In this context, "attending" denotes activity necessary for the study of the law, a theme that recurs frequently in the Rabbinic literature. What is it, exactly, that the students are being charged with? On one interpretation, the students were unable to attend their teachers because of political upheaval that interfered with the development of close bonds with their masters, their teachers. That is, on this interpretation, controversy is perceived as an outcome of a historical contingency rather than as a punishment for wrongdoing.

On another reading, however, one that appears to be more in line with the context of the baraita, which lists various manifestations of social decline, controversy is seen as inflicted upon the nation as a result of the students' moral deterioration.

### iii Adverse effects of controversy

Having considered the factors put forward here as causes of controversy, let us now say a few words about the alleged result of its proliferation—"the law became like two sets of laws" [literally, like two Torahs]. Now what is the concern here? We can distinguish between two possible problems the baraita may be alluding to: sectarianism and doctrinal disagreement.

The following passage from the Mishnah describes types of halakhic controversies that are potentially divisive:

> The house of Shammai permit the rival-wives to the brothers, but the house of Hillel prohibit it. If they [widows] had undergone the ceremony of *halitza*–the house of Shammai declare them ineligible for [marriage to] the priesthood, but the house of Hillel declare them eligible; if they had been taken in levirate marriage, the house of

39 This additional sentence also appears in bHulin 7a, prefaced by "*detenan*" (for we have learned) which usually signifies that the quotation is of mishnaic origin. However, it is not in the Mishnah.

> Shammai declare them eligible, but the house of Hillel declare them ineligible.
>
> mJebamot 1:4

Although concerned about the potentially segregative effects of controversy, the Mishnah goes on to say that the feared outcome did not materialize:

> Nevertheless, though one house prohibit what the other house allow, and one house declare unfit what the other house declare fit, yet the house of Shammai did not refrain from marrying women of the house of Hillel, nor the house of Hillel from marrying women of the house of Shammai. In spite of all the disputes regarding purity and impurity, in which one side declare pure what the other side declare impure, they did not refrain from making use of whatever pertained to the other in matters connected with purity.

To be sure, this idealized account is not corroborated by other traditions regarding the controversy between the two schools, which indeed confirm that the fears were not exaggerated. For example,

> It was taught in the name of R. Joshua Onia, The students of the house of Shammai stood below and killed the students of the house of Hillel. It was taught, Six of them went up and the rest blocked their way with swords and spears.
>
> jShabat 1:4 (3c)[40]

This tradition can explain the great sensitivity of the Sages to the potentially dangerous social implications of controversy.

Concern over the proliferation of controversy is reflected in the punishment of the rebellious elder,[41] which is mandatory and cannot be abrogated.

> Come and hear. R. Josiah said: Three things did Zeira, an inhabitant of Jerusalem, tell me: If the husband renounced his warnings [to his wife whom he suspected of adulterous conduct], they are null; if the father and mother wished to pardon a stubborn and rebellious son, they may do so; and the court may pardon a rebellious elder, if it so desires. But when I went to my colleagues of the south, they agreed to the first two,

40 A parallel passage is found at the end of Megilat Taanit: "On the ninth of Adar, they decreed a fast, to mark the controversy between the house of Shammai and the house of Hillel, wherein three thousand of their students were killed." And see bShabat 17a.

41 "Rebellious elder" denotes a judge who seeks a ruling from the high court in Jerusalem, and upon receiving it, rules otherwise in his own court; he is subject to capital punishment. See Chapter Four below, "Erroneous Rulings."

> but not to the rebellious elder, so that controversy would not increase in Israel. This is an irrefutable answer.
>
> bSanhedrin 88a

Above, we noted that concern about controversy and its possible repercussions was, to some extent, also motivated by theological considerations. A remark in this vein is made, for instance, by the Ritba, in commenting on a key talmudic *sugya* dealing with controversy, bJebamot 13b-14a, part of which is discussed below:

> Since you are the children of one Father and one God, it is proper that you not form factions, as if there were two Torahs and two deities.
>
> *Hidushei Haritba*, bJebamot 13b

In any event, whether motivated by apprehension about adverse social or theological outcomes, fear that the law will become two distinct bodies of law is discernible as a thread running through the talmudic corpus alongside the voices in favor of tolerating, or even encouraging, controversy. The alleged deleterious consequences of controversy are seen as an argument for minimizing the degree to which controversy can have more than purely theoretical significance, that is, the degree to which it can be acted upon.

Averting controversy remained a priority in the post-talmudic era. This is evident from discussion of the talmudic *sugya* about an enactment concerning the precise procedure for blowing the shofar on Rosh Hashana.

> R. Abbahu ordained in Caesarea that there should be a long blast (*tekia*), three short blasts (*shevarim*) [groans], one wailing blast (*terua*) and another long blast (*tekia*). How can this be justified? If the sound [required by the Bible] is a kind of wailing, then there should be *tekia*, *terua* and *tekia*, and if it is a kind of groaning, should there not be *tekia*, three *shevarim*, and *tekia*? He was in doubt whether it was a kind of groaning or a kind of wailing.
>
> bRosh Hashana 34a

In addition to the non-disputed requirement of blowing *tekia*, R. Abbahu required that two additional kinds of blowing sounds be issued. Concerning this passage, R. Hai Gaon was asked how it could be that there was no clear tradition regarding the blowing of the shofar, which takes place every year.

> Our master [R. Hai Gaon] of blessed memory, was asked: Should we assume that before the time of R. Abbahu, the [obligation to fulfil the] precept of blowing the shofar was not discharged? Apparently, the sound of the *terua* was subject to doubt among them, as it is said, "this

is surely a matter of controversy" (bRosh Hashana 33b), but there is no doubt that the issue must have been decided: Is it conceivable that they did not know the true procedure for a duty that had to be performed every year? Had they not seen how it was performed, each generation showing the next, one hearing the tradition from another, continuously, back to Moses our teacher, of blessed memory?

And our master, of blessed memory, answered that the *terua* as prescribed by the Torah is certainly discharged with either a wailing or a groaning blast, because the Torah intended that the *terua* be composed of sounds and broken blasts. And in earlier times it was performed either as broken blasts or as wailing; it was a matter of individual preference, and the duty was in any event discharged. This was known to the learned, but ordinary people mistakenly thought that there was a difference between them, and therefore that one or another group was not discharging its obligation with respect to the precept. So to dispel this view held by the ignorant, and in order to prevent the Torah from becoming like two sets of laws [lit., two Torahs], R. Abbahu ordered that both customs be followed, and added one more *terua* blast at his own initiative, because he resolved to establish the *terua* in every possible customary broken sound. Since simple folks thought that there was controversy among them over this, the Talmud presents this in the style of a debate, that is, with objections raised and a resolution offered.

*Ritba* ad loc., quoting a responsum by R. Hai Gaon

## 3.2 Sifre Deuteronomy 96–the injunction against factionalism

The normative formulation of the critical stance on controversy is the "do not form factions" injunction, the earliest source for which in the Rabbinic literature is Sifre Deuteronomy.

> "Ye shall not cut yourselves" (*lo titgodedu*) (Deut. 14:1). Do not form factions, but be united, as it is written, "It is He that buildeth His upper chambers in the heaven, and hath founded His bunch[42] on earth" (Amos 9:6).
>
> Sifre Deuteronomy, Ree, 96 (Finkelstein edition p. 158)

The somewhat indefinite significance of this general injunction, which at first sight might seem directed against the formation of sects outside the halakhic framework altogether, is ultimately endowed with a well-defined halakhic meaning in a celebrated controversy between Abbaye and Rava:

> Said Abbaye: The admonition against forming factions is only applicable to a case such as that of two courts of law in the same town,

42 The term for bunch, "*agudato*," is in the singular.

> one of which rules in accordance with the views of the house of Shammai while the other rules in accordance with the views of the house of Hillel. However, in a case of two courts of law in two different towns, it is irrelevant. Said Rava to him, surely the case of the house of Shammai and the house of Hillel is like that of two courts of law in the same town? Whereas, said Rava, the admonition against forming factions is only applicable to a case such as that of a court of law in a given town, part of which rules in accordance with the views of the house of Shammai while the other part rules in accordance with the views of the house of Hillel. However, in a case of two courts of law in the same town, it is irrelevant.
>
> bJebamot 14a

This talmudic injunction is the subject of a tremendous amount of discussion and explication in the post-talmudic literature. The development of this discussion is too sweeping to be addressed here, and merits separate examination. Two central questions, on which much of the debate has focused, are the following. Does this injunction address the halakhic authority, or the individual? And with respect to the injunction, is there any difference between conduct grounded in custom (*minhag*) and conduct grounded in law?

### 3.3 mEduyot 1:6—rejection of minority views

Above, in exploring the positive attitude to controversy, we saw that mEduyot 1:5, manifesting a favorable attitude, presents the recording of minority views as a means of introducing some flexibility into the decision-making process, by empowering the judge to rely on a rejected minority view.

The contrary view, however, is also to be found there, immediately following that paragraph:

> R. Judah said: If so, why do they record the opinion of the individual against that of the majority to no effect? So that if one should say, "I have received such a tradition," another may say, "You have heard it only as the opinion of so-and-so."
>
> mEduyot 1:6

The position of R. Judah here[43] is that the recording of minority views is motivated by the desire to strip them of any normative validity. This view is more pronounced in a variant reading of this Mishnah, which, instead

43 The Tosefta records the same dispute, except that the positions expressed are reversed, with R. Judah upholding rather than disparaging controversy (tEduyot 1:4 [Zuckermandel edition]).

of construing the phrase "to no effect" as part of the question, sees it as part of the answer, reading it as, "To invalidate them!"

### 3.4 mEduyot 8:7–the eradication of controversy

We will conclude by looking at the final passage in mEduyot.

> R. Joshua said: I have received a tradition from Rabban Johanan b. Zakai, who heard it from his teacher, and his teacher from his teacher, as a law given to Moses at Sinai, that Elijah will not come to pronounce impure or to pronounce pure, to send away or to bring near, but to send away those brought near by force and to bring near those sent away by force. The family of Bet Zerephah was on the other side of the Jordan, and Ben Zion sent it away by force; and yet another family was there, and Ben Zion brought it near by force. Elijah will come to pronounce such cases impure or to pronounce pure, to send away or to bring near. R. Judah says: to bring near, but not to send away. R. Simon says: to reconcile controversy. And the Sages say, neither to send away nor to bring near, but to make peace in the world, for it is said, "Behold I send to you Elijah the Prophet ... and he shall turn the heart of the fathers to the children and the heart of the children to their fathers" (Mal. 3:23–24).
>
> mEduyot 8:7

Here we see Elijah the Prophet in a role different from that which he played in the passages above. In those passages, he served as an intermediary between the heavenly and the mortal spheres, whereas here he represents the end of days, the ideal future that mankind hopes to merit. This Mishnah describes several views on the ways in which the world will be perfected, one of them being the elimination of controversy.[44] Here, we must keep in mind the distinction discussed above between two senses of "controversy"—debate and social strife. However, it appears that in saying, "to reconcile controversy," R. Simon is referring to controversy as debate.

## 4 Conclusion

Our examination of sources evincing a negative attitude to controversy opened with tSanhedrin, which described the idyllic past when there was no controversy, and ends with the messianic period to come, when there

44 This Mishnah is the basis for the popular understanding of the Aramaic word "*teiku*," used to denote unresolved disputes in the Talmud, and derived from the word "*kum*," to stand. On this popular conception, *teiku* is an acronym for *tishbi* [Elijah] *yetaretz kushiyot ubeayot* (Elijah will resolve difficulties and problems).

will once more be no controversy. The assumption underlying this utopian vision is that controversy is an unfortunate phenomenon. Human society, however, is not situated in these contention-free circumstances, but in historical eras that, as we have seen throughout this chapter, have been replete with controversy and differences of opinion. Mankind, with its limitations and failings, has become involved in controversy in the course of a sincere search for truth. The pragmatic wisdom of the Sages was, therefore, to accept the reality of controversy and not attempt to muzzle or deny it. Indeed, they had the perspicacity to view it as a positive, enriching, inspiring and engaging process that allowed all segments of the learned community to express themselves, as we have seen. The only constraint limiting debate pertained, not to the content of the views expressed, but to the modes of expression used. Civility, respect and a positive attitude to one's interlocutors, both past and present, were put in place as safeguards that enabled dissenting views to remain within the collective discourse. Tolerance of controversy indeed attests to strength and self-confidence, and it is hoped that this tolerance will continue to characterize the Jewish scholarly community, in the future, as it has in the past, and to make itself felt even beyond.

# 2 Legal formalism



## 1 Two methods of formulating laws

'Formalism' in the legal context has a number of meanings. It can refer to formalism in the wording or formulation of rules of law, judicial formalism, and formalism in the procedural rules constituting the overall process of achieving a legal objective. Formalism in the formulation of rules of law is the method of precisely defining rules and their scope, as well as stating them in a concrete rather than an abstract manner. This method prefers to issue its directives in the form of well-defined rules rather than broad principles. The outcome of a case governed by such rules will depend on fulfillment of the specific formal conditions enumerated in the laws. Judicial formalism refers to how the law is interpreted by the judge. The interpreter adheres strictly to the letter of the law rather than seeking to identify, and rule in accordance with, the spirit of the law. Formalism with respect to procedural rules refers to the official requirements pertaining to legal documents and the submission of writs and warrants, as, for example, the use of proper application forms, stamps, and so on.

This chapter deals with formalism in the first sense, that is, formalism in the formulation of laws.

The formalistic method can be effectively illustrated by comparing a formalistically-worded law to a non formalistically-worded law. Consider the following Israeli laws:

> Where the tenant of a dwelling has died, his spouse shall become the tenant, provided they had been spouses for not less than six months immediately preceding the death of the tenant and had lived together during that period.
>
> *Tenants' Protection Law (Consolidated Version), 5732–1972*, 26 LSI 204 1971–72 §20(a)

> (a) The lawful possessor of any immovable property may use a reasonable amount of force to prevent trespass thereon or the unlawful denial of his control thereof.
> (b) Where a person occupies any property unlawfully, the lawful possessor thereof may use a reasonable amount of force to take it from the occupier, provided he does so within what, in the circumstances of the case, is a reasonable time.
>
> *Land Law 5729–1969*, 23 LSI 283 1968–69 §18(a), (b)

Under certain circumstances, Israeli law recognizes the right of a tenant and his or her spouse to occupy their apartment after the expiration of the original lease. The aim of the quoted law is to prevent fictitious marriage contracts, the sole purpose of which is to transfer rights of tenancy. The formalistically-formulated law quoted here does not concern itself with the relationship of the married couple, or define the needs of the surviving partner. The right to occupy the apartment is to be decided solely on the basis of the fulfillment of formal requirements: the date of marriage and the length of time the apartment was jointly occupied.

Such formalism is absent in the second law. This law is formulated in a general manner, using terms such as "reasonable force" and "reasonable amount of time," without defining how these instructions are to be applied in practice. Unlike the first example, where a period of six months is mentioned, the law does not fix the duration of the "reasonable time" in which the owner is permitted to exercise his right to evict the trespasser, nor does it define the extent of the "reasonable force" that may be used.

Laws can also be formulated in a 'mixed' manner, that is, partly formalistically and partly non-formalistically. In 1981, clause (b) of the second law was amended to read as follows:

> Where a person occupies any property unlawfully, the lawful possessor thereof may, within thirty days from the date of the occupation, use a reasonable amount of force to remove him therefrom.
>
> *Public Land (Removal of Squatters) Law 5741–1981*, 35 LSI 108 1980–81 §7

### 1.1 Merits and drawbacks of formalistic and general formulation

The inherent advantage of formalistic formulation is that it clearly delineates lawful actions from unlawful actions. By unambiguously demarcating the limits of legal responsibility, it obviates the need for debate and deliberation each time the law is followed. Formalistic formulation provides straightforward instructions to the addressees of the law, those who must abide by it.

On the other hand, this method has drawbacks: the legislator cannot foresee all future cases to which the law might apply; sometimes a formalistically-formulated norm may not cover a case to which it seems relevant, and its strict application may lead to injustice. General formulation has the opposite drawbacks: though a law that has been formulated in general terms will be broad enough to cover unforeseeable cases, it often leaves open what particular action should be taken in a given case.

Consider the following example. A sign at the entrance to a municipal park states: "No entry to motor vehicles." The aim of this prohibition is to ensure the safety of children playing in the park, and to minimize noise and exhaust fumes. Prima facie, the sign is unequivocal and leaves no room for doubt. But what about a disabled person in a motorized wheelchair?

The sign denies entrance to motor vehicles and the motorized wheelchair is such a vehicle. It is clear, however, that the legislator did not intend to exclude people with disabilities from entering the public park, thereby denying them access to facilities available to every other citizen. It would have been possible to solve this problem by wording the sign differently: "It is forbidden to cause any disturbance or create any danger on park property." This general formulation would remove any doubts concerning the motorized wheelchair, but would leave open the question of what constituted a disturbance. The ordinary citizen would have difficulty interpreting the sign, and this would likely lead to disputes and friction. The agreeable and harmless pastimes of one park-goer, say skateboarding and playing the flute, would be regarded as dangerous nuisances by another, whose interests are different. Lacking specific instructions as to precisely which activities are permissible, and which are not, each would claim that his interpretation of the rule was the correct one.

In commenting on the biblical verse, "You shall do that which is right and good in the eyes of God" (Deut. 6:18), an example of a generally-formulated norm, Nahmanides assserts:

> At first he [Moses] stated that you are to keep His statutes and His testimonies which He commanded you, and now he is stating that even where He has not commanded you, give thought, as well, to do what is good and right in His eyes, for He loves the good and the right. Now this is a great principle, for it is impossible to mention in the

> Torah all aspects of man's conduct with his neighbors and friends, and all his various transactions, and the ordinances of all societies and countries. But since He mentioned many of them—such as, *Thou shalt not go up and down as a talebearer* [Lev. 19:16]; *Thou shalt not take vengeance, nor bear any grudge* [Lev. 19:18]; *Neither shalt thou idly by the blood of your neighbor* [Lev. 19:16]; *Thou shalt not curse the deaf* [Lev. 19:14]; *Thou shalt rise up before the hoary head* [Lev. 19:32]; and the like—He reverted to state in a general way that, in all matters, one should do what is good and right.[1]

The Ramban is asserting is that the principle "You shall do that which is right and good in the eyes of God" is a general norm that fills gaps engendered by the more formalistic formulation of the Torah's other laws.

The great English legal philosopher, H.L.A. Hart, offers a similar account of the need for general norms: there are some spheres in which the legislator's expertise does not suffice to precisely articulate the relevant parameters, and she must therefore content herself with broad abstract principles, leaving specification of the more detailed requirements to those who are closer to the field:

> Sometimes the sphere to be legally controlled is recognized from the start as one in which the features of individual cases will vary so much in socially important but unpredictable respects that uniform rules to be applied from case to case without further official direction cannot usefully be framed by the legislature in advance. Accordingly, to regulate such a sphere the legislature sets up very general standards and then delegates to an administrative, rule-making body acquainted with the varying types of case, the task of fashioning rules adapted to their special needs....
>
> A second similar technique is used where the sphere to be controlled is such that it is impossible to identify a class of specific actions to be uniformly done or forborne and to make them the subject of a simple rule, yet the range of circumstances, though very varied, covers familiar features of common experience. Here common judgments of what is 'reasonable' can be used by the law. This technique leaves to individuals, subject to correction by a court, the task of weighing up and striking a reasonable balance between the social claims which arise in various unanticipatable forms. In this case they are required to conform to a variable standard before it has been officially defined, and they may learn from a court only ex post facto when they have violated it, what, in terms of specific actions or forbearances, is the standard required of them....

1 *Ramban (Nachmanides): Commentary on the Torah*, trans. Charles Chavel (New York: 1976), Deuteronomy, 88.

> The most famous example of this technique in Anglo-American law is the use of the standard of due care in cases of negligence. Civil, and less frequently criminal, sanctions may be applied to those who fail to take reasonable care to avoid inflicting physical injuries on others. But what is reasonable or due care in a concrete situation?... But owing to the immense variety of possible cases where care is called for, we cannot *ab initio* foresee what combinations of circumstances will arise nor foresee what interests will have to be sacrificed or to what extent, if precaution against harm is to be taken.[2]

### 1.2 The problematics of formulating laws—an example from the Talmud

Let us now turn to talmudic law, and examine a law that highlights the differences between the formalistic and general modes of formulation.

> If fire break out, and catch in thorns, so that the shocks of corn, or the standing corn, or the field are consumed; he that kindled the fire shall surely make restitution.
>
> Exodus 22:5

This verse states that one who starts a fire must pay for the damage it causes. Although the verse does not state the extent of his responsibility, it is clear that it would be unjust to hold him liable if he took reasonable care to prevent the spread of fire.

The subject of the following Mishnah is the liability of one who lit, on his own property, a fire that later spread to his neighbor's property.

> If one kindles a fire on his own property, how far must the fire [have room to] spread [within his own domain to render him exempt from liability]? R. Eleazer b. Azariah says, [For him to be exempt], they consider [the fire] as though it were in the centre of a *kor*'s area of land.[3] R. Eliezer says, Sixteen cubits, like a public thoroughfare. R. Akiva says, Fifty cubits. R. Shimon says, "He that kindled the fire shall surely make restitution"—it all depends on the nature of the fire.
>
> mBaba Kama 6:4

The debate between the Sages and R. Shimon focuses on what type of norm is preferable—a norm that is specific and unambiguous, or a norm that is open to a range of interpretations, and therefore covers a wide variety of particular cases. The first three Tannaim, R. Eleazar b. Azariah, R. Eliezer, and R. Akiva, state an exact distance from the boundaries of his

2 H.L.A. Hart, *The Concept of Law* (Oxford:1961), 127.
3 75,000 square cubits (nearly 274 cubits square).

property to be maintained by the fire-kindler to ensure his exemption from liability if the fire spreads to a neighbor's domain. If the owner of the field lit a fire in the middle of his field, so that it was at least that distance from the field's boundary, then even if the fire spread, damaging the adjoining field, he is not liable for the damage. In R. Eleazar b. Azariah's view, the minimum distance should be 137 cubits (about 280 feet); according to R. Eliezer, it should be 16 cubits, and according to R. Akiva, 50 cubits. If the distance was smaller, the fire-kindler would be held responsible; if it was greater, he would be exempt.

There is obviously an arbitrary element in these definitions, since even if the distance is only slightly greater than that specified, the fire-kindler is not liable, a few inches making all the difference. The purpose of the definitions is to settle the matter of legal responsibility by distinguishing between those who will be held liable, and those who will not. The logic behind having an arbitrary definition is that it allows someone planning to light a fire to take precautions that will enable him to avoid financial injury. Presumably, the various minimum distances suggested by the Sages were arrived at after observing various fires.

A very different view is upheld by R. Shimon, who maintains that "it all depends on the nature of the fire." In other words, he holds that liability must be determined on a case by case basis, taking the size of the fire and the prevailing conditions into consideration. While the other Sages seek to define the extent of the fire-kindler's liability in general, R. Shimon argues that there is no way to pre-define the extent of liability. Liability can only determined, he asserts, when the specific conditions that obtained at the time the fire was lit have been established. If the fire was small and conditions were such that it was not reasonable to suppose that the fire would spread, then, even though the fire nonetheless did spread, the fire-kindler is not liable, even if the distance from the fire to the boundary of his field was small. Conversely, if the fire was large and conditions were conducive to its spreading rapidly, the fire-kindler is accountable for the damage even if the fire was started far from property line. R. Shimon's approach is in harmony with that of halakhic tort law, and it is interesting to note that the law is decided in accordance with his view.

Let us now compare the mishnaic rule with the rule as set down in the Tosefta.

> If one kindles a fire on his own property, how far must the fire [have room to] spread [within his own domain to render him exempt from liability]? R. Eliezer says, sixteen cubits, like a public thoroughfare; when it is windy, thirty cubits. R. Judah says, Thirty cubits; when it is windy, fifty cubits. R. Akiva says, Fifty cubits; when it is windy, three hundred cubits. An incident occurred in Arav, where a flame leapt more than three hundred cubits and did damage.... Under what circumstances? When it jumped across. But if it was going along and

> smoldering, or if there was brush there, even over a distance of up to a *mil*, the one who kindled it is liable.
>
> tBaba Kama 6:22

In one sense, the Tosefta's approach replicates the formalistic approach favored by the first three Tannaim of the Mishnah, however, it also encompasses an element of the context-sensitivity championed by R. Shimon, insofar as it invokes environmental conditions, namely, wind and the presence of brush.

## 2 The formalistic method–some talmudic examples

Talmudic law generally prefers the formalistic method of formulation, for reasons discussed in section 3 below. Let us consider a number of examples.

### 2.1 Finding a young pigeon

> If a young pigeon is found within fifty cubits, it belongs to the owner of the dovecote; but if beyond fifty cubits, it belongs to the finder.
>
> mBaba Batra 2:6

This Mishnah deals with the laws of lost and found property. It discusses a baby pigeon, as yet unable to fly, found near a dovecote. The question is whether the finder may keep it, or has to return it to its owner. The answer turns on another question: whether the bird has fallen from the dovecote, or was from elsewhere, and had been lost by its owner when passing through the area. In the latter case, the finder can keep the bird. Regarding the factual question as to the origin of the pigeon, the Mishnah defines an exact measure: if the fledgling was found within fifty cubits of the dovecote, then it belongs to the dovecote owner, and the finder must return it to him. If it was found more than fifty cubits from the dovecote, the finder may keep it. The Talmud gives the following reason for this decision: "Nothing that hops, hops more than fifty cubits." If the fledgling was found more than fifty cubits from a dovecote, it can be assumed that it was dropped by passers-by, and did not fall out of the dovecote. Since it has no identifying markings, its owners have 'despaired' (a technical talmudic term) of finding it, meaning they have written it off as a loss, and thus by law, the finder may keep it.

It is not difficult to imagine a scenario in which application of the mishnaic ruling would be unreasonable. Suppose the fledgling was found within fifty cubits of a dovecote, but the dovecote is surrounded by a high fence that it could not possibly have climbed, and the bird was outside the fence. A more general wording, such as, "a young pigeon belongs to its finder if in the given circumstances it is reasonable to suppose that it did not come from a nearby dovecote," would be more flexible, and would provide a solution in this hypothetical case. But this wording would likely lead to arguments between the finder and the owner of the dovecote, each of whom would interpret the expression "in the given circumstances" to his own advantage.

The rigidity of the Mishnah's ruling is criticized in a question raised by one of the Sages.

> R. Jeremiah raised the question: if one of its feet is within the fifty cubits and the other is outside the fifty cubits—what do we say?
>
> bBaba Batra 23b

To highlight the inflexibility of the mishnaic rule and its lack of utility for solving real-world problems, R. Jeremiah describes a hypothetical situation, a fledgling straddling the fifty-cubit demarcation line. This challenge to the fundamental adequacy of formalistic wording, emphasizing the absurdity of its specificity, remains unanswered. The Talmud relates only that as a result of this question, R. Jeremiah was expelled from the house of study for causing annoyance.[4]

The young pigeon case is an example of formalistic wording regarding measures of distance. The following example deals with formalistic wording regarding time.

### 2.2 The widow's waiver

> As long as she [the widow] lives in her father's house, she is entitled to collect [the amount specified in] her *ketuba* forever. As long as she lives in her husband's house, she may collect [the amount specified in] her *ketuba* until twenty-five years [have elapsed]. For over the course of twenty-five years, she benefits as much as her *ketuba* is worth—so says R. Meir in the name of Rabban Shimon b. Gamaliel. But the Sages say: As long as she lives in her husband's house, she may collect [the amount specified in] her *ketuba* forever. As long as she lives in her father's house, she may collect [the amount specified in] her *ketuba* until twenty-five years [have elapsed].
>
> mKetubot 12:4

A widow whose husband left an estate may choose between two alternatives: she may either claim her *ketuba*[5] and forgo all further claims

4 The Talmud relates other questions in the same vein posed by R. Jeremiah in different contexts (see bRosh Hashana 13a; bSota 16b). bBaba Batra 165b tells us that R. Jeremiah was re-admitted to the House of Study after presenting his views with great humility—when asked for his opinion, he replied: "I am unworthy of having this question addressed to me, but your pupil [referring to himself] is inclined toward the view that…."

5 *Ketuba*: A document in which the groom undertakes a number of duties toward the bride. One of the clauses promises the bride a sum of money if she is widowed.

on her husband's estate, or she may draw maintenance. In the latter case, she may still claim her *ketuba* and terminate her legal relationship with the estate if she acts within a given period of time. The length of this time is debated in the Mishnah.

R. Meir is of the opinion that a widow who chooses to stay in her husband's household may make use of the estate to benefit others–for example, by inviting her friends for tea[6]–something that, strictly speaking, she has no legal right to do. After these fringe benefits have been enjoyed for twenty-five years, they equal the worth of her *ketuba*, which is thus forfeited. But if she lives in a different household, without making any use of her late husband's property, she may claim her *ketuba* forever.

The Sages hold the opposite view. A widow who remains in her husband's household, and is supported by his heirs, never loses her right to claim her *ketuba*. They reason that no matter how much time has elapsed, the widow does not waive her right to the *ketuba*, because she would be uncomfortable suing her husband's heirs for her rightful due. But if she lives in a different household, and her husband's heirs merely forward to her the maintenance payments to which she is entitled by law, then she draws no extra benefits and has no emotional ties to the heirs. In this case, if twenty-five years have elapsed without her claiming the *ketuba*, it is to be assumed that she has waived her rights, and she cannot suddenly decide to claim it.

This rule is similar to a statute of limitations in contemporary law, with one key difference. Limitation laws are based on public policy–there must be a time limit to one's responsibility for his acts, and a time limit for keeping evidence. Here, there is a clear element of arbitrariness in fixing the time limit, and there is no specific empirical justification for this determination. By contrast, the rule in the Mishnah is based on an assumed waiver of rights for which an exact time period is defined: twenty-five years after the husband's death, the widow is regarded as having waived her right to claim her *ketuba*. Here, the time limit, though a general rule and not based on case-by-case assessment, reflects a attempt to reconstruct a widow's mind-set, and hence purports to be objectively justified.

The type of challenge raised in the case of the young pigeon is encountered here too. It is raised by Abbaye, who objects to a definite time limit.

> Abbaye said to R. Joseph: the poorest in Israel until twenty-five years [have elapsed] and Martha the Boethusian [someone from a very affluent family][7] until twenty five years? He said to him: The load must fit the camel [i.e., it is a relative matter, and just as the load varies with the size of the camel, so the benefit varies with the wealth of the family].
>
> bKetubot 104a

6 Literally, "lending salt to her neighbors."
7 bGitin 56a.

Abbaye is asking how the arbitrary time limit of twenty-five years can be set without regard to the particular case or the amount settled on the woman in the *ketuba*. He contends that the time limit should vary with the sum in question.

R. Joseph justifies R. Meir's view by saying that the widow's use of the estate is proportional to her wealth. A wealthy widow whose *ketuba* settles on her a large sum spends proportionally more to benefit others from the estate than one whose *ketuba* settles on her a smaller sum. Abbaye accepts R. Joseph's reasoning concerning R. Meir's opinion, but follows up with a query about the view of the Sages.

> Abbaye said to R. Joseph: She comes before sunset and may claim her *ketuba*, and after sunset she may not claim it? Has she waived her right in this short time?[8]

Abbaye is referring to the last day of the twenty-fifth year and questions whether—given that this rule is based on the widow's waiver of her *ketuba*—it is reasonable to assume that the psychological process of deciding to waive her rights indeed took place precisely as the sun was setting.

R. Joseph understands that Abbaye, in raising this question, is objecting to the formalistic formulation of laws in general, and therefore answers by making a generalization:

> He [R. Joseph] said to him: Yes. All the measures of the Sages are thus—in forty *seah* one can immerse, in forty *seah* less a *kortob*, one cannot immerse.
>
> bKetubot 104a, quoting mMenahot 12:4

R. Joseph deduces the prevailing view concerning measures from the rules of the ritual bath (mikve). For the purpose of ritual purification, one must immerse oneself in a bath containing at least forty *seah*. If even a minute amount is missing from this volume, the mikve is invalid for immersion. In answer to Abbaye's question, R. Joseph in effect says that the measures defined by the Sages are fixed even if they seem to be unreasonable in a particular case. This point will be discussed below in 3.2.ii.

The validity of fixed measures can be attacked in two ways: by bringing a case where the rationale for fixing the measure does not apply, or by focusing on the measure's limiting case, and thereby implying the absurdity of the fixed measure in general. Abbaye's first objection to the formalism endorsed by the Sages in the case of the widow's waiver pivots on an instance where the rationale given for the measure, namely, the fact that it captures the amount of time within which the widow would have incurred a benefit equal to her *ketuba*, is inapplicable. From his first

8 In Jewish law the day runs from sunset to sunset.

objection, we can conclude that Abbaye objects to **arbitrary** measures, but he is not attacking the very notion of setting fixed standards and measures. Abbaye's second objection, however, pivots on a limiting case, which is of the very nature of fixed standards. This attack implies a wholesale rejection of legal formalism, and calls to mind R. Jeremiah's query.

### 2.3 The obligation to assist

The following verses further demonstrate the use of formalistic wording in the development of a legal standard.

> When you encounter your enemy's ox or donkey straying, you shall surely take it back to him. When you see the donkey of someone who hates you lying helpless under its load, you shall refrain from leaving it for him, but you shall surely release it with him.
>
> Exodus 23:4–5

These verses set out the general obligation to aid others, even one's enemies. The Talmud raises the question of the distance one must go out of his way to render aid, particularly since the conditions mentioned in the two verses that set out the obligation appear to be inconsistent. If one is obliged to render assistance upon encountering ("when you encounter") such a stray animal, the obligation is more limited than it would be if such assistance must be rendered even when one merely sees ("when you see") a stray animal.

The Sages sought to combine the directives, and came up with the following:

> The Sages estimated the measure to be a $7.5^{th}$ part of a *mil*, which is a *ris*.
>
> bBaba Metzia 33a

The Sages precisely defined the distance one must go out of one's way to help someone else. Rendering assistance beyond that limit is not obligatory. The general biblical obligation to assist has thus been transformed by the Sages into a formalistically-formulated norm. This is, in essence, the same process we saw above regarding the liability of the fire-kindler.

There is an arbitrary element in defining concepts that have a clear meaning, yet lack well-defined limits. This problem was familiar to the ancient Greeks, who formulated it as a paradox, known as the sorites paradox, or the ancient paradox of the heap:

> If removal of a single grain always leaves a heap, then, by mathematical induction, removal of all the grains leaves a heap. Russell's[9] latter-day

9 Referring to Bertrand Russell, famous twentieth-century logician and philosopher.

> version is no less familiar: if the loss of a hair renders no man bald, then neither does the loss of any number of them.[10]

Is there a point at which the premise that removal of a single grain leaves a heap is not true? How do we decide where it is? In the legal context, it must be decided whether the legislator should set arbitrary limits—that is, use formalistic formulations, or leave the decision to the discretion of the judge—that is, use abstract formulations. The examples we have discussed show that Jewish law tends to prefer the former. The talmudic term for the formalistic method is '*midot veshiurin*,'—literally, 'standards and measures.'

That Jewish law prefers the formalistic method, that the halakha is to a great extent formulated in terms of standards and measures, can be ascertained from the following Mishnah:

> These are the things that have no prescribed measure: the corners [of the field],[11] the first fruits,[12] the appearance offering,[13] loving-kindness, and studying the Torah.
>
> mPeia 1:1

The Tanna enumerates a number of obligations that are not subject to precise measures. Since the Mishnah presents them as exceptions, it can be inferred that as a rule, halakhic obligations are framed in terms of exact standards and measures.

Commenting on this Mishnah in his *Commentary on the Mishnah*, Maimonides notes that the list is not exhaustive. There are further examples of obligations that are not subject to precise measures, such as the dust of the Sotah,[14] the spittle of the levir's brother's widow,[15] the ashes of the red heifer,[16] and the blood of the leper's bird[17]–examples the Tanna did not bother to mention, Maimonides argues, because "however important they may be, [fulfillment of] these [obligations] does not carry an additional reward [if carried out in excess]."[18] But regarding those that are mentioned, "the more one adds to them, the greater the reward." Although the obligations mentioned in mPeia are fulfilled by minimal amounts, the Mishnah

10 See W.V. Quine, *Theories and Things* (Cambridge MA: 1981), 32.

11 See Leviticus 19:9; 23:22. The corners of fields were to be left unharvested for the poor.

12 First fruits–Deuteronomy 26:1–11; the first fruits were brought to the Temple as a gift.

13 Appearance offering–Deuteronomy 16:16; on the three Pilgrimage Festivals (Passover, Shavuot, Sukkot), the Israelites were to visit Jerusalem, bringing with them an "appearance-offering." The amount of the offering, however, was not specified.

14 Dust of the Sotah–Numbers 5:17. A suspected adulteress was made to drink a mixture of dust and water.

15 The spittle of the levir's brother's widow–Deuteronomy 25:9. As part of the levirate release ceremony, the widow had to spit in front of her levir (brother-in-law).

16 The ashes of the red heifer–Numbers 19:17.

17 The blood of the leper's bird–Leviticus 14:6.

18 Maimonides' explanation of this point follows jPeia 1:1 (15a).

shies away from delineating these minimums, thereby tacitly encouraging increased observance of these precepts.

## 2.4 'Standards and measures' in tort law

The function of 'standards and measures' in tort law is debated in tractate Baba Batra. The Mishnah sets down precisely-articulated measures to be taken by homeowners with respect to matters where there might be risk to neighbors. But is the owner liable if he complied with the standards, yet damage to his neighbor's property nonetheless occurred? One possibility is to regard the owner's liability as conditional on non-compliance with the standards. Another possibility is to hold the owner liable in any event, even if he complied with the standards; the setting of standards merely gives the other side, namely, the neighbor, the right to seek an injunction if the standards are not complied with.

> One must not place an oven within a house, unless there is a space of four cubits above it.[19] If he placed it in an upper chamber, under it there must be it cement flooring of [at least] three handbreadths [in thickness][20]; and in the case of a small stove, only one [handbreadth].[21] But if it caused damage, he must pay for whatever damage was caused.[22] R. Shimon says, They prescribed all these measurements only so that if damage is caused, [the homeowner] will be exempt from having to pay.
>
> mBaba Batra 2:2

## 2.5 Casuistic formulation and formalistic formulation

Every legal rule has at least two parts: a description of a factual situation, and a norm applicable to the factual situation. The factual situation can be described either by way of concrete examples (casuistically), or by way of generalization. Characterization of a law as having casuistic wording thus relates to its description of the factual situation. Characterization of a law as having formalistic wording, on the other hand, relates to the norm applicable to the said factual situation. This norm can be conveyed either by way of precise standards and measures (i.e., formalistically), or by way of abstract directives. It follows that there are two types of casuistic laws: those that are formulated formalistically, and those that are formulated abstractly.[23]

19 As a precaution against fire.

20 Also as a precaution against fire.

21 A small stove generates less heat than an oven.

22 Compliance with the above regulations does not confer exemption from paying damages when damage ensues despite compliance.

23 Of the two possible types of general (i.e., non-casuistic) laws – those formulated formalistically, and those formulated abstractly – the former is implausible.

Some scholars have failed to distinguish the two components of legal rules, and consequently, have conflated formalistic formulation of a legal rule's normative component with casuistic formulation of the rule as a whole. Menachem Elon, for instance, has asserted:

> A legal rule may be formulated in either of two ways: casuistically, by specific instances, or normatively, by prescriptive generalization. Casuistic formulation sets forth the law by describing specific cases detailing the concrete factual circumstances to which a given law is applicable. The normative style, on the other hand, states the norm, the abstract legal principle, without reference to any concrete factual situation.
>
> Contemporary statute books are generally drafted in the normative style and set forth legal principles without casuistic examples. By contrast, the Mishnah is for the most part drafted casuistically; indeed, the casuistic style is typical of Jewish law from its beginnings in the Written Law until the present day. Jewish law developed and grew out of life's circumstances, which, in turn, affected the way the law was determined and handed down from generation to generation. This does not mean, however, that there are not occasionally paragraphs in the Mishnah combining the casuistic and the normative styles, or even passages that are couched in a purely normative manner.[24]

Elon adduces the following mishnaic law as a "classic example of casuistic style."

> No person may dig a pit near the pit of his neighbor; nor may he dig a ditch, a cave, a water-channel or a washpool, unless he separates it by three handbreadths from his neighbor's wall, i.e., the wall of his neighbor's pit, and plasters it with lime.[25]

He describes the legal norm "implicit" in it as the prohibition against creating a situation that may be damaging to one's neighbor, and "the obligation to keep the possibly harmful substance as far away from his neighbor's property as is necessary to avoid causing damage."

But is this analysis apt? If we examine the mishnaic law, we clearly see that the first part is indeed casuistically formulated. It lists a series of concrete circumstances, or what I have called 'factual situations': digging a pit near one's neighbor's pit, digging a ditch, a cave, and so on near one's neighbor's property. But the second part does not merely "imply" a general

24 M. Elon, *Jewish law: History, Sources, Principles* (Philadelphia: 1994), 3:1072–73, citing mBaba Batra 2:1.

25 Ibid., 1074.

legal norm, specifically, "the obligation to keep the possibly harmful substance as far away from his neighbor's property as is necessary to avoid causing damage." Rather, the law explicitly sets down a **formalistically**-worded norm, to wit: 'no person may dig a pit ... unless he separates it by three handbreadths from his neighbor's wall.' Elon's analysis fails to appreciate that the precise measure set down in the Mishnah is not incidental, nor is it merely an example of the supposedly-implicit "as far away as is necessary to avoid causing damage" principle. It is, rather, an essential aspect of the norm.

## 3 The underlying rationale for 'standards and measures'

An examination of the 'standards and measures' method of formulation, in which laws are formulated with great specificity, raises two important questions, which will be discussed in turn. First, what is the rationale underlying the institution of 'standards and measures'? Are standards and measures to be viewed as reflecting an existing state of affairs, in which case they are not arbitrary, or are they to be regarded as a legal instrument denoting an arbitrary, though not totally fictitious, reality? That is, are they based on generalization of some empirical fact, which is then deemed a fixed measure regardless of its correspondence to future instances? And second, why does Jewish law employ the method of standards and measures to such a great extent?

### 3.1 Laws given to Moses at Sinai

According to a well-known Rabbinic dictum, standards and measures are "laws given to Moses at Sinai."[26] What is the significance of this assertion in our context? When a norm is characterized as a "law given to Moses at Sinai," this means that, being regarded as of divine origin, it is unequivocal and immutable. Taking this view precludes any queries about the justification for standards and measures, inasmuch as they are inherently justified by virtue of their having been revealed to Moses at Sinai, just as the Torah was. On this approach, standards and measures are seen as divinely-ordained, not man-made. Those who take this approach to standards and measures fall on a spectrum, with some interpreting it in a more extreme way, and others, more liberally. A particularly categorical expression of this view is put forward by Maimonides: "All the measures, and all their details, were given to Moses at Sinai."[27]

26 bEruvin 4a; jPeia 1:1(15a).

27 Maimonides, *Code*, Laws concerning Forbidden Foods 2:11. See I. Gilat, "Were not all measures given by the Sages?" (Hebrew), in *Studies in the Development of the Halakha* (Hebrew), (Ramat-Gan: 1992), 191–204; Haim H. Cohn, "The fictions of measurements," in A. Katsh and L. Nemoy (eds.), *Essays on the Occasion of the Seventieth Anniversary of the Dropsie University* (Philadelphia: 1979), 39–47.

Some halakhic authorities endorse the principle that standards and measures were given at Sinai, but restrict its application in various ways.

Tractate Kelim discusses issues related to the impurity and purity of utensils. Standards and measures play an important role in the laws of purity. One of the chapters of tractate Kelim (ch. 17) constitutes an informal lexicon of standards and measures pertaining not just to vessels, but to several halakhic spheres. The Mishnah explicates the meanings of various measures: the egg measure, the *grogeret* measure (the bulk of a dried fig), the barleycorn measure, the lentil measure, the olive measure, and the cubit, and distinguishes between different sizes of these measures. What is the import of this lexicon, and in particular, what is the relationship between this lexicon and the dictum that measures were given at Sinai? Was the lexicon itself given to Moses at Sinai? If not, how are we to understand the claim that measures were given at Sinai?

In the opinion of the Hazon Ish, a twentieth-century decisor, the dictum that measures are Sinaitic refers only to the **units** of measurement: the cubit, the barleycorn, the lentil, olive, and so forth. In his view, the dictum that standards and measures are "laws given to Moses at Sinai" refers only to the **types** of measures that are halakhically relevant, that is, in terms of which the law is articulated—the cubit, the barleycorn measure, and so on—but not their specific magnitudes. The latter were established by the Sages on the assumption that the Torah intended the average values to be taken as the standard measure for each type of measure. Such stipulative definitions set down by the Sages are not absolute, but vary from one age to the next, and from place to place. In the words of the Hazon Ish:

> And so when the Sages defined the measures [in mKelim 17] [such as] ... the barleycorn and the lentil, they did so as long as it was available to them. But if they are not available, it is within the authority of the sages of future generations to define for all Israel what they take to be the medium-sized measure [of each kind], or authorize the individual to set these medium-sized values as he sees fit and in accordance with local conditions. And if these sages have not issued a ruling, the decision reverts by default to each individual according to what he perceives to be the case.[28]

On this view, the measures in terms of which Jewish law is articulated were indeed given at Sinai, but the Sages specified how these designations were to be 'translated' into specific quantities of concrete and familiar entities. Let us now examine part of the mishnaic lexicon of measures, which reflect the average sizes of the various types of measures according to the then-prevailing conditions.

28 *Hazon Ish*, Tractate Shabat, Essay On Measures (Kuntres Hashiurim), at the beginning.

Mishnah Kelim 17:5–11 (Blackman translation)

Mishnah 5

[The size of] the pomegranate of which [the Sages] have spoken refers to one that is neither large nor small, but applies to one of medium measure. And why were Badan[29] pomegranates mentioned? Because [only in their case, if one of them from *orlah* fruit or from *forbidden-junction* fruit or forbidden for other reason, was confused with other pomegranates] in any quantity whatever, it renders them prohibited. This is the opinion of R. Meir. R. Jochanan b. Nuri says, [They are mentioned] in order to measure with them [the breaches in] utensils. R. Akiba says, [They are mentioned] for both these reasons, [namely] in order to measure with them [the breaches in] utensils and because [if one of them from *orlah* fruit or from *forbidden-junction* fruit or forbidden for other reason were confused with other pomegranates in any quantity whatever], it renders them prohibited. R. Jose[30] said, *Badan pomegranates* and *Geba*[31] *leeks* were mentioned only for the reason that tithes must be separated everywhere from them as [there is uncertainty whether they are] undoubtedly tithed.[32]

Mishnah 6

[The size of] the egg of which [the Sages] have spoken [namely, an egg's bulk of unclean food will communicate *uncleanness*] refers to one that is neither large nor small, but applies to one of average bulk. R. Judah says, [to determine this medium measure] they should get the largest [egg possible] and the smallest [egg possible] and place [them both] in [a vessel quite full of] water and divide [into two equal parts the volume of] the [overflowing] water, [then one half will be the measure of a middle size egg]. R. Jose said, But who can tell me which [egg] is the largest and which is the smallest [egg]? But rather, leave all such estimation to be determined by the eye.[33]

Mishnah 7

[The measure of the bulk of] a dried fig of which [the Sages] have spoken refers to one that is neither large nor small, but applies to one of medium size. R. Judah says, [The fig that is deemed] large in the land of Israel is but as one of average bulk in other lands.

29 Badan in Samaria, famed for its pomegranates.

30 According to some, R. Judah.

31 A town in Samaria.

32 Cutheans (viz., Samaritans) who inhabited these two towns were wont to tithe only what they themselves consumed, but not what they sold; the pomegranates and leeks that grew in those districts were special species and easily recognized, and had to be tithed even when bought from those that were not inhabitants of these localities.

33 i.e., to decide which egg is deemed medium-sized, visual assessment suffices.

Mishnah 8

[The measure of the size of] the olive of which [the Sages] have spoken refers to one that is neither large nor small, but applies to one of average bulk, such as an olive of exceptionally good quality. [The measure of the bulk of] the barleycorn of which they have spoken refers to one that is neither large nor small, but applies to one of average bulk, such as grows in the wilderness. [The measure of the size of] the lentil of which they have spoken refers to one that is neither large nor small, but applies to one of middle bulk, such as the Egyptian [lentil]. Any movable object communicates (the) *uncleanness* if it be as thick as a plough handle, and it refers to one that is not big or small, but to one of average size. What [plough handle] is deemed of medium size? Every one that is a handbreadth in circumference.

Mishnah 9

The *cubit* [measure] of which [the Sages] have spoken refers to the medium size cubit. There were two [standard] cubit [measures deposited] in [a chamber at the *Eastern Gate* of the *Temple Mount* whereon was sculptured a representation of] the *Castle of Shushan*, one [cubit measure] at the north-east corner and the other at the south-east corner; the one at the north-east corner exceeded [the *cubit*] of Moses[34] by half a *fingerbreadth*, [and] that at the south-east corner was half a *fingerbreadth* longer still, [and thus] it is found [that the latter] was one *fingerbreadth* longer than [the *cubit* measure] of Moses. And why did they enjoin [the use of] a larger [*cubit* measure] and a smaller [*cubit* measure]? In order that the craftsmen contracted [to carry out Temple work] according to the smaller [*cubit* measure], but who used the larger [*cubit* measure] in the actual work not be guilty of the misappropriation of sacred property (*meila*).[35]

Mishnah 10

R. Meir says, All [the measurements in the Temple were made with] *cubits* of medium length[36] with the exception of those of the *Golden Altar*, and the [four] horns[37] [of the *Brazen Altar*], and the *gallery* [around the *Altar* for the priests to walk on], and the [*Altar]* base. R. Judah says, The *cubit* used for the [Temple] structure was six *handbreadths* and that for the utensils[38] *five handbreadths*.

34 This was a six-handbreadths cubit used in building the Tabernacle [Maimonides].

35 They were not to derive any profit from any labor or materials pertaining to the Temple. See Leviticus 5:15.

36 Each six handbreadths long.

37 Each one cubit square.

38 E.g., the *Ark*, the *Table*, the *Golden Altar*.

Mishnah 11
And there were cases where [the Sages] enjoined the use of a smaller measure: for *liquid measures* and *dry measures* [in Temple usage they prescribed] *Italian measures* which were equivalent to those used in the Wilderness [at the time of Moses]; and there were cases where they prescribed all [measures] in accordance with [the physical measurements of] a person himself, [for instance as when one is bidden] to take a *handful* of the *meal-offering*,[39] or both *handfuls* of the *incense*,[40] or [is forbidden] to drink a *mouthful* on the Day of Atonement, or when one is enjoined to prepare food sufficient *for two meals* for the *erub* [of Sabbath limits] such as he would consume on a weekday but not on the Sabbath. This is the view of R. Meir. R. Judah says, [Fare such as he would consume] on the Sabbath but not on a weekday. [But in fact both R. Meir and R. Judah] were minded to give a lenient ruling. R. Simon says, [The *erub of Sabbath limits* must consist of] two-thirds of a loaf [of a bulk that three such loaves are made] from a *kab* [of flour]. R. Jochanan ben Baroka says, [The *erub of Sabbath limits* must be at least] a loaf worth a *pondion* [and made of wheat sold at] a *sela* for four *seahs*.

Note that the measures listed in the Mishnah are related either to parts of the body, for example, the cubit and the handbreadth, or to the natural environment, for instance the egg, and various grains and fruits. This is also the case in other cultures.

In ancient times, people had recourse, for measurement purposes, to parts of the body, such as limb length, or natural phenomena from the plant and animal world, such as the size of seeds and the volume of hollowed-out pods and shells. Protagoras[41] already asserted that people found the units of measurement they required in their bodies and their surroundings. And indeed, the ancient measures, some of which are still in use today, are derived from parts of the human body (cubit, little fingerbreadth (*zeret*), handbreadth, fingerbreadth, hand and foot).

The "cubit" or "ell" usually represents the arm's length from the elbow to the tip of the middle finger … the "handbreadth" represents the width of the four adjacent fingers of the hand; and the "fingerbreadth"—the width of one finger. The units of measurement that are based on the human body varied from region to region, and changed from time to time, since people's limbs do not have a fixed size.

Encyclopedia Hebraica, 'Weights and measures,' 229

39 Leviticus 2:2.
40 Leviticus 16:12.
41 Protagoras, pre-Socratic Greek philosopher and Sophist, 5th century BCE.

The Geonim, heads of the Babylonian talmudic academics of the fifth to eleventh centuries CE, made the following observation:

> Hence the Torah gave us measures such as eggs and fruits… for eggs and fruit are to be found everywhere, because it was revealed and known to 'He who spoke and the world was created' that the people of Israel would be scattered among the nations, and their weights and measures from the time of Moses, to which the Sages of the land of Israel had added further measures, would not be preserved. And measures vary by generation and country, for in each generation, the sages define weights anew.… Even relatively recent measures have changed, and all the more so the ancient ones, the dimensions of which we are completely ignorant. So the Sages standardized their measures using as units fruits and eggs, which exist in every period and do not change. But the size of the eggs and fruits is left to the discretion of the beholder.
>
> *Otzar Hageonim*, bEruvin 83b

Having elucidated the Hazon Ish's exposition of the Rabbinic dictum of the Sinaitic origin of standards and measures, an exposition that moderates its thrust significantly, taking only the names for measures to have been revealed at Sinai, but their concrete meanings to have been assigned by the talmudic Sages, and subject to variation in accordance with environmental conditions, let us consider yet another moderate reading of the dictum. This account further qualifies the claim that standards and measures were given at Sinai, by restricting it to specific spheres of the law. On this view, the Sages emphasized that only some, but not all, measures were given to Moses at Sinai. For example, bYoma 80a states that "the measures of punishments were given to Moses at Sinai," that is, only those measures that define the thresholds for incurring punishment were given at Sinai.

Moreover, the contrary view, namely, that measures are all man-made, can also be found in the Talmud. For example, with regard to the view just elucidated, namely, that "the measures of punishments were given to Moses at Sinai," the dictum continues: "Others say, the court of Yaavetz enacted them."[42]

A more general expression of this position can be deduced from the following passage:

> R. Hosheia says: One who eats forbidden food in these times [after the destruction of the Temple] had better take note of the exact amount,

42 In the talmudic tradition, Yaavetz is identical with Othniel b. Kenaz, a contemporary of Joshua b. Nun; see bTemura 16a. By attributing a ruling to Yaavetz and his court, the Talmud emphasizes its antiquity.

> lest another court convene and change the measure, so he should know what quantity he has eaten.
>
> jPeia 1:1(15b)

This law has to do with forbidden food consumed inadvertently. While the Temple was in existence, one who unintentionally consumed forbidden food had to bring a sin-offering for the inadvertent transgression. The Sages set a threshold, such that if the amount of forbidden food inadvertently consumed was less than the set amount (which was very small), consumption of the food did not render one a transgressor obligated to bring a sin-offering. R. Hosheia considers the possibility that such measures might be changed by new legislation. It could, therefore, happen that one who had eaten forbidden food would be exempt according to the old measure but liable according to the new one. R. Hosheia does not mention the possible motives for such legislation, but the feasibility of such an occurrence indicates that measures are determined by the Sages, and are not absolute and unchangeable quantities, as implied by the phrase "given to Moses at Sinai."

A parallel passage is found in the Babylonian Talmud:

> R. Eleazar said: one who eats [forbidden] fat in these times should write down the exact amount, lest another court convene and increase the measure.
>
> bYoma 80a

Note that according to the Jerusalem Talmud, the new measure set down by the later court could be either greater or smaller; if it was smaller, the inadvertent consumption of even a minute amount of forbidden food—an amount that had formerly rendered its consumer exempt—might be retroactively rendered a transgression. But on the Babylonian Talmud's version of the law, the new measure could only be larger, meaning that retroactively, transgressions would be rendered permissible acts, but not the reverse. Here, the concern was that a gratuitous sin-offering would be brought, which is itself a transgression.[43]

Moreover, the familiar talmudic expression "the Sages estimated the measure" would also seem to indicate that the Sages routinely set measures themselves. Indeed, the word for "measures" (*shiurin*) has another meaning—estimates—and it has been suggested that this is due to the fact

43 Note that on both versions, the court's new legislation has retroactive application. The motivation of the later court—that which changed the measures—might be either policy considerations, or a new understanding of the truth of the matter. The present-day aversion to retroactive legislation is understandable with regard to the former motivation, but is less relevant in cases where legislation purports to reflect the newly-discovered truth of the matter.

that measures were estimated and set down on an ongoing basis, and were not absolute.

### 3.2 How were standards and measures determined?

Let us return to a question posed above. Assuming, now, that standards and measures were indeed introduced into the halakhic system at the Sages' initiative, we must ask what constituted the basis for their specific normative determinations, for example, the determination that a cistern should not be dug less than three handbreadths from a neighboring property. It is reasonable to suppose that when the Sages introduced a given norm, they did so on the basis of personal experience—their observation of nature, human psychology, commerce, and interpersonal relations. But the question remains: did the Sages regard their determinations as objective correlates of objective realities, or merely as convenient legal instruments that facilitated the workings of the law, regardless of whether these determinations reflected some objective reality?

Talmudic discussion, by its very nature, does not engage in philosophical self-reflection, and does not offer general and comprehensive analyses of its own methods. An indirect answer to the question just posed may, however, be arrived at by examining a number of representative cases involving standards and measures. Although we will look at only a few cases, they suffice to enable us to answer this question, and can at the same time serve as an example of how the inductive method is applied in halakhic research.

#### i Adverse possession

In mBaba Batra 3:1, the Mishnah rules that one who has no title deeds can sustain his claim to rightful ownership of property if he can prove three years of undisputed possession.

The Talmud reports the following debate between Rava and Abbaye over the reason for the three year period.

> Rava said: A person is not particular [about his property rights] in the first year, he is not particular in the second year, but he is particular in the third year.
>
> bBaba Batra 29a

Rava's view is that the mere fact that someone was in possession of a field for one or two years does not prove his rightful ownership, because the rightful owner might disregard a trespasser for two years and not complain about this unauthorized occupation. But no one would allow trespassing for three years. Therefore, if someone has been in undisputed possession for three years, we may regard his ownership as proven.

Abbaye raises the following difficulty:

> Abbaye said to him: If so, those such as the people of Ben-Eliashiv, who are particular even about someone crossing their fields—in their case, should not occupation confer presumptive ownership immediately [if they do not object]? If you agree, then you are introducing an element of variability into your determinations (*natata dvarekha leshiurin*)!

Let us analyze Abbaye's argument. Assuming that the measure of three years fixed in the Mishnah is based on observation of human nature, asserting that owners ordinarily disregard trespassers for two years but no longer, what would be the ruling regarding a petty, short-tempered, selfish individual known to stand up for his rights in every matter, no matter how trivial—a person who would never keep silent even for an instant? In such a case, would the presumptive ownership by adverse possession apply immediately, or at any rate within a period shorter than three years? Suppose we answer in the affirmative vis-à-vis assertive individuals. This would compromise the uniformity of the rule's application, which would vary with the owner's temperament. In dispossession cases brought by assertive individuals, courts might award ownership to the possessor before three years have elapsed. In cases brought by less-assertive individuals, possession would not be awarded until three full years had passed. This lack of constancy would lead to social and legal instability.

Rava concedes that Abbaye is right, and suggests another rationale for the mishnaic ruling, which we will discuss shortly. But first, it should be noted that the underlying assumption here is that specific determinations involving measures fixed by the Sages must reflect an objective reality in each and every case, and it is not sufficient if they are adequate for most cases and persons. For were measures simply a legal instrument, Rava could have replied: 'It is true that in the case of someone assertive, the period of adverse possession could have been shortened, but for the sake of legal uniformity, we ignore this particular aspect of the case.' Abbaye's objection, and the fact that it was accepted by Rava, who offers an alternative rationale for the Mishnah, shows that both Abbaye and Rava justify the use of predetermined measures in their legal determinations because they are deemed to reflect reality. We can conclude that both Abbaye and Rava hold that laws that invoke standards and measures are not merely a legal instrument, but a reflection of reality.

Let us now look at the alternative rationale offered by Rava:

> But Rava said: A person safeguards his documents in the first year, and he safeguards them in the second year and third year. Beyond that, he does not safeguard them.

Rava's first argument was based on the assertiveness of one whose field is occupied by someone else. His second argument is based on the period of time it is reasonable to expect owners to keep title deeds. The latter argument is, or at least so it seems, impervious to Abbaye's objection, because it not meant to be a descriptive statement, but rather a prescriptive norm: owners ought to keep their deeds for three years. The first argument focused on the psychological disposition of the property owner, something that varies from person to person, whereas the second argument focuses on a standard that can be imposed on everyone.

### ii Sabbath boundaries

Let us now consider another talmudic case that illustrates the distinction between the approach on which the Sages' determinations with respect to standards and measures are, though empirically-generated, merely instrumental, and that which regards them as reflecting facts about the world. On the Sabbath, one is allowed to walk within an urban area and 2000 cubits beyond the town boundaries. If he has not prepared an *eruv*,[44] he may move only four cubits beyond this limit, and go no further. This measure of four cubits is derived by a baraita:

> Where in Scripture are these four cubits written? As we have learned, "Let each man stay where he is" (Exod. 16:29). And how much [is 'where he is']? Three cubits for his body, and one cubit for him to stretch his arms and legs. These are the words of R. Meir. R. Judah said: Three cubits for his body, and one cubit to enable him to take an object at his feet and put it down at his head. What is the difference between them? The difference between them is that [according to R. Judah], the measure of the four cubits is to be exact.
>
> bEruvin 48a

This measure, which prescribes the movement permitted beyond the Sabbath limits, is the measure of someone stretching out his limbs on the ground. The Talmud follows with a query about the definition of the cubit.

> R. Mesharsheya said to his son: When you go visit R. Papa, ask him whether the four cubits of which the Rabbis have spoken are determined by the arm of each individual concerned or determined by the standard cubit used for sacred objects. If he tells you that they are

44 *Eruv*: There are three types of *eruv*. The type relevant here is '*eruv tehumim*.' By placing foodstuffs that would constitute a meal at the 2000 cubit limit on the eve of the Sabbath, one symbolically indicates that the place is his home, which enables him to walk a further 2000 cubits.

> determined by the cubit used for sacred objects, [ask him:] What should be done in the case of Og, the King of Bashan?[45] And if he tells you that they are determined by the arm of each individual concerned, say to him: Why wasn't this measure taught among those that the Rabbis have set down as being in accordance with each individual?
>
> When he came before R. Papa, [R. Papa] said to him: Had we been so punctilious, we would never have learned anything. It is determined by the arm of each individual, and as to your objection—why was this measure not taught among those that the Rabbis have set down as being in accordance with each individual? [mKelim 17:11]—their list cannot be regarded as comprehensive, since [even a normal-sized person] may have stumped limbs.
>
> bEruvin 48a

The question is whether the "cubit" in the baraita is an absolute measure [the cubit for sacred objects], or a relative measure, namely, the length of the arm of the individual concerned. The following passage addresses this issue.

> The cubit (*amah*) is the measure of the length between the elbow and the tip of the middle finger, which is also called *amah* for this reason. In ancient times, the human body and its parts, such as the feet, hands, both or singly, and even half, or a half of a half, served as measures for different purposes. Obviously, the cubit is inevitably a relative measure that varies from person to person and from nation to nation. Hence, even in early times, there was a need for a fixed standard unit, which gave rise to the need to indicate, in certain contexts, which cubit was being referred to: the relative cubit or the standard one.[46]

The standard cubit, or to be more precise, one of several types of standard cubit, is known as the 'Temple' cubit. The relative cubit, which is determined on a case-by-case basis, is referred to as the 'personal' cubit. The Temple cubit is a typical unit of measurement, whereas the personal cubit is a peculiar hybrid, inasmuch as while the unit itself is fixed, and does not vary from individual to individual, its size does indeed so vary.

If the baraita refers to the Temple cubit, which has a fixed length, what would be the rule for a giant like Og, for whom this measure is obviously inadequate? He would be unable to move around at all in such a confined space. This part of R. Mesharsheya's question is premised on the assumption that a measure ought to fit the purpose for which it was introduced. The implicit assumption is that measures are not merely a legal instrument, but a reflection of reality. On the other hand, if the baraita

45 Og—a giant, see Deuteronomy 3:11.
46 J. Brandt, "On our ancient cubit" (Hebrew), *Sinai* 40 [Jubilee Volume], (1958), 573.

refers to a personal cubit to be determined anew in each case, then why is it not mentioned in mKelim 17:11, which enumerates the instances where personal measures are referred to? R. Papa, to whom this question was posed, answers that the baraita is referring to the personal cubit, but was not included in the list because of the exceptional case of someone whose limbs are undeveloped, where the standard or Temple cubit would apply. Here too, then, the principle adopted is that measures should conform to the real world, to the objective circumstances of each particular case. If the rationale for fixing a length of four cubits is to enable one to stretch one's limbs, then the measure invoked must render this possible in every case.

### 3.3 Measures as a legal instrument

Notwithstanding the aforementioned examples, there are numerous instances in the Talmud where measures are regarded as no more than legal instruments, as average values adduced for convenience, without regard to the actual dimensions of the entities involved. One example is a law pertaining to the ritual bath (mikve). By law, one who is ritually impure and wishes to be purified must immerse himself in water, for it is written in the Torah, "and shall wash all his flesh in water" (Lev. 15:16).

The Talmud elaborates on this requirement:

> "All his flesh in water"—his entire body must be immersed in it—and how much is that? A square cubit to the height of three cubits, which the Sages have estimated to be a volume of water of forty *seah*.
>
> bEruvin 4b

The rationale the Talmud gives for this rule is that there must be a quantity of water large enough for one to immerse himself completely, yet there is no differentiation to accommodate persons of various sizes. Though one may be completely immersed in less than forty *seah*, this immersion is not valid. Or as the Mishnah puts it:

> All the measures of the Sages are thus—in forty *seah* one can immerse, in forty *seah* less a *kortob*, one cannot immerse.
>
> mMenahot 12:4 (bKetubot 104a)

Note that the missing *kortob* is a minute amount (.0054 litre), and in practice, it cannot be determined whether such an amount is missing.

A commentator observes:

> We have to assume that the rule that a missing *kortob* makes the mikve unfit is a genuine rule, even though in practice it is impossible to know

whether a mikve containing 260,000 drops is 20 drops short. The measure is subject to our own discretion, to ascertain that the required minimal measure exists.

R. Menahem Kasher, *Tora Shleima*, 5:10–11; addenda, 2

The fictitious element in the rationale alluded to with respect to the mikve is explicitly referred to in the following argument for the thesis that any coherent legal system requires standards and measures:

> Standards and measures are indispensable to legal logic, which is based on presuming the existence of identical events. To allow for logical thought and logical conclusions, these identical events must first be created (or defined)—this identity is fictionally created. As long as these fictions are not regarded as truth, but are accepted as artificial formulas or abstractions, as supplementary instruments created and provided for a particular aim, fiction will not detract from law but will enrich it.
>
> The existence of fictions[47] is a precondition that enables the law to exercise its role of providing the formal context for social coexistence. The aim of legal logic is but to simplify the legal structure, and to render it as predictable, consistent and applicable as possible: the fiction of standards and measures is a tool, a prop enabling legal logic to achieve its goals.[48]

The thesis that standards and measures are a fiction can also be understood somewhat differently. Obligations must be 'translated' into concrete terms in order to be carried out in daily life. That is, the law must be concretized. Standards and measures can be seen as a manifestation of this process of concretization. This approach is implicit in the following passage from Maimonides' *Guide for the Perplexed*. In addressing the question of the rationale for the precepts (*mitzvot*), Maimonides differentiates between the precept, which has a rationale, and the procedure by means of which the precept is observed.

> The true reality of particulars of commandments is illustrated by the sacrifices. The offering of sacrifices has in itself a great and manifest utility, as I shall make clear [referring to *Guide for the Perplexed* III:46]. But no cause will ever be found for the fact that one particular sacrifice consists in a *lamb* and another in a *ram* and that the number of the

47 For our purposes, the following definition of 'legal fiction' will suffice: a legal stipulation that a statement that is, or may be, false, is true, or, that certain conditions exist even though they have never actually existed.

48 Haim H. Cohn, "On measures and measurements" (Hebrew), 3–4 *Shenaton Hamishpat Haivri* (1976/77), 231; see too Cohn, n. 27 above.

> victims should be one particular number. Accordingly, in my opinion, all those who occupy themselves with finding causes for something of these particulars are stricken with a prolonged madness in the course of which they do not put an end to an incongruity, but rather increase the number of incongruities. Those who imagine that a cause may be found for suchlike things are as far from truth as those who imagine that the generalities of a *commandment* are not designed with a view to some real utility.
>
> Know that wisdom rendered it necessary—or, if you will, say that necessity occasioned—that there should be particulars for which no cause can be found; it was, as it were, impossible in regard to the Law that there should be nothing of this class in it. In such a case the impossibility is due to the circumstances that when you ask why a *lamb* should be prescribed and not a *ram*, the same question would have to be asked if a *ram* had been prescribed instead of a *lamb*. But one particular species had necessarily to be chosen. The same holds for your asking why *seven lambs* and not *eight* have been prescribed. For a similar question would have been put if *eight* or *ten* or *twenty* had been prescribed. However, one particular number had necessarily to be chosen. This resembles the nature of the possible, for it is certain that one of the possibilities will come to pass. And no question should be put why one particular possibility and not another comes to pass, for a similar question would become necessary if another possibility instead of this particular one had come to pass. Know this notion and grasp it.
>
> *Guide for the Perplexed* III:26 (Pines translation)

Examples can be adduced for both interpretations of measures, that is, the view that they reflect features of the world, and the view that they are legal instruments. It would seem, however, that the dominant view of the talmudic legal literature is that measures are a convenient legal instrument, that, by specifying precise instructions, facilitates the application and enforcement of legal rules.

## 3.4 Why does Jewish law use 'standards and measures' to such a great extent?

Let us now turn to the second question raised above: why does Jewish law make such wide use of the method of formalistic formulation?

The extent to which formalistic formulation is used varies among legal systems, with some more inclined to it, and others less. So too it varies from era to era. But no legal system can completely free itself of the need for formalistic wording. It is common, indeed, virtually universal, for rules pertaining to worship and ritual to be laid down in minute detail. Great pains are taken to ensure that religious ceremonies are carried out exactly as prescribed. This phenomenon exists in Jewish law too, for example, in connection with forbidden food, and even more so in matters of ritual purity, for example, the size of the mikve, as we saw.

But Jewish law is equally strict regarding matters pertaining to interpersonal legal relationships apparently unrelated to worship or ritual. Most of the examples discussed above reflect this tendency. Jewish law exemplifies a legal system characterized by formalistic formulation of laws. Critics of talmudic law, both from within and without, have attacked this feature, perceiving it as evidence of narrow-mindedness and excessive pedantry.[49] Let us, then, consider two explanations that have been offered for the pervasiveness of formalistic formulations in Jewish law.

### i R. Joseph Soloveitchik's view

In an abstruse but much-acclaimed essay, "Halakhic man," a twentieth-century halakhic authority, R. Joseph Soloveitchik, considers the meaning of measures in the halakha, and offers an explanation of the phenomenon. He first describes the halakhic propensity to use standards and measures extensively:

> Halakhic man resembles somewhat the mathematician who masters infinity only for the sake of creating finitude, delimited by numbers and mathematical measures, and cognizing it. The Halakhah, from the perspective of the process of contraction, also uses the method of quantification; it quantifies quality and religious subjectivity in the form of concrete, objective phenomena that are standardized and measurable. 'The laws relating to standards, interpositions, and partitions are laws revealed to Moses on Mount Sinai' [Eruvin 4a; Sukkah 5b]. The Halakhah fixes firmly established and clearly delimited laws, statutes, and measures for each and every commandment—what constitutes eating and what are its measurements, what constitutes drinking and what are its standards, what constitutes a fruit and what are its stages of development and distinguishing characteristics, the thirty-nine categories of work on the Sabbath and their measurements, the measurements of a tent that defiles, partitions, units of monetary value, and many more. [Here Soloveitchik quotes from *Likutei Amarim*.[50]]
>
> Now because the commandments were given to us by way of being clothed in the attribute of strength and by the contraction of the light.... therefore, most commandments have a delimited, 'contracted' measure. For instance, the length of the *tzitzit* [must be]

49 See H. Ben-Menahem, "Is talmudic law a religious legal system? A provisional analysis," 24 *Journal of Law and Religion* (2008/2009), 379–402, esp. 398.

50 Seminal work by R. Shneur Zalman of Liadi, founder of Chabad hasidism.

> twelve times the width of the thumb; the phylacteries, two fingers by two fingers and necessarily square; the *lulav*, four handbreadths; the *sukkah*, seven handbreadths; the *shofar*, one handbreadth; the *mikvah*, forty se'ahs. Similarly, the sacrifices have a delimited, 'contracted' measure as regards age, as, for instance, 'lambs of the first year' (Exodus, 29:38).[51]

We can distinguish two levels of explanation here, one metaphysical, the other psychological. Vis-à-vis the former, Soloveitchik argues that measures are an expression of the divine will. Just as this will is manifested in our tangible world by the act of genesis and the creation of the universe, so it is reflected in the world of ideas in the creation of the halakha. In the continuation, Soloveitchik asserts:

> The fundamental method of the Halakhah is that act of quantification which is so integral a part of the mystery of *tzimtzum*. This wondrous principle expresses itself in two parallel dimensions: in the real world—in empirical reality—and in the ideal world—in Halakhic constructions. The supernal will clothes itself in these two creations and becomes embodied through them in the attribute of strength (*gevurah*) and contraction, from whose midst there flows the method of quantification.... The supernal will is reflected both in the mirror of reality and the mirror of the ideal Halakhah, through the medium of objective, quantitative measurements.[52]

In other words, he is saying that measures are an expression of the divine will. This approach accords with the dictum "Measures were given at Sinai"—indeed, R. Soloveitchik prefaces his own view by invoking this dictum approvingly.

But R. Soloveitchik also argues that measures have an important role at the psychological level: they were defined in order to create an objective dimension in religious experience. He contrasts religion that speaks to emotion, discounting the need for specific modes of conduct, with religion that prescribes a mode of conduct and way of life. This is, he argues, the difference between subjective and objective religion. Formalistic formulation of laws is an integral part of the Jewish religion, and sustains its existence. Without formalistic formulation, Judaism is not an objective religion, but is open to personal and idiosyncratic reconstruction.

> A subjective religiosity cannot endure. And all those tendencies to transform the religious act into pure subjectivity negate all corporeality

51 J. Soloveitchik, *Halakhic Man*, translated by Lawrence Kaplan (Philadelphia: 1983), 55–56. The quotation from *Likutei Amarim* is from Igeret Hakodesh, 10, 115a.

52 Ibid., 56–57.

> and all sensation in religious life and admit man into a pure and abstract world, where there is neither eating nor drinking, but religious individuals sitting with their crowns on their heads and enjoying their own inner experiences, their own tempestuous, heaven-storming spirits, their own hidden longings and mysterious yearnings—will in the end prove null and void. The stychic power of religion that seizes hold of man, that subjects and dominates him, is in force only when the religion is a concrete religion, a religion of the life of the senses, in which there is sight, smell, and touch, a religion which a man of flesh and blood can feel with all of his senses, sinews, and organs, with his entire being, a sensuous religion which conative man will encounter, in a very palpable way, wherever he may go. A subjective religiosity comprised of spiritual moods, of emotions and affections, of outlooks and desires, will never be blessed with success.[53]

How is this objective religiosity to be attained?

> The Halakhah, which was given to us from Sinai, is the objectification of religion in clear and determinate forms, in precise and authoritative laws, and in definite principles. It translates subjectivity into objectivity, the amorphous flow of religious experience into a fixed pattern of lawfulness.[54]

According to R. Soloveitchik, Judaism teaches that "religion which does not lead to definite actions, to clearly formed solid laws and precepts, is sterile." Therefore, "the Halakhah sets down statutes and erects markers that serve as a dam against the surging, subjective current coursing through the universal *homo religiosus*, which, from time to time, in its raging turbulence, sweeps away his entire being to obscure and inchoate realms."

### ii Silberg's view

In contrast to Soloveitchik, the Israeli scholar Moshe Silberg takes a jurisprudential approach to Jewish law. Silberg too puts forward a theory to explain why Jewish law makes such considerable use of standards and measures.

> Jewish jurisprudence—if we may say so—is a jurisprudence which does not depend on judges. The function of the law is not to prescribe

53 Ibid., 57–58. The word "stychic," derived from the Greek word for 'order,' is used in religious literature to denote the elements of nature operating in the cosmos; in sociological literature, it denotes processes that are beyond the individual's consciousness and will.

54 Ibid., 59.

> for the judge how to decide; it prescribes for the person how to conduct his life.[55]

This statement calls for some clarification, for Silberg could not have meant that Jewish law does not recognize the judiciary, without which no legal system can be conceived. Tractate Sanhedrin and the many details pertaining to the functioning of the judicial system demonstrate that this institution is well-rooted in the talmudic tradition.

Silberg argues, however, that Jewish law is primarily addressed to the individual, its objective being to guide the individual's conduct. This thesis is particularly significant if we bear in mind certain influential jurisprudential theories, such as that advocated by, among others, Hans Kelsen,[56] which postulate that laws are addressed to judges. According to Kelsen, the legal system turns directly to the judge, instructing him how to rule in a given case. Individuals are addressed only indirectly, by implication. The legislator may use abstract norms such as 'reasonable care' and so on, and leave it for the judge to decide, in applying them to particular cases, their precise meaning.

This is not the case with talmudic law, which, Silberg emphasizes, addresses the individual. As an illustration, Silberg quotes the Mishnah about the young pigeon, cited above: "If a young pigeon is found within fifty cubits, it belongs to the owner of the dovecote; but if beyond fifty cubits, it belongs to the finder." A more flexible wording of the Mishnah would have been: 'a young pigeon belongs to its finder if in the given circumstances it is reasonable to suppose that it did not come from a nearby dovecote.' However, as Silberg points out,

> It is clear that if the matter should become subject to litigation and the dispute come before the judge, after listening to witnesses and experts, he will be able to clarify all the circumstances in the case and draw from them the most plausible conclusion. But what is the ordinary citizen, who does not have command of this complex apparatus, to do—how can he clarify the subject, and what is he to do in order to be able to decide whether he is indeed obligated to return the bird or not?[57]

Flexible wording would afford little help to the well-intentioned individual. If the legislator's objective is to provide the individual with direct instruction regarding his conduct, the law must be worded in a particularistic manner.

55 M. Silberg, *Talmudic Law and the Modern State*, trans. Ben Zion Bokser (New York: 1973), 48.
56 Hans Kelsen (1881–1973), legal philosopher who formulated a kind of positivism known as the "pure theory of law."
57 Ibid., 89.

If the goal before the legislator, if the ideal towards which he aspires, is not to resolve post factum conflicts between man and man, but to provide, in the first place, moral guidance for each person, then the first consideration—precision and clarity—will prevail, and the inevitable result is legal formalism.[58]

58 Ibid., 90.

# Judicial process

# 3 Exigency authority



## 1 Certainty versus applicability

All legal systems are confronted by a serious dilemma. On the one hand, they aspire to constancy, seeking to treat similar cases in a similar way, so that their outcomes can be predicted with reasonable certainty. Legal certainty thus requires adherence to existing rules, even if this generates unjust or ineffective judgments in particular instances. On the other hand, if the law is to be able to adjust to new circumstances arising out of social or economic changes, it must maintain some degree of flexibility.

The river of life, by its very nature, constantly reshapes its banks. Rules that are reasonable and adequate one day may be obsolete or irrelevant the next. Novel phenomena that have not been addressed by the legislature may generate problems that require immediate legal solutions. The solutions provided for by the law on the books may be obsolete or inadequate, and may conflict with current social and cultural thinking. Western jurisprudential thought generally takes the view that laws can only be changed by legislative action. But this is a long and tedious process, and changes in the law may be urgently needed before legislation can be drafted, passed, and implemented. Following the letter of the law in such cases may debase it and thwart its purpose.

We must distinguish between the way judges actually resolve this dilemma in a given legal system, and the course of action prescribed by the system. Examination of court decisions reveals that judges adopt various strategies to overcome the problem of obsolete or irrelevant laws, including reinterpretation of existing law, the creation of new legal rules and legal fictions, or simply disregarding existing law. How judges **should** rule, however, depends on general theories of adjudication and the given legal system's prescribed course of action for such occasions. Although legal systems generally do not explicitly address conflicts between laws on the books and new socio-cultural conditions, they may suggest a course of action inexplicitly. Jewish law is aware of this dilemma, and has laid down principles empowering courts to deal with novel situations.

## 2 Two understandings of the nature of a legal system

In describing legal systems, it is useful to differentiate between norms and practices, that is, between that which ought to be, and that which is, or as philosophers say, between 'ought' and 'is.' The normative approach to describing a legal system is theoretical in nature, seeking to infer its rules, principles, and ideals from the system's normative sources, without regard to the extent of their implementation. The realistic approach to describing a legal system seeks to describe the rules and principles actually employed in the judicial process. The focus is on how the law is administered, rather than on the nature of its norms.

As an example, consider section 351 (abolished in 1990) of the *Israeli Penal Law, 5737—1977*, which explicitly forbids homosexual acts. Such acts, even in private and between consenting adults, constituted a felony punishable by ten years of imprisonment. Nevertheless, the Attorney General instructed state prosecutors to refrain from bringing offenders to trial.

It should be noted that this directive was binding on government officials, but not on the courts. Were a state prosecutor to have ignored it, and brought such a case before the courts, the latter would not have been bound by the instruction to ignore the law. In practice, state prosecutors always refrained from pressing charges against suspected violators of this law. So if we ask whether homosexuality was punishable under Israeli law, the answer is: from the normative perspective, it was punishable under section 351; from the realistic perspective, it was—in light of the Attorney General's directive—not punishable.

## 3 American legal realism

In the 1920s, a school of thought referred to as 'legal realism' gained popularity among legal scholars in the United States. Its most enthusiastic proponents, however, were practicing lawyers and judges. Realism rejected traditional Anglo-American jurisprudence, which defined the legal system as an autonomous, consistent, and self-contained set of rules and principles. The traditional view was norm-based, describing the legal process as a matter of choosing and applying the appropriate rule from an existing body of laws. In opposition to the traditional approach, legal realism proposed that in describing a legal system, attention should be paid only to the law as applied in practice. Legal realism suggested that litigants were in fact subject to the judge before whom they appeared rather than to a set of abstract legal norms. Its proponents considered the norm-based approach, with its emphasis on rules and laws, misguided. They argued that legal rules merely serve as a point of departure for the judge, who never in fact applies them in their pure form. In practice, the legal realists claimed, judges use their discretion in deciding whether or not a precedent is applicable to the case at hand. Furthermore, the human element also had to be taken into consideration. Rules are applied by judges of flesh and blood, whose decisions are influenced by their cultural and political background, personalities and experience.

Justice Oliver Wendell Holmes (1841–1935) coined what became the motto of legal realism: "The prophecies of what the courts will do in fact, and nothing more pretentious, are what I mean by the law."[1] A prominent forbear of legal realism, John Chipman Gray, quotes with approval a remark made by an English cleric in 1717: "Whoever hath an absolute authority to interpret any written or spoken laws, it is he who is truly the law-giver to all intents and purposes, and not the person who first wrote or spoke them."[2]

Legal realism had a significant jurisprudential impact. It drew attention to the human, social, and economic aspects of the legal process, elements that are not captured by a description of abstract norms. But to dwell on these aspects exclusively is also a mistake. In depicting a legal system, due consideration must be given to its underlying ideals, principles, and concepts, even if they are not fully reflected in practice. These concepts reflect social norms that, though not necessarily put into practice, are nevertheless not repudiated, and implicitly influence the behavior of those operating within the system.

1 Oliver Wendell Holmes, *Collected Legal Papers* (New York: 1920), 173.
2 John Chipman Gray, *The Nature and Sources of the Laws* (New York: 1909), 125.

In this chapter, we will discuss a talmudic *sugya* addressing the question of judicial conduct when there is a gap between the law on the books and societal needs, as perceived by the court. Much of the chapter will be devoted to analysis of the most important talmudic treatment of this problem, the rule of R. Eliezer b. Jacob.[3]

## 4 R. Eliezer b. Jacob's rule

It is taught: R. Eliezer b. Jacob[4] said, I heard that courts mete out lashes (*makin*) and punishment [in a manner that is] not in accordance with the law.

### 4.1 Talmudic sources

R. Eliezer b. Jacob's rule, which is not disputed in the halakhic literature, concerns the powers of the court. There are three different versions of the rule in the Rabbinic sources; apparently, the different versions reflect the gradual development of the rule's scope. Let us now explore the passages in which the rule is found.

*The Babylonian Talmud version*

> It is taught: R. Eliezer b. Jacob said, I heard that courts mete out lashes (*makin*) and punishment [in a manner that is] not in accordance with the law, and not to transgress the law, but to safeguard the law. And it happened that a man rode a horse on the Sabbath during the time of the Greeks, and they brought him to the court and stoned him to death, not because he deserved it, but because it was an exigency of the times. And again, it happened that a man had relations with his wife under a fig tree, and they brought him to the court and flogged him (*vehilkuhu*), not because he deserved it, but because it was an exigency of the times.
>
> bSanhedrin 46a; bJebamot 90b

The passage apparently consists of two parts: the rule stated by R. Eliezer b. Jacob, and two precedents adduced to illustrate it.

3 This rule has been treated extensively in the literature; see e.g., E.B. Quint and N.S. Hecht, *Jewish Jurisprudence*, vol. 1 (New York: 1980), 139–213, and N.S. Hecht and E. B. Quint, "Exigency jurisdiction under Jewish law," 9 *Dine Israel* (1978–1980), 27–99.

4 We know of two Tannaim with this name. One lived in the 1st century CE (at the end of the Second Temple period); the other, a student of R. Akiva, and a founder of the Usha academy, lived in the 2nd century CE. The Talmud states various laws in the name of R. Eliezer b. Jacob without specifying which of the two is being referred to. In any case, both flourished prior to the redaction of the Mishnah.

*The Jerusalem Talmud version*

> We learned: R. Eliezer b. Jacob said, I heard that they punish [in a manner that is] not in accordance with the halakha, and they punish [in a manner that is] not in accordance with the law. How far [does their discretion extend]? R. Lazar b. R. Jose says, [it extends] even to hearsay; R. Joseh says, witnesses [are always required], but [it extends to cases where there was] no forewarning. And it happened that a man went on his way riding his horse on the Sabbath, and they brought him to the court and stoned him to death. Was it not [merely] a Rabbinic prohibition? But it was an exigency of the times. And again, it happened that someone went on his way and his wife was with him, and he turned aside behind a fence and did what he had to with her, and they brought him to the court and flogged him (*vehilkuhu*). And was she not his wife? But he conducted himself shamefully.
>
> jHagiga 2:2 (78a)

It is clear that in this version, something not found in the Babylonian Talmud version has been added between the two parts—the rule itself, and the illustrative precedents—namely, the discussion about the extent of judicial discretion to impose extra-legal punishment. The significance of this debate between R. Lazar and R. Joseh, Amoraim of the fourth generation, will be addressed below.

*The version in the scholium to the Scroll of Fasts (Megilat Taanit)*

The passage is constructed in the same way as its Babylonian variant: the rule in the first part and its illustration in the second. In addition, there is a dispute about the validity of the rule.

> ***"On the 22nd [of the month] of Elul they again executed apostates"***
>
> [Scholium] R. Eliezer b. Jacob said, I heard that courts flog (*malkin*) and execute [in a manner that is] not in accordance with the law. Of the school of Levi, R. Shimon said, I heard that the courts punish with fines and mete out lashes (*makin*) [in a manner that is] not in accordance with the law, not because it is written in the law, but because Scripture says, "so shalt thou put away the evil from the midst of thee" (Deut. 22:21; 22:24). And it happened that a man had relations with his wife under a fig tree, and the court had him flogged (*vehilkuhu*); and was he, then, guilty? But it was due to the exigency of the times, to teach a lesson to others, because they conducted themselves promiscuously. And again, it happened that a man rode a horse on the Sabbath, and they brought him to the court and stoned him to death; and was he, then, guilty? But it was an exigency of the times.

Megilat Taanit (The Scroll of Fasts) is a short list enumerating thirty-six days considered to have been historically joyous or happy occasions for the Jewish people, and hence fasting on these days is prohibited. In its current form—it is written in Aramaic in a laconic style—Megilat Taanit dates back to either the first or second century CE, and is therefore one of the earliest extant documents from the Tannaitic period, predating redaction of the Mishnah.[5] The first, italicized, line of the above passage is the text of Megilat Taanit, describing an event of which we have no historical knowledge.

After the redaction of the Talmud (circa 500 CE), a commentary or scholium was appended to Megilat Taanit. It is written in mishnaic Hebrew and based on several different sources, including the Hebrew version of Maccabees I, the Talmud, and other unidentified sources. R. Eliezer b. Jacob's rule is quoted in the scholium. This source is therefore the latest of the three sources of the rule.

Let us compare the three versions of the rule itself, without the preceding and subsequent text:

*Babylonian Talmud*

> It is taught: R. Eliezer b. Jacob said, I heard that courts mete out lashes (*makin*) and punishment [in a manner that is] not in accordance with the law, and not to transgress the law, but to safeguard the law.

*Jerusalem Talmud*

> We learned: R. Eliezer b. Jacob said, I heard that they punish [in a manner that is] not in accordance with the halakha, and they punish [in a manner that is] not in accordance with the law.

*Megilat Taanit*

> R. Eliezer b. Jacob said, I heard that courts flog (*malkin*) and execute [in a manner that is] not in accordance with the law. Of the school of Levi, R. Shimon said, I heard that the courts punish with fines and mete out lashes (*makin*) [in a manner that is] not in accordance with the law, not because it is written in the law, but because Scripture says, "so shalt thou put away the evil from the midst of thee" (Deut. 22:21; 22:24).

Let us now consider the earliest passage of the three, namely, the Jerusalem Talmud's version of the rule.

5 See Vered Noam, *Megillat Ta'anit: Versions, Interpretation, History* (Hebrew), (Jerusalem: 2003).

> We learned: R. Eliezer b. Jacob said, I heard that they punish [in a manner that is] not in accordance with the halakha, and they punish [in a manner that is] not in accordance with the law.

The second sentence, which is, according to the received reading, regarded as part of the statement of the rule, and therefore would seem to be redundant, is in fact the Jerusalem Talmud's amazed reaction to the rule: "And they punish [in a manner that is] not in accordance with the law!?"[6] It is, in fact, the beginning of an interpolation, which records the Amoraic debate mentioned above, about the scope of R. Eliezer b. Jacob's rule. This interpolation will be discussed below. In this source, then, that is, in the Jerusalem Talmud, the continuity between the rule and the precedents is disrupted by the question and ensuing debate.

When we pare away the interrogative repetition and ensuing debate, the Jerusalem Talmud's version of the rule itself reads: "I heard that they [the courts[7]] punish [in a manner that is] not in accordance with the halakha."

Now in analyzing ancient texts, there is a heuristic principle that the shortest version can be assumed to be the earliest. The first writer presumably knew what he intended to convey, whereas a later expositor or transcriber would tend to expand the text to make sure that it was properly understood. If we regard brevity as an indication of antiquity, it is more than likely that the Jerusalem Talmud records the earliest version of the rule.

Before continuing our comparative analysis of the three versions, some semantic clarifications of legal terms they contain are in order.

## 4.2 Meaning of the term "punish"

What does the term "punish" mean in the context of the Jerusalem Talmud? Ordinarily, it means one of the following: fines, corporal punishment, or capital punishment. The question, then, is, does the Jerusalem Talmud authorize courts to mete out all three kinds of punishment "in a manner that is not in accordance with the halakha"? The precedents seem to support an answer in the affirmative. However, this conclusion is only

6 It is not unusual for the Jerusalem Talmud to reiterate a puzzling statement in the interrogative. For example, jSanhedrin 9:11 (27b): "We learned: It was done against the will of the Sages. And Pinhas [did it] against the will of the Sages?"; jTaanit 2:8 (65d): "And the prophet Elijah stepped forth.... And Elijah offered a sacrifice on the prohibited High Places?"

7 It should be noted that, in contrast to the Babylonian Talmud and the scholium to Megilat Taanit, the Jerusalem Talmud does not explicitly refer to "the courts" here. Indeed, its usual style is to refer to the courts implicitly. E.g., mSanhedrin 9:5 states: "If someone kills another person, but there were no witnesses, they confine him to a cell, and feed him the bread of adversity and water of affliction." It is clear that this imprisonment of a murderer is based on a judgment handed down by the court.

valid if the rule and precedents are an integral unit, a point that will be discussed below. For the present, let us consider whether one of the three ordinary meanings of the term "punish" is dominant.

One way to define the exact semantic field covered by a term is by examining parallel sources that shed light on its meaning in different contexts. Other Tannaitic sources using the term "punish" should therefore be examined to elucidate its meaning in the context of R. Eliezer b. Jacob's statement. Unfortunately, this method is not helpful in our case, since perusal of the sources reveals that the term is used in the various senses in an apparently random fashion, as the following examples illustrate.

### a Release from vows

> Regarding all of these [cases], they [persons seeking release from a vow] do not have to inquire [since the vows in question are not binding], but if they do inquire, they are punished, and the stringent ruling is applied to them—so says R. Meir.
>
> mNedarim 2:5

This Mishnah deals with the law concerning non-binding vows. R. Meir maintains that those who make such vows and, ignorant of the fact that their vows are not binding, consult a rabbi as to whether and how they can be legally released from their vows, should be treated severely and "punished," to discourage people from making such vows in the future. The punishment in question here is that the rabbi would not inform them that they are not, in fact, bound by the vows, and thus not in need of release, but would keep them in suspense.

### b Slandering one's bride

> And the elders of that city shall take the man and chastise him. And they shall punish him a hundred silver coins.
>
> Deuteronomy 22:18–19

A baraita in tractate Ketubot interprets the biblical verse as follows:

> Our Rabbis taught: "and they shall punish him"—this means money [a fine]; "and [they shall] chastise him"—this means flogging.
>
> bKetubot 46a

### c Conspiring witnesses (*zomemim*)

> And you shall do to him as he conspired to do to his brother.
>
> Deuteronomy 19:19

The Midrash comments:

> "As he conspired": if by money, money; if by lashes, lashes; if by punishment, punishment.
>
> Sifre Deuteronomy, Shoftim, 190 (Finkelstein edition, p. 231)

A conspiring witness who intended to cause someone undeserved punishment incurs the same punishment himself. The Midrash comments that this norm is applicable to various kinds of punishment: fines, flogging, and unspecified punishments.

### i Maximalist interpretation of the term "punish"

The Israeli scholar Menachem Elon interprets the term "punish" in line with a remark made by Rashi in his commentary on bSanhedrin 46a, a remark not found in any version of Rashi prior to the Amsterdam edition of the Talmud, printed over a three year period beginning in 1644. Rashi, commenting on the *sugya* in the Babylonian Talmud, takes "punishment" to mean capital punishment; his comment would seem to be equally applicable to "punishment" in the Jerusalem Talmud. Elon adopts this interpretation, asserting:

> "Mete out lashes" means "flogging" and "punish" refers to the death penalty. Both sentences can be imposed even in cases where, under the law of the Torah, the defendant could not be convicted or punished. See Rashi, Sanhedrin 46a.[8]

This maximalist view does not reflect the original meaning of the talmudic text. Note that the scholium to Megilat Taanit differs from both the Jerusalem Talmud and the Babylonian Talmud in referring explicitly to capital punishment: "I heard that courts flog (*malkin*) and execute [in a manner that is] not in accordance with the law." But the inclusion of capital punishment as part of the rule articulated by R. Eliezer b. Jacob is disputed by R. Shimon, who asserts: "I heard that the courts punish with fines and mete out lashes (*makin*) [in a manner that is] not in accordance with the law." Now, how can the explicit reference to capital punishment, at variance with the other sources, both of which are earlier, be explained? And what is the import of R. Shimon's dissenting view?

The context of the reference to R. Eliezer b. Jacob's rule in the scholium may be instructive. The rule is quoted to legitimize, or provide support for, a statement in Megilat Taanit that on the 22nd day of Elul courts regained the authority to execute apostates. The event is reported as follows:

8 Menachem Elon, *Jewish Law: History, Sources, Principles* (Philadelphia: 1994), 2:515.

> Because Gentiles occupied the land of Israel, the Israelites could not lay a hand on the wicked who were in their midst, until they [the Gentiles] went away from there; and once they left, the wicked were given three days of grace, to repent. When they saw that they did not repent, they took a vote and executed them. The execution day they turned into a festival.
>
> Scholium to Megilat Taanit

The report seeks to provide an authoritative source as justification for execution of "the wicked," seeing as they apparently were not subject to the death penalty by the strict law. To fill this need, the scholium reads R. Eliezer b. Jacob's reference to "punishment" as connoting "execution." However, in addition to this internal textual requirement, another problematic element in this passage, to which we will now turn, may also explain the rendering of "punishment" as "execution."

### 4.3 The rule–precedent relation

In all the sources where the rule in question appears, it is accompanied by two precedents, which are presumably intended to exemplify its application. But what, precisely, is the relationship between the rule and the precedents? Do they constitute a single textual entity, or were they originally distinct entities that were, in light of their shared subject matter, subsequently conjoined? The importance of this inquiry is that it may illuminate the original meaning of the rule—as opposed to its exposition by later halakhic authorities. If the passage was originally a single unit, then its exact meaning can be deduced from the precedents. If the precedents were added later, however, they only serve to show how the rule was understood by those who added them, without shedding light on the rule's original meaning.

Careful reading of the *sugya* in tractate Sanhedrin of the Babylonian Talmud reveals various considerations indicating that the passage is composed of two distinct units:

1. In the Babylonian Talmud version, the first precedent says that someone was executed, but the rule itself does not explicitly permit capital punishment. It is reasonable to suppose that had R. Eliezer b. Jacob, the author of the rule, been aware of the precedent, and had he intended to authorize capital punishment, he would have been more explicit.
2. The rule speaks of the authority to "mete out lashes," whereas the second precedent mentions "flogging." These are different technical terms in talmudic law. "Lashes" generally refers to the punishment of 39 lashes prescribed in Scripture for transgression of biblical law. "Flogging," on the other hand, was ordered by courts for rebellious

conduct. Had R. Eliezer b. Jacob himself been adducing the precedent, uniformity of expression would be expected.

3. The order of the precedents does not parallel the structure of the rule. The rule first mentions the authority to mete out lashes, whereas the first precedent demonstrates that the court has the authority to execute transgressors, while the second precedent speaks of the authority to order an offender flogged.

These three discrepancies are eliminated in the scholium to Megilat Taanit. Let us examine it once more (eliding R. Shimon's view, which is not germane to the present analysis).

> R. Eliezer b. Jacob said, I heard that courts flog (*malkin*) and execute [in a manner that is] not in accordance with the law.... And it happened that a man had relations with his wife under a fig tree, and the court had him flogged (*vehilkuhu*).... And again, it happened that a man rode a horse on the Sabbath, and they ... stoned him to death.

In this version, there is continuity between the rule and the precedents. The rule specifically mentions the authority to impose capital punishment, the locution "mete out lashes (*makin*)" has been changed to "flog" (*malkin*), and the order of the precedents has been changed to correspond to the components of the rule. However, it is precisely this harmony that renders the passage suspect. The extension of R. Eliezer b. Jacob's rule to encompass capital punishment was probably not accepted by his colleagues with equanimity. The existence of reservations about this extension is acknowledged by quoting the view of R. Shimon, who reiterates the rule in its original limited sense: "R. Shimon said, I heard that the courts punish with fines and mete out lashes (*makin*)." The word "fines" is added to show that the authority to impose extra-judicial punishment extends only to fines and corporal punishment, but stops short of capital punishment. R. Shimon's statement should thus not be regarded as an independent tradition, but as an exposition of R. Eliezer b. Jacob's original rule. Note also that the version of the rule presented by R. Shimon retains the original verb "*makin*," rather than the "*malkin*" as in the 'edited' formulation of the rule. It is typical of legal documents that new and controversial interpretations are read into the original in order to impart to them authority and credibility.

Although we have suggested that the rule was propounded first, and the precedents were added on later, some scholars have claimed that the opposite is true, that the precedents predate the rule itself. Gedaliah Alon, for instance, argued as follows:

> The Jerusalem Talmud (*Hagiga* ii, 77d) explains Simeon b. Shetah's action in hanging eighty women in one day, which, contrary to the law, was an emergency measure called for by the circumstances of the time.

Thus the Babylonian Talmud also cites the Baraita: 'R. Eliezer b. Jacob said: 'I have heard that the Bet Din beat and impose[d] penalties on an offender though not required by the Torah, not with the intention of transgressing against the ordinances of the Torah, but in order to safeguard it,' etc. But it is doubtful if there existed such a directive that gave the court permission to put a person to death, contrary to Torah law, even if 'called for by the circumstances of the time.' For the case of the one who rode on a horse on the Sabbath in the days of the Greeks and was brought before the Bet Din and was stoned may be explained by the premise that the ancient Halakha was stringent in regard to desecration of the Sabbath and imposed the penalty of death even on one who committed a transgression that was only a 'Rabbinic' prohibition according to the new Halakha.... The author of *The Book of Jubilees* likewise prescribes death for one who draws water on Shabbat (1, 8). Similarly Philo explains *(De Vita Mosis* ii, 220) the death of the stick-gatherer, that he became liable to capital punishment because he collected wood for kindling, which was intended for lighting a fire. Thus he became liable to stoning on account of *muqse* [something that may not be used or handled on the Sabbath or Holy Day, because its use is not counted on (cf. *Sifre Num.*, §113; *T.B. Shabbat* 96b; *T.P. Sanhedrin* iv, 22d). It appears that the ancient Halakha did not differentiate, in regard to penalties, between Torah law and 'Rabbinic enactment', and ordained death for every kind of work forbidden on the Sabbath. As for the case of the man who had intercourse with his wife beneath a fig tree and was brought before the court and flogged, it is a daily occurrence for the Bet Din to inflict corporal punishment for disobedience on the basis of Rabbinic enactment; thus 'Rav ordered a lashing for anyone who betrothed his wife by intercourse without previous negotiations [*shiddukhe*]' (*T.B. Qiddushin* 12b; so, too, did Samuel according to *T.P. ibid.* iii, 64b). It should be noted that in the Palestinian Talmud (*Hagiga* ii, 78a) the account of the second incident does not conclude (as in the Babylonian Talmud, and also in the Palestinian Talmud, earlier, in connection with one who rides on a horse) with the words 'not because he merited this punishment legally, but because the circumstances of the time called for it'; instead it reads: 'But was she not his wife? Only he behaved disgracefully.' It may therefore be assumed that this ruling of R. Eliezer b. Jacob was based on incidents that occurred in early generations who convicted and punished not in conformity with the *new* Halakha, and we simply have here an attempt to explain the earlier and contrary Halakha as 'a temporary measure.'[9]

9 G. Alon, *Jews, Judaism and the Classical World: Studies in Jewish History in the Times of the Second Temple*, trans. Israel Abraham (Jerusalem: 1977), 121.

In Alon's opinion, the precedents for the rule predated the rule itself, and reflected the severe "ancient law," on which transgressors were put to death for transgressing Rabbinic prohibitions. Since it was no longer the judicial practice to carry out such executions, there was a gap between the law recorded in the precedents, and that current at the time. Alon argues that the rule was invoked to close the gap by suggesting that the old precedents were extra-legal, but imposed on the authority of R. Eliezer b. Jacob's rule. While there is no doubt that the Talmud downplays the problem of these precedents by invoking the principle of extra-legal punishment, it is by no means clear that that was indeed the motivation for its formulation in the first place. It stands to reason that the rule was formulated independently, as an expression of a judicial policy that sought to strengthen the power of the court, a hypothesis supported by the many linguistic discrepancies discussed above.

### i Word order and its significance

If we accept the premise that in the context of R. Eliezer b. Jacob's rule, "punishment" indeed refers to capital punishment, the passage in the Babylonian Talmud lists the punishments imposed by the court in ascending order of the severity: "mete out lashes and punishment." Corporal punishment, which is clearly less severe than capital punishment, is mentioned first. However, if we accept the suggestion that "punishment" denotes fines, the order is the reverse, since the punishment of fines is less severe than corporal punishment. If the editor of the *sugya* indeed sought to list the punishments logically, in ascending order of severity, the text should have been 'mete out punishment and lashes.'

It may well be, however, that the existing word order reflects, not logic, but a classic stylistic consideration, characterized as follows by the Talmudist Shamma Friedman:

> Students of language and stylistics are familiar with the rule stating that "in a sequence of names or words there is a tendency to put the shorter words first and the longer words last." This rule was known to the ancients. Today it is called the "law of increasing members." It applies to many languages: Greek (even in Homer), Latin, German, English, etcetera. It is found in lists of names, rhetoric, poetry, in ritual and religious incantations, and so on.[10]

More specifically, the rule states that in phrases and collocations (words often used together) of words of various lengths (measured by number of syllables), the shortest will tend to precede the others. The phenomenon is

10 Shamma Friedman, "The law of increasing members in mishnaic Hebrew" (Hebrew), *Leshonenu* 35 (1971), 117, reprinted in M. Bar-Asher (ed.), *Studies in Mishnaic Hebrew* (Hebrew), vol. 2 (Jerusalem: 1980), 299–326.

commonplace: consider the expression 'thunder and lightning'— which event really comes first? As Friedman demonstrates, the phenomenon is also found in the Rabbinic literature. Examples in Hebrew include 'favor and charity' (*hen vehesed*); 'poor and destitute' (*ani veevion*); 'law and order' (*hok vaseder*), 'day and night' (*yom valaila*). The somewhat peculiar collocation '*hupa vekidushin*' (marriage ceremony and betrothal) is also accounted for by this rule. Logically, the order should have been the reverse—'*kidushin vehupa*,' given that in the talmudic period, the events always took place in the latter sequence—since medieval times, the two components have been conjoined into a single event—but due to this stylistic consideration, the word order is changed.

The expression "mete out lashes and punishment" is "*makin veonshim*" in Hebrew. The second word in this idiom is longer by a syllable, albeit an unstressed one. This may well be the reason for the apparently illogical word order.

To sum up our comparative analysis of the three versions of R. Eliezer b. Jacob's rule, let us recapitulate the historical process the rule underwent. The earliest document, the Jerusalem Talmud, records the earliest version of the rule, that is, where not warranted by law, courts can only inflict monetary punishments. The first extension of the rule occurs in the Babylonian Talmud, which extends the rule to cover corporal punishment. A more radical extension occurs in Megilat Taanit, which authorizes the courts to impose capital punishment. Normatively speaking, however, the passage in the Babylonian Talmud was usually understood broadly, as encompassing capital punishment.

## 4.4 Is the court a legislative or judicial institution?

In both the Tannaitic and the Amoraic sources, the term "court" (*beit din*) can denote either a legislative or a judicial institution. Which of the two meanings is the correct one is ascertained by considering the context.

As a judicial institution, the court acts after the fact to resolve disagreements between litigants. Its rulings are binding on the parties who appear before it. By contrast, in its legislative capacity, the court acts prospectively, by passing laws and enactments to safeguard society and maintain a suitable level of social harmony. These laws are binding on the general public.

Even though the same term—'*beit din*'—is used in both senses, and sometimes the same individuals serve in both capacities, that is, as both judges and legislators, this does not mean that there is no difference between the court's legislative role and its judicial role. Consider the following rule:

> One court cannot annul the decision of another unless it is greater both in wisdom and in number.
>
> mEduyot 1:5

Maimonides, who formulates this rule in the *Code*'s Laws concerning Rebels 2:1–2, regards it as referring to the court as a **legislative** institution: a law passed by one court cannot be annulled by another unless it is greater in both wisdom and number. This does not, however, prevent a court that is adjudicating a case from deviating from a precedent set by a different court. Furthermore, by definition every court has judicial power, but only a court with a certain status is qualified to enact laws binding on the general public. Three persons, even if they lack judicial qualifications, may pass judgment on an individual, but they cannot enact laws binding on the public at large.

Consider the following talmudic passages, the first five of which use the term 'court' in its judicial sense, and the latter four, in its legislative sense.

1 If the judges' assessment valued the property by one-sixth below or above its worth, their sale is void. R. Shimon b. Gamaliel says: Their sale is valid; otherwise what good is the court's power? (mKetubot 11:5)
2 R. Nahman said in the name of Samuel: Where orphans [who are minors] wish to divide the property of their father, the court appoints a guardian for them and [the guardian] chooses a suitable portion for them. When they reach the age of majority, they are entitled to enter a protest. (bJebamot 67b)
3 R. Hisda stated in the name of Mar Ukba: If one became insane, the court takes control of his property and feeds and maintains his wife, his sons, and his daughters. (bKetubot 48a)
4 R. Katina said: The court takes on a case even for less than a penny's worth [i.e., there is no minimum threshold amount for litigation]. (bBaba Metzia 55a)
5 If someone was flogged and flogged again [i.e., transgressed repeatedly], the court puts him in a cell and feeds him barley until his stomach bursts. (mSanhedrin 9:5)
6 Can the court make a stipulation abrogating a law of the Torah!? (bJebamot 89b)
7 Rabbi [Judah the Prince] assembled a court and they decided by vote that if the property had been in the hands of the Sicaricon[11] for twelve months, then whoever bought it first acquired title, but had to give a quarter [of the purchase price] to the original owner. (mGitin 5:6).
8 It was taught: R. Ishmael the son of R. Johanan b. Beroka says: It is a stipulation of the court that [an owner of a swarm of bees] is entitled to enter his fellow's field and cut down the bough [on which the

11 *Sicaricon*–Variant of *sicarius*. Fiscal official of the Roman Empire who confiscated or extorted property of Jews who had fought against the Romans. See Chapter 13, "Unjust Enrichment," section 3.3.i.

swarm has settled] to save his swarm, and he pays him the value of the bough. (bBaba Kama 81b)

9 R. Simlai expounded in Netzivin: R. Judah and his court voted on oil [made by Gentiles] and permitted it. (bAvoda Zara 36a)

The distinction between the court in its judicial capacity and in its legislative capacity comes to the fore in the following mishnaic discussion:

> If one died and left a wife, a creditor and heirs, and had property in trust or on loan in the hands of others, R. Tarfon says: It should be given to the party that is at greatest disadvantage. R. Akiva says: They must not show compassion in adjudicating a legal case. Rather, it must be given to the heirs.
>
> mKetubot 9:2

This Mishnah concerns division of an estate that is insufficient to satisfy all the legitimate claims on it. R. Tarfon is of the opinion that the poorest claimant should be given priority. R. Akiva disagrees, saying that compassion is irrelevant in this context; the issue should not be decided on the basis of the claimants' respective means, but the legitimate heirs should be given priority. R. Abraham Isaac Kook was asked how R. Tarfon's view can be reconciled with the scriptural injunction, "Neither shalt thou favor a poor man in his cause" (Exod. 23:3), which forbids any bias in favor of the weaker party in a court of law. He replied:

> We must therefore say that when the Sages, in their legislative capacity, see fit to set down legislation that is—from the perspective of the attribute of compassion—worthy of being set down as the law, they have the power to do so. And afterwards, the ordinary judge who engages in adjudication, must rule in accordance with that legislation, and is forbidden to disregard it, even if his own personal sense of compassion would incline him to do so.
>
> *Pri Haaretz* 4 (1982), p. 20

R. Kook, then, distinguishes between the court acting in its capacity as a legislative body, which is indeed empowered to factor empathetic considerations into its pronouncements, and the court acting in its judicial capacity, which may not do so.

### 4.5 R. Eliezer b. Jacob's rule: legislative or judicial?

With this distinction in mind, let us consider whether R. Eliezer b. Jacob's rule that a court may punish in a manner that is not in keeping with the law, refers to a court acting in a judicial capacity, or a court acting in a legislative capacity. In other words, does the rule authorize the court to issue verdicts that are contrary to the law, or to issue new legislation that is contrary to biblical law?

The importance of this question can hardly be exaggerated. If the rule refers to judicial institutions, its thrust is to liberate the court from subjection to the law and allow it to decide cases as it sees fit, though with certain restrictions. If this is indeed the correct reading of the rule, it endorses an approach that is unique to Jewish law and has no parallel in contemporary western law, which construes the judiciary as entirely subject to the law. In western law, the sole situation in which a court is authorized to deviate from the law is when a state of emergency has been declared and special emergency regulations are in force. But it is the legislature and not the judiciary that issues a declaration of a state of emergency, and such declarations are not retroactive: emergency regulations cannot be applied to actions performed before the state of emergency was declared. Furthermore, even if a state of emergency has been declared, courts are bound by emergency regulations, just as they are bound by the law in normal times. They must apply the emergency regulations, and are not authorized to deviate from them.

In his *Jewish Law: History, Sources, Principles*, Menachem Elon discusses R. Eliezer b. Jacob's rule in the chapter entitled "Legislation: Nature, Objectives and Principles of Legislation by the Halakhic Authorities":

> The second exception to the general principle that denies the power to permit performance of what the Torah prohibits is the legislative principle that authorizes the halakhic authorities to enact *takkanot* in criminal law, even in capital cases, and even if these enactments prescribe action the Torah prohibits.... This legislative principle was stated by the Tanna, R. Eliezer b. Jacob: "It was taught: R. Eliezer b. Jacob said: I have heard that the court may impose flogging and punishments not prescribed by the Torah—not to transgress the law of the Torah, but to make a fence around the Torah."[12]

Elon does not distinguish, in this context, between the court's legislative and judicial powers. He deems R. Eliezer b. Jacob's dictum to be unambiguously legislative in nature. But this view is open to question, and the textual evidence suggests that the rule should be associated with the judicial rather than the legislative process.

First, the expressions "mete out lashes," "mete out punishment," "flogs," and "executes" would seem to denote judicial activity. Second, the rule is accompanied by two court rulings, not two examples of legislation. Above, we noted that the accompanying precedents may be later additions, and not an integral part of the original rule. If so, this second point is not decisive proof that the rule pertains to the judicial process rather than the

12 Elon, n. 8 above, 2:515.

legislative. Yet if they are additions and not part of the original rule, the illustrations attest to how the rule was understood by the editor of the *sugya*. Finally, as the following analysis will demonstrate, the very wording of the rule itself appears to indicate that it is speaking of the court as a judicial institution.

## 4.6 The meaning of "I heard"

All versions of the rule of R. Eliezer b. Jacob contain the locution "I heard that...." This locution is a technical Tannaitic term that qualifies the dictum it precedes. It is familiar from other Tannaitic statements in the Mishnah and Baraita, and, like other formulaic expressions, indicates something about the provenance of the dictum it introduces. Indeed, the first step in the analysis of any Tannaitic or Amoraic source consists in the identification and clarification of technical terms. Scholars have stressed the importance of standard formulae in understanding talmudic *sugyot*:

> Most of the problems connected with talmudic terminology are methodological. It is no accident that they have occupied scholars from the time of the Geonim to the modern age. This is reflected in a considerable number of works, starting with various introductions to the Talmud and other writings of the Geonim and R. Samuel Hanagid, *Sefer Keritut, Halikhot Olam, Darkhei Hatalmud, Klalei Hatalmud* (R. Bezalel Ashkenazi), *Klalei Hatalmud* (R. Joseph Caro), *Sheeirit Yosef, Tehilat Hokhma, Kneset Hagedola, Yad Malachi*, and up to the works of Horowitz (author of *Shnei Luhot Habrit*) and others of the traditional school, followed by such modern works as W. Bacher, *Die Exegetische Terminologie der Jiidischen Traditionsliteratur, Introduction to the Mishnah* by I. Epstein, and *Studies in the Baraita and Tosefta*, by H. Albeck. A thorough understanding of the talmudic debate is impossible without an appreciation of the terminology which forms the framework of the talmudic *sugya*.
>
> This matter goes beyond the formal methodology of the *sugya*; it serves as a starting point for examination of the various sources of which the Talmud is comprised, since use of different terminologies indicates different redactors (Epstein and Albeck discuss this point in reference to the terms "*tania*" and "*tana*" in bNedarim). Hence this seemingly 'marginal' subject is certainly deserving of more attention, to ascertain whether further conclusions can be drawn from terminology in dating the redaction of talmudic passages, tractates, and perhaps the Babylonian Talmud as a whole.
>
> The investigation of the origins and development of talmudic terms is thus important to our study. As a rule, each standard term or expression is the outcome of an editing process. When actively debating a point or engaged in argument, people do not necessarily

> use precise language. Later on, however, when things are laid down in a permanent fashion, and the debate is presented in a literary form, standard terms and markers are introduced to denote or set off quotations, punctuation, questions and answers, formulae, rules, definitions, and traditions from various periods. Since these edited transcriptions reflect a long process, from the beginnings of the Mishnah to the redaction of the Talmud, such terminology has itself undergone changes at various stages, nor was it identical in every center of learning.[13]

When the expression "I heard" precedes a dictum, this indicates that its content was not widely known, but was transmitted orally from teacher to pupil in a more or less private manner. Furthermore, the term suggests that the statement is deficient in some way. There are a number of examples of this in the Tannaitic literature. For example, the term "I heard and I have no explanation" (mJebamot 8:4; tZevahim ch. 2; bMenahot 18a) indicates an unclear, unfamiliar oral tradition. "I heard out of context" (mPara 1:1) also indicates that the dictum in question is unclear. "I heard [a tradition attributed to] R. Eliezer... and persistently searched among all his students for a colleague [to verify it], but I failed" (mEruvin 2:6) indicates an oral tradition that is not current among the students. When an "I heard" type of tradition is being characterized as reliable, the expression "I heard it explicitly" is used (mSheviit 6:5, 6:6; mOrla 1:7).

That the locution "I heard" is used to qualify the reliability of a tradition can also be shown by examination of another term used to introduce talmudic traditions. Tractate Eduyot of the Mishnah records testimonies of various Sages regarding traditional teachings imparted to them by their teachers in an official setting. The term most commonly used to introduce such testimony is: "R. So-and-So testified." De Vries, whose remarks on terminology were quoted above, discusses this locution:

> Already in one of the earliest Mishnayot [mEduyot 8:4]—some say the earliest—we find a technical term with a special meaning. It begins with: "Jose b. Yoezer of Zeredah testified." The term "testified" has a specific meaning. It is from the judicial lexicon and thus denotes that a law was issued in the presence of an official or official body—a council, a court, or the head of the court. This is the source of the term "testimony" in the sense of an officially-presented law **as opposed to a law transmitted from teacher to student**.[14]

Like "testified," "I heard" is also taken from courtroom terminology. But as is well known, hearsay evidence is neither admissible in court nor

13 Benjamin De Vries, *Studies in Talmudic Literature* (Hebrew), (Jerusalem: 1968), 223.
14 Ibid. (emphasis added).

deemed reliable. Use of the term "I heard" to introduce a tradition thus hints that the dictum being introduced is problematic for some reason, and cannot be "testified" to. In the present context, it indicates that R. Eliezer b. Jacob's rule that the court can mete out lashes and punishment that is not in accord with the law, is in some way problematic. It would appear that the rule's novelty is the problematic element.

How does awareness of the significance of the technical term "I heard" contribute to our understanding of R. Eliezer b. Jacob's dictum? Research by I. Gilat has established that the court's **legislative** power to issue enactments contrary to the Torah—"the court can make stipulations abrogating Torah law"—was recognized and accepted by the Tannaim. To be sure, the issue was the subject of controversy during the Amoraic period, but at the time of R. Eliezer b. Jacob, there had as yet been no dissent.

> It seems, therefore, that in the early period, the Sages did not refrain from pronouncing decrees and enacting legislation, when they saw a need for it, even if doing so occasionally uprooted something [prohibited] in the Torah, by mandating action contrary to it. This custom is anchored in ancient tradition, reflected in the books of the Prophets, which relate acts and injunctions that manifest deviation from the precepts of the Torah.... It would be impossible, then, to sustain the early sources of the halakha on an approach that restricts the Sages' power to order religious life. The courts, in pronouncing decrees or enacting legislation, beheld the needs of the time so as to 'strengthen religion and enhance the social order.' They fixed the law for [future] generations and reinforced their decrees, even if as a result it occasionally happened that a law of the Torah was uprooted by an injunction against acting [lit., "sit and do nothing"] or an injunction mandating an action [lit., "rise and do"].[15]

It can be stated with considerable confidence that a tradition that was well-known, established, accepted by the Sages and implemented in practice would not have been introduced by "I heard." The court's power to set down legislation in contravention of the Torah was not a novel concept, and would certainly not have been introduced by the "I heard" formula. On the other hand, the notion that the court has **judicial** power to punish in a manner at variance with the law and not previously set down by the established legislative process is not mentioned in any halakhic source prior to R. Eliezer b. Jacob, and it is highly likely that many were opposed to it. Hence it was appropriate for the dictum to be introduced by the locution "I heard." In summary, R. Eliezer b. Jacob's rule

15 Isaac Gilat, "A rabbinical court may decree the abrogation of a law of the Torah" (Hebrew), in *Studies in the Development of the Halakha* (Hebrew), (Ramat-Gan: 1992), 204.

can be seen as the judicial counterpart to the legislative principle that "the court can make stipulations abrogating Torah law."

### 4.7 The scope of the rule's application

As we said, it may be that the rule's accompanying precedents were added later, and do not allow us to draw any conclusions as to the rule's original meaning. But this reservation is important only with respect to historical investigation of the rule. If we seek to understand the normative implications of the rule as presented by the talmudic *sugya*, the rule and the precedents can be regarded as a single unit.

Analysis of the rule and the precedents shows that its application is limited to the imposition of punishment. This may be inferred from the terms appearing in the rule: "mete out lashes," "punishment," and "execute," and from the precedents describing punishment of offenders. The rule does not address the court's authority to deviate from the law in civil matters, that is, monetary law.

Let us now examine the precedents by comparing the different versions:

*Jerusalem Talmud*

> And it happened that a man went on his way riding his horse on the Sabbath, and they brought him to the court and stoned him to death. Was it not [merely] a Rabbinic prohibition? But it was an exigency of the times. And again, it happened that someone went on his way and his wife was with him, and he turned aside behind a fence and did what he had to with her, and they brought him to the court and flogged him (*vehilkuhu*). And was she not his wife? But he conducted himself shamefully.

*Babylonian Talmud*

> And it happened that a man rode a horse on the Sabbath during the time of the Greeks, and they brought him to the court and stoned him to death, not because he deserved it, but because it was an exigency of the times. And again, it happened that a man had relations with his wife under a fig tree, and they brought him to the court and flogged him (*vehilkuhu*), not because he deserved it, but because it was an exigency of the times.
>
> bSanhedrin 46a, bJebamot 90b

*Scholium to Megilat Taanit*

> And it happened that a man had relations with his wife under a fig tree, and the court had him flogged (*vehilkuhu*); and was he, then, guilty? But it was due to the exigency of the times, to teach a lesson to others, because they conducted themselves promiscuously. And again,

> it happened that a man rode a horse on the Sabbath, and they brought him to the court and stoned him to death; and was he, then, guilty? But it was an exigency of the times.

These parallel sources differ in a number of ways, some of which were discussed above, and some of which are irrelevant. But one more difference between them calls for examination, namely, the reasoning or justification adduced for the court's decision.

Aside from the Jerusalem Talmud's justification for the ruling in the public fornication case, all the justifications offered for the anomalous rulings invoke the rubric of an 'exigency of the times.' In the court's opinion, the prevailing social circumstances made it necessary to mete out severe punishment as a deterrent, literally, to 'build a fence for [i.e., to prevent a breach of] Torah law.' On this reasoning, the offenses in and of themselves did not deserve such severe punishment, but the prevailing circumstances constituted a state of emergency, and justified deviation from the law. In each case, had the same offense been committed at a different time, it would have met with a more lenient reaction.

The Jerusalem Talmud's reasoning in the case of the public fornicator is markedly different: "He conducted himself shamefully." Here, the punishment is not imposed because the prevailing conditions mandate drastic measures, but because of the nature of the offense. By law, the act in question was not punishable, but the court imposed a severe punishment. Its aim was not to prevent improper conduct from proliferating, but to reform the offender.

The term 'exigency situation' may refer either to an existing state of rampant misconduct, where unseemly behavior has become widespread, or to a situation where there is a serious risk of widespread misconduct, but it has not yet materialized. Let us consider two passages from the responsa literature that discuss such situations.

R. Jacob b. Asher, author of the *Tur*, quotes a Geonic responsum regarding a case where an inebriated man attacked and killed someone on the Purim holiday. The question is whether he is to be tried as a murderer.

> Now, my dear gentlemen, do not encourage criminals, so that every one of them is wild and shoots off sparks, and then says, 'I did it inadvertently.'[16] Rather, convene a court, and beat him and punish him, to safeguard the law, as in the examples of the one who rode on the Sabbath, and the one who had relations with his wife [in public]. As our Rabbis explained, we do not impose punishments in order to safeguard the law against the misconduct of a single individual, but only to erect a fence around the law when there is a

16 Alluding to Proverbs 26:18–19: "As a madman who shoots off sparks, arrows and death; so is the man that deceives his neighbor, and says, do I not act in jest?"

communal need, in which case we punish in accordance with the exigency of the times.

*Tur*, HM 425[17]

The Gaon differentiates between two categories of offenses: those that are widespread, and those limited to individual miscreants. He rejects the notion that the court may impose fines in order to reform individual offenders, as in the second precedent mentioned in the Jerusalem Talmud.

On the other hand, a sixteenth century commentator on the Talmud, R. Meir of Lublin, adduces this same Geonic responsum, but offers a limiting interpretation of it:

> It cannot be argued that [the Gaon] wanted to say that when a single individual is wont to commit a certain transgression, he is not to be fined so as to safeguard the law, but only where there are many who are wont to commit that transgression.... But rather, he meant that where no widespread flouting of the law is likely to occur, but the transgression will be limited to that individual, then no punishments [lit., fines] are imposed. However, where widespread flouting of the law is likely to occur—even if at the moment only one individual is transgressing, but by not punishing him, this will cause many to transgress the law in that way, and this will generate a damaging and pervasive breach of the law—since this is a communal exigency, we impose punishments, to erect a fence [around the law], in accordance with the exigency of the times.
>
> *Responsa R. Meir of Lublin*, #138

R. Eliezer b. Jacob's rule can be understood as a power-conferring rule, or as a duty-imposing rule. As a power-conferring rule, it empowers the court, on occasion, to deviate from the law, but it does not make such deviation—even when called for—mandatory. As a duty-imposing rule, however, it obliges the court to be more severe than the law requires whenever the authority of the law is at risk. The received opinion is that the former interpretation of the rule is correct. Nevertheless, as the following passage attests, the duty-imposing reading of the rule has also been defended.

> R. Yudan says: Every judge who is not stringent will leave this world before his appointed time.... He [strives to] hand down an absolutely just ruling and yet he is punished. For example, a judge who is punctilious about the fine points [of the law], so as to exonerate the

17 Simha Assaf has identified this responsum as written by R. Abraham b. Isaac (d. 1158) of Provence, and not a Babylonian Gaon, see S. Assaf, *Sifran Shel Rishonim* (Jerusalem: 1935), 42 n. 3.

> evil-doer. As we have learned: Courts mete out lashes and punishment [in a manner that is] not in accordance with the law, in order to safeguard the law, or due to the times, and the judge who shies away from punishment, and is punctilious about the law, seeking an opening to render [the offender] exempt from punishment according to strict law … when the Holy One, blessed be He, judges the world, such a judge will be held accountable for that, and for that will leave this world before his appointed time.… There are some who do not judge in accordance with the law, and yet are rewarded, for instance my father. He saw someone embracing and kissing a married woman, he ordered them to be taken to the execution place and killed. Not that they deserved to be put to death, but to safeguard the law, lest you should say that a judge discharges his obligation by following the law, and that suffices for him. But rather, a judge who does nothing to safeguard the law will not himself be safeguarded, either in this world or in the world to come.
>
> *Beit Yosef*, *Tur*, HM 2[18]

## 5 Scope of R. Eliezer b. Jacob's rule

### 5.1 Restrictive interpretations

Notwithstanding the widespread acceptance of R. Eliezer b. Jacob's rule, and its central role in defining the court's power and authority, it was qualified in various ways, with a view to restricting its scope. The first of these qualifications appeared in the Jerusalem Talmud, and reflects opposition to the concentration of too much power in the hands of the courts.

It should be noted that this problem does not arise if R. Eliezer b. Jacob's rule is taken to pertain to legislative authority. Above, we saw that Menachem Elon so interprets the rule. It may well be that this interpretation reflects, to some degree, a desire to preempt the problem of excessive judicial power.

#### i The Jerusalem Talmud: limiting the rule to procedural deviations

There is an insertion in the Jerusalem Talmud that is absent in the parallel sources:

> "Not in accordance with the law?" How far [does their discretion extend]? R. Lazar b. R. Jose says, [it extends] even to hearsay (*zimzum*)[19];

18 Quoting from the Kabbalistic *Midrash Neelam* on the Book of Ruth.

19 Lieberman interprets "*zimzum*" (lit., buzzing), as hearsay: "there is no hard evidence, only rumors," see S. Lieberman, *Studies in Palestinian Talmudic Literature* (Hebrew), (Jerusalem: 1991), 202.

> R. Joseh says, witnesses [are always required], but [it extends to cases where there was] no forewarning.[20]
>
> jHagiga 2:2 (78a)

R. Lazar and R. Joseh, two Amoraim of the fourth generation of Palestinian Amoraim, debate the extent to which R. Eliezer b. Jacob's rule is to be applied. Indeed, the question that opens the debate—"How far?"—already implies that the court's power to deviate from the law should have clearly demarcated boundaries, or in other words, should be institutionalized.

The feature common to the limitations introduced by the two Amoraim is that the court's authority to deviate from the law is restricted to points of procedure. R. Lazar says that the rule allows for punishment of an offender even in the absence of direct evidence, as long as there is a rumor that a transgression has been committed. In the opinion of R. Joseh, however, no one can be convicted without direct evidence. On his view, the rule allows for more limited deviation from the law: the offender may be punished even if he was not forewarned that his act constituted a transgression. Both qualifications of R. Eliezer b. Jacob's rule restrict the scope of its application significantly.

### ii Restricting the authority to deviate from the law to the High Court in Jerusalem

Another way of circumventing or at least minimizing the problem engendered by the far-reaching scope of R. Eliezer b. Jacob's rule, namely, excessive judicial power, is by limiting recourse to the rule—that is, limiting the authority to decide the law in a manner that diverges from the law on the books—to the High Court in Jerusalem.

In the Middle Ages, the talmudic text was sometimes emended due to apprehension about the censor's response, or at his demand. Obviously, the dictum of R. Eliezer b. Jacob was one of the problematic passages. Indeed, one of the 'corrections' introduced under the pressure of Christian censorship was insertion of the phrase "in the period of the Temple." The emended version reads, "R. Eliezer b. Jacob said, I heard that courts in the Temple period meted out lashes (*makin*) and punishment [in a manner that is] not in accordance with the law." The insertion strips the rule of any practical significance, turning it into a mere historical anecdote. This 'correction' and others appear in a booklet entitled *Kuntres Hesronot Hashas* (Koenigsberg, 1860), which lists the changes made to the text of the Babylonian Talmud by medieval Christian censors. A vestige of this correction can be found in some of the printed editions of the Talmud, which read: "I heard that the court **used to** mete out lashes...."

20 By law, an offender must be forewarned that the act he is about to commit constitutes a transgression, otherwise he is not liable to punishment; see tSanhedrin 11:1–5.

Aside from such emendations, the restriction of the validity of the rule to decisions of the High Court in Jerusalem prevails in a number of commentaries on the Talmud. Let us look at three of them, the commentaries of three late medieval Spanish commentators: Rabbenu Nissim Gerondi (Ran), R. Joseph Habiba, and Don Isaac Abarbanel.

### a R. Nissim of Gerona

In tractate Sanhedrin, the Babylonian Talmud relates an incident involving a suspected murderer named Bar Hama. The Exilarch (the secular leader of the Jews of Babylonia, who ruled by authority of the Gentile monarch) appointed R. Aha b. Jacob to bring the suspect to trial, instructing him:

> Go and investigate this case. If it is certain that he slayed [someone], dim his eyes.[21]
>
> bSanhedrin 27a

The commentators are at a loss to explain these instructions, since blinding is not one of the punishments meted out in Jewish law. Moreover, since the authority to try capital cases had lapsed with the destruction of the Temple, the rabbinical courts in Babylonia could not sentence offenders to death. Rashi and others suggest that the Exilarch ordered this punishment in reliance on R. Eliezer b. Jacob's rule. Rashi gives a similar explanation of another case, recounted in bSanhedrin 48b, where R. Huna ordered the hand of an assailant chopped off. This too is not a punishment recognized by the halakha.

R. Nissim raises the following objection with respect to the case of the blinded murderer:

> The rule to mete out lashes and punishment that is not in accordance with the law is more severe than the Torah law, so there is a greater need for great and expert judges. How could they act thus in Babylonia, where they had no authority to try capital charges at all, even according to the law of the Torah?
>
> *Hidushei Haran*, bSanhedrin 27a[22]

R. Nissim therefore argues that the Exilarch had the authority to act as he did, that is, to impose extra-legal punishment, not by virtue of R. Eliezer b. Jacob's rule, but because he had been granted the authority to rule by the Gentile king.[23] Rabbenu Nissim assumes that ordinary courts are not

21 This translation is in line with Rashi's commentary.

22 There is some doubt as to whether the Ran himself actually authored the work known as *Hidushei Haran* (Novellae of the Ran). The true author may have been one of his students.

23 This view is set out in *Derashot Haran*, #11.

endowed with the authority to impose punishments that are at variance with the law. How can it be imagined, he asks, that a court with even more limited halakhic authority could enjoy this prerogative?

R. Nissim does not explicitly state which courts are authorized to invoke the rule of R. Eliezer b. Jacob. He implies, however, that full halakhic authority is a prerequisite for deviating from the law, and only judges in the land of Israel have such authority.[24]

### b R. Joseph Habiba

One of the four modes of execution by the court is burning, described by the Mishnah as follows:

> The obligatory procedure for execution by burning: They immersed him in dung up to his knees, rolled a rough cloth into a soft one and wound it about his neck. One pulled it one way, one the other until he opened his mouth. Thereupon one ignites the [lead] wick and throws it into his mouth, and it descends into his bowels and sears his bowels.
> mSanhedrin 7:2

The body of the convict was not burned; molten lead was poured into his mouth, from which he died. The Babylonian Talmud (bSanhedrin 52b) recounts the incident of Imrata bat Tali, the daughter of a priest, who committed adultery. Scripture states: "And the daughter of a priest if she profanes herself by harlotry ... shall be burnt with fire" (Lev. 21:9). Accordingly, the Amora R. Hama b. Tobiah,[25] sentenced Imrata to death. He ordered her to be surrounded by a pyre of twigs and burned.

The Talmud comments that R. Hama made a double error. He erred in the method of execution, which according to the mishnaic law should have been by pouring molten lead into her mouth. And he also erred in ignoring the fact that after the destruction of the Temple, no court had the authority to try capital cases. The commentaries on the Talmud ponder the question of why R. Hama's action could not be justified by adducing R. Eliezer b. Jacob's rule, which sanctions deviation from the law.

R. Joseph Habiba addresses this point:

> If this [the fact that R. Eliezer b. Jacob's rule was not invoked to justify R. Hama's action] seems problematic, since it is established that the court metes out lashes and punishment [in a manner that is] not in accordance with the law, as for example, [in the case of ] the one who

24 This view differs from that of Alfasi, who explicitly states that courts in Babylonia can, on the strength of R. Eliezer b. Jacob's rule, impose punishments that are contrary to the law. See *Alfasi*, bBaba Kama 96a (Alfasi pagination).

25 A variant reads "Hama b. Tobiah," omitting the title R(av).

> rode a horse on the Sabbath, who was brought to court and stoned to death, the rejoinder is that in that instance, [the anomalous punishment was imposed by] the High Court, which had comprehensive authority, but a regular court does not.
>
> *Nimukei Yosef*, bSanhedrin 16a (Alfasi pagination)

The Nimukei Yosef thus restricts the authority to have recourse to R. Eliezer b. Jacob's rule to the High Court in Jerusalem, denying ordinary courts this privilege.

#### c Don Isaac Abarbanel

Don Isaac Abarbanel, like R. Joseph Habiba, distinguishes between the authority of the High Court in Jerusalem and the authority of local courts. The former may deviate from the law, but the latter may not. In support of his opinion, he quotes the rule of R. Eliezer b. Jacob as follows:

> Therefore our Rabbis, of blessed memory, stated: "R. Eliezer b. Jacob says: I heard that the High Court in the land of Israel used to mete out lashes and punishment [in a manner that was] not in accordance with the Torah." (bSanhedrin 46a)
>
> *Abarbanel*, Deuteronomy 17:8

It is exceedingly doubtful that Abarbanel had before him a text of the Talmud with this wording, given that R. Eliezer b. Jacob, who lived in the land of Israel, would not have expressed himself in this way. It is more likely that the Abarbanel is interpolating his own interpretation into the talmudic text, so that the text accords with the political theory he expounds in his commentary on the Bible.

### 5.2 Non-restrictive interpretations

#### i R. Isaac b. Sheshet (Ribash)

Another prominent scholar of the Spanish school, R. Isaac b. Sheshet Perfet, is of a different opinion.

In a responsum to a rabbinical court judge named R. Menahem the Tall, he comments on the subject of trying capital cases after the destruction of the Temple:

> As you well know, all the capital cases that we try nowadays, where this is permitted us by the state authorities, are not in accordance with the law, because the authority to try capital cases has been abrogated. However, in order to safeguard the law, courts mete out lashes and punishment [in a manner that is] not in accordance with the Torah, if

> it is an exigency of the times, as is stated in the Talmud.[26] ... And there were instances where the Sages acted thus, putting to death those who were not liable to incur the penalty of death by the court according to the laws of the Torah. For example, the case of someone who rode a horse on the Sabbath[27]; and also the case involving Shimon b. Shetah, who hanged eighty women in Ashkelon on one day[28]; and R. Eleazar b. R. Shimon, who held a royal warrant licensing him to execute Jewish evildoers, without witnesses or forewarning.[29] Similarly, in the days of the Amoraim, R. Huna ordered that an evil man's hand be cut off, because he habitually struck people with his fist.[30] And he said, "And let the uplifted arm be broken" (Job 38:16). There was also the case of Bar Hama, who killed a man. And the Exilarch said [to the judge]: "If it is certain that he slayed [someone], dim his eyes."[31] For the Exilarch saw that, given the exigency of the times, this chastisement was sufficient, and did not command that he be executed. And in any event, as the Talmud says elsewhere,[32] blinding involves mortal danger.
>
> And if for these transgressions offenders were put to death not in accordance with the law, due to exigency of the times, needless to say this was authorized in cases of bloodshed, regarding which the Sages ruled severely.
>
> *Responsa Ribash*, #251

We can see, therefore, that there is a significant difference between the approach espoused by the Ribash, and the approach of the Ran and those who uphold his view. Comparison of these opposed views suggests another question about R. Eliezer b. Jacob's rule: does it only extend the power of a fully authorized court, or does it also delegate power to a court that lacks full halakhic authority?

The Ribash, contra R. Nissim, maintains that the rule authorizes expansion of the powers of a court that lacks full judicial authority, such as a court in our times. According to R. Meir of Lublin, this view is the majority view of the halakhic authorities:

> The definitive basis, on which most of the decisors rely, in ruling that in our time too, a court has the authority to punish, both by corporal punishment and by death, is the statement found in bSanhedrin 46a and bJebamot 90b: It is taught: R. Eliezer b. Jacob said, I heard that courts mete out lashes (*makin*) and punishment [in a manner that is]

26 bJebamot 90b.
27 Ibid.
28 bSanhedrin 45b.
29 bBaba Metzia 83b.
30 bSanhedrin 58b.
31 bSanhedrin 27a.
32 bAvoda Zara 28b.

> not in accordance with the law, and not to transgress the law, but to safeguard the law. And it happened that a man rode a horse, during the time of the Greeks, on the Sabbath, and they brought him to the court and stoned him to death, not because this was the law, but because it was an exigency of the times.
>
> *Responsa R. Meir of Lublin*, #138

For additional examples, from the responsa literature, of non-restrictive interpretations of the rule, see Appendix.

### ii The rule in the classic law codes

The rule of R. Eliezer b. Jacob is set out in the codes of Maimonides, R. Jacob b. Asher, and R. Joseph Caro. There are certain differences between their respective formulations of the law.

*Maimonides*

> 4 The courts are empowered to flog those who are not liable to be flogged, and to execute those who do not incur the punishment of death; not to transgress the law, but to safeguard it.... But all such measures are of a temporary nature, and do not establish law that is binding for all times. Thus a man who had relations with his wife under a tree was flogged, and another, who rode a horse on the Sabbath during the days of the Greeks, was brought to the court and executed by stoning.
>
> 5 So too the courts may, in all places and at all times, flog one whose reputation is bad, and about whom the people talk, ascribing to him sexual transgressions—provided the rumors about him are persistent, as has already been stated, and he has no avowed enemies who may be spreading evil rumors about him. Similarly, one of ill repute may be disdained, and she who bore him shamed in his presence.
>
> *Code*, Laws concerning the Sanhedrin 24:4–5[33]

*R. Jacob b. Asher*

> Though cases where death sentences are meted out, criminal cases, and cases punishable with fines are not tried outside the land of Israel,

33 Note that Maimonides' formulation of the rule is in line with the Megilat Taanit version of R. Eliezer b. Jacob's rule, despite the fact that this is the least authoritative source of the three sources of the rule. This indicates that Megilat Taanit was known to Maimonides. His preference for this source is presumably due to the fact that it has undergone systematic editing, and thus is more coherent than the other two sources.

> nevertheless, if the court declares it an exigency of the times, because the people are wont to commit transgressions, it may impose capital, monetary or any other kind of punishment.... This rule applies only if [the judges are] the greatest of the generation ... or leaders of the town appointed to the court by the community, but the rule does not apply to local judges.
>
> *Tur*, HM 2

*R. Joseph Caro*

> *A court is empowered to flog and to punish according to the needs of the time.*
>
> Any court, even if not ordained in the land of Israel, that sees that people are behaving lawlessly, may impose capital, monetary or any other kind of punishment, even if there is no conclusive evidence.
>
> And if the defendant is a violent man, they may ask Gentiles to beat him. And all their deeds should be for the sake of heaven. This rule applies only if [the judges are] the greatest of the generation, or leaders of the town appointed to the court by the community.
>
> *Shulhan Arukh*, HM 2

Although the *Tur* and the *Shulhan Arukh* quite explicitly authorize courts (though not all courts) in our day to act on the strength of R. Eliezer b. Jacob's rule, whether this is Maimonides' view is somewhat controversial. The problem arises from a comparison of laws 4 and 5 from the Laws concerning the Sanhedrin 24. The source of law (5)—which allows punishment of an alleged fornicator—is not the rule of R. Eliezer b. Jacob, but bKidushin 81a. Here, Maimonides explicitly asserts that this applies to courts "in all places and at all times." This locution is absent from law (4), which codifies the rule of R. Eliezer b. Jacob. It would thus appear that Maimonides is restricting the applicability of R. Eliezer b. Jacob's rule. However, law (5) begins with the words "So too," which can be taken to imply that the provisions articulated in law (4) are also universally applicable.

### iii R. Isaac Arama

Let us reiterate the dilemma with which we opened this chapter, namely, that of the choice between legal certainty, on the one hand, and complete applicability, on the other. That is, the dilemma between strict adherence to the law, even at the cost of handing down an unjust or unreasonable sentence in a particular case, and rendering just and effective judgment in a particular case by deviating from the law on the books. R. Isaac Arama, yet another renowned Spanish commentator, raises this dilemma in his commentary on Exodus:

> For example, it is a fundamental principle of monetary law that the burden of proof falls on the one who seeks to take something that is in his fellow's possession (bBaba Metzia 2b), and also a fundamental principle that there is a presumption that one does not pay his debt before it is due (bBaba Batra 5a). But it may happen that a claimant is making a true claim but has no evidence, or a defendant paid his debt before it was due, but no one saw it, and other such eventualities are possible. And it will be unavoidable that the judge will either rule in accordance with the truth of the particular case, and thereby harm the general law; or conversely, his ruling will do justice to the general law, but harm the particular case, and so on.
>
> *Akeidat Yitzhak*, Exodus, gate 43, p. 96a

He suggests the following solution to the problem:

> They authorized the court of each and every generation to adjudicate, afflict, and punish both in accordance with the law, and not in accordance with the law, where by "in accordance with the law" they meant, ruling in accordance with [the details of] the particular case, and by "not in accordance with the law" they meant, ruling in accordance with the general law. As they said, "not because of the law, but because it was an exigency of the times" (bJebamot 90b), that is, not because the general law is thus, but because this is in accordance with the details of the particular case.... the Torah covers all of humanity, and all the details of their deeds, for it is possible to have a divinely perfect law and divine ethics that comprehend in their infinite wisdom all that exists, in all its detail.

R. Isaac Arama thus views the ruling of R. Eliezer b. Jacob as highly significant. The authorization to deviate from the law and rule in accordance with the "particular case" applies, in the opinion of R. Isaac Arama, to all courts at all times. The rationale thus appears to be jurisprudential rather than historical: it expresses a philosophy of adjudication that seeks to ensure that courts will be able to render individualized decisions. Arama goes even further, asserting that a judge who always decides in accordance with the law thwarts justice:

> But judges who always decide in accordance with the directives of the law, even if they decide in accordance with the true law, bring havoc and destruction to this world, as it is said in the Talmud, "Jerusalem was destroyed because they judged in accordance with the strict truth" (bBaba Metzia 30b), that is, in accordance with the general truth without regard to the circumstances of the particular case. But rather say, "let the law pierce the mountain" (bJebamot 92a; bSanhedrin 6b).

## 6 Conclusion

As we have seen, Jewish law recognizes the court's authority to deviate from the law and hand down a ruling that contravenes the law.[34]

We have surveyed the historical evolution and expansion of the scope and meaning of R. Eliezer b. Jacob's rule, as well as its normative status. What has not been clarified, however, is the extent to which the rule was in fact employed. Evidence from the responsa literature can be adduced to show that the rule was indeed invoked frequently over the centuries.

Contemporary western law does not countenance such far-reaching judicial power. It sees the law as the ultimate authority, and demands total obedience to it. Western jurisprudence seeks to neutralize the role of personal, social and economic factors in the administration of justice, so as to ensure legal certainty and stability. It upholds the ideal that society should be guided by rules and laws, not decisions made by individuals. The following passage illustrates this ideal and its underlying rationale:

> *Non sub Homine sed sub Deo et Lege*—Not under Man, but under God and Law. So reads the inscription over the entrance to the magnificent library of one of the oldest and greatest law schools in America. The imposing presence in such a place of this ancient aphorism of the English common law is symptomatic of one of the strongest traits in the character of man—the quest for certainty. It finds its counterpart in the more modern phrase, so often repeated, that ours is the government of laws, and not of men. Man, himself, is apparently not to be trusted. He is an undependable being, given to capricious and arbitrary thought and deed. Accordingly, to place a man under the rule of man is to give him no certainty or security but to subject him to the selfish whims of a potential tyrant or despot. One need take but a hasty glance about the world today to realize that such an outcome of government by man is at least a possibility.
>
> So it is that man seeks to assure himself that he lives under the government of laws. "Equal Justice under Law" we read as we enter the gleaming, marbled home of the United States Supreme Court in the city of Washington. In our minds takes shape a picture of impartial, impersonal judges applying traditional and immutable principles of law so as to render absolute justice to all men. Here there is no uncertainty, no mere whim or caprice, no arbitrary edict by man over man. Instead, here is unchanging, beneficent rule of law, whereby a judge as a seeker of the truth ... discovers the principles on which his conclusions bearing on a case may be based and from which a judgment follows, subject to no variance or turning.[35]

34 See H. Ben-Menahem, *Judicial Deviation in Talmudic Law* (Chur, Switzerland: 1991).

35 R.K. Carr, *The Supreme Court and Judicial Review* (New York: 1942), 1.

The author of this passage contends that courts should under no circumstances be allowed to deviate from the law, and this is the only way to ensure equality and legal certainty. If the price of implementing these ideals is an unjust or inefficient decision in a particular case, then it is a price well worth paying.

Unlike western legal thought, which advocates total subjection of the judiciary to the law and nothing but the law, Jewish law allows judges to deviate from the law if such a course is, in their opinion, justified and necessary. But can we conclude that Jewish law does not recognize the importance of legal certainty and stability?

The halakha is well aware that in practice, good law does not suffice to protect people, just as bad law does not necessarily lead to injustice. Good will—or the lack thereof—on the part of the judge is always a factor. As contemporary history demonstrates, the written law offers no guarantee that the judge will act in accordance with it. There are dictatorships that have enlightened written constitutions that guarantee full protection of personal rights, including free speech, where human rights are systematically disregarded, while England, the epitome of parliamentary government, has no written constitution at all. Even so, it is among the world's most advanced states as far as civil rights are concerned.

The only guarantee against arbitrariness is the judges' sense of responsibility and restraint, and their esteem for the law, the society they live in, the office they hold. A judge who lacks integrity can easily circumvent any law, or assume authority he does not have, while an honest judge is not tempted to exploit his office for corrupt ends.

The Talmud (bSanhedrin 7a) states that a judge should always behave as if a sword was suspended over his head (literally, at his loins), with "hell gaping from beneath." Many of the Sages' injunctions emphasize the great self-discipline required of the judge, and the great responsibility he bears, since these are the only guarantees against biased and arbitrary judgments.

Maimonides, known for his concise language, goes to uncharacteristic length to register his reservations about judicial power:

> Whatever action he [the judge] sees fit to resort to, and the times require—all his deeds should be done for the sake of Heaven. Let human dignity not be light in his eyes.
>
> *Code,* Laws concerning the Sanhedrin 24:10

Historical experience makes clear that when R. Eliezer b. Jacob's rule was invoked in practice, courts were wary of using their almost unlimited authority, and the rule was used with great restraint. The fact that judges had at their disposal virtually unlimited power did not in fact lead to any abuse of power. Even though the rule is recognized as a norm authorizing courts to deviate from the law, it is invoked only in a controlled manner. Judges who were apprehensive about deviating from the received law are much more common in the annals of Jewish law than those who exploited their authority to the full.

Judges administering justice under western law may confront cases where the law enables criminals who have planned their crimes carefully to escape punishment. They can do nothing but lament the shortcomings of the law. By contrast, a judge acting on the basis of Jewish law is able to convict and punish an offender who planned his crime in such a way that the written law was not broken. Under the Jewish legal system, even the spirit of the law cannot be violated with impunity.

## Appendix Examples of non-restrictive interpretations of R. Eliezer b. Jacob's rule from the responsa literature

1. *Responsa Ri Migash*, #161
2. *Responsa R. Gershom, Light of the Exile*, #9
3. *Responsa Rashba*, 5, #238
4. *Responsa Rashba*, 3, #393
5. *Responsa Rashba attributed to Nahmanides*, #279
6. *Responsa Ribash*, #251
7. *Responsa Trumat Hadeshen*, Psakim Ukhtavim, #210
8. *Responsa Rashba*, 4, #311

### 1. *Responsa Ri Migash*, #161

The Talmud says that one who hires false witnesses to testify is exempt from the laws of man, but liable by the laws of heaven.[1] This only applies if he hired them for another person, but if he hired them for himself, he is liable even by the laws of man. And even though the Sages said he was exempt, meaning, completely exempt, nevertheless, if there is a sitting judge in the town, and he thinks it proper to punish him for it, he may do so. As they said, "I heard that courts mete out lashes and punishment [in a manner that is] not in accordance with the law, and not to transgress the law, but to safeguard the law," and so on,[2] provided that the circumstances of the times require it. If, for example, the man who hired false witnesses had committed this act a number of times before, or if in that country there were many people who had committed it, so that there was cause for apprehension that should [the judges] be lax about punishing them for these acts, more and more people would commit similar deeds. But if either one of the two conditions is not satisfied, the courts cannot hold those who commit such acts liable for anything, and it goes with saying that this is true with regard to judges who do not constitute a sitting court. The public is not regarded as a sitting judge in this respect.

### 2. *Responsa R. Gershom, Light of the Exile*, #9

About a Jew who appraised a horse on the Sabbath, received it and took possession of it.[3]

1 bBaba Kama 55b.

2 bSanhedrin 46a.

3 He did not pay the vendor, but they agreed on a certain price. Cf. bKetubot 108b–109a, the case of someone who promised a sum of money to his [prospective] son-in-law and then claimed he was insolvent.

I do not know of an explicit law about this, however, it seems to me that it cannot be compared to [the case of] one who cooked on the Sabbath, which is a serious offense punishable by stoning,[4] or to [the offense committed by] one who sells his field during the Jubilee year.[5] In the latter case Rav says that it is sold [i.e., the sale is valid] but must be immediately returned; it is sold because he already took it and the transaction was completed and he acquired possession by paying money, but it is returned, since the Merciful One said, "In this year of Jubilee ye shall return every man unto his possession" (Lev. 25:13). Samuel says that the sale is not valid: the buyer thought he would buy it after the Jubilee year, and the money was a gift. He regards this transaction as analogous to the case in which one betrothed his sister. Everyone knows that betrothal is not binding with respect to a sister, so the money paid was obviously intended as a gift.[6] But the present case is different. We cannot say that the man knew that transactions carried out on the Sabbath are invalid.[7] We learned that one who steals a purse on the Sabbath is liable, and acquires it when he takes hold of it. Nor can the case be compared to that of one who sold his slave to an idolater,[8] because in such a case the seller prevents the slave from observing the religious precepts.

It seems to me that since this is a lesser prohibition, and a Rabbinic prohibition,[9] the man should be flogged for rebelling against Rabbinic injunctions, the horse sold, and if the proceeds of the sale exceed its purchase price, the difference should be distributed among the poor, so that the sinner is not rewarded. And if that place is rife with laxity regarding the observance of the Sabbath laws, you may be more strict with him, as you see fit, in order to safeguard the law and put up a fence to fence it in—as was said about Rav in the Talmud: "Rav found an open field and fenced it in.[10] [It is taught that] R. Eliezer b. Jacob said, I heard that courts mete out lashes (*makin*) and punishment [in a manner that is] not in accordance with the law, and not to transgress the law, but to safeguard the law. And it happened that a man rode a horse on the Sabbath during the time of the Greeks, and they brought him to the court and stoned him to death, not because he deserved it, but because it was an exigency of the times."[11]

4 bShabat 74b.
5 bGitin 44b.
6 bArakhin 30a.
7 bShabat 91b.
8 bArakhin 29b: the sale is void.
9 *isur shvut*, see bBeitza 36b.
10 bEruvin 6a. Rashi ad loc. states: "meaning, was more strict and instituted safeguards in order to distance people from transgressions, just as one fences in an open field in order to protect it."
11 bSanhedrin 46a.

3. *Responsa Rashba*, 5, #238

This was my reply to the learned R. Jacob b. Hakashaf, head of the yeshiva in Tolitula [Toledo], about the government of the country, and the chastisement of offenders.

And bear in mind: "a gentle tongue can break bones" (Prov. 25:16) and it always straightens and makes straight, and clears the way for the people. And to remove stumbling blocks that are before the people we have to proceed from the easy to the difficult. The whole burden must not be lifted at once. I speak, of course, allegorically. And you are already familiar with the talmudic statement, "a well-intentioned transgression is better than fulfilling a precept out of ulterior motives."[12] And we have already been given sound advice and understanding in what the Talmud relates in tractate Avoda Zara about the house of Rabbi [Judah the Prince]: They had to present a fatted ox to the Romans for their festival, and a sum of forty thousand coins was paid for the concession not to present it on the day of the festival but on the morrow ... then forty thousand was again paid to be freed altogether from presenting it. And they said: Rabbi was anxious to abolish the thing entirely, but he considered it advisable to abolish it little by little.[13] That much we know. But you should also bear in mind, that not all people can be treated the same way. Remember the conduct of King David, our lord and king, who was accustomed to overlooking the deeds of Joab and Shimei, though they had forfeited their lives. And this was his argument: "do not I know that on this day I am King over Israel?" (II Samuel 19:23). For everything has its own time, and overlooking an offender is sometimes a religious duty–everything according to the needs of the time. And a wise person can easily overlook something now and then.

I think that there is a need to strengthen the institution of enactments first, and avoid getting involved in controversies. And you know well what happened to our first king, Saul, who kept silent. And overlooking things, as called for until the bodies responsible for implementing the enactments are strengthened, is indeed highly commendable. And whoever follows this command can make the rules authoritative, and they will readily be fortified and protected. After you have gained sufficient strength, you can rule in any way you desire.

As you know, the Sanhedrin chose to be exiled from its abode [Jerusalem], as the Talmud relates, to avoid trying capital cases, for they saw that murderers were becoming more numerous.[14] How much more so is this true for us, who lack the authority endowed by scriptural law to try capital cases, or impose fines, except when it is an exigency of the times, and this is "not to transgress the law but to safeguard the law," as noted by the

12 bNazir 23b.

13 mAvoda Zara 1.

14 bSanhedrin 41a.

Talmud.[15] And if silence sometimes serves to safeguard the law, you need have no qualms that the opposite view might take hold. My advice is that you should try to appeal [to the people] with gentle language; once, and then another time. Make more friends than enemies, using the carrot and the stick [lit., the left pushes away, the right draws near]—perhaps they will be rewarded, and repent of their evil ways, "and the wicked will be no more" (Ps. 104:35). "But if they do not obey, they shall perish by the sword" (Job 36:12). Pluck and tear them out, take a stick and hit them on the head a thousand or so times. There are matters on which it is necessary to weigh losses against gains. There is a need for moderation, consent, and thoughtfulness, but these [virtues] will turn the many to the way of heaven. For the greater the issue is, and the call to use force, so grows the need for care and dissipation of anger. The judge must take care lest his zeal for God, may He be blessed, inflames him and causes him to depart from the good and right path. This being so, when vengeance comes to him, while it is still in his hand, let him not consume it, lest he swallow it half-ripe. Let him ripen it and sweeten it, in accordance with the secrets of the elders, "whose hearts are upright" (Ps. 125:4).

4. *Responsa Rashba*, 3, #393

ANSWER

I have considered all the arguments in this pamphlet, and here is my view. If the witnesses were credible to the judges, they may impose a monetary fine or corporal punishment, as they see fit, for this preserves society [lit., the world]. For if you sought to resolve everything according to laws specified in the Torah, and to mete out punishment only as prescribed by the Torah, in torts and so forth, society would be ruined, because we would need witnesses and forewarning. And it is as the Sages, of blessed memory, said: "Jerusalem was destroyed only because they judged according to the letter of the scriptural law."[16] Even more so outside the land of Israel, where there is no authority to implement the laws imposing fines, and those whose dispositions lacked gravity would breach every societal boundary, and society would become desolate. And the Sages, of blessed memory, already imposed fines for striking someone with one's hand, or kicking him, as it says in the Talmud.[17] Now even though these are fines, which cannot be imposed in Babylonia, as it says in the same passage in the Talmud, nevertheless, in every single locale, fines of this sort are imposed for the sake of public order.[18] The Talmud relates the strongest such measure: Shimon b. Shetah hanged eighty women in Ashkelon on

15 bSanhedrin 46a; Jebamot 90b.
16 Paraphrasing bBaba Metzia 30b.
17 bBaba Kama 27b.
18 Lit., in order to fence in the generation.

one day, even though according to the law, women are not punished by hanging, nor can two capital cases be judged on the same day.[19] And the reason was not to transgress the law, but to safeguard the law. And in tractate Jebamot they stated, "a man rode a horse on the Sabbath during the time of the Greeks, and they brought him to the court and stoned him to death.... and ... a man had relations with his wife under a fig tree ... and they ... flogged him."[20] All this because it was an exigency of the times. And this is done in every single generation, and every single place, when they see that the times require it, to chastise the fools and the immature, and those who turn to crooked ways.[21]

And they also related that R. Huna, who was in Babylon, ordered a man's hand to be cut off,[22] and the incident of the Exilarch [who, instructing the judge in a murder case], said, "If it is certain that he slayed [someone], dim his eyes."[23] And even though the laws of the Torah do not include the cutting off of a limb, nevertheless, it was a safeguard, and an exigency of the times. Therefore the magistrates who did this—provided that they considered it to be a need of the times to impose monetary fines or corporal punishment in order to straighten out society, in light of the exigency of the times—acted legally. All the more so where they have a royal warrant, as was the situation with regard to R. Eleazar b. R. Shimon.[24] Nevertheless, the magistrates must explain themselves and be thoughtful, and their intention should always be to act for the sake of heaven.

### 5. *Responsa Rashba attributed to Nahmanides*, #279

The community appointed magistrates in order to uproot transgression. And in their charter it is written: they may inflict corporal chastisement and punish by imposing fines, as they see fit. And even if they have witnesses who are relatives [of the accused],[25] or hearsay evidence, and so on, [nevertheless,] if the indictment seems to them to be true, they may render judgment and impose fines. Because there is no need for witnesses [who meet all the scriptural requirements completely], other than in cases where Torah law is being applied, for example, in cases that come before the Sanhedrin, and so on. But as to someone who infringes the enactments of the country, he is dealt with according to the needs of the times. For if you do not say this, they would not even be able to impose fines, or deal with unusual cases, nor could they try charges such as robbery and battery. And forewarning would be required. Yet the Sages said, "they mete out

19 bSanhedrin 45b.
20 bJebamot 90b.
21 Alluding to Psalms 125:5.
22 bSanhedrin 58b.
23 bSanhedrin 27a.
24 bBaba Metzia 83b.
25 And thus, by law, unfit to testify.

lashes and punishment [in a manner that is] not in accordance with the law, and not to transgress the law, but to safeguard the law."[26]

6. *Responsa Ribash*, #251

To the learned Rabbi, R. Menahem the Tall, may God protect and redeem him.

ANSWER

As you well know, all the capital cases that we try nowadays, where this is permitted us by the state authorities, are not in accordance with the law, because the authority to try capital cases has been abrogated. However, in order to safeguard the law, courts mete out lashes and punishment [in a manner that is] not in accordance with the Torah, if it is an exigency of the times, as it is stated in the Talmud.[27] And there were instances where the Sages of the Talmud acted thus, putting to death those who were not liable to incur capital punishment according to the laws of the Torah. For example, the case of someone who rode a horse on the Sabbath[28]; and also the case involving Shimon b. Shetah, who hanged eighty women in Ashkelon on one day[29]; and R. Eleazar b. R. Shimon, who held a royal warrant licensing him to execute Jewish evildoers, without witnesses or forewarning.[30] Similarly, in the days of the Amoraim, R. Huna ordered that an evil man's hand be cut off, because he habitually struck people with his fist.[31] And he said, "And let the uplifted arm be broken" (Job 38:16). There was also the case of Bar Hama, who killed a man. And the Exilarch said [to the judge]: "If it is certain that he slayed [someone], dim his eyes."[32] For the Exilarch saw that, given the exigency of the times, this chastisement was sufficient, and did not command that he be executed. And in any event, as the Talmud says elsewhere,[33] blinding involves mortal danger.

And if for these transgressions offenders were put to death not in accordance with the law due to exigency of the times, needless to say this was authorized in the case of bloodshed, regarding which the Sages ruled severely. The Mishnah says that when someone murders and there are no witnesses, he is put in a cell [and caused to perish].[34] And there is no similar procedure for other offenses punishable by death imposed by the court. I need not dwell on this because you are well versed in the Talmud. But in

26 bJebamot 90b; bSanhedrin 46a.
27 bJebamot 90b.
28 Ibid.
29 bSanhedrin 45b.
30 bBaba Metzia 83b.
31 bSanhedrin 58b.
32 bSanhedrin 27a.
33 bAvoda Zara 28b.
34 mSanhedrin 9:5.

any event, even with respect to exigency convictions, not all punishments are equal. For it is more appropriate to mete out punishment to one who murdered than to one who only committed battery. [Also relevant is ] whether there are two reliable witnesses to the transgression, or none, or only one reliable witness, or there is only circumstantial evidence. For according to the Mishnah, one who murders someone, but there are no witnesses, is not put to death, but put into a cell and caused to die. The Talmud explains that the witnesses to the said murder were competent to testify in monetary cases, but not capital cases.[35] Hence, on the testimony of only one witness, or on the testimony of women, or relatives, a murderer is not put into a cell. And Samuel's explanation is that the murder took place without proper forewarning, and there are some who explain that the witnesses' testimony was disproved on minor points but not with respect to the actual event. And it is proper for us to try and approximate the [strict legal] procedures when trying cases, in order to safeguard the law.

... As to that judge who brazenly appeared in the synagogue in the presence of the city notables, and spoke with malice, and said that he commanded the execution, and ordered the thing–his sin is unbearably great, and he should be condemned and severely punished. For he was a judge in that community, and in place of the law, there was iniquity. And he commanded the execution of one of his brethren, a fellow Jew, and two others have already carried out the execution. Furthermore, he should have condemned his son for pursuing his fellow with a drawn sword, but he saw him acting thus in the presence of the community's notables, and instead of restraining him, encouraged him, saying that it was a religious duty to so act. Now the judge is legally exempt, on the basis of the principle "the teacher's instructions and the student's instructions—which ought one follow?" But Maimonides, of blessed memory, already ruled regarding one who hired an assassin to kill his fellow, or sent his servants to kill him, and so on, that while he is exempt by the laws of men though liable by the laws of heaven–[nevertheless], if the court sees fit to punish him by means of an exigency ruling, if this is required by the times, they have the authority to do so, as they see fit, by royal warrant.[36] And Maimonides, of blessed memory, also says: "If the hirer of the assassin was not put to death, because it was not an exigency of the times, in any event it is the duty of the court to flog him severely, almost to death, and incarcerate him in prison for many years, and to afflict him with all kinds of afflictions, in order to frighten and threaten the other wicked people, so that [the temptation to do violence] will not be an inner impediment and stumbling block, and they will not be able to say, 'I am about to kill my enemy, as did so-and-so, and I will not be found guilty.'

35 bSanhedrin 81b.

36 *Code*, Laws concerning Murder and the preservation of Life, ch. 2.

Therefore this wicked judge is not excused due to the fact that witnesses say that he seemed to them to be saying these things out of great anger, because this is the way of all murderers: to kill out of anger and quarrels. It is written, "And if men contend, and one smote the other," and so on (Exod. 21:18)—from this the Sages learned that the aggressor should be imprisoned. "For anger resteth in the bosom of fools" (Eccles. 7:9)—and ought not rest in the hearts of civic judges. And in my opinion, in addition to what you inflict on this judge for his evil deeds, in terms of punishment, fines, imprisonment and so on, it is also fitting to demote him from his high status–the Asherah should be uprooted from the altar.[37] And he should never again be appointed to hold public office, as is the law with respect to an inadvertent manslaughterer, who returns from banishment upon the high priest's demise, and does not regain his former high position. As the Sages, of blessed memory, expounded, "He returns to his family, but not to the offices held by his forefathers."[38] This is what seems right on my evaluation.

As you are aware, we do not judge capital cases in this country, nor do we cut off hands and feet, because the law is in the hands of the King. And you are a sitting judge, and familiar with the administration of the law in the land, and its judges. And you know how the judges are accustomed to ruling, according to the needs of the time, in this sort of case. Act as they do, and "forsake not thy mother's Torah" (Prov. 1:8). For in truth, as I write this, my hands shake, and my knees knock against each other. So do not rely on my opinion, but on your own, as guided by heaven. For a judge must rely only on that which his eyes behold, and my hearing the case is not better than [your deciding based on] what you see for yourself.

7. *Responsa Trumat Hadeshen*, Psakim Ukhtavim, #210

Two persons appeared before me for judgment, R. Eliezer b. Shalom and R. Gershom b. Shalom. R. Eliezer clamored against R. Gershom that he rammed and pushed him during the Hoshanot procession during the festival of Tabernacles (Sukkot), with harmful intentions, as he had hated him for years. And he was pushed so hard that he broke his collarbone and was in need of a doctor and medical treatment. And R. Gershom replied that he had participated in the procession, which was conducted in the customary way, and that generally there is much pushing during these processions. And if he pushed him, it happened without any intent to harm him. And they went on at length in telling me about their quarrel, and I scrutinized their testimony with care, but found no clear evidence that R. Eliezer was indeed forcibly pushed by R. Gershom; I found in the evidence only subjective assessments and arguments. But there was one

37 The Asherah was a pole used in pagan rites; see bSanhedrin 7b, Deuteronomy 16:21.
38 bMakot 13a.

witness who testified that R. Gershom told him the night before the day of the procession that he planned to push R. Eliezer the following day, and also said so upon leaving the synagogue. And [I asked], 'why did you not help your master when he was pushed?' And this piece of testimony is clearer than the other testimony in the case. In any event, if we were to pursue the depth of the biblical law, there would not be sufficient evidence. For what R. Gershom told this witness on the night before is inconclusive, because sometimes people exaggerate but do not act, as it explicitly says in the Talmud.[39] And also, what he said upon leaving the synagogue, as I mentioned above, was not in court, it was self-incriminating, and it was not against the litigant—so it is not valid evidence, as explained in *Or Zarua*.[40] And on the basis of such subjective assessments and arguments, R. Gershom should not be held liable and punished. For it has been established in the Talmud, "There was an ox grazing on a river bank and a dead ox lying next to it; even though the one ox was a recidivate gorer and the other was gored, we do not say that the one gored the other."[41] This is the ruling of Alfasi. And in the present case, all the more must we have additional evaluations that are tantamount to proof of intent to harm, because if he did not intend to harm him—even though the other person was certainly harmed by him—he is exempt from any charges, because the injury occurred while they were celebrating the observance of a precept, as stated in *Or Zarua* and *Asheri*, citing the *Tosafot*.[42]

Nevertheless, I can see, and so my heart tells me, that this matter calls for putting into place a significant safeguard and qualification. For should it transpire, heaven forbid, that someone would wait in ambush for his fellow in this setting, then the holy precept of the procession would be abandoned, for every person would fear that his enemies might do him bodily harm. And if a person does bodily harm to his fellow on such an occasion, his sin is greater than if he had done it at a different place and a different time. First, he has been contemptuous of the sanctity of the synagogue; secondly, he has sinned while fulfilling one of the precepts of God, may His memory be exalted. In addition, on the pulpit at the time was the Torah scroll, in which is written "he shall not exceed, lest, if he should exceed" (Deut 25:3), which our Rabbis have interpreted to mean that even if there is an evil person among Israel, anyone who strikes him transgresses a negative injunction, for he has already received his punishment.

Since it appears, and has been demonstrated, that R. Gershom did intend to strike and to cause R. Eliezer bodily pain, and in instances such as this courts mete out punishment even [in a manner that is] not in accordance with the law, therefore I rule that R. Gershom should express remorse and

39 bBaba Batra 33b.

40 By R. Isaac b. Moses of Vienna (Riaz).

41 Paraphrasing bBaba Batra 93a.

42 At the end of tractate Suka.

beg for pardon. He is to do the following. On a day when the Torah is read,[43] while the Torah scroll is on the pulpit, he should leave his seat and go over to R. Eliezer, passing in front of the ark on his way. And the notables of the community should go over there as well. And he should say to R. Eliezer: 'Eliezer, I have sinned, [first] against the God of Israel, and then against you, because I was contemptuous of the sanctity of the synagogue and of the commands of God, may His memory be exalted. I also transgressed the Torah's admonition that one must not strike or cause bodily pain to his fellow. And for this I beg for forgiveness and atonement from the God of Israel, and then beg your pardon, because I am remorseful for what I have done.'

I have assessed the medical expenses at the average rate. R. Gershom will also give R. Eliezer two gold coins. And to honor the synagogue of Grätz, R. Eliezer will, on the cognizance of two reliable witnesses, donate these two gold coins, to any good cause (*mitzva*), because they only came to his hands as a fine imposed in order to strengthen the safeguard, as I explained above. And for that reason, I did not award anything for loss of income, because it is not clear what that amounts to, unlike the doctor's fee, which will be known when R. Eliezer will have to pay it.

So says the most insignificant and junior in Israel.

8. *Responsa Rashba*, 4, #311

QUESTION

The community came to an agreement to appoint us as magistrates, in order to uproot transgression, and we swore to do so. And it is stated in the agreement that was enacted that we are permitted, by the government of the state, to inflict chastisement and punishment, both corporal and monetary, as we see fit. Please inform us [what to do in circumstances such as the following]: if witnesses who are close relatives of Reuben testify that he transgressed a vow, and the witnesses are reliable, or if a woman and a minor testify [to this], relating it casually—is Reuben to be chastised or not? And if the witnesses, or one of them, are related to Reuben, and we have good reason to believe that these witnesses are telling the truth, are we permitted to act in accordance with their testimony, even that it is essentially not [valid] evidence?

ANSWER

These matters seem to be obvious. You are permitted to act as you see fit. For the matters you mention apply only for a court that judges according to the Torah—a Sanhedrin or court of that caliber. But a court whose mandate is to maintain social order does not judge strictly according to the letter of the law of the Torah, but as dictated by the demands of the time,

43 The Torah is read on Mondays and Thursdays, as well as on the Sabbath and on Festivals.

as permitted by the [Gentile] government. Were this not so, they could not impose fines or corporal punishment, because courts do not have the authority to implement the laws imposing fines in Babylonia, nor to try cases pertaining to unusual occurrences. Because nowadays we have no authority to judge even cases of debt by the laws of the Torah, as that calls for expert judges, and we are but commoners. But rather, we act as the agents of the expert judges [of the past], and as their agents, we discharge our duty with respect to commonplace things such as loans and affidavits, but as to infrequent things, such as robbery and battery and other transgressions, we do not. Furthermore, one cannot be flogged or punished on the basis of self-incrimination, for by law, one cannot incriminate himself. Furthermore, even if there are proper witnesses, we cannot flog without forewarning, because the courts only impose flogging after the offender has been forewarned. But all these things apply only to courts that judge according to the law of the Torah. And you can observe that David killed the Amalekite stranger by himself.[44] Furthermore, it is said that "courts mete out lashes and punishment [in a manner that is] not in accordance with the law, and not to transgress the law, but to safeguard the law. And it happened that a man rode a horse on the Sabbath during the time of the Greeks, and they brought him to the court and stoned him to death." Not because that was the law, but because it was an exigency of the times; as it is stated in the Talmud.[45] It applies much more in your case, because the main thrust of your appointment was to enable you to act as you see fit, as stated in the letter of enactment, as you said. And the matter is obvious to us, and applies to all places where there is an enactment of the community that addresses this issue.

44 II Samuel, ch. 1.
45 bJebamot 90b.

# 4 Erroneous rulings



## 1 Introduction

### 1.1 The dilemma posed by erroneous rulings

According to the prevailing western understanding of the judicial process, courts are duty-bound to apply the rules of the legal system within which they operate, however these rules were generated. A question immediately presents itself: what is the status of a court ruling that is perceived by its addressee as being based on a misunderstanding on the part of the judge, and thus, perceived as going against the system's rules? Is the ruling's addressee obligated to obey the ruling despite its alleged erroneousness? Note that this question differs from that of the case where the addressee is critical of the ruling's **moral** implications. In the latter case, the addressee is unwilling to abide by the system's determination, on moral grounds, whereas in the former case, she simply wants the court to generate the correct ruling.

The former question can also be presented in the following way: is the binding nature of a court ruling dependent on its **substantive** correctness, or is its validity solely a function of **procedural** correctness?

The position of Jewish law on the question of what renders a ruling valid differs from that endorsed in contemporary western legal theory. According to talmudic law, the validity of legal rulings does not rest exclusively on procedure, but is also conditioned on substantive correctness, that is, consistency with the law. In Jewish law, there may indeed be circumstances in which someone who believes that a ruling is not consistent with the law will not be bound by it. The practical import of this conclusion is that under certain circumstances, the law itself directs an individual not to follow a ruling that was handed down by the court. We will explore precisely when this scenario is deemed to occur.

More specifically, the paradigm case on which we will focus is that of the duty to obey a halakhic judgment in a situation where one of the judges disputes the ruling because he considers it erroneous. Elsewhere in this volume,[1] we saw that the phenomenon of controversy is a hallmark of halakhic literature. In many instances the Sages took pride in the existence of controversy regarding the correct understanding of the law, and even encouraged the parties to various controversies to uphold, teach and defend their respective views. But in this chapter, our focus will not be on theoretical controversy in the context of study in the *beit hamidrash* (yeshiva, talmudic academy), but on the adducing of controversial laws in actual legal decision-making. Consider the following scenario: a court hands down a ruling that conflicts with the view held by one of the judges, and, as he is convinced of the correctness of his position, this judge claims that the court has erred, and has issued a ruling that runs counter to the law. Does the halakha require this judge to abide by the court ruling he considers to be erroneous, or does it recognize a more limited obligation to obey, one that permits the scholar who is convinced of the halakhic correctness of his own position to maintain it in the face of a ruling to the contrary? Does such a scholar have the right to act, or maybe even rule in his community, in a manner that deviates from the said ruling, or might he even have an obligation to do so?

Once again, it must be stressed that the dilemma in question does not arise out of a legal ruling that conflicts with an individual's moral outlook, creating a disparity between his legal obligations and his personal worldview. Rather, the dilemma arises out of rulings that, in the opinion

1 See Chapter One above, "Controversy."

of one of the members of the court, contravene the law itself, or in other words, are erroneous in their substantive interpretation of the law.

The dilemma posed by erroneous rulings has significant social and existential implications. Permitting scholars to conduct themselves, or even to rule, on the basis of their own reasoning and understanding of the law, contrary to rulings of the courts, will undermine the stability of the legal system in general, which will, in turn, threaten the broader social order. The ability to project a sense of reliability and integrity in its application of the law is crucial to the operation of any legal system, and without it, communal unity will crumble. On the other hand, true justice is also a paramount value, and desirable standards of truth and justice cannot be maintained by a judicial system without mechanisms that enable it to quickly correct mistakes, even at the expense of stability. This desideratum mandates a weakening of the obligation to abide by the court's legal determinations in the event of a mistaken judgment, so as to ensure that the legal system is not held hostage to erroneous rulings.

The question of the scope and limits of the duty to abide by erroneous halakhic rulings has garnered considerable attention from contemporary scholars.[2] In particular, they have grappled with the fact that for approximately the past two hundred years, Orthodox Judaism has endorsed the notion of deference to the halakhic pronouncements of preeminent authorities (*daat torah*). This phenomenon has motivated scholars to explore whether this far-ranging obligation has its roots in the Rabbinic sources, or is a more modern development.

Many scholars claim that two approaches to this issue can be found in the classic halakhic sources, one mandating a limited duty of compliance with legal authority, and the other—often presented by contemporary halakhic authorities as the sole legitimate stance—mandating full and thorough deference to the pronouncements of halakhic authorities. The law of the "rebellious elder" (*zaken mamre*), which will be discussed in section 2, is often claimed to reflect the latter approach, whereas the stance taken in tractate Horayot of the Mishnah, which will be discussed in section 3, is said to reflect the approach espousing a more limited duty to obey. In this chapter, we will claim, however, that the different Rabbinic sources do indeed present a coherent position on the duty of deference to legal authority. The Sages emphasize that the Sanhedrin's rulings are authoritative, and uphold a comprehensive obligation to comply with them. Generally speaking, they do not permit those holding dissenting opinions to act contrary to the rulings of the court. Moreover, they declare that the Sanhedrin has the power to establish the normative and binding law with respect to as-yet undecided legal questions. Nevertheless, they

2 See M.Z. Sokol (ed.), *Rabbinic Authority and Personal Autonomy* (Northvale NJ: 1992); J. Roth, "The justification for controversy under Jewish law," 76 *California L. Rev.* 337 (1988); M. Walzer et al. (eds.), *The Jewish Political Tradition* (New Haven: 2000), vol. 1, ch. 7.

did limit the obligation of obedience to rulings of the Sanhedrin in those exceptional cases where an obvious and objective mistake had been made. Indeed, a sage is not permitted to abide by the erroneous ruling. We will see that these two principles—the principle of the authoritativeness of Sanhedrin rulings, on the one hand, and that of the duty not to abide by a clearly erroneous ruling, on the other—reinforce and complement one another, ensuring that obedience to rulings issued by the court will be intelligent, critical, and subject to the overriding constraint of truth.[3]

### 1.2 The High Court in Jerusalem

The Sages based their understanding of the role and status of the High Court on Deuteronomy 17:8–13:

> **8** If there arise a matter too hard for thee in judgment, between blood and blood, between plea and plea, and between stroke and stroke, even matters of controversy within thy gates; then shalt thou arise, and get thee up unto the place which the Lord thy God shall choose.
> **9** And thou shall come unto the priests the Levites, and unto the judge that shall be in those days; and thou shalt inquire; and they shall declare unto thee the sentence of judgment.
> **10** And thou shalt do according to the tenor of the sentence, which they shall declare unto thee from that place which the Lord shall choose; and thou shalt observe to do according to all that they shall teach thee.
> **11** According to the law which they shall teach thee, and according to the judgment which they shall tell thee, thou shalt do; thou shalt not turn aside from the sentence which they shall declare unto thee, neither to the right hand, nor to the left.
> **12** And the man that doeth presumptuously, in not hearkening unto the priest that standeth to minister there before the Lord thy God, or unto the judge, even that man shall die; and thou shalt exterminate the evil from Israel.
> **13** And all the people shall hear, and fear, and do no more presumptuously.

3 This chapter touches on several philosophical issues that have been the subject of much debate in recent years: (1) Is Jewish law divine, i.e., does its obligatory nature derive from the fact that it is divinely revealed, or is it autonomous, i.e., is its source human?; (2) Is Jewish law monolithic, upholding one unequivocal stance on any legal issue, or is it pluralistic, recognizing multiple and possibly incompatible stances?; (3) Is Jewish law conservative, advocating slow—if any—development of its rules in response to changing circumstances, or is it innovative, easily adjusting its norms to address contemporary needs?

This biblical rule establishes that the High Court will sit in Jerusalem ("the place which the Lord thy God shall choose") as the ultimate authority on all areas of the law: purity and impurity, the Temple service, and even civil matters (verse 8). In all these realms, in the event that the law is not known ("there arise a matter too hard for thee in judgment"), one must go to the High Court to seek a ruling, and one is obliged to follow that ruling (verse 10). This obligation is repeated in verse 11 with a metaphor that likens obedience to the court to taking a specific path from which no divergence is brooked ("neither to the right hand, nor to the left").

The Rabbinic discussion of this passage focuses on the parameters of the obligation to obey the court, though not on the obligation to go to Jerusalem to seek a ruling, a point that was apparently considered obvious. The focal point of the Rabbinic deliberation is the right of an individual sage to claim that the court has handed down an erroneous ruling, and to conduct himself, or even issue a ruling for his community, in accordance with his own (contrary) opinion. The discussion of this question reflects the dilemma that confronted the Rabbis as they went about their decision-making: ought they give precedence to the values of stability and communal unity, or to the value of correctly and truly interpreting the law? In other words, ought they place more weight on the need to preserve unity within the halakhic enterprise, even in the absence of consensus with regard to a particular law, or on the desideratum of allowing each sage to follow his own path—that is, his own understanding of the law—when convinced of its truth?

It is important to clarify the basis of the Rabbinic position regarding obedience to court rulings. Is obedience required because of the presumption that the court always acts rightly—that is, that the court is infallible—or is it grounded in the court's fundamental authority? We must also investigate whether authority is invested in judges as individuals, due to the high esteem in which they are held, or granted to the court as an institution, due to its importance to the maintenance of society. Let us now begin this examination with a look at the key Rabbinic sources relating to the 'rebellious elder' (*zaken mamre*), a sage who does not comply with a ruling handed down by the Sanhedrin.

## 2 The rebellious elder (*zaken mamre*)

On the strength of the biblical injunction regarded as the prooftext for the obligation to abide by the ruling of the High Court in Jerusalem, the Rabbis set down the law of the "rebellious elder," a sage who contests the ruling of the High Court, claiming that it is erroneous.

The law of the rebellious elder is set out in the Mishnah:

> An elder who rebels against the court's decision [is put to death], as it is said, "If there arise a matter too hard for thee in judgment" (Deut.

> 17:8). Three courts were [in Jerusalem]: one convened at the entrance to the Temple Mount, one convened at the entrance to the Temple Court, and one convened in the Hall of Hewn Stone. They come to the one at the entrance to the Temple Mount, and he [the elder] says, "Thus I expounded and thus my fellows expounded, thus I taught and thus my fellows taught." If they [the court] had heard [a tradition regarding the matter], they tell it to them ; if not, they go on to those [judges] at the entrance to the Temple Court, and he says, "Thus I expounded and thus my fellows expounded, thus I taught and thus my fellows taught." If they had heard [a tradition regarding the matter], they tell it to them; and if not, these and those come to the High Court that is in the Hall of Hewn Stone, from which Torah goes forth to all Israel, as it is said, "from that place which the Lord shall choose" (17:10). If he returned to his town, and yet again taught in the manner he had before—he is exempt; but if he ruled that the teaching was to be acted upon—he is liable, as it is said, "And the man who acts presumptuously" (17:12); he is not liable until he rules that it is to be acted upon.
>
> mSanhedrin 11:2

According to the mishnaic account, the deliberations move through successively higher instances, finally reaching the High Court in Jerusalem that convened in the Hall of Hewn Stone. Although the High Court rules against the stance taken by the sage in question, he nonetheless 'rebels' and continues to instruct his followers to act in a manner contravening the ruling handed down by the court. It is at this stage that the Rabbis impose the punishment specified in the biblical passage: "that man shall die; and thou shalt exterminate the evil from Israel."

### 2.1 Rationale for the obligation to comply with court rulings

Why does the Talmud relate to the rebellious elder with such severity? Does the gravity of the rebellious elder's offense reside in the very fact that he dares to challenge the law, or is it that he challenges the High Court in Jerusalem? In other words, does the gravity ascribed to his offense arise from the assumption that the rulings of the court are ipso facto correct, and thus in disputing the court's ruling, he is in essence rejecting the authority of the law itself, or does it arise solely from the fact that he rejects the authority of the court and the legal establishment?

In the continuation of the Mishnah, the scope of the law of the rebellious elder is further limited in such a way that we can conclude that the law of the rebellious elder is intended to defend the authority of the **court**, and not necessarily the authority of the halakha itself. The rebellious elder is punished by death not because he weakens the rule of law, but because he undermines the standing of the highest court in the judicial system. The

Mishnah distinguishes between the sage who rules that a Torah law is to be abrogated, and one who rules that a law established by the Rabbis is to be abrogated:

> Greater severity applies to [an elder who contradicts] the words of the Scribes than to [an elder who contradicts] the words of the Torah. [One who says] "There is no [precept of] phylacteries (*tefilin*)," in order to transgress the words of the Torah—is exempt [from the law of rebellious elder]; [one who says] "[Phylacteries have] five[4] compartments" in order to add to the words of the Scribes—is liable.[5]
>
> mSanhedrin 11:3

The precept of donning phylacteries is set down in the Torah, but the details of the precept, such as the structure of the phylactery boxes, were promulgated by the Sages. The Mishnah asserts that a sage who disputes the law of phylacteries itself is exempt, whereas a sage who disputes the details of the law, which were set down by the Sages, is liable.

The Early Authorities give different explanations for the exemption of the rebellious elder from liability for disputing the law of phylacteries. According to Rashi, the rationale is as follows: "This is not considered a legal ruling, since one can go and read it in the schoolhouse." In other words, the precept of phylacteries is a matter so obvious that even schoolchildren know it.[6] Hence, such a ruling is inherently repudiated, and cannot even be considered a legal ruling.

Maimonides, on the other hand, explains the exemption as follows:

> [The Sages of the Mishnah] said that he [the elder] is exempt if he admitted that it [the precept of phylacteries] is obligatory but he disobeys it due to rebelliousness, as [the Mishnah] says: "in order to transgress the words of the Torah," while admitting that it is a transgression. Therefore, he does not incur death by the court, because we do not put to death one who disobeys a positive commandment. But, if he said that there is no precept of phylacteries due to heresy, he is executed because he is a sectarian, not because he is a rebellious elder.... Have you ever seen a case where one who expresses belief and conviction that there are two or three deities—which is undoubtedly a repudiation of the biblical declaration that 'God is One'—about which we say that this person is not to be executed, or

4 The Sages specified that there are to be four compartments; see bMenahot 3b.

5 Although all of the halakha is often referred to under the rubric "words of the Torah" (*divrei torah*), here the term is used in a more restricted sense to refer to laws specifically stated in the biblical text. The expression "words of the Scribes" (*divrei sofrim*) refers to laws introduced by the Sages via tradition or interpretation.

6 See bSanhedrin 33b, bShavuot 14b, bHorayot 4a.

> that he is a rebellious elder?! Rather, he is executed because he excluded himself from the community, that is to say, the community of Israel.
>
> Maimonides, *Commentary on the Mishnah*, mSanhedrin 11:3

The mishnaic account portrays the rebellious elder as seeking to usurp the authority of the High Court in Jerusalem, as Maimonides goes on to assert:

> Because the rebellious elder does not destroy the edifice of the Torah or repudiate the whole Oral Law in its entirety, he is not considered like the Sadducees or the Boethusians, but rather, he is someone who considers his own opinion to be above that of the High Court, and Scripture deems him liable to be put to death to preserve [the court's] honor.

The following baraita[7] sharpens this Mishnah and enables us to distinguish two rationales underlying the law of the rebellious elder:

> R. Joshia said: Three things did Zeira, an inhabitant of Jerusalem, tell me: [In the case of] A husband who wishes to retract (*limhol*) his having suspected his wife [of unfaithfulness]–his having suspected her is retracted. A stubborn and rebellious son whose father and mother wish to excuse (*limhol*) him–he is excused. A rebellious elder whom the court wishes to excuse (*limhol*)–he is excused. And when I came to my colleagues in the south, about two of the things they agreed with me, but about the rebellious elder they did not agree with me, so that controversy would not proliferate among Israel.
>
> bSanhedrin 88a-b[8]

The baraita is premised on the assumption that one who has been harmed may ordinarily waive his rights with regard to the person who harmed him—for example, a parent may forgive his wayward son and thus release him from the punishment specified in the law of the "stubborn and rebellious son," and a husband may forgive his wife and thus release her from the need to undergo the waters of bitterness ordeal[9] to prove her innocence.

It appears that, in the opinion of Zeira, the transgressive aspect of the rebellious elder's offense is the injury he inflicts on the **personal honor and prestige** of the members of the court. Hence, they are permitted to forgive him for his actions and exempt him from punishment. Zeira's colleagues opposed this interpretation and its implications. In their opinion, the culpable aspect is not the insult to the judges' personal honor and prestige,

7 See also bSota 25a.

8 See also jSanhedrin 8:6 (26b); Sifre Deuteronomy, Ki Teitze, 218 (Finkelstein edition p. 251).

9 See Numbers 5:11–31.

but rather, to the standing of the High Court as an **institutional authority**, the body that unites the world of Jewish law and ensures that "controversy will not proliferate among Israel." Hence members of the court do not have the authority to forgive the rebellious elder for his actions.

## 2.2 The rebellious elder's ruling

As we stated above, the rebellious elder is convicted for issuing a directive contrary to the ruling of the High Court, thereby undermining its authority. But what distinguishes acceptable criticism from directives considered confrontational and subversive? Is the rebellious elder punished for every expression of a position contrary to that upheld by the High Court? Is he punished for a ruling that he alone follows, or only if he instructs others to follow his ruling? We will see that a range of different positions on these questions can be found in the sources, reflecting the different views as to the obligation to obey the court.

Clearly, expressing an opinion must be distinguished from carrying out an action. The rebellious elder is entitled to oppose the High Court's ruling in various ways. He can simply express his opinion, and assert that the ruling of the High Court is in error; he can also carry out an act that contravenes the court's ruling. But he can also go beyond merely expressing his opinion as a theoretical view, and direct others to act in a manner that contravenes the High Court ruling.

In which of these situations should the rebellious elder be punished? What is the underlying rationale for punishing the rebellious elder—to prevent incitement, or to prevent rebellion against the legal establishment? If preventing incitement is the rationale, the focus will be on punishing the rebellious elder when he causes others to refuse to abide by a ruling of the High Court—for instance, when he directs others to act contrary to the court ruling, or so acts himself, thereby serving as a role model. From this perspective, it would be less serious for the rebellious elder to act contrary to the ruling of the High Court in the privacy of his own home, where others are unaware of his behavior, or if the rebellious elder emphasizes that his conflict with the court is theoretical in nature, and as regards his actual practice, he accepts the court ruling. On the other hand, if preventing rebellion against the judicial establishment is the rationale, we would expect that any infringement of a court ruling, even if carried out in private, would be deemed serious—indeed, perhaps even the mere expression of theoretical opposition to the court's opinion would be deemed serious.

Keeping these considerations in mind, let us examine in parallel three Rabbinic sources that address this issue—the Mishnah we considered above, a baraita, and a Tosefta—beginning with the first two.

i. If he returned to his town, and yet again taught in the manner he had before—he is exempt, and if he ruled that the teaching was to be acted upon—he liable, as it is said, "And the man who acts presumptuously" (17:12); he is not liable until he rules that it is to be acted upon.

mSanhedrin 11:2

ii. The Rabbis taught: he [the elder] is not liable unless he acts in accordance with his ruling, or directs others [to act in accordance with his ruling] and they act in accordance with his ruling.

baraita in bSanhedrin 88b

It is clear that in two cases, the rebellious elder is exempt from punishment for his action: (1) if he expressed theoretical opposition to the court's ruling, but did not instruct others to act in accordance with his own view; and (2) if he acted in a manner contravening the court's ruling, but did not issue a ruling that such conduct was lawful.

Beyond this, the Mishnah and the baraita seem to diverge. From the Mishnah it seems that the very fact that the rebellious elder issues a ruling that contravenes the court's ruling is sufficient to render him liable, and it is not necessary that he or others actually act in accordance with his ruling. In contrast, the baraita deems him liable only if his directive leads to performance of an act that contravenes the court's ruling.

In contrast to the Mishnah and the baraita, the Tosefta is more nuanced, and open to various interpretations:

A rebellious elder who ruled and acted in accordance with his ruling is liable; if he ruled but did not act in accordance with his ruling, he is exempt; if he ruled in order that it be acted upon (*hora al menat laasot*), then even if he did not act, he is liable.

tSanhedrin 14:12

At first glance, the Tosefta seems to be inconsistent. From the first two clauses, the rebellious elder seems to be deemed liable if his ruling leads to an action that contravenes the court's ruling (as in the baraita). But the last clause appears to indicate that he can be found liable on the basis on his ruling even if it does **not** lead to an action (as in the Mishnah).

The key to resolving this apparent inconsistency lies in the difference between the expression "ruled" (in the first two clauses), and "ruled in order that it be acted upon" (in the last clause). To understand the significance of the difference, we must adduce a distinction widely invoked in Jewish law, namely, the distinction between a ruling "intended as a statement of the law" (*lehalakha*) and a ruling "intended for implementation" (*halakha lemaase*). The former is a halakhic ruling that does not call for its own implementation. It is given with the recognition that it may remain a purely theoretical injunction. In contrast, a ruling that is intended for implementation is issued with the intention that it be implemented in practice.

The first two parts of the Tosefta deal with instances where he ruled "as a statement of law." This explains why the rebellious elder is not to be punished in cases where he issues a ruling contravening that of the court, but no action is carried out in accordance with his ruling. He is to be punished only in cases where his ruling results in the performance of actions that contravene the court's ruling. The last clause in the Tosefta passage, however, deals with a law "intended for implementation," *horaa lemaase*, or as the Tosefta puts it, "he ruled in order that it be acted upon." Here, the ruling itself suffices to convict the rebellious elder, regardless of whether it was actually implemented.[10]

The distinction is also found in jSanhedrin 11:3 (30a): "If he ruled **not** in order that it be acted upon–he is exempt, [if he ruled] in order that it be acted upon, even if it was not acted upon–he is liable."

We can conclude from these sources that when a court's ruling is contrary to the position of a particular sage, he is permitted (and perhaps even obligated) to continue to teach his tradition or his line of reasoning, though it is contrary to the court's ruling. However, when he teaches this position, he must emphasize that in practice it is not to be acted upon, but rather, the ruling issued by the court is to be acted upon.

The principle that a sage may publicly dispute the court's ruling and seek to disseminate his own ideas, as long as he emphasizes that they are not to be acted upon unless the court changes its ruling, reflects the very essence of the talmudic enterprise. Talmudic debate does not seek only to establish the law to be applied in practice, but also to clarify and profoundly understand the various opinions on any given issue. Hence it is legitimate to publicly take issue with a court ruling, but illegitimate to act or instruct others to act in a manner conflicting with that ruling. The fact that it is permissible for the sage to continue to teach his opinion, to disseminate it, and to try to convince students of its correctness, clearly demonstrates that the elder's transgression is not that he challenged the correctness of the High Court's ruling.

It is important to note that the very fact that the sage is permitted to teach his dissenting opinion sharpens the obligation to obey the court. Where the sage is convinced of the correctness of the court's ruling, obeying it is not a manifestation of true obedience, since the sage does so not merely because the court ruled that is was the law, but on the basis of his own understanding and belief that the ruling is correct. Real obedience to the court is manifested only when the sage claims that the court ruling

10 R. David Pardo's commentary, *Hasdei David*, explains the Tosefta as follows: "With regard to 'he ruled,' a distinction is to be made. For even if he so ruled, if he did not so rule as the law intended for implementation (*halakha lemaase*), but rather, as a hypothetical principle, he is exempt. But if he ruled in order that it be acted upon, even if no one acted in accordance with his ruling, neither he nor anyone else—he is immediately liable."

is flawed, and publicly teaches his arguments against it, yet obeys the ruling nevertheless.

This may shed light on another mishnaic law that defines who can be considered a rebellious elder:

> A sage not yet authorized to render legal rulings who rules that his teaching is to be acted on is exempt. Hence his more severe offense turns out to be a leniency for him. [Rashi: the stringency applied to him, [namely,] that he is not considered fit to issue rulings ... becomes a leniency that exempts him from death].
>
> mSanhedrin 11:2

At first glance, this exemption seems surprising. We might think that a dissenting ruling issued by a student would be more serious than such a ruling issued by an elder, inasmuch as it is characterized by brazenness and lack of awareness of the student's status as but a 'sage in training,' so to speak. Indeed, the Mishnah emphasizes that a ruling issued by a student **is** more serious, but nevertheless rules that he is exempt from the punishment meted out to the rebellious elder. The logic behind this exemption becomes clearer in light of our analysis that the essence of the rebellious elder's offense is his undermining of the High Court's authority. The student who issues a ruling contrary to that of the High Court does not jeopardize the status of the court, as he has no standing as a legal authority. Hence the punishment is reserved for the elder alone, that is, the sage who by virtue of his high standing undermines the court's authority.

### 2.3 The rebellious elder's argument

The Mishnah describes the controversy between the rebellious elder and his colleagues, but does not spell out the arguments put forward by the two sides. The *sugya* in the Babylonian Talmud addresses this point, and can shed further light on the obligation to abide by court rulings. Theoretically speaking, one who argues for a particular legal position may seek to do so on the basis of either logic or tradition. He might seek to convince others of the correctness of his position by arguing that it is more logical or more accurate from an exegetical perspective (e.g., by claiming that it can be deduced using the standard exegetical principles, whereas the opposed position cannot). On the other hand, he might argue that his position should be adopted, not because it is more logical or deductively valid, but because it reflects the halakhic tradition, that is, earlier legal sources.

Keeping in mind this distinction, we can better understand an Amoraic controversy over the nature of the dispute between the rebellious elder and his colleagues. We will first examine the position of the Amora, R. Kahana:

> R. Kahana said: If he [the rebellious elder] says, '[My ruling is] based on tradition,' and they [the other judges] say, '[Our ruling is] based on tradition'—he is not killed. If he says, 'So it seems to me,' and they say, 'so it seems to us'—he is not killed. All the more so if he says, 'It is based on tradition,' and they say, 'so it seems to us'—he is not killed. Only when he says, 'So it seems to me,' and they say, 'It is based on tradition' [is he killed].
>
> bSanhedrin 88a

In R. Kahana's opinion, tradition is superior to interpretation. The High Court's unique status, the factor mandating the punishment of death for one who undermines its decisions, does not derive from the quality of its judicial judgment, but from the superiority of its legal traditions. The idea here is that the High Court's traditions of the law are weightier than any interpretation that might be proposed by an individual on the basis of his own understanding.

In practice, R. Kahana significantly limits the scope of the law of the rebellious elder. R. Kahana takes the view that a claim based on tradition is stronger than a claim based on logic. Hence, the rebellious elder is guilty only if he bases his claim on an argument **weaker** than that of his colleagues. If his claim is based on an equally-strong or stronger argument, he is not punished. It follows from R. Kahana's approach that when the High Court's position is based on exegesis and reasoning, the rebellious elder who rules against it will not be punished, since his claim will be justified by an argument of equal or greater strength. The fact that he questions the High Court's ruling is not in itself a transgression. The rebellious elder is only liable when, on the strength of his own logic alone, he seeks to deviate from a received tradition.

There is no question that R. Kahana's understanding of the law reflects an agenda that seeks to limit the scope of the law of the rebellious elder, and thereby reduce the institutional authority of the judicial establishment. R. Kahana was a Babylonian Amora, and his opinion is consistent with the Babylonian Talmud's anti-establishment attitude. At the time, the Jewish community in Babylonia did not have official institutions, and this engendered a fundamental tendency to restrict the power and status of those institutions that did emerge. This, in turn, gave rise to a strengthening of the duty not to obey an erroneous court ruling, and, as we will see, more severe punishment for one who does acquiesce in such a ruling.[11]

R. Eleazar, an Amora from the land of Israel, disagrees with R. Kahana's approach, objecting to the limitation he seeks to impose on the law of the rebellious elder. R. Eleazar remains loyal to the simple and more inclusive

11 On the differences between the attitudes of the Amoraim of Babylonia and those of the land of Israel with respect to the judicial process, see H. Ben-Menahem, *Judicial Deviation in Talmudic Law–Governed by Men, Not by Rules* (Chur, Switzerland: 1991), 55–98.

meaning of the Mishnah, which does not mention any of the distinctions employed by R. Kahana. The continuation of the talmudic *sugya* reads:

> R. Eleazar said: Even if he says, "[my ruling is] based on tradition," and they say "so it seems to us"—he is killed, so that controversy will not proliferate within Israel.

The thrust of R. Eleazar's stance is expressed in his concluding remark, "so that controversy will not proliferate within Israel." This reason applies equally to all the situations in which the rebellious elder disputes the High Court's ruling, regardless of the epistemic grounds for the elder's and the court's respective views. On this approach, the rebellious elder's offense is not his divergence from the High Court's ruling on the strength of a weaker argument, but the divergence itself. The grounds for the views upheld by the rebellious elder and his colleagues are irrelevant; the only relevant point is whether the **substance** of the elder's view is in keeping with that of the High Court. We can therefore characterize R. Eleazar's view as encapsulating an expansive approach to the obligation to obey rulings handed down by the High Court.

In the *sugya* in tractate Sanhedrin of the Babylonian Talmud, the law is decided in accordance with the view of R. Eleazar.[12] The proof adduced for this decision is the baraita, discussed above, that implies that the principal rationale for the law of the rebellious elder is "so that controversy will not proliferate within Israel"; that is, to preserve the unity of the law, as determined by the High Court.

## 3 Tractate Horayot of the Mishnah

Tractate Horayot deals with mistakes by community and national officials. It discusses the status of erroneous court rulings and mistakes made by the High Priest or the *nasi* (Prince), as well as the sacrifices to be brought by these office-holders if they err. The first two *mishnayot* of tractate Horayot set down the law pertaining to the individual who acts upon an erroneous court ruling. These *mishnayot* appear to endorse an approach quite different from that taken in the *sugya* of the rebellious elder. The Mishnah establishes that there are situations in which not only is there no obligation to obey an erroneous court ruling, but there is actually an obligation to refuse to obey.

### 3.1 The prohibition against acting upon an erroneous ruling

The first chapter of mHorayot assumes as a given that it is forbidden to obey an erroneous court ruling, and addresses the punishment incurred for acting upon such a ruling:

12 See bSanhedrin 88b and Maimonides, *Code*, Laws concerning Rebels 4:1.

> If the court handed down a ruling [entailing the] transgressing of any of the commandments in the Torah, and an individual went and acted upon its ruling ... he is exempt, because he relied on the court. If the court handed down a ruling, and one of its members knew that it had made a mistake, or a student himself qualified to rule went and acted upon its ruling [knowing that it had made a mistake] ... he is liable, because he did not rely on the court [i.e., he did not have available to him the excuse that he relied on the court]. This is the general rule: whoever relies on himself is liable, and whoever relies on the court is exempt.
>
> mHorayot 1:1

Jewish law distinguishes between one who transgresses under duress (*anus*) and one who transgresses inadvertently (*shogeg*). In both cases, the transgression is not intentional. The latter's transgression is the result of a deficiency in either his knowledge of the law or his perception of reality. One who transgresses under duress is generally completely exempt from punishment and any other legal sanctions, whereas the inadvertent transgressor often must atone for his transgression by bringing a sin-offering, though he does not incur the punishment meted out for a transgression committed willfully. The Mishnah raises the question of whether one who acts in accordance with an erroneous court ruling is required to bring a sin-offering, or is deemed completely exempt from doing so. In determining the answer, the Mishnah distinguishes between a sage and a layman. A layman who innocently follows the court's ruling is exempt from bringing a sacrifice "because he relied on the court." In effect, he can be viewed as someone who was forced (*anus*) to act contrary to the law, since his reliance on the court ruling was reasonable, given that it can be assumed that the court will hand down the correct ruling.

The sage, however, who knows that the court's ruling is mistaken, is not exempt from bringing a sin-offering. since he is not 'forced' to act contrary to the law. He should have used his own judgment, and refused to obey the court's erroneous ruling.

Thus, the Mishnah is clearly premised on the assumption that there is no obligation to obey an erroneous court ruling, and in certain circumstances doing so is indefensible. These circumstances will be discussed below.

### 3.2 Degrees of exemption

In certain cases, those who have complied with an erroneous court ruling do not incur any legal consequences, and are deemed exempt from punishment or the sin-offering requirement. In the Tannaitic and Amoraic sources, different accounts of who is exempt are presented. As we saw, the Mishnah declares that a layman who obeys an erroneous court ruling is completely exempt, as he is not expected to apply his own critical judgment to rulings handed down by the court, inasmuch as the court is authorized to render such decisions. In contrast, in obeying the court's ruling without exercising his own judgment, a sage, who knows the law, errs.

The Talmud takes a more severe approach with regard to both the sage who obeys an erroneous ruling, and a layman who does so. With regard to the former, the Talmud asks why the Mishnah considers him to have transgressed unintentionally (*shogeg*) rather than willfully (*mezid*). Presumably, given his knowledge that the ruling was mistaken, he knew it was forbidden to carry out the act in question. Therefore, the Talmud claims, this sage should receive the full punishment meted out for the act in question, and it ought not suffice for him to simply bring a sin-offering, the sanction applicable in the case of an inadvertent transgressor. "It is a case where he knew [the said act] is prohibited, but erred with regard to the commandment of hearkening unto the words of the Sages" (bHorayot 2b).

In other words, the Talmud is suggesting that the mishnaic law is restricted to the case of a scholar—someone well-versed in the intricacies of the law, and in possession of professional legal judgment—who is indeed aware that the court ruling is mistaken, but errs in his understanding of the obligation to obey the court, taking it to be absolute, and thus to apply even to erroneous rulings. This interpretation would render most cases of erroneous action in accordance with a court ruling—where the individual in question is not a layman but someone capable of issuing legal rulings—instances of willful transgression.

Thus, it appears that the obligation to follow the High Court's ruling is by no means absolute, and in practice, one who knows that the court has erred is forbidden to defer to its ruling.

The Babylonian Talmud also strengthens the law articulated in mHorayot with respect to the layman who follows an erroneous ruling. Adducing a baraita, the Talmud claims that although the opinion put forward in mHorayot is indeed upheld by some Tannaim, it is only a minority opinion. The majority opinion does require this individual to bring a sin-offering. Regarding the law in mHorayot, the Amora R. Judah said the following in the name of Samuel:

> This [that the layman is exempt from having to bring a sin-offering] is the opinion of R. Judah, but the Rabbis said: "An individual who acts in accordance with the [erroneous] ruling of the court is obligated [to bring a sin-offering]."
>
> bHorayot 2b

We have seen, then, that the Talmud tends to strictness in its interpretation of the law governing one who acts on an erroneous court ruling. The layman, who the Mishnah considers to have acted under duress, is regarded by the Talmud as one who erred inadvertently, and is thus obligated to bring a sin-offering. And the scholar, who the Mishnah considers to have erred inadvertently, is regarded by the Talmud as one who acted willfully.

### 3.3 Types of rulings

The scope of the obligation to obey court rulings can also be viewed from another perspective: the type of ruling and the nature of the error involved. The law does not regard all errors in the same way. mHorayot 1:3 addresses the **court's** obligation to bring a sacrifice called the "bullock [brought] because of the hidden thing" (*par heelem davar*) if it inadvertently issues an erroneous decision. It also addresses the type of error referred to in the mishnaic passage we have been discussing, mHorayot 1:1.

In a situation where most or all of the community acted upon an erroneous court ruling and transgressed, they are exempt from having to bring a sin-offering. Instead, the court is obligated to bring a sin-offering called a "communal bullock [brought] because of the hidden thing" (*par heelem davar shel tzibur*) or "bullock brought for transgressing any one of the precepts" (*par haba al kol hamitzvot*). The Rabbis derived this law from the biblical verse: "And if the whole congregation of Israel shall err, the thing being hid from the eyes of the assembly, and do any of the things which the Lord hath commanded not to be done, and are guilty: when the sin wherein they have sinned is known, then the assembly shall offer a young bullock for a sin-offering, and bring it before the tent of meeting" (Lev. 4:13–14). In essence, the offering brought by the communal leaders exempts the individuals within the community from having to bring a sin-offering.

The types of mistaken rulings that obligate the court to bring such an offering are as follows:

> If the court issued a ruling uprooting an entire percept, saying that there is no precept of marital separation [during menstruation] (*nida*) in the Torah; there is no [precept of the] Sabbath in the Torah; there is no [precept prohibiting] idol worship in the Torah—they are exempt. If they issued a ruling annulling part and sustaining part, they are liable. How so? If they said, "There is a law of the menstruant in the Torah, but if [a husband] lay with [his wife] while she maintains a day-to-day observation [but has not immersed in the mikve], he is exempt; there is a [precept of the] Sabbath in the Torah, but one who carries something from a private domain to a public domain[13] is exempt; there is [a precept prohibiting] idolatry in the Torah, but one who merely bows down [to an idol, but does not prostrate himself] is exempt—they [the court] are liable, for it is said, "the thing being hid" (Lev. 4:13)—some thing, but not the entire precept.
>
> mHorayot 1:3

13 Carrying objects from a private to a public domain is prohibited on the Sabbath.

In contrast to what we might expect, the Mishnah establishes that the court is liable to bring a sin-offering in cases where its ruling was inconsistent with one of the component details of a precept, but not in cases where it negated the whole thrust of a precept. How is this rather paradoxical position to be explained? Apparently, a ruling that negates the whole thrust of a precept does not obligate the court to bring a sin-offering because it is so radical that it is not considered a bona fide court ruling at all. Conversely, one who follows such a ruling is obligated to bring a sin-offering because he ought to have known that such a ruling was not to be obeyed. But in the case of a ruling that negates a component detail of a precept, it is plausible that a layman might err and comply with the ruling. Should that transpire, he is exempt, and it is the court that must bring the sin-offering.

There is, then, a parallelism between the distinctions established in this Mishnah and the distinctions set out in the Mishnah of the rebellious elder discussed earlier. We saw that a rebellious elder is punished if he rules that a Rabbinic law is to be transgressed, but not if he rules that a law explicitly set out in the Torah is to be transgressed. Rashi explains that the latter is not considered a bona fide ruling because it is inherently repudiated: "This is not considered a ruling, since one can go and read it in the schoolhouse." Here, in mHorayot, we find the same basic principle: a court ruling that is radically and patently erroneous, such as a ruling that uproots in its entirety one of the precepts of the Torah, is not considered a bona fide ruling. Those who act upon such a ruling are obligated to bring a sin-offering. In the case of a less serious mistake by the court, however—though here too, the ruling is unlawful and not to be complied with—an individual's claim that he acted on the ruling in good faith is accepted.

## 4 Compatibility of the Mishnah in Horayot and the Mishnah of the rebellious elder

Analyzing the types of judicial error referred to in the two main mishnaic passages we have examined, mHorayot and the law of rebellious elder, is instructive. These passages deal with judicial error in different circumstances. mHorayot deals with instances where court rulings are erroneous in an absolute sense. The Mishnah uses the term "mistake" (*taut*), indicating that the error can be proven.[14] Hence the continuation of the first chapter of mHorayot addresses the question of a court that recognizes its mistake.

14 An interesting question that the Mishnah does not address is how it came about that the court issued such a patently erroneous ruling. One explanation invokes the historical background: "This Mishnah is talking about a court, composed of Hellenists during the time of the evil Antiochus, that permitted things that were specifically forbidden in the Torah" (Sifra Devei Rav [Finkelstein edition], vol. 1, 203). Nevertheless, in the Talmud, the discussion is preserved without reference to its historical context.

It speaks of an objective error that is clear and unequivocal, and therefore invalidates the ruling. Moreover, the scenario under consideration is one where the court is not seeking to decide an interpretive controversy or an open legal question. On the contrary, the court is addressing a legal matter regarding which the law has long been decided, and revisiting the law would exceed the court's authority. In other words, the cases in question are cases where the court's role is solely to apply the decided and unequivocal law, as expressed in available legal sources, to a given situation. Given this scenario, mHorayot establishes that erroneous court rulings have no validity, and one who hears of such a ruling should refuse to comply with it. It follows that the court itself, having recognized and retracted its mistake, is obligated to bring a sin-offering for its transgression.

In contrast, the Mishnah of the rebellious elder addresses a situation in which a controversy is brought to the court for a decision. Each side to the controversy is convinced of the correctness of its position, but cannot unambiguously prove it. The point of contention is an open legal question that can, in theory, be decided either way; though the court issues its ruling, the rebellious elder contends that the question should not have have been decided as the court decided it.

It is significant that mSanhedrin's description of the process by which it is determined that a sage is a rebellious elder describes a scenario where the legal point at hand is an open legal question, a precedent-setting issue on which a definitive and binding decision has not yet been rendered. The Sages present different solutions, based either on tradition or logical arguments: "Thus I expounded and thus my fellows expounded, thus I taught and thus my fellows taught." The open question is brought to the High Court for a decision. From this point on, the High Court's decision obligates all members of the judiciary, even those who initially presented an opposing opinion. A sage who refuses to adopt the court's decision is deemed a "rebellious elder," and his punishment is death. He is not punished for attacking the law itself, but for undermining the court's status as an institution with the authority to decide the law.

Now an open legal question is not necessarily an interpretive controversy, and the controversy could arise due to the existence of opposing traditions, or because although the court has a tradition–"If they [the court] had heard [a tradition regarding the matter]"—this tradition was hidden and did not become part of the halakhic corpus, the corpus of decided and well-known law. In the latter situation, the controversy conducted by the Sages is essentially a mechanism that transforms the hidden tradition into a binding component of the halakhic corpus.

It is important to remember that the High Court in Jerusalem is not an ordinary court, and functions not just as a judicial body, but also as a legislative body. Hence the matters brought before it are often precedent-setting questions that cannot be left in limbo and must be decided.

Not all contemporary theorists of Jewish law interpret the two mishnaic passages we have examined—the rebellious elder and mHorayot—as **complementary** sources that together offer a comprehensive answer to the question of the duty to defer to legal authority, as has been argued here. Those who challenge the account presented here claim that the passages represent two **opposing** approaches to the obligation to defer to legal authority, approaches that compete with each other in the rabbinical literature. This position is expressed in the following passage:

> What makes an individual or an institution an authority? Several different answers to this question can be discerned in the Jewish tradition. One approach suggests what might be called a 'knowledge' model of halakhic authority. This model assumes that the validation of authority emerges from specific knowledge of a clearly defined area that gives the authority an advantage over those who do not have such knowledge.... The premise of this approach is that the Sages' authority is based only on knowledge, hence when contrary to the truth, their rulings need not be obeyed. Moreover, this truth is not the exclusive province of the Sages, but freely knowable by everyone, since it is that which determines the veracity of the Sages' ruling. In truth, the Sages' authority is not grounded in powers granted them to create and establish the law as they wish, but rather, its source is the Torah, which they know. Therefore, where they make a mistake, obedience to their ruling is a mistake, and is even forbidden. And we find this idea expressed explicitly in ... mHorayot....
>
> But the Jewish tradition also suggests another model of halakhic authority, the 'command' model. According to this model, a legal authority is granted the prerogative to command, to issue directives that prescribe acts be carried out, and to subject members of the community to his authority. The latter have an absolute obligation to obey the rulings of the authorities. On the command model, authority is not necessarily based on the specific knowledge base of the authority, but rather on the power granted to individuals or institutions to establish obligatory societal norms. Therefore, in cases where it appears to those under this authority that the authority figure has erred, they still have an obligation to obey.[15]

Those who uphold the thesis that there is an unresolved tension in the Talmud between two opposing stances on obedience to legal rulings often cite, in support of their claim, a purported corresponding tension in traditional Rabbinic exegesis of the verse "thou shalt not turn aside from the sentence which they shall declare unto you, neither to the right hand, nor to the left" (Deut. 17:11).

15 A. Sagi and Z. Safrai, *Between Authority and Autonomy in Jewish Tradition* (Hebrew), (Tel Aviv: 1997), 10–13.

The Jerusalem Talmud suggests that the verse be read as asserting that since one who comes before the court can distinguish between right and left, he is **forbidden** to follow an erroneous ruling:

> Is it possible that if they say to you regarding right that it is left and regarding left that it is right, you should listen to them? Therefore Scripture teaches that one is to go right and left–when they say to you regarding right that it is right, and regarding left, that it is left.
>
> jHorayot 1:1 (45d)

A different exegesis reaches the opposite conclusion, namely, that the verse seems to establish an absolute obligation to defer to legal authority:

> "Neither to the right hand, nor to the left" (Deut. 17:11)–even if they show you [lit., show to your eyes, *marim beeinekha*] regarding right that it is left, and regarding left that it is right, listen to them.
>
> Sifre Deuteronomy, Shoftim, 154 (Finkelstein edition, p. 207)

This Midrash uses an uncommon turn of phrase: "even if they show to your eyes," giving rise to a number of variant readings in various MS.[16]

a. The reading in *Yalkut Shimoni*, Oxford manuscript: "even if they **rule** (*morin*) regarding right that it is left."
b. The reading in the Oxford MS of Sifre: "even if they show (*marim*) regarding right that it is left."
c. The reading in *Pesikta Zutra*: "even if it **seems** ("*dome beeinekha*") in your eyes regarding right that it is left"
d. The reading in Song of Songs Rabbah (Vilna edition, parasha 1, "*ki tovim dodekha miyayin*," 2): "even if they **say** to you (*sheyomru lekha*) regarding right that it is left."

Despite these attempts to harmonize, by means of textual emendation, what seem to be expressions of opposing views as to the duty to comply with court rulings, it is difficult to reconcile these Rabbinic exegeses. Nevertheless, another contemporary scholar has convincingly argued that there is no contradiction between them, as they refer to two different situations:

> It seems that no one paid attention to one particular word in the phrasing of the baraita in the Jerusalem Talmud: "one is **to go** (*lalekhet*) right and left." In the verse (Deut. 17:11), it does not say that. Rather, it says: "the sentence which they shall declare unto you, neither to the right hand, nor to the left." In fact, this word [*lalekhet*] supports a

16 These are listed in the Finkelstein edition of Sifre.

> different explanation of the matter, and in particular, a different source, namely, Deuteronomy 28:14: "And you shall not turn aside from any of the words that I command you this day, to the right hand, or to the left, to go (*lalekhet*) after other gods to serve them." The explanation is that the exegesis in the Jerusalem Talmud addresses the situation where "the court handed down a ruling [entailing the] transgressing of any of the commandments in the Torah," namely, "the words that I command you this day." In this situation, one is not to hearken to the words of the Sages unless they rule that right is right and left is left, and there is no doubt as to what is right and what is left. The question is whether "to go" to the right or the left [i.e., to deviate from the true law, as the court has done]—and [the answer is that] one should not turn aside from the words [of the Torah]. On the other hand, in the law of the rebellious elder (Deut. 17:11) [i.e., the dictum in the Sifre], the discussion relates to "the sentence which they shall declare unto you," that is, the pronouncements spoken by the Sages, which, regardless of whether they are right or left, are not to be turned aside [i.e., deviated] from.[17]

This resolution of the apparently contradictory approaches to compliance with court rulings distinguishes between the dictum in the Jerusalem Talmud, which addresses the case where a court rules that a law from the Torah is to be transgressed, stating that such a ruling is not to be obeyed, and the dictum in the Sifre, which speaks of a ruling handed down by the Sages, stating that even if it appears to be erroneous, such a ruling is indeed to be obeyed.[18] This distinction corresponds, to a considerable extent, to the distinction drawn in this chapter between the Mishnah in Horayot, which deals with a court ruling that is patently erroneous insofar as it is contrary to the decided law, and the law of the rebellious elder, which deals with a court ruling that decides an open legal question.

## 5 Interim summary

The Mishnah seeks to outline the role and authority of the High Court in Jerusalem. Its point of departure is that the Torah, like any text, is in need of interpretation, and the interpretive process is likely to lead to controversy. The High Court is given the authority to resolve controversies and create uniform law that is binding on all. A sage who directs others to contravene a High Court ruling is a 'rebellious elder' who is liable to be put to death, as he has threatened the court's stability and authority. Yet the Mishnah

17 S.Z. Havlin, "On 'literary redaction' as a basis for periodization in Jewish law" (Hebrew), in Shamma Friedman (ed.), *Saul Lieberman Memorial Volume* (Jerusalem and New York: 1993), 164.

18 See Ben-Menahem, n. 11 above, 165–73.

also makes a strong statement as to the limits of judicial authority and the obligation to obey court rulings. The court has incontrovertible authority only where the law is in need of definitive interpretation. Where the law is clear and is not in need of interpretation, and a court ruling undermines the law—the situation discussed in mHorayot—the Mishnah concludes that the ruling is invalid and should not be obeyed.

In mHorayot, examples are adduced to establish the principle that a court ruling contrary to an uncontroversial law is not a valid ruling but a mistake, and not to be acted upon. The biblical idiom that serves as a prooftext for mHorayot is "and the thing be hid" (Lev. 4:13), or in the mishnaic formulation, "and one of its members knew that they had made a mistake." These locutions presuppose that there is indeed an **objective legal truth**, and what is needed to bring it to light is **knowledge**, not interpretive acumen. One can know it, forget it, or be mistaken about it, but its meaning is not in question. Tractate Horayot does not deal with the obligation to obey court rulings, but rather, with the results of mistaken obedience. An erroneous court ruling has no validity, hence there is no obligation to heed it. The only question is whether one who complies with such a ruling in good faith is deemed to have acted under duress (exempting him from bringing a sin-offering) or inadvertently (obligating him to bring a sin-offering).

## 6 Medieval understandings of the obligation to comply with court rulings

Although we have cast doubt on the claim of some scholars that the **Rabbinic** sources reflect profound disagreement over the obligation to comply with court rulings, it is clear that among the medieval commentators, there was indeed such a disagreement. Some saw the obligation to defer to legal authority as far-reaching, others sought to limit the duty to defer and broaden the space for judicial discretion. There are also a number of intermediate positions. The different views are all anchored in the Rabbinic sources, some of which we explored above. Let us now take a closer look at some medieval understandings of the obligation to defer to the court.

### 6.1 Maimonides

Maimonides' position appears to echo the Rabbis' position as presented above.

On the one hand, Maimonides sets down a broad and far-reaching obligation to comply with rulings of the High Court. In his *Book of Precepts*, Maimonides articulates this obligation as follows:

> We are commanded to hearken to the High Court and do everything they command, be it a prohibition or a dispensation. And in this regard

> there is no difference between that which they decide on the basis of reasoning, and that which they derive by way of the exegetical principles by which the Torah is expounded, or that which they agree reflects a secret of the Torah, or for that matter, anything that they take to be correct and to strengthen the Torah. All [that they mandate], we are obligated to hearken to and to carry out, and to uphold what they say and not transgress it.
>
> Maimonides, *Book of Precepts*, positive commandment 174[19]

In the continuation of his remarks, Maimonides adduces Sifre Deuteronomy as a supporting allusion (*asmakhta*), citing the sentence that precedes the one quoted above:

> And the language of the Sifre is: "'And according to the judgment which they shall tell thee, thou shalt do" (Deut. 17:11)—this is a positive commandment.'"

Yet it seems that Maimonides takes the opposite position elsewhere:

> If the court ruled that it is permissible to eat all of the *heilev* [prohibited fat] of the stomach, and one person in the community knew that they had erred and that the stomach *heilev* was prohibited, and he ate it in reliance on the court's ruling, because they thought that heeding the court even when it erred was a commanded act—the one who ate it is obligated to bring a fixed[20] sin-offering for having eaten.... What case are we talking about? When the one who knew that they erred was a sage or a student who had reached the level of being able to issue rulings. But if it was an ordinary person, he is exempt, since his knowledge of forbidden things is not certain.
>
> *Code*, Laws concerning Offerings for Transgressions Committed through Error, 13:5

The relationship between these two Maimonidean passages seems to mirror that between the Rabbinic ruling in mHorayot and the law of the rebellious elder, as explained above. In the *Book of Precepts*, in which Maimonides establishes the obligation to obey court rulings, he is speaking of an open legal question for which there is no definitive answer in the halakhic sources. The obligation to obey exists where the court has rendered its opinion on an interpretive question: "that which they decide on the basis of reasoning, and that which they derive by way of the exegetical principles by which the Torah is expounded," and so on. By

19 Maimonides repeats this point in detail in *Code*, Laws concerning Rebels 1:1–2.

20 I.e., a sin-offering with a fixed value, as opposed to an offering that varied in accordance with the offerer's means.

contrast, in the *Mishne Torah*'s Laws concerning Offerings for Transgressions Committed through Error, Maimonides is addressing situations similar to those discussed in tractate Horayot, namely, where the court has made a clear and unequivocal legal mistake, and it is therefore forbidden to act in accordance with the court's ruling. It is no coincidence that in the Laws concerning Offerings for Transgressions Committed through Error, Maimonides adduces clear-cut examples similar to those given in mHorayot, for instance, "If the court ruled that it is permissible to eat all of the *heilev* [prohibited fat] of the stomach." For no court has—nor could it have—the authority to permit something that is forbidden by the Torah. The law constitutes the limit of the court's authority, and no court has the authority to diverge from it. In a situation where one knows that the court's ruling is mistaken, one is forbidden to comply with it.

### 6.2 Nahmanides

Nahmanides is widely viewed as having set out a comprehensive, well-ordered and cohesive position as to the authority of the court and the nature of its rulings. He is seen as an unyielding advocate of the court's institutional authority. It has even been claimed that Nahmanides put forward a forced interpretation of mHorayot because it was compatible with this outlook.[21]

With regard to the passage in Deuteronomy that establishes the obligation to defer to court rulings, Nahmanides discusses the question of whether there is an obligation to comply with a mistaken ruling. Citing the Sifre's exegesis of the biblical verse "you shall not turn aside from the sentence which they shall declare unto you, neither to the right hand, nor to the left," Nahmanides made the following oft-quoted comment:

> Even if in your heart, you know that they are mistaken, and it is clear in your eyes, just as you know right from left, you must do as they command you. And do not say, 'how can I eat this completely forbidden fat,' or 'how can I kill this innocent person,' but say, 'so the Master who commands the commandments has commanded me, to observe all His commandments as I will be directed by those who stand before Him in the place that He shall choose; and He gave me the Torah subject to their opinion—even if they are mistaken.'
>
> Nahmanides, *Commentary on the Torah*, Deuteronomy 17:11[22]

21 G. Blidstein, "'Even if he tells you right is left': the validity of moral authority in the *halakha* and it limitations" in M. Beer (ed.) *Studies in Halakha and Jewish Thought Presented to Rabbi Emanuel Rackman* (Hebrew), (Ramat Gan: 1994), 230.

22 Note that other Early Authorities take this same position, e.g., Rabbenu Nissim, *Drashot Haran*, lecture 11; *Sefer Hahinukh*, commandment 496; Maharal of Prague, *Gur Arye*, Deuteronomy 17:11.

Thus, Nahmanides' view is unequivocal: it is obligatory to heed the court's ruling in every instance, "even if they are mistaken." Note that one of the examples used by Nahmanides to demonstrate the obligation to obey court rulings, the ruling that forbidden fat is to be eaten, is similar to the rulings mentioned in mHorayot, which expressly **forbids** acting upon an erroneous ruling.

Nahmanides presents two arguments for his position, arguments that to some extent contradict each other. The first invokes apprehension about the danger of rifts and discord that might be engendered by controversy. Granting every individual the authority to act in accordance with his own judgment could cause the societal fabric, and halakhic uniformity, to unravel. To forestall such a situation, it was established that the court was to be the authoritative interpreter of the Torah, and that compliance with its rulings was obligatory:

> For the Torah was given to us in writing, and it is known that all the opinions that derive from it will not be the same, and controversies will proliferate, and the Torah will become many Torahs. And Scripture definitively set down the law that we must heed the High Court that stands before God in the place that He shall choose.... For He gave the Torah subject to their opinion, even if in your eyes it is as if they interchange right and left.

The second argument takes a different tack. Nahmanides claims that one must assume that the court is correct because its members are infallible:

> And even more so, you should think that they say of right that it is right, for the spirit of God rests on those who serve in His holy place, and He will not abandon His righteous ones. They are always protected from mistakes and failure.

There is an important difference between these rationales. Consider the case of a sage who sought to teach—strictly as a matter of theory—an opinion contrary to the court's ruling. If Nahmanides' second rationale for compliance with court rulings is deemed correct, we would expect that the sage would not even teach the rejected opinion as a theoretical possibility, stressing that it was not to be put into practice. Whereas if we uphold the first rationale, teaching a dissenting view would be permissible as long as the sage expounding it emphasizes the distinction between theory and practice and does not instruct others to act on the dissenting view, contrary to the court's ruling.

An anecdote from tractate Rosh Hashana of the Mishnah provides a good illustration of the practical import of the first rationale. Before presenting the story itself, some background is useful. During the Tannaitic period, the beginning of each new month (*rosh hodesh*) (and thus the calendar and festivals occurring in that month), were determined by a judicial process in which witnesses testified that they had seen the new moon, the re-emergent lunar crescent. The Mishnah describes a controversy that arose from an incident in which Rabban Gamaliel accepted testimony relating to the new moon, and R. Joshua thought that it should be rejected:

> It once happened that two [witnesses] came and said, "We saw [the new moon] in the east in the morning and in the west in the evening." R. Johanan b. Nuri said, "They are false witnesses!" When they came to Yavne, Rabban Gamaliel accepted them [i.e., their testimony]. And another two [witnesses] came and said, "We saw it at its proper time, but by [the next] night, it was not visible," and Rabban Gamaliel accepted them. R. Dosa b. Horkinos said, "They are false witnesses! Can they testify about a woman that she gave birth, and on the morrow her belly is between her teeth[23]?" R. Joshua said to him, "I see [the point of] your words." Rabban Gamaliel sent for him, "I order you to come before me, with your staff and with your money, on the day on which Yom Kippur falls, according to your calculation." R. Akiva went and found him in distress; he said to him, "I can adduce [Scriptural] proof that whatever Rabban Gamaliel has ruled is [valid]." .... He [R. Joshua] took his staff and his money in hand, and went to Yavne to Rabban Gamaliel on the day on which, according to his calculation, Yom Kippur fell. Rabban Gamaliel stood up and kissed him on the head, and said to him, "Come in peace, my master and my student! My master in wisdom, and my student because you accepted my words."
>
> mRosh Hashana 2:8–9

From the way the incident is reported, it is clear that R. Joshua did not accept Rabban Gamaliel's opinion in principle. Nevertheless, at the level of practice, that is, in the way he actually conducted himself, he chose to defer to Rabban Gamaliel's ruling. Moreover, the Mishnah indicates that R. Joshua was, to use the talmudic expression, greater in wisdom, hence his opinion was probably the correct one, yet even so, R. Gamaliel's view was deemed authoritative. It appears that the Mishnah is endorsing the idea of obedience to court rulings in the realm of conduct, but does not demand that the court's position be accepted on the theoretical level as well.

Returning to Nahmanides, it remains to be determined whether the two rationales are indeed distinct and to some degree inconsistent with each other, or whether the second rationale is simply an attempt on Nahmanides' part to reassure those who fear that in following the court they might not be acting in accordance with the 'true' law. They need not fear, he may be

23 I.e., she is noticeably pregnant.

declaring, since the possibility of error is minimal, given that those on whom "the spirit of God rests" are not prone to err.[24]

Regardless of whether the rationales are distinct, Nahmanides' position on the duty to obey the court is problematic. First, it is difficult to reconcile with mHorayot. How can we reconcile Nahmanides' teaching that it is permissible to eat meat that the court rules kosher though we have certain knowledge that it is forbidden fat, with mHorayot, which teaches that under those circumstances it is forbidden to act upon the court's ruling? Sensitive to this problem, Nahmanides addressed it elsewhere as well. In that context, he offers a different and novel interpretation of the *sugya* in Horayot. He still maintains that the obligation to defer to legal authority is broad and far-reaching, but notes that a basic condition, established in mHorayot, must be met:

> But there is a condition, which can be discerned by one who looks carefully at the first chapter of mHorayot. And it is that if, at the time of the Sanhedrin, there was a sage who was competent to issue rulings, and the High Court ruled that something was permitted and he thought that they erred in their ruling.... he must appear before them and present his claims to them, and they must debate the matter with him. And if most of them agree to reject his opinion, and find fault with his reasoning, he must retract, and afterwards, after they have removed him and rendered a decision as to his claim, conduct himself in accordance with their opinion. This is what follows from those laws [of tractate Horayot]. But in any case, he must accept their opinion after the final decision.
>
> *Hasagot Haramban*, *Sefer Hamitzvot*, root 1

For a court ruling to be binding on a sage who disagrees with it, even when he believes that the judges have made an unequivocal objective error, they must have considered and discussed his claim. Only then does the ruling bind the sage, even if he continues to oppose it. But if his view has not been considered, he is not obligated to comply with the court's ruling.

According to Nahmanides, then, compliance with court rulings is obligatory, even according to mHorayot. But this is so only if the court has considered dissenting opinions. If an opinion has not been deliberated on by the court, its ruling does not obligate the sage who holds the dissenting view. Some contemporary scholars take this 'concession' by Nahmanides to be rather forced, and driven by a desire to reconcile the two Rabbinic sources, mHorayot and the law of the rebellious elder.[25] We maintain, however, that the novel condition introduced by Nahmanides is consistent with his advocacy of strong judicial authority. Though compliance is

24 See Blidstein, n. 21 above, 222.
25 Ibid., 230.

obligatory, if court rulings are to be valid, any opposing views must have been considered and refuted, for if the court has not weighed the opinion of a sage who disagrees with its ruling, we cannot say that the court has indeed rejected the dissenting opinion.

## 6.3 The Riva and the Abarbanel: distinguishing erroneous legal rulings from acceptable judicial divergence from the law

The Tosafist R. Isaac b. Asher (Riva) takes a very different approach to the question of the obligation to defer to the court. His point of departure is the impossibility of an obligation to follow an erroneous ruling. In response to Rashi's comment (based on the Sifre) that one is obligated to obey the court even if it rules that right is left, the Riva retorts: "And do we listen to a sage who says that something impure is pure and something prohibited is permitted?"

The Riva makes an innovative distinction. He maintains that we must distinguish between two types of court rulings. When the court makes a mistake in applying a law from the Torah, there is no obligation to follow the mistaken ruling. One who believes that the court's ruling is inconsistent with Torah law should not heed it, but rather, do what he deems correct. But when the court **knowingly** deviates from the Torah law on the strength of the legislative authority with which it is endowed, it is obligatory to follow the court's ruling, even if at first glance it appears contrary to Torah law:

> Necessarily, the solution [to the paradoxical nature of Rashi's comment] is that we must apply it [only] to the decrees (*gezerot*) and enactments (*takanot*) of the Sages: "regarding right that it is left"–such as [the injunction that] blowing the shofar does not supersede the Sabbath[26] … "and regarding left that it is right"–such as adding to those with whom sexual relations are prohibited.[27]

In the Riva's opinion, the Sifre's exegesis, which Rashi upholds, does not address the obligation to comply with erroneous rulings. Rather, it deals with rulings the court hands down on the basis of its legitimate authority to deviate from Torah law. These rulings might appear mistaken to one who is unaware that the court has this authority, but are not, in fact, mistaken. In essence, the Riva construes the dictum as addressing, not erroneous court rulings, but the court's legislative authority to deviate

26 "The blowing of the shofar does not supersede the Sabbath"—The blowing of the shofar is a central commandment of the Rosh Hashana holiday. Despite its centrality, and despite the fact that the Torah permits the blowing of the shofar on the Sabbath, the Sages decreed that when Rosh Hashana falls on the Sabbath, the shofar is not blown.

27 "Adding to those with whom sexual relations are prohibited"—the Torah defines a specific group of relatives with whom sexual relations are prohibited (*arayot*): one's mother, father, child, sibling, etc. The Sages added additional relatives.

from Torah law by way of decrees and enactments. On his interpretation, the court's authority to set norms that, in effect, deviate from Torah law, is anchored in the Sifre's exegesis of Deuteronomy 17:11. The Riva is thus **limiting** the scope of the obligation to comply with erroneous court rulings, asserting that one ought **not** heed a ruling that something impure is pure or something prohibited is permitted.

A somewhat different approach is taken by the Abarbanel, a renowned late medieval commentator. The Abarbanel addresses a classic jurisprudential problem: the relationship between laws, which are inherently general, and their implementation in particular circumstances.[28] The central dilemma was already formulated by Aristotle, who noted that the general law cannot possibly cover all possible situations to which it is intended to apply. This could give rise to a miscarriage of justice in certain cases, even though it is clear that the law itself is good and appropriate in a general sense. The Abarbanel upholds the Aristotelian view that in a particular case where the general law is not appropriate, judges are permitted to deviate from the law, so that they can achieve a just outcome in the particular circumstances of the case before them. He argues that the emphasis on obedience to court rulings is motivated by the desire to reinforce the authority of judges who find it necessary, in particular cases, to deviate from the law as written in order to avert an unjust outcome. Though it might appear, he explains, that such judges have deviated from the law and therefore erred, and that the legally-correct decision would have been the very opposite of what they decided, one is obliged to comply with their ruling. Judges, Abarbanel explained, take into account not only the relevant legal principles, but also the unique circumstances of the case under consideration:

> And on this issue, [the Torah] warned that one should "not turn aside from the sentence which they shall declare unto thee, neither to the right hand, nor to the left." This means to say: even though they went outside the letter of the general law and shifted it to the left, or if the correct outcome was to the left, they issued a decree to the right, one may not turn aside from their decision. For as to that which they have decreed in this case, even though in relation to the general principles it appears to [render] right left and left right, nevertheless, in terms of the truth of this particular case and the nature of this localized matter, they are only saying of right that it is right and of left that it is left, for that is what it is appropriate to do, and nothing else.
>
> *Abarbanel*, Deuteronomy 17

We thus see that, like the Riva, the Abarbanel takes neither the biblical verse nor the Sifre's exegesis to apply to an erroneous court ruling. He

28 See Chapter Eight below, "Equity."

does not construe these sources as applicable to a situation where someone has knowledge of the factors taken into consideration by the court, and on that basis contends that the court erred, but rather, as applicable to a situation where someone has knowledge of the law, but not of the particular circumstances of the case in question. The Abarbanel claims that such an individual must obey the court ruling even if it is not in harmony with the law on the books, for in deciding the law the judge must demonstrate not only mastery of the relevant legal principles, but also sensitivity to the unique features of the case in question.

### 6.4 R. Issachar Eilenburg

Later, in the seventeenth and eighteenth centuries, we find a different approach to the problem of erroneous rulings, an approach less enthusiastic about categorical deference to the legal establishment. This approach views the individual as obligated to use his own independent judgment to critically evaluate the correctness of court rulings. Those he deems erroneous are not to be acted upon.

One of the chief advocates of this position was R. Issachar Ber Eilenburg, author of the *Beer Sheva* commentary on the Talmud. In explaining mHorayot, which asserts that an erroneous ruling is not to be followed, R. Eilenburg points out the contradiction between this law and the Sifre's exegesis of Deuteronomy 17:11, which, as we saw, appears to call for obedience even to a ruling wherein the judges declare that right is left and left is right. To reconcile this apparent inconsistency, he offers a novel reading of the Sifre:

> That which was stated in the Sifre, "even if they show you [lit., show to your eyes] regarding left that it is right," can be explained as follows: even if you think in your heart, according to your own assessment, that they erred in judgment, and ruled of left that it was right, but do not know for certain that they made a mistake in the law. And the Sifre's formulation was precise–"even if they show to **your** eyes," and so on. And that which we learned in the baraita that I quoted above–"Is it possible that if they say to you regarding right that it is left and regarding left that it is right, you should listen to them? Therefore Scripture teaches that one is to go right and left–when they say to you regarding right that it is right and regarding left that it is left" (jHorayot 1:1 (45d))—this means, [do not act upon their ruling] when you know with certainty that they made a mistake in the law by permitting something forbidden; that is my opinion.[29]
>
> *Beer Sheva*, Horayot 2:2 s.v. *kehai gavna mezid hu*

29 See also *Peirush Amudei Yerushalayim*, jHorayot 1:1 (45d) s.v. *kehada detani.*

On R. Eilenburg's interpretation, the Sifre is not speaking of one who **knows with certainty** that the court has erred, but of one who **suspects** this is so, but does not know with certainty. R. Eilenburg bases this exegesis on the formulation: "even if they show to your eyes," taking this to refer to subjective conjecture that the court may be wrong, rather than objective, unequivocal knowledge. According to R. Eilenburg, the Sifre asserts that one who merely **thinks** that a ruling is erroneous is to defer to the judges and their discretion. However, if one has come to a firm conclusion that the court has erred, this overrides the obligation to defer to the court's ruling.

## 7 Erroneous lower court rulings

Thus far, we have discussed instances in which the High Court in Jerusalem issued a determinative ruling as to the law. Such determinations are not, obviously, the sole or even the primary activity of the legal system. The legal system is also called upon to adjudicate cases involving conflict between two parties. Decisions in such cases are generally not issued by the courts of higher instance, often called the Supreme Court or High Court, but rather the lower courts, usually local courts that address practical matters as opposed to matters of principle. This is a particularly important distinction in the context of the Jewish legal system, which, for the greater part of its history, has not had a functioning high court. Judicial decisions can, therefore, be issued only by courts of lower instance. Historically, such courts have not always operated as formal institutions.

In this section, we will examine how the principles discussed above in the context of rulings of the High Court in Jerusalem apply in the context of halakhic rulings issued by lower courts. We will first look at two categories of unambiguous and objective error that invalidate legal rulings: mistakes relating to facts and mistakes relating to law. We will then examine two other categories of halakhic error, which, though they cast doubt on a ruling's veracity, are not considered unambiguous and objective, and hence do not render the ruling invalid.

### 7.1 Mistake of fact versus mistake of law

The erroneous rulings discussed in mHorayot are legal errors, that is errors in interpreting or applying the law. At times, however, court rulings may be found to be in error with respect to facts: the court may err in its determination of the facts of the case.

The Tosefta discusses a case where, on a particularly cloudy Sabbath day, it had not been clear whether the sun had set and it was permitted to do work, or had not yet set and the prohibition against working was still in force. According to the Tosefta, if the court ruled that the Sabbath had ended, and it later became clear that the sun had not set and the ruling was in error, the decision would not be a "[valid] ruling" (*horaa*), but a "mistake" (*taut*): "If the court ruled that the Sabbath had ended and afterwards the sun shone–this is not a [valid] ruling, but a mistake."[30]

In other words, although the law provides a defense for one who acts in accordance with a court ruling that embodies a legal error, no such defense is available to one who acts on a ruling that was based on a mistake of fact. The factual error renders the court's decision devoid of the status of a valid court ruling and makes it simply a mistake, compliance with which is forbidden. One who acts upon such a mistake is transgressing, though this transgression is not considered a malicious act, but rather, an unwitting one. The important point is that in contrast to a ruling based on a 'mistake of law,' a judicial decision that is based on a mistake of fact is not considered a valid legal determination at all. It is important to note that the 'facts' in question are not necessarily common knowledge, and a factual error is not necessarily a mistake that is manifest and widely recognized. On the contrary, if the overcast sky misled the judges, causing them to think the sun had set, it is reasonable to conclude that others would also have made the same mistake and therefore should not be blamed for acting in accordance with the ruling. Nevertheless, the principle here is that an erroneous factual determination renders the ruling invalid whether the error is recognizable or not.

An interesting Amoraic controversy relating to this point arose with regard to family law. The Mishnah states that if, after being informed that her husband had died, a woman remarries, and subsequently it becomes clear that the information was incorrect and her first husband is still alive, she must be divorced from both husbands. The question that arises in this context is whether—since it is known, retrospectively, that the woman violated the prohibition against adultery, albeit unwittingly—she should be subject to sanctions for her transgression.

The Mishnah states that a distinction must be made between a woman who decided to remarry on her own, and a woman who consulted a court and remarried on the basis of its ruling.

> If she married with the court's authorization—she has to leave [both husbands], and she is exempt from [having to bring] a [sin-]offering. If she did not marry with the court's authorization—she has to leave [both husbands], and she is obliged to bring a [sin]-offering. The court's power is such that it exempts her from [having to bring] a [sin-] offering.
>
> mJebamot 10:2

It follows from this Mishnah that one who acts in accordance with an erroneous court ruling is exempt from any punishment. As Rashi puts it:

30 tHorayot 1:6 (Zuckermandel edition).

"One who acted in accordance with a court ruling is exempt" (bJebamot 87b). And clearly, the court being referred to here is not necessarily the Sanhedrin in Jerusalem.

Yet the Mishnah's assumption that such a court decision is a valid ruling and serves as a legitimate defense for the woman who heeds it and transgresses, is revisited in the talmudic discussion in bJebamot 87b. Some Amoraim, specifically, Zeiri and Rava, take such a ruling to be analogous to the case where the court erred in deciding that the sun had set and the Sabbath had ended. If so, they argue, the court ruling does **not** serve as a defense for the woman who has, on the basis of the ruling, gone ahead and remarried, hence she must bring a sin-offering. These Amoraim maintain that the law is not in accordance with this Mishnah, for given that the error in question is factual rather than legal, the court's decision is a mistake (*taut*), not a valid ruling (*horaa*). By contrast, R. Nahman upholds the mishnaic law, arguing that the court's decision is indeed a valid ruling, and that a woman who remarries on the strength of the ruling is exempt from having to bring a sacrifice. In his opinion, despite the fact that it later became clear that her first husband was still alive, the ruling permitting her to marry cannot be considered a "mistake."

It seems, then, that these Amoraim differ regarding the question of whether to characterize the pronouncement of the husband's death as a statement of fact, or as a statement of law, namely, a declaration that the woman's legal status is such as to permit her to remarry. The position of Zeiri and Rava would seem to be plausible, inasmuch as the court declared the husband dead, yet later it became apparent that he was still alive, and thus according to the principle established by the aforementioned Tosefta, the decision was not be a "[valid] ruling" (*horaa*), but a "mistake" (*taut*). But what can R. Nahman's reasoning be? Does he accept the law established by the Tosefta? And if so, how is the court's determination that the sun had set and the Sabbath had ended different from the determination that the husband had died and the widow was free to remarry?

Addressing this question, the Talmud explains that according to R. Nahman, the ruling in the remarriage case differs from other factual determinations. According to the halakhic rules of evidence, a court ruling must generally be based on the testimony of two witnesses. An exception to the rule is made in the case of a woman seeking the court's permission to remarry. The Rabbis issued an enactment stipulating that in this situation, the testimony of just one witness will suffice to establish the husband's death. This is the basis for R. Nahman's argument that the court ruling permitting the woman to remarry is not a **factual** determination, since factual determinations can only be made on the basis of the testimony of two witnesses. Rather, it is a legal determination made in accordance with the ritual laws, viz., the laws governing that which is prohibited and that which is permitted. The court does not, and cannot, determine whether the husband is dead or alive, since two witnesses have not testified before it regarding the matter. In such a situation—that is, in a situation of uncertainty, a situation in which there is a legal doubt, given that only one witness has attested to the husband's death—what the court can, and does, do, is establish, from a legal perspective, that the woman is permitted to remarry. If so, on R. Nahman's reasoning, this decision is deemed to be a legal ruling (*horaa*), not a determination of fact. Hence when the ruling is later found to be in error, the woman who has remarried on the strength of the ruling is exempt from having to bring a sin-offering.

The case where a woman is granted a dispensation to remarry is thus a difficult case to categorize, as it can plausibly be seen as generating a factual determination (Zeiri and Rava), but also as generating a legal determination (R. Nahman). Despite the existence of this case, the classification of which is controversial, all the halakhic authorities accept the conceptual distinction between a court decision that is based on a mistake of law, which is regarded as a valid ruling, and a court decision that is based on a mistake of fact, which is not regarded as a valid ruling, but as a mistake.

This distinction seems to support the point made above regarding a court ruling that is objectively mistaken, with which one who is cognizant of the error is forbidden to comply. In bJebamot a distinction is made between different types of objective error. In the case of an objective **legal** error, one who acts upon the ruling, even though he ought not to have acted as he did, has a valid defense. In the case of an objective **factual** error, such as a determination that the sun has set when in fact it has not, one who acts upon the ruling has no valid defense.

## 7.2 Mistakes in judgment (*shikul hadaat*) versus mistakes in legal knowledge (*dvar mishna*)

The principle that a court decision that is objectively and unequivocally erroneous is not considered a valid ruling is also evident in another aspect of the judicial process. A *sugya* in tractate Sanhedrin addresses the question of how to rectify a miscarriage of justice caused by an erroneous ruling. The Talmud points out a contradiction between two Tannaitic sources. A Mishnah asserts that an erroneous decision can be reversed.

> In monetary cases, a decision—whether it was to acquit or to hold liable—can be reversed: in capital cases, a decision can be reversed [in order] to acquit, but not to hold liable.
>
> mSanhedrin 4:1

In other words, the Mishnah is asserting that any erroneous ruling in monetary cases can be reversed. Yet a baraita in the Babylonian Talmud implies that a court that has issued an erroneous ruling cannot reverse its decision. The ruling remains valid, but the judge must compensate the party injured by his erroneous ruling:

> If [a judge] judged the case and acquitted the liable party while holding the non-liable party liable, or declared impure that which was pure, and declared pure that which was impure–what he did is done [i.e., cannot be undone], and he must pay [compensation] from his own property.
>
> bSanhedrin 33a

This seeming contradiction between the sources posed a challenge to the Amoraim, who sought to resolve it in various ways. R. Sheshet suggested that the conflict be reconciled by distinguishing between two types of errors that can mar court rulings. Errors of the more serious type render court rulings invalid, whereas those of the second type do not.

> Rav Sheshet said: Here he erred regarding a point of legal knowledge (*dvar mishna*), there he erred in judgment (*shikul hadaat*). For R. Sheshet said in R. Asi's name: If he erred regarding a point of legal knowledge, the decision is reversed, if he erred in judgment, it is not reversed.
>
> bSanhedrin 33a

Let us try to demarcate the categories "*dvar mishna*" and "*shikul hadaat*." The Talmud explains that a mistake classified as an error regarding "a point of legal knowledge" (*dvar mishna*) results from the judge's having overlooked an important legal source that, had it been taken into account, would have resulted in his handing down a ruling contrary to that which he in fact handed down. The judge's having overlooked this source, which expressed a view contrary to his own, conclusively establishes that the judge's ruling is mistaken. Since, had he been familiar with this source, he would have reached a different decision, his ruling is invalid. Once again, we see that an objective mistake by the judge, in this case a mistake of law stemming from ignorance of a binding halakhic source, renders the ruling invalid. A twentieth century halakhic authority, R. Meshulam Rata, noted that a mistake arising from ignorance of a binding halakhic source is similar to a mistake "as to the reality [of the situation]," that is, to what we have called a mistake of fact.[31] Both bring about the same legal outcome: the ruling is deemed invalid.

The concept of an error in judgment (*shikul hadaat*) is vaguer and more difficult to define. Indeed, an explanation given by the Amora R. Papa, far from elucidating the notion, makes it even harder to understand:

> If, for example, two Tannaim or two Amoraim hold opposed views, and the law has not been declared to be in accordance with the view of this one, or in accordance with the view of that one, then should it happen that [a judge] rules in accordance with one of the views, while

31 *Responsa Kol Mevaser*, 1, #51.

the general practice is to rule in accordance with the other—this is [a mistake in] judgment (*shikul hadaat*).

bSanhedrin 33a

This question has garnered much contemporary scholarly interest. In the opinion of Asher Gulak, a mistake in *shikul hadaat* is an instance where the judge's **reasoning** is found wanting and draws criticism. Gulak took R. Papa's description, not as a definition or general characterization, but rather as just an example of an instance of the exercise of *shikul hadaat*. He then abstracted from this example to formulate a general principle, namely, that a mistake in *shikul hadaat* is an error in the judge's reasoning.[32]

Hanina Ben-Menahem explains the term 'mistake in judgment' (*shikul hadaat*) differently. In his opinion, whereas a mistake regarding a point of legal knowledge (*dvar mishna*) results from the judge's overlooking an important legal **source**, a mistake in judgment results from the judge's overlooking a salient **judicial practice**. This refers to a legal matter regarding which, though that the law has not been conclusively decided one way or the other, the judiciary's practice is to rule in a certain way. The judge who has made a mistake in 'judgment,' has erred, according to Ben-Menahem, by ruling in a manner that diverged from the prevailing judicial practice at the time. According to this explanation, R. Papa's statement is, contrary to Gulak's opinion, not merely an **illustration** of behavior exemplifying error in judgment, but rather an exhaustive **characterization** of such error.[33]

Regardless of which interpretation of the notion of 'error in judgment' is accepted, all agree that according to talmudic law, when a legal ruling overlooks a valid and unquestionably authoritative legal source—that is, when there has been a mistake regarding a point of legal knowledge (*dvar mishna*)—the ruling is void, and not to be complied with.

### 7.3 'A sage has already ruled'

We have seen that an unequivocal mistake nullifies an erroneous ruling. This is consistent with the principle established in mHorayot, namely, that one is not to comply with an erroneous legal ruling. But this same principle mandates that in the case of a ruling that cannot be deemed erroneous with absolute certainty, one is obligated to act in accordance with the ruling. This principle is reflected in a *sugya* in bSanhedrin 29b, which raises the question of the scope of the judge's obligation vis-à-vis rulings, handed down by earlier courts, with which he does not concur.

In the *sugya*, the Talmud discusses the legal value of an individual's declaration regarding his debts. Is it viewed as a declaration that obligates

32 Gulak, *The Foundations of Jewish Law* (Hebrew), (Berlin: 1922), 4:180.
33 Ben-Menahem, n. 11 above, 136–37.

him and can serve as the basis for a legal claim by the lender, or is the declaration purely rhetorical—say, to present a poverty-stricken 'front' so as to keep creditors and beggars at bay— and devoid of evidentiary value? The Amora R. Nahman set down the presumption that "One is wont to disclaim abundance [of wealth]," viz., that we must be skeptical about declarations of debt, since people tend to declare that they have no money, or that they owe money they do not really owe, so as not to appear wealthy in the eyes of others. Hence such a declaration cannot serve as evidence for one who claims to be a creditor. Given this presumption, the Amoraim disagreed over how to address a similar declaration made by someone on his deathbed. The question arose in the context of the following case: "A certain man was nicknamed 'the mouse lying on the *denarii*[34]' [the miser]. Before his death, he declared: 'I owe money to so and so and to so and so.'"

The Talmud recounts that after he died, the named men came and made a claim against the heirs for payment of his debts to them. R. Ishmael b. R. Jose ruled that R. Nahman's presumption does not apply in this case, since the person in question made the declaration just before his death, a time when people do not lie. Hence the declaration is to be viewed as obligating him, and the heirs are thus obligated to discharge the debts that their father acknowledged. After this ruling, the heirs paid only half of the debts, and the creditors therefore turned to another judge, R. Hiya, seeking payment of the second half of the debt. Contrary to R. Ishmael b. R. Jose, R. Hiya responded in accordance with R. Nahman's presumption, ruling that it applies even to someone about to die, and that the heirs were thus exempt from repaying the debt. The creditors then asked R. Hiya whether they had to return the half they had already been paid on the basis of R. Ishmael's ruling. R. Hiya said they did not have to, asserting: "A sage has already ruled."[35]

The upshot of the story is that though R. Hiya disagreed with R. Ishmael b. R. Jose with regard to the law, and contended that the ruling should be the opposite of what R. Ishmael had decided, he refused to void R. Ishmael's ruling. The import of the "a sage has already ruled" principle is that the first ruling retains its force, and another judge does not have the authority to overturn it even when he clearly disagrees with it.

Let us examine R. Hiya's position more closely. If it was clear to R. Hiya that his view was correct, and not that of R. Ishmael b. R. Jose, why didn't he agree to overturn the first decision? And why didn't he allow the heirs to recover the monies taken from them contrary to the law? The key to understanding R. Hiya's position is to note that the difference of opinion between the two judges arose from their divergent views of human nature,

34 *Denarius* (pl. *denarii*)—a Roman coin.

35 bSanhedrin 29b. Some commentators read the *sugya* as saying that it was the heirs who approached R. Hiya, seeking repayment of the half of the estate that they had paid to the creditors.

and was not a disagreement over a decidable point of law. Hence we cannot say that in R. Hiya's opinion, R. Ishmael's view was indisputably mistaken. Had R. Hiya maintained that there had indeed been such a mistake, it stands to reason he would have declared the judgment mistaken and annulled it. But given that there is no 'right answer,' R. Ishmael's ruling stands and is final. Alfasi, an eleventh-century codifier, explains this as follows:

> As to the judgment exercised when R. Ishmael b. R. Jose and R. Hiya disagreed: R. Hiya had no proof to confirm that R. Ishmael b. R. Jose had made a mistake. Therefore, he did not have the power to overturn his action, and because of this, said, "A sage has already ruled."[36]

This example further underscores the point that disagreement over a legal question does not necessarily indicate that one side is mistaken. In most cases where there are two opposed rulings, the legal system will seek to decide between them. Yet in the case under discussion, **both** the opposed rulings are accepted as valid **concurrently**: the ruling of R. Ishmael b. R. Jose with respect to the first half of the debt, leaving the heirs' money in the creditors' possession, and that of R. Hiya with respect to the second half of the debt, rejecting the creditors' claim. Even if it is disputed, a ruling that cannot be conclusively demonstrated to be erroneous is valid and binding with respect to the case in which it was handed down. R. Hiya cannot overturn R. Ishmael's ruling vis-à-vis the situation in which it has already been applied, and his own stance can be expressed only in adjudicating other issues that come before him for judgment.

## 7.4 'If a sage has declared something forbidden, his colleague may not declare it permitted'

The principle that 'finality of judgment' applies to rulings that cannot be proven to be in error is also manifest in a case, reported in the Tosefta, where someone sought to have an already-decided matter brought before a new judge. A baraita in tEduyot ruled:

> If he asked one sage and he declared it impure, he may not ask another sage. If he asked a sage and he declared it pure, he may not ask another sage.
>
> tEduyot 1:5 (Zuckermandel edition)[37]

36 *Alfasi*, bSanhedrin 12b (Alfasi pagination); see also *Piskei Harosh*, Sanhedrin, ch. 3, sec. 26.

37 On some versions of this Tosefta, the prohibition against asking for another opinion applies only in the first case, where the first judge declared it impure.

As formulated in the Tosefta, the addressee of this law is the individual who requested a court ruling. As noted in a recent scholarly analysis of this issue, however,

> in a number of talmudic *sugyot*.... the baraita is invoked as an argument against a sage who has permitted something that his colleague had forbidden. For example, "Has it not been taught: 'If a sage declares something impure, his colleague is not authorized to declare it pure, or if he has declared something forbidden, his colleague is not authorized to declare it permitted'?"[38]

In both formulations, the law does not address theoretical questions about purity and impurity, but rather, it addresses the status of a ruling handed down in a concrete case. With respect to abstract discussion of legal questions, discussion that is not connected to an actual case, there are almost no limitations on a sage who wishes to take issue with views expressed by his colleagues. Controversy is a cornerstone of the Rabbinic sources, and indeed, of halakhic discourse in general.[39] The law in question, however, is not about abstract discussion, but, as we said, about an attempt to dislodge a legal ruling that has been handed down.

It should be noted that the law does not require the second judge to rule, in new cases that come before him, as did the first judge. On the contrary, in those cases he is at liberty to render a decision as he sees fit. It only prevents the second judge from ruling on a case that has already been decided by another judge.

What is the rationale for the law of the 'sage who declared something impure'? Why does the first judge's ruling commit the second judge to accept that ruling only with respect to the specific case on which the first judge ruled, but not with respect to cases that come before him in the future? Would it not make sense, for the sake of halakhic uniformity, for the ruling of the first judge to bind the second judge from that point on, that is, with respect to any future cases he might adjudicate? This would correspond to the common law doctrine of **binding precedent**–a ruling that has been issued is binding in other similar cases.

On the other hand, if the second judge is not committed to this ruling in future cases, why is he obliged to accept this ruling in this particular case, and not allowed to re-hear the case and perhaps overturn it? Consistency would require that the first ruling not bind the second judge at all and that he be free to overturn the first decision if he sees fit.

38 S. Ettinger, "The prohibition against consulting two authorities and the nature of halakhic truth," 18 *Jewish Law Annual* (2009), 1–2. Ettinger notes that the passages where the baraita is formulated as a directive addressed to judges include, among others, bHulin 44b; bNida 20b, bBerakhot 63b.

39 See Chapter One above, "Controversy."

The explanation offered by most of the Early Authorities is based on the principle of finality of judgment.[40] The Ritba explains the prohibition against the second sage's rendering an opinion in the case as follows:

> Do not say that "he may not ask" applies only *ab initio*, in deference to the honor of the first [sage]. For if he asked, [it applies] even ex post facto. The purity declared, and the dispensation issued by the second [sage], are of no consequence. For the first one is a sage who is qualified to issue a legal ruling that something is prohibited or impure, which he did, hence he turned it into a 'prohibited thing.'... and it is so even if the second is greater than the first "in wisdom and in number"[41].... And it stands to reason that since the first sage has turned it into a 'prohibited thing,' it can never be permitted, even if it transpires that he was mistaken.
>
> *Hidushei Haritba*, bAvoda Zara 7a

On this understanding, when the first sage issued his ruling, and no categorical error was discovered in it regarding a point of legal knowledge, it became final and binding, and what he ruled impure became completely forbidden. The ruling, however, did not become a precedent-setting ruling, and **in other cases** the second sage–or even the first—can rule differently.

Note that not only does the second judge not have the **right** to hand down a ruling contrary to the first judge, he does not have the **legal authority** to do so. Hence if he nonetheless proceeds to hand down a ruling contrary to that of the first judge, his ruling is void. Moreover, the ruling remains in force even if the first sage later changes his mind and adopts the second sage's view, and even if the second sage is wiser than the first.

In commenting on the law of the 'sage who declared something impure,' the Rabad of Posquières invokes the distinction, discussed above apropos bSanhedrin 33a, between mistakes in judgment (*shikul hadaat*) and mistakes regarding legal knowledge (*dvar mishna*).

> If a sage declared something impure, his colleague may not declare it pure; if he declared it forbidden, his colleague may not permit it–and if he permitted it, it is not permitted. And it seems to me that this is so when they disagree as to a matter of judgment (*shikul hadaat*), but if the first made an error regarding a matter of legal knowledge (*dvar mishna*),

40 See Chapter Five below, "Finality of judgment," and see Ettinger, n. 38 above, 1–19.

41 Alluding to the rule that one court may not reverse decisions made by another unless it is greater "in wisdom and in number" (mEduyot 1:5).

> [his ruling] is retracted and his colleague may permit [the matter in question].
>
> *Rabad*, bAvoda Zara 7a (Sofer edition, p. 12)

It is important to reiterate that in saying that a ruling is binding, and precludes other sages from disputing the matter further, this refers only to the realm of actual legal rulings in concrete cases, but not to the domain of theoretical study of the law. Even when the law has been definitively decided, another sage can challenge it at the theoretical level, as long as he acts in accordance with what has been declared the normative practice. The Rosh, R. Asher b. Yehiel, stressed this distinction in discussing the obligations of the second sage, who wishes to express a position contrary to that handed down by the first:

> And if the second believes that the first is mistaken, he should go and argue with him. If he can prove that he erred regarding a matter of legal knowledge, he should make him retract it. And if he disagrees with him as to a matter of judgment, that is, if his reasoning leans toward permitting that which the first prohibited, but he cannot prove it from the Mishnah or the Amoraic teachings, he should say: 'I say this, but I am not permitting what you have prohibited, since you declared it prohibited, and rendered it a prohibited thing, and I do not have the power to make you retract.'
>
> *Piskei Harosh*, Avoda Zara, ch. 1, sec. 3

The doctrine of finality of judgment, *res judicata*,[42] bars repeated consideration of a case on which a final decision has already been rendered, for two main reasons: to strengthen the status of the court within society, and to protect the individual from having to defend in court a position he has already defended. Important as these desiderata are, it is clear that the doctrine of finality does, in some cases, lead to miscarriage of justice, the perpetuation of error, and obstruction of attempts to ascertain the truth. The talmudic Sages' approach to the question of obedience to legal rulings seeks to balance these considerations. On the one hand, legal rulings, once rendered, are taken to be final. It was clear to the Rabbis that a legal system in which rulings are subject to incessant critical review was untenable, and would gravely impair the halakha as a normative system. On the other hand, they could not ignore the cardinal Torah value of seeking and upholding truth. Hence they mandated that if a ruling is objectively mistaken, it is not to be complied with. Moreover, even when a legal ruling has been handed down and is valid and final, it does not constitute a binding precedent that constrains judges adjudicating future cases, nor does it limit the study and teaching of contrary positions.

42 See Chapter Five below, "Finality of judgment."

# 5 Finality of judgment



## 1 *Res judicata*

This chapter will explore a central element of legal procedure, finality of judgment—*res judicata*.[1] The notion of finality of judgment raises numerous questions, chief among them being, of course, that of whether a judgment ever becomes irrevocable and absolute, or is always open to reconsideration. If so, who is entitled—or obligated—to initiate reconsideration? Is it permissible for one of the litigants to request a new trial after a ruling has been issued, and if so, under what conditions? This chapter will clarify the position of Jewish law on these procedural issues. We will also explore the extent to which positions taken on putatively procedural issues have substantive implications for both the actual outcomes of concrete legal proceedings, and for our understanding of the essence of the law, and its role in society.

The question of whether we can fix a point at which a ruling on a particular issue becomes final, or it remains open for continual review, involves a variety of considerations. On the one hand, there are clearly important considerations, such as the public good, and reducing the cost of the legal system, against permitting repeat deliberations on matters that

1 The Latin term means 'a thing [already] adjudicated.' Various other terms are also used for this concept, among them 'former adjudication,' 'claim preclusion,' and 'estoppel by judgment.' Although law dictionaries articulate nuances of difference between these terms, here we will use them interchangeably.

have already been decided. Another important such consideration is the prestige of the court, which would appear to call for the acceptance of its decisions as binding and not subject to being reviewed and possibly overturned. Furthermore, allowing a second trial on an issue that has already been decided could produce conflicting judgments on the same matter, undermining public confidence in the legal system, and threatening its stability. Another consideration in favor of finality of judgment is protection of the litigant's right not to have to deal with an adversary who seeks to avenge his loss in court by having the matter adjudicated yet again. On the other hand, there are, it would seem, considerations no less significant in favor of the court's taking up all claims and petitions brought before it, even if this entails renewed deliberations on a matter already adjudicated. The principle that justice should be done for all parties speaks to allowing the court to re-consider an issue even if it was raised previously and a final decision was rendered. So too, the court's prestige may be enhanced if its public image is that of an institution ready to admit the need to reconsider a previous decision, demonstrating its unwavering commitment to the pursuit of truth and justice. Obviously, the reason one of the litigants offers for requesting a new trial must be taken into consideration. A reason that could have been raised at the previous trial, and was not raised, is not comparable to a reason that emerged only after the court's ruling was rendered. It would appear that new witnesses of whom there was no knowledge during the previous trial, and whose testimony could affect the court's decision, cannot be compared to a new argument that one of the sides now seeks to introduce, even though it could have been raised previously, but wasn't.

It goes without saying, however, that formulation of a doctrine of finality of judgment is complex, raising a wide spectrum of issues. For example, the question of finality of judgment in the criminal context differs markedly from its counterpart in the civil context. Whereas in the latter context, a faulty judgment will at most have detrimental consequences with respect to the affected litigant's property rights, in the criminal context, the fundamental and protected rights of the individual—a central value in most contemporary legal systems—may be violated, an immeasurably more serious outcome.

Various legal systems uphold the principle of "former adjudication"–*res judicata*: when, in a given case, all the legal processes to which there can be recourse have been exhausted and a final decision has been handed down by the court, the case may not be reopened. In the words of the great Lord Coke:

> For as it hath been well said, "*interest reipublicae, ut sit finis litium*"; otherwise great oppression might be done under color and pretence of law; for if there should not be an end of suits, then a rich and malicious man would infinitely vex him who hath right by suits and actions; and

> in the end (because he cannot come to any end) compel him ... to leave and relinquish his right; all which was remedied by the rule and reason of the ancient common law, the neglect of which rule ... hath therewith introduced four great inconveniences: 1. Infiniteness of verdicts, recoveries, and judgments in one and the same case. 2. Sometimes contrarieties of verdicts and judgments one against the other. 3. The continuance of suits for 20, 30 and 40 years, to the utter impoverishing of the parties. 4. All this tends to the dishonour of the common law, which utterly abhors infiniteness, and delaying of suits.[2]

The *res judicata* principle rests on three main considerations: (a) it is in the public interest that litigation of a case not be interminable, but rather that as soon as the status of a particular object or the rights of a particular person have been established, there be no doubt that the said status or rights were acquired legally; (b) no plaintiff should be permitted to use the services that the state puts at his disposal for the purpose of filing suit more than once; (c) it is unfair to pursue a defendant more than once in connection with a given matter. Accordingly, on the *res judicata* principle, if a plaintiff brings an action and is unsuccessful, he will not be permitted to reopen the case.

The question of the finality of judgment can be presented as reflecting a tension between utilitarian considerations and considerations related to achieving justice. It seems plausible to argue that utilitarian considerations favor finality of the legal process and limitations on the parties' ability to turn to the court regarding a matter it has already adjudicated. Recurrent deliberations render the legal process cumbersome and expensive. Their elimination also builds confidence in the stability of the legal solution set down by the court, confidence that is necessary if the parties are to rely on the judgment that is handed down concerning their petition. Were it possible that the judgment as to their claim might at any subsequent point be overturned, in other words, were there no finality of judgment, litigants would be constantly apprehensive that this might occur, and thus would have difficulty acting on the basis of the ruling in question. On the other hand, if the courts have as their mandate the execution of justice, then to avoid perpetrating an injustice, surely they should be allowed to revisit previous judgments when there is concern that newly-raised arguments and evidence would mandate a different decision.

But things are not so straightforward: pragmatic arguments against finality can be put forward, and finality can be seen as advancing the pursuit of justice. For while reconsideration of a judgment after it has been handed down indeed allows the court to rectify an erroneous decision

2 *Ferrer v. Arden* (1599) 6 Co. Rep. 7a, 77 ER 263, 266.

made in the past, it also allows one litigant to abuse the other with repetitive claims regarding a matter already adjudicated. In this respect, finality of judgment is a protection the legal system affords the litigants against the possibility of incessant pursuit in the corridors of justice. Similarly, utilitarian considerations can be invoked to argue against finality and in favor of allowing new deliberations on matters already decided by the court. Although this makes the legal process more cumbersome, and increases its cost, it nonetheless strengthens the court's status as an institution that assiduously pursues truth and justice. This in turn strengthens public trust in the courts, and reinforces the inclination to solve conflicts and problems through due process and orderly recourse to the courts rather than by means of confrontation and vigilante justice.

But *res judicata* is by no means an all-or-nothing principle. There need not be either categorical support for finality of judgment, nor complete rejection of this principle and support for allowing renewed consideration of cases already decided. It is certainly possible to take a non-polar position that distinguishes between different circumstances and seeks a balance between the conflicting considerations noted above.

An example of a radical endorsement of the doctrine of *res judicata* is found in ancient Roman law.[3] In the pre-Justinian period, the plaintiff exhausted his right to adjudication merely by submitting his claim to the court. Consequently, whatever the decision of the court, he had no right to apply to the court again regarding the same matter, even when he lost his case on purely formal grounds. If, for instance, a claim regarding payment of a debt was lodged before the payment was due, and on that ground, denied, the plaintiff who lost his case could not apply to the court again after the said date.

Later legal systems, which inherited the doctrine of *res judicata* from Roman law, uphold a more nuanced take on the doctrine, emphasizing public policy: the interest of the State in reducing redundant recourse to the judiciary, and the interest of the public in preventing incessant harassment of defendants.[4] The preeminent jurist John W. Salmond unequivocally endorsed this view of *res judicata*:

> A judgment is conclusive evidence as between the parties, and sometimes against all the world, of the matter adjudicated upon. The Court of Justice may make mistakes, but no one will be heard to say so. For their function is to terminate disputes and their decisions must be accepted as final beyond question.[5]

3 See *The Institutes of Justinian*, trans. J.B. Moyle (Oxford: 1945), 595–96 n. 5; R.W. Lee, *Elements of Roman Law, with a Translation of the Institutes of Justinian*, 2nd ed. (London: 1949), 457; A. Berger, *Encyclopedic Dictionary of Roman Law* (Philadelphia: 1953), "*Res judicata*," 678.

4 See *Phipson on the Law of Evidence*, 9th ed. (London: 1952), 421–26, 430–35.

5 John W. Salmond, *Jurisprudence*, 10th ed. (London: 1947), 484.

Even stronger is the following description of this doctrine: "*Res judicata* changes white to black and black to white, it makes the crooked straight and the straight crooked."[6]

In this chapter, we will consider these and similar questions from the perspective of Jewish law, exploring the conceptual foundations of the halakhic stance on these questions, and how these principles generate a balanced understanding of finality of judgment. We will also gain insight into the theological roots of the halakhic approach.

### 1.1 *Res judicata*—procedural or substantive?

*Res judicata* might, at first glance, appear to be a purely procedural issue. And indeed, in the past, law was assumed to be readily divisible into two main areas: procedural law and substantive law. With regard to the former, obviously, no legal system can exist without established guidelines for the conduct of its proceedings. Until the beginning of the twentieth century, it was assumed that such rules, governing elements of the legal system such as trial procedures, methods of presenting and accepting evidence, representation of litigants, and decision-making, could be clearly delineated from substantive law, namely, laws defining obligations, rights, and remedies. The rules of legal procedure, it was thought, do not address such issues, but merely establish the methods for answering questions about them.

Legal procedure was defined by Salmond as follows:

> Substantive law is concerned with the ends which the administration of justice seeks; procedural law deals with the means and instruments by which those ends are to be attained. The latter regulates the conduct and relations of courts and litigants in respect of the litigation itself; the former determines the conduct and relations in respect of the matters litigated.... What facts constitute a wrong is determined by substantive law; what facts constitute proof of a wrong is a question of procedure. For the first relates to the subject-matter of litigation, the second to the process merely.... So far as administration of justice is concerned with the application of remedies to violated rights, we may say that substantive law defines the remedy and the right, while the law of procedure defines the mode and conditions of the application of one to the other.[7]

But as realistic approaches to law gained ascendancy in the first half of the twentieth century, the complexity of the relationship between procedural

6 *Jeter v. Hewitt* 63 U.S. 352, 363–64 (1859); *Brown v. Felsen* 442 U.S. 127, 132 (1979); 18 C.A. Wright, A.R. Miller & E.H. Cooper, *Federal Practice and Procedure* §4403 (1981).

7 Salmond, n. 5 above, 467.

and substantive elements in the law was increasingly recognized. The very distinction between substantive and procedural law was called into question. Rules of procedure, which had previously been considered neutral with respect to legal outcomes, came to be seen as an integral part of substantive law.[8]

The interrelationship between process and substance is manifested in the courtroom, most importantly in the content of the judgment itself. Courts can use procedure in a manipulative manner so as to achieve a preconceived legal outcome. This may happen when it is more comfortable for the court, for a variety of reasons, to achieve a particular legal outcome indirectly, through the implementation of procedural rules, than through the direct application of substantive legal principles. Thus, for example, the court may rule that a particular claimant has not met the minimum requirements for filing a petition, with the hidden agenda of not wanting to deal with the essence of his petition. Critical analysis of procedural rules reveals that they are by no means merely technical regulations designed to ensure standardized courtroom practice. Indeed, the manner in which procedural rules are used reflects the worldview and ideology of the trial judge. We find, however, that the opposite can also be the case—procedural rules can influence the substance of the law, and indeed, can come to be foundational principles that shape a society's outlook and culture. For instance, extension of the right to petition the court, so that all citizens are granted the right to bring claims for any wrong inflicted by the government, though seemingly a 'neutral' procedural matter, actually promotes a value system vis-à-vis the rule of law and proper governance.

Why does the law tend to 'camouflage' important substantive norms as technical procedural regulations? As noted, this may result from uneasiness about a particular legal outcome—its morality, say—though it is thought to be valid nonetheless; its justification through technical procedural arguments obviates the need to deal directly with the substantive issue. At times, however, substance may be clothed in the rhetoric of procedure because the issue in question is so fundamental to the essence of the legal process that it is presented as a procedural principle to enhance its perception as self-evident. The latter appears to be the case with regard to finality of judgment both in law in general, and in Jewish law.

## 2 Jewish law and finality of judgment

The position taken by Jewish law on the issue of *res judicata* is fundamentally different from that upheld in Roman law and the legal systems that followed it. The operative principle in Jewish law, broadly speaking, is that a party may always reopen a case after the decision has been handed down. Moreover, Jewish law permits a case to be reopened on the basis of

8 See Robert M. Cover and Owen M. Fiss, *The Structure of Procedure* (New York: 1979), ch. 2.

a wide range of claims that can be raised by the sides to the dispute. There are certain exceptions to this rule, where reopening the case is not possible, but these exceptions do not change the fact that Jewish law fundamentally rejects the concept of *res judicata.* This rejection is not limited to specific contexts, but applies across the board to the many and diverse areas governed by the halakha. Generally speaking, in Jewish law, a party seeking to demonstrate that a court decision against him is incorrect is not barred from so doing. The grounds for challenging a decision and reopening the case include error that has been discerned in the logic of the decision, new evidence found by a litigant after the decision was handed down, and new arguments that the litigant did not raise during the first hearing.

In Jewish law, arriving at a correct—that is, a truly just—decision is the overarching desideratum. If, in its view, a decision different from that which has been handed down is truer and more correct, the court can void its earlier decision and hand down a new one. Correctness takes precedence over the other considerations mentioned above, such as the need to put an end to the process of litigation, the court's prestige, and so on, but does not completely override them.

Below, we will consider situations where all the relevant evidence was not brought before the judge (§3.1), and situations where the relevant legal arguments were not presented (§3.2). In §3.3, we will discuss situations where it is claimed that the judge's conclusion was incorrect. As we will show, error raises unique difficulties with respect to reopening a case on which a ruling has been handed down.[9] After considering the various scenarios that call for reconsidering a judicial decision, we will explore the theological perspective underlying the Jewish legal approach to this issue (§4). The chapter will conclude (§5) with an examination of the dramatic change that took place in Jewish law at the beginning of the twentieth century—introduction of the institution of the appellate court—and the extent to which it has bearing on the traditional position of Jewish law vis-à-vis finality of judgment.

## 2.1 The duty to consult with colleagues

Before examining how Jewish law handles rulings discovered to be in error, it is important to review the safeguards put in place to prevent legal errors from occurring in the first place.

The importance of ensuring that true justice is achieved manifests itself not only after a ruling has been handed down, but at all stages of the legal process. Jewish law seeks to minimize the likelihood of erroneous rulings, and thus imposes upon the judge a responsibility to consult with judges from higher courts. This obligation is addressed in the following baraita:

9 See Chapter Four above, "Erroneous rulings."

> It has been taught: R. Jose said: Originally there were no disputes in Israel.... If a matter of inquiry arose, the local court was consulted. If they had a tradition thereon they stated it; if not, they went to the nearest court. If they had a tradition thereon, they stated it, if not, they went to the court situated at the entrance to the Temple Mount; if they had a tradition, they stated it; if not, they went to the one situated at the entrance of the Courtyard ... if they had a tradition thereon, they stated it, and if not, they all proceeded to the Hall of Hewn Stone where [the Great Sanhedrin] sat from the morning burnt offering (*tamid*) until the evening burnt offering; on the Sabbath and festivals they sat within the fortifications of the Temple. The question was then put before them: if they had a tradition thereon, they stated it; if not, they took a vote: if the majority voted 'impure,' they declared it so; if 'pure,' they so ruled.
>
> bSanhedrin 88b

This baraita portrays a legal system where judges are permitted to claim that they lack the knowledge needed to answer a legal question that has been presented to them, that is, to decide a given case. Indeed, under those circumstances, the judge (*dayan*) is not merely permitted, but **obliged** to consult with additional experts who can advise him and share with him their legal expertise. This requirement increases the likelihood that the judge will reach an accurate judgment. The process of consultation was the standard practice not only at the time of the Sanhedrin,[10] but even afterwards, when the Sanhedrin was no longer in existence:

> R. Safra said: If two litigants vehemently disagree with respect to a lawsuit, and one says, Let us have the matter adjudicated here, and the other says, Let us go to the place where scholars assemble, the latter is forced to have the matter adjudicated in the court in [the plaintiff's] town. And if there is a need to ask [the assembly] about something, they [the court] write it down and send it [to the assembly].
>
> bSanhedrin 31b

10 The Sanhedrin, which functioned during the Second Temple Period, served two important functions in the institutional hierarchy of the court system in Israel. It served as the highest judicial instance, but also had a decisive legislative role. That is, it not only served to adjudicate the law, but also to make law. When the Sanhedrin ceased to exist, the legal hierarchy disappeared with it. In the talmudic and post-talmudic periods, Jewish legal authority, with respect to both religious–ritual and civil–criminal matters, was reestablished in a non-hierarchical fashion, on the basis of expertise in Torah study, charisma, leadership, and so on. Throughout the generations, there have been several failed attempts to revive the Sanhedrin. The establishment of the Supreme Rabbinical Court in Jerusalem at the beginning of the twentieth century placed the possibility—and attendant problematics—of reestablishing a formal judicial hierarchy on the agenda of the halakhic decisors.

The practice of consulting with other scholars remained an integral part of the halakhic system even in later periods. The *Shulhan Arukh* asserts: "And if there is a need to ask the High Court about something–they write it down and send it and ask."[11] It is clear that this rule does not refer to the High Court in Jerusalem (that is, the Sanhedrin), for the laws in the *Shulhan Arukh* deal only with conduct 'in our day.' And indeed, a considerable portion of the responsa literature, one of the primary genres of halakhic literature, contains questions posed by judges in one locale to their colleagues or teachers in other places, often distant. Elon describes this phenomenon as follows: "Complex problems that local courts could not resolve ... ultimately reached one of the recognized respondents active in the various centers of the Diaspora."[12]

Thus, the right of judges to consult another court does not depend on the existence of the Sanhedrin or any other institutional hierarchy. A judge may consult with any rabbinical authority he deems appropriate. In the words of the nineteenth century decisor R. Yehiel Mikhel Epstein:

> If the judges need to ask a question concerning the matter they are adjudicating, they can ask [someone residing] anywhere they wish, and the litigants need not approve this step, and the responder replies to the judges, and not to the litigants.
>
> *Arukh Hashulhan*, HM 13:11

The difference between sending a question to the Sanhedrin and sending a question to another court or a great scholar of the time is significant: the Sanhedrin had binding authority, and the inquiring court had to submit to its instructions, whereas courts and halakhic scholars 'in our day' have no such power.

It is interesting to compare this position with the doctrine of 'certification' in American law, on the strength of which the court may direct a question to the Supreme Court regarding an issue about which it is in doubt. This allows the lower court to get an authoritative opinion on the matter at hand. In contrast to Jewish law, here the consultation process is formal, and lower courts have no leeway with regard to which court they wish to consult.

> [Certification is a] method of appeal whereby a lower court requests that the Supreme Court answer certain questions of law so that a correct decision may be made. The Supreme Court may answer the questions, after which the lower Court may reach a decision in light of the answers provided; or, in instances when a Court of Appeals has certified questions, the entire record to the case may be ordered up for decision by the Supreme Court itself. This method of appeal is not

11 HM 14:1.

12 M. Elon, *Jewish Law–History, Sources, Principles* (Philadelphia: 1994), 3:1460.

> within the control of the litigants, since the lower court may determine whether or not clarifications on points of law are required.[13]

Another tenet of Jewish law that is conducive to preventing error of law in judicial rulings is the judge's **obligation** to consult his teacher or, alternatively, any other higher halakhic authority, when a case before him cannot be decided on the basis of sources that deal with the issue in question explicitly, and an analogy must be made to sources dealing with similar cases. The Talmud states:

> R. Isaac said … "Evil after evil" [alluding to "Evil awaits he who…" in Prov. 11:15] comes upon … he who rivets himself to the word of the law … [This applies] to a judge who, when a lawsuit is brought before him, and he knows of a halakhic judgment [relating to a similar case], compares one case with the other and, though he has a teacher, does not go to him to ask about it. And R. Samuel b. Nahmani further said in the name of R. Jonathan: A judge should always see himself as having a sword hanging over his head[14] and Gehenna gaping open beneath him.
>
> bJebamot 109b

Maimonides cites this dictum, not simply as an expectation, as morality to be aspired to, but as a halakhically binding legal principle:

> Any judge who presides over a case and begins by drawing an analogy between it and a previous ruling known to him, and though there is a judge greater than he in wisdom in the region, does not go and consult with him, is considered among the evil ones who are crass with respect to the rulings they hand down. And the Rabbis said: "Evil after evil comes upon him" (bJebamot 109b), for all the said rulings and their like, that are due to his crassness, bring about a distortion of the law.
>
> *Code*, Laws concerning the Sanhedrin 20:8

It seems plausible that Maimonides is referring to a situation where the judge has misgivings about the analogy, either because he is unsure of its correctness, or because he is utilizing it in a mechanical fashion, without sufficient consideration. In this case he is required to consult with someone who has more expertise than he does. This interpretation was put forward by a twentieth century decisor, R. Haim David Halevi:

> This is, nevertheless, the intent of our teacher [Maimonides], who wrote "begins by drawing an analogy"–at the outset, it appears to him

13 28 U.S.C. §1254(2).
14 Lit., resting between his thighs.

> [the judge] that the cases are similar, but in reality they are not similar in every respect. With regard to this situation, our teacher said that he is "among the evil ones who are crass with respect to the rulings they hand down." However, if the cases are indeed similar in every respect, he should certainly not be required to consult the local sage.
>
> *Dvar Hamishpat*, 20:8

Despite the consultation requirement, the attempt to prevent judicial error does not always bear fruit. As we said, Jewish law does not invoke the *res judicata* principle, but takes a different approach to the problem of judicial error.

## 3 Grounds for reopening a case

### 3.1 New evidence

In legal systems that accept the doctrine of *res judicata*, in most cases it is rare for the court to call for reconsideration of an already-adjudicated matter when new evidence comes to light. This policy, as we saw, is anchored in the fact that legal proceedings must have an end. Both sides already had a clear opportunity to gather evidence and present it to the court, and they are not normally granted a second such chance, except under extraordinary circumstances.

The following Mishnah leaves no doubt that the position of Jewish law on this issue diverges markedly from that of legal systems that espouse finality of judgment. The first part of the Mishnah deals with evidence that one of the sides seeks to bring after a judgment has already been rendered. The second part of the Mishnah, which we will discuss later on, deals with an unusual scenario, in which the evidence one of the sides seeks to present is suspected of being fabricated.

> Whenever he brings proof, it overturns the judgment. But if they said to him, Bring all the proof you have between now and thirty days [from now]—if he adduces it within thirty days, it overturns [the judgment], but after thirty days, it does not overturn [the judgment]. Rabban Shimon b. Gamaliel said: What is he to do if he did not find [such proof] within the thirty days, but found it after thirty days?
>
> mSanhedrin 3:8

The Mishnah opens with the undisputed rule that the handing down of a decision does not bar a litigant from attempting to overturn it by bringing new evidence. In the continuation of the Mishnah, however, a dispute is reported between the first opinion, which is adduced anonymously (*tanna kama*), and that of Rabban Shimon b. Gamaliel, concerning the question of whether the court can set a time limit such that if the litigant brings his evidence after it has passed, the decision can no longer be overturned. The *tanna kama* contends that the court can set such a time limit. According to Rabban Shimon b. Gamaliel, however, the court cannot set a time limit, for what is a litigant to do if he does not succeed in gathering the evidence for his claim before the deadline? He is, Rabban Shimon b.Gamaliel maintains, always entitled to reopen the case, and the court has no power to deprive him of this right. In the opinion of Rabban Shimon b. Gamaliel, when the consideration of the public interest in not allowing cases to be reopened once a decision has been handed down is set against the consideration that decisions should be truly just, the latter consideration prevails.

As we see from the following responsum, by the late medieval Spanish authority R. Shimon b. Tzemah Duran, the law was decided in accordance with the opinion of Rabban Shimon b. Gamaliel.

> Question: Two brothers were partners, and one of them died, and his heirs claimed [their father's share of the partnership] from the remaining brother, and a compromise had to be worked out [between the heirs and their uncle]. Later, a statement was found in the dead brother's handwriting, worded as follows: I, Reuben, hereby acknowledge to my brother Shimon and attest regarding myself that I have received from him all the outstanding monies he owed me.... This is the entire text of his handwritten statement, no more and no less, and the question is whether this voids the compromise.
>
> Answer: According to Reuben's handwritten statement, Shimon is free of any obligation.... even though the arbitrators who worked out the compromise ruled that he should be liable, because he did not have any proof [that he had discharged his obligations to his brother]. Now that he has found proof, the decision is overturned, for we follow the opinion of R. Shimon b. Gamaliel, who said that even in a case in which a litigant was told, Bring all the proof you have between now and thirty days [from now]—the decision may always be overturned, since we say: What is he to do if he did not find [such proof] within the thirty days, but found it after thirty days?
>
> *Responsa Tashbetz* 2, #202

This responsum shows that Rabban Shimon b. Gamaliel's principle applies not only to witnesses, but also to written documents. The law does not distinguish between the two kinds of evidence, and legal proceedings may be reopened if a litigant finds either witnesses or documents that attest to his claims.[15]

15 This clarification was articulated by R. Yekutiel Judah Teitelbaum in *Responsa Avnei Tzedek*, HM 1. It should be pointed out that with respect to arbitration proceedings, as opposed to formal rabbinical court proceedings, parties who wish to forestall the possi-

In principle, it is possible to distinguish between new evidence that it would have been difficult to adduce previously, and new evidence that could have easily been adduced. From the fact that the decisors refrained from making such a distinction, and allowed the litigant to bring any type of new evidence, we can deduce that their main concern was preventing, at any cost, the issuance of an erroneous judgment.

Thus far we have discussed the general question of litigants who seek to reopen legal proceedings regarding an already-adjudicated matter because new evidence has come to light. Now we must determine whether both parties are entitled to do so, or it is only the defendant who is entitled to seek to have a decision overturned. It would seem logical to distinguish between the plaintiff and the defendant, for whereas in relation to the defendant, the argument 'what is he to do if he did not find the proof until now?' seems reasonable, in relation to the plaintiff it seems more plausible to maintain that if he did not have evidence against the defendant, he ought not to have proceeded against him. The public good requires, apparently, that a party not be allowed to bring an action against another without having to take into account that if his action fails, he will lose the right to bring it again.

The majority view among the decisors, however, is that the right to reopen a case following the discovery of new evidence belongs not only to the defendant, but to the plaintiff as well. And although the public interest must indeed be accorded greater weight when it is the plaintiff who seeks to reopen legal proceedings, even in such cases, the imperative that true justice be done prevails over any other consideration.[16]

### i Evidence suspected of being forged

The Sages added an important limitation to the principle allowing the litigants to bring new evidence that they have found in order to open a new trial on a matter regarding which a decision has already been rendered:

> If they [the court] said to him, Bring witnesses, and he said, I have no witnesses, or they said, Bring proof, and he said, I have no proof, yet some time later he produced proof or found witnesses, then it is of no value. Rabban Shimon b. Gamaliel said: What is he to do if he did not know that there were witnesses [who could testify] for him, but found them [later], or did not know that there was proof, but found it [later]?

bility that one of them will challenge the decision by adducing new evidence, can include in the arbitration agreement a clause in which they both declare that they explicitly waive their right to bring any new evidence after the arbitrator's ruling is handed down. See *Responsa Rashba*, 2, #278; *Responsa Radbaz*, 4, #1235.

16 See the *Bah* and the *Sema* on *SA*, HM 16:1.

> ... But if, when he saw that he was about to be pronounced liable, he said, Bring in so-and-so and have him testify for me, or he produced proof from his money belt, then it is of no value.
>
> mSanhedrin 3:8

Whereas in the first part of the passage Rabban Shimon b. Gamaliel rules that the litigant should have the right to bring new evidence, at the end of the passage he agrees with the *tanna kama* that the litigant should not have this privilege. The circumstances described, namely, presentation of the new evidence at the last minute, when a conviction seems imminent, raise the suspicion that the evidence is fraudulent.

The *Shulhan Arukh* appears to rule in accordance with the view of the *tanna kama* that in a case where the judges instructed the litigant to bring his proofs, and he claimed that he had no further proofs, he may not bring any new evidence. However, the ruling significantly limits the Sages' rule, by deeming it applicable only to circumstances in which the evidence could have been known to him previously (e.g., if he already had the evidence, or the witnesses were in his locale). However, in the case of evidence the litigant could not have known about previously, such as witnesses who arrived from afar, he may bring the new evidence despite his declaration that he had no further evidence:

> To what does this refer? To a case where he had the proof available to him and the witnesses were in the area. But if he said, I have no witnesses and I have no evidence, and afterwards witnesses came to him from abroad, or there was a purse belonging to his father containing the relevant documents had been entrusted to others, and the person to whom it had been entrusted came and produced the proofs for him–then the party brings it to court and the decision is overturned, since he can now claim, I stated that I do not have witnesses or proof because they were not available to me; and as long as he can plead and say, For such-and-such a reason I said that I had no witnesses or proof, and there is substance to these claims, then his arguments have not been refuted, and the decision is overturned. Therefore, if [at the time of his original assertion] he elaborated and said, I have no witnesses at all, not here and not abroad, and no proof at all, either in my possession or in the hands of others, he cannot [seek to] overturn the decision.
>
> *Shulhan Arukh*, HM 20:1

Above, we saw that with respect to the reopening of legal proceedings, the desideratum of achieving true justice superseded public policy and other pragmatic considerations; if so, why does it not prevail here too? The reason the litigant forfeits his right in the situation under discussion is that there is a suspicion that the evidence the party adduces in order to have the case reopened is forged, and the witnesses are perjurers.[17] In making an express declaration that he has no further evidence to adduce, the litigant has admitted that he has no witnesses, and if, despite this admission, he later seeks to bring witnesses and reopen the case, the suspicion arises that they are false witnesses.

### ii Application of the law in practice

In the following responsum, R. Solomon ibn Adret, a thirteenth-century Spanish halakhic authority, addresses the community's right to enact a procedural rule that deviates from talmudic law and restricts the right to bring new evidence:

> Question: The leaders of a certain community made an enactment that anyone who did not claim certain tax privileges within a specified time period would lose them. Someone came and claimed that he was not in town at the time or was unable to establish his privilege within the time limit.... Do we say in such a case: what could he do? He didn't find it within the specified time, and now he has found it, and, by swearing an oath, he should therefore be given credence [viz., allowed to claim the privilege]? Or do we say that since communal enactments have the power to expropriate money ... he is not to be given credence, for if so, then everyone in the community will make a similar claim?
>
> Answer: According to the letter of the law, anyone who claims that he was not in town at the time, and did not hear the proclamation—it is not right that he should lose out. Why should he lose out, what has he done? Even of one who comes to court and they said to him, Bring all the proof you have between now and thirty days [from now]—of such a case R. Shimon b. Gamaliel said, What is he to do if he did not find it within the thirty days, but found it after thirty days?[18] And that is the accepted law in such cases.... That is the letter of the law. As regards the communal agreement, however, I do not know precisely what they agreed upon.
>
> If they specifically agreed that whoever did not present himself within a certain time, whether they heard about it or did not hear about it, whether they were heirs [to the property in question] or not; and, if this enactment was made because they deemed it to be for the good of the town, in order to prevent the corrupt from evading [their responsibilities], then whatever they agreed upon and enacted and all concurred in imposing—whatever they did, they did and enacted,

17 See *Rashi*, bSanhedrin 31a s.v. *harei ein ze klum*; *Sema*, *SA*, HM 20:4.
18 bSanhedrin 31b.

> whether in accordance with the law or not in accordance with the law; they are authorized to do it, and what they have appropriated is appropriated. And this is derived from the talmudic dictum in bBaba Batra 8b: "the townspeople are at liberty to use the soup kitchen like the charity fund and to inflict penalties for the infringement of their rules."
>
> *Responsa Rashba attributed to Nahmanides*, #59

The Rashba's responsum implies that in the context in question (the validity of time limits for claim-submission in communal enactments), the community leadership can issue a regulation even if it conflicts with the talmudic law regarding limitations on the introduction of new evidence after a case has been decided. It seems that the goals of enhancing the public good and preventing evasion and corruption are sufficiently compelling to justify deviation from the talmudic stance and imposition of time limits for presenting evidence to the court.

Sources such as this responsum serve to illustrate a distinction that is fundamental to Jewish law, namely, the distinction between ideal law and real-world law, or as it is sometimes referred to, the distinction between theoretical law and applied law. The talmudic law reflects an ideal worldview and embodies important values, particularly that of ascertaining the truth so that justice can be done. Nevertheless, it is not always possible for actual communities and concrete legal institutions to perfectly exemplify these ideal values. In the responsum, the Rashba demonstrates acute awareness of the fact that many communities will enact ordinances that are, in essence, very close to the spirit of the *res judicata* doctrine, by means of which the said communities will be able to prevent introduction of new evidence after rulings have been issued. The primary motivation for this willingness to deviate from the talmudic law is the pragmatic need to neutralize the insidious intentions of those who would seek to bring fabricated evidence, and indeed, this is also, as we saw, one of the basic intuitions underlying the finality of judgment principle.

At the same time, as is evident from the following responsum by R. Moses Isserles, the Rema, the ideal embodied in the talmudic law—namely, that achieving true justice outranks all other considerations—is maintained in the spheres of criminal law and personal status. The enactment of ordinances limiting the period within which evidence can be presented to the court is sanctioned only with regard to civil law.

> And as to the husband's claim that he still has other proofs elsewhere, it seems to me that even though the rabbis of Prague decided among themselves that whoever does not bring his evidence to our court forfeits his claim ... nevertheless, if the husband obtains clear evidence after this time, it is impossible not to accept it, and the court does not have the power to override a prohibition.
>
> *Responsa Rema*, #12

What is the logic behind the distinction between civil law, with respect to which the community can enact an ordinance limiting the period within which new evidence can be introduced, and the laws governing personal status (marriage and divorce), with respect to which such an ordinance would have no validity? The difference may derive from the legal basis underlying the community's power to enact binding ordinances. The validity of communal ordinances can plausibly be understood as grounded in the fact that, from a legal standpoint, all members of the community are perceived as associates in a large partnership. The partners determine the rules of the partnership. Hence, with regard to money matters, the community members can set down the rules of civil procedure. Personal status issues, on the other hand, are not encompassed within the communal partnership, but are, rather, between man and God. Hence the community cannot change the legal status of an individual, though he is part of the community, by means of ordinances. Therefore, if someone has new evidence that is of relevance to the court's determination of his personal status, the communal organs cannot hinder him from presenting it.

### 3.2 New arguments

Thus far, we have discussed the reopening of legal proceedings on the strength of new evidence. Another possible ground for reopening a case is that of new arguments—arguments that were not raised during the proceedings, but which, had they been raised, might have changed the decision. Here we are not speaking of the introduction of new evidence that will strengthen a legal argument already raised, but rather, the introduction of new legal arguments that are not necessarily based on new facts. Can a litigant seek to reopen the case on this basis?

From the perspective of the claimant's responsibility, there is a consideration that supports making a distinction between new evidence and new arguments. The discovery of new evidence is often an unexpected occurrence. However much investigation and research has been conducted, additional witnesses and documentation can turn up unexpectedly. Thus there is only limited control over the discovery of evidence. By contrast, legal arguments are raised on the basis of known facts. To arrive at the appropriate arguments, adequate preparation is essential, including consultation with experts. There is, then, a certain logic to the fact that there is often more openness to accepting new evidence than new arguments. On the other hand, from the perspective of the pursuit of truth, both should be treated equally, for the presentation of new legal arguments can contribute as much to the correction of errors in the original ruling as can new evidence.

It is interesting that the principal halakhic sources do not address this situation directly and explicitly. As we saw above, the Mishnah and Talmud discuss the possibility that a litigant will seek to present new evidence after the judgment has been handed down, and as we will see below, they also discuss the possibility that the judgment was erroneous. They do not, however, discuss new **arguments** that a litigant might seek to introduce after the judgment has been issued. The principal legal codes, the *Shulhan Arukh* for example, do not address this situation either. Hence our examination of this question will focus on opinions from the responsa literature, and in particular, the view of a relatively recent halakhic authority.

The silence of the sources on this issue can be interpreted in various ways. We could conclude that the law allowing new evidence to be introduced after a judgment has been issued does not apply to new arguments. And one decisor indeed asserts that there is a right to a new trial only where there is new evidence, but not when a new legal argument is put forward, a point he argues for by citing the fact that the *Shulhan Arukh* does not establish such a right.[19]

But the silence of the sources can be viewed differently. It could be argued that the decisors addressed the issue of introducing new evidence after a judgment has been handed down because that was the issue raised by the Mishnah, but in doing so, did not intend to exclude the introduction of new legal arguments. Had the decisors intended to distinguish between new evidence, which they deemed introducible, and new legal arguments, which the aforementioned *argumentum ex silentio* alleges are non-introducible, they would have stated that explicitly, for prima facie, distinguishing between new evidence and new legal arguments is not in keeping with the principle that the truth is to be pursued, which, we have stressed, Jewish law seeks to implement. In support of this contention, we can invoke a responsum written by the Rashba, and the position of *Sefer Meirat Einayim* (*Sema*), which is in line with the Rashba's view.

The Rashba was asked the following question: What is the rule when two parties agree to submit written pleas and respond to each other within a given time, but one of them does not respond within the specified time? He answered as follows: "The court may not set a time limit for pleadings, after which a party will not be able to respond with a further argument, and thereby deny his rights."[20] In other words, the court is not authorized to set out a delimited time for the hearing of arguments. The Rashba was not referring specifically to the right of a party to present an argument even after the judgment has been handed down and by so doing cause the case to be reopened. But R. Joshua Falk, author of the *Sema*, cites this ruling in connection with the issue of the court's authority to set a time for bringing evidence, with respect to which, he states, the rule is that "even though he brought evidence after [the allotted] thirty days—he may reopen the case."

19 See *Responsa Shoel Venishal* (R. Moses Khalfon Hakohen), 5, HM #8.
20 *Responsa Rashba*, 1, #899.

> And this is so even if the court set a time within which the litigant could come and plead, and he did not come at the appointed time–he may still plead later, for the court is not authorized to set a time after which he is not able to come and plead.
>
> *Sema, SA,* HM 20:1

While R. Falk does not explicitly state that it is possible to bring new **arguments** after the judgment has been issued, it is very clear from the context of his remarks that this is his intent. Thus, it seems that according to the view expressed in the *Sema,* the case may be reopened even on the basis of new arguments raised after the court handed down its decision. Nevertheless, it must be conceded that the statement in the *Sema* is not conclusive, for the Rashba was talking about raising new arguments within the context of the original legal proceeding itself after the time set by the court had elapsed, and did not specifically address the possibility of raising new arguments after the judgment had been handed down.

There is, however, another source that appears to explicitly permit the introduction of new legal arguments after the issuance of a judgment. In the following responsum, the Rosh discusses a particular case that had been decided on the basis of the arguments put forward by the parties to the dispute. Later on, the losing side sought to reopen the case on the grounds that, due to lack of knowledge, he had not made the argument that would have allowed him to win the case:

> The judge [who ruled on the case] did not want to accept his [new] argument, because when they first sued, he did not raise the matter ... and he accepted the ruling and cannot now return [to the court] and offer a [new] argument, because we say: they taught him this argument. [The judge's] opinion does not appear correct to me, for they certainly did well to teach him that which he did not know, and he thought that the judgment that obliged him to pay ....was proper and fair. And when he was informed that he was not liable to pay ... it was proper that he could then bring an argument refuting the judgment that had been handed down to him.
>
> *Responsa Rosh,* 108:15

In the opinion of the Rosh, when it became evident that the said litigant's original pleading was the result of lack of knowledge, he ought to have been allowed to reopen the case. The judge whose position is critiqued by the Rosh opposes reopening a case on the strength of new arguments taught to the litigant by third parties. It is possible that the judge's concern is that if such new arguments are deemed acceptable, there might be no end to the legal process: a litigant could continually solicit legal advice from others as to new arguments to bring before the court, precluding any possibility of ending the litigation. Alternatively, the judge may be apprehensive that arguments suggested by third parties may simply be legal manipulations and not authentic claims. He therefore seeks to prevent such arguments from being put forward. According to the Rosh, however, the pursuit of truth always overrides other considerations. Hence it is inappropriate to prevent a litigant from introducing a legal argument that he was apprised of by others. On the contrary, the Rosh praises those who instruct him as to how best to argue his case, as their efforts, too, contribute to arriving at the truth.

Just as is the case with respect to the reopening of a case on the basis of new evidence, so too a litigant may not reopen the case on the basis of new arguments when he has expressly declared, in reply to a question from the court, that he has no further arguments. This principle, too, is articulated in the Rosh's responsa:

> And they [the defendants] are permitted to come [later on] with other arguments, because the judges did not ask them whether they had other arguments for holding Reuben liable; for surely, if they asked them, and they replied, We have no further claims and proofs for holding him liable, then they cannot come [later on] and bring such evidence.
>
> *Responsa Rosh*, 13:20

Indeed, the *Arukh Hashulhan* maintains that raising new legal arguments after a judgment has been issued is tantamount to bringing new evidence:

> And so too with regard to arguments: if, when the judges asked him if he had other arguments for holding Reuben liable, and he was silent, and they held him liable, and afterwards he raised [new] arguments that refute the judgment, the arguments he introduces are heard and considered, because he did not say, I have no further arguments.
>
> *Arukh Hashulhan*, HM 20:3

In this context, it is instructive to keep in mind the distinction between adversarial and inquisitorial legal systems. In legal systems that take an adversarial approach, the trial process is essentially conducted by the litigants: they raise the legal arguments, and to a certain extent, set the parameters of the legal deliberations. On this approach, the judge has no authority to consider arguments that are not raised by the litigants. Jewish law, however, is closer to the inquisitorial approach, on which the role of the judge is far more central. The judge is authorized, and even obligated, to consider the relevant legal arguments, even those not raised by the litigants. On this approach, raising arguments is not a privilege granted to the litigants, but a responsibility that devolves upon the judge. In legal systems that take this approach, the right to raise new legal arguments—even at relatively late stages of the proceedings—is of great importance.

And if this is the case with respect to legal **arguments** not raised by the sides themselves, how much more so is it the case with respect to legal **sources** that are not adduced by the litigants. The judge has a duty to consider all the relevant legal sources, even if the litigants themselves are unaware of them. If he overlooks a relevant legal source, he cannot defend himself by arguing that the litigants did not adduce this source when presenting their respective cases.

### 3.3 Error

It can indeed happen that a judge hands down an erroneous ruling: he may have overlooked a relevant legal source, made a faulty analogy, or drawn an incorrect conclusion. Does a litigant have the right to request a reopening of the proceedings with regard to a matter that has been adjudicated, if, in his opinion, an error has been made? On this scenario, the litigant's claim is that, given the legal arguments that were raised in court, and the evidence presented, the court erred in its decision. The accepted way to handle such a claim in western law is to take the case to a court of appeals, whose role it is to consider putative errors in lower court rulings. This course of action is, however, for the most part not an option in the context of Jewish law, which for nearly all its history has not encompassed the institution of the court of appeals.[21] Later in the chapter, we will examine the salient exception: in the twentieth century, a court of appeals was incorporated into the rabbinical court system in Israel.

In a way, this situation is less problematic than the other scenarios envisaged above. It seems reasonable that if a litigant can request a new trial on the basis of new legal arguments or new evidence, how much more so should he be able to request a new trial on the basis on an error in the court's ruling. And this is indeed the position of Jewish law. Nevertheless, this situation raises a number of significant questions.

Already in the Talmud, Rav Sheshet set down the following directive: "If [the judge] erred on a point of law, he must retract."[22] In other words, if there is a clear error in the judge's ruling, in that he forgot an explicit legal

21 See Z. Warhaftig, "Precedent in Jewish law," in H. Ben-Menahem and N. Hecht (eds.), *Authority, Process and Method: Studies in Jewish Law* (Amsterdam: 1998), 1–32.

22 bSanhedrin 6a. The simple case is "if he erred on a point of law," that is, overlooked a legal source that is important and relevant. The Talmud also discusses more complex mistakes it refers to as "errors in judgment." In such cases, it is not possible to identify an unambiguous error in the ruling, even though a strong argument for its incorrectness can be made. Rav Papa explains that this refers to cases where the relevant law is controversial and has not been conclusively decided, but it has become customary for judges to rule in accordance with one of the views, and the judge in question deviated from this practice, and ruled in accordance with the other view. In this section, we will not explore such cases, which, because they do not revolve around a clear and unequivocal error, in essence raise a different question, namely, that of the judge's authority to decide controversies as to the law. See above, Chapter One, "Controversy," and Chapter Four, "Erroneous rulings."

source that, had it been taken into account, would have led to a decision that was the opposite of the decision he actually reached, the judgment is nullified. This principle was codified in the *Shulhan Arukh*:

> Any judge who adjudicates a matter of monetary law and errs—if he erred regarding that which is well-known and familiar, such as explicit laws in the Mishnah or the Gemara, or laws laid down by the decisors, the decision is retracted, and re-adjudicated in accordance with the law.
>
> *Shulhan Arukh*, HM 25:1

The fact that the court is required to recognize any errors it has made and nullify its erroneous decisions indicates a willingness to jeopardize the court's honor and prestige for the sake of arriving at a substantively correct and just ruling. In the following responsum, R. Yair Bacharach, a seventeenth century authority, advises a judge to forgo his honor and admit his mistake, since it is preferable to suffer shame in this world rather than in the world to come when one stands before his Creator:

> Question: Two judges were selected [by the sides] to adjudicate a dispute between the sides, and to do so fully in accordance with the law, and not by mediating a compromise agreement. They decided what they decided, but afterwards, one of the litigants cried out and said that the judgment seemed to him to be in error, and one of the judges agreed with him. But his colleague, who sat with him on the bench, did not want to listen to him at all, and said that since they had already handed down the judgment in writing to each side, [to call it into question now] would engender contempt for the court, and so on.
>
> Answer: In truth, my esteemed colleague, what you have written to ask me about is quite puzzling. With regard to the second judge, if he admits that he has erred, but is too embarrassed to retract [his decision], then pressure should be brought to bear on him so that he does retract. For it is stated in tractate Shevuot, "How do we know that a judge must not advocate for his own decision? Because Scripture says, 'Keep thee far from a false matter' (Exod. 23:7)."[23] And Rashi explains that [a judge] should not serve as a defense counsel for his own decision if he realizes that he has erred. And undoubtedly, one who acts as an advocate for his own decision does so due to the embarrassment, for he is not at ease with having to retract and admit his error.... Nevertheless, the Torah admonishes the judge to be ashamed before God, may He be blessed, [rather than before his fellow judges], [as it

23 bShevuot 30b.

> says,] "Keep thee far from a false matter." ... In any case, it is better to cringe in embarrassment in this world than in the world-to-come.
>
> *Responsa Hut Hashani*, #60

This illuminating responsum allows us a glimpse of one manifestation of the existential–religious dimension that is a sub-text of the halakhic legal process. The judge's obligation to admit his error, even at the cost of the embarrassment this will bring him, is justified in terms of his responsibility to provide a full accounting of his deeds when he comes before God. Below, we will see that other religious elements can be detected in the halakhic approach to the question of finality of judgment.

We now have three grounds for reopening legal proceedings on a matter that has already been decided: new evidence, new legal arguments, and apparent error in the ruling itself. The question of which grounds for revisiting a decision are most defensible depends on the perspective from which we approach the matter.

From the perspective of the degree of responsibility borne by the claimant for submitting a request to reconsider only after the decision was rendered, the simplest case is the claim that the judgment was erroneous. Such a claim certainly could not have been made before the ruling was issued. In this situation, it seems quite plausible that, due to concern that an error was made, a new proceeding should be conducted. Somewhat less plausible, but still credible, is the request to reopen the proceedings in order to present new evidence, for it is indeed possible that the evidence was discovered only after the ruling had been issued. The more difficult case, from this perspective, is the request to reconsider on the grounds that a new legal argument merits being put to the court, since, for the most part, any argument could have been presented at the original hearing.

From the perspective of the court's standing, the simplest case is the presentation of new evidence, as this does no damage to the prestige of the court, since it cannot be faulted for not having considered the said evidence. The request to present new legal arguments does undermine the court's prestige to some degree, since it should have been aware of the arguments during the original proceeding. Most problematic, from this perspective, is the claim of judicial error. This is a real blow to the prestige of the court, since it implies that the judges erred in their deliberations. From the perspective of striving for truth, however, it would seem that the three grounds are equally defensible, as all facilitate correction of an erroneous ruling.

### 3.4 Whose obligation is it to inform the court of deficient rulings?

There is a difference between reopening the legal proceedings on the basis of an error in the court's ruling, and doing so on the basis of new evidence or new legal arguments. In the event of an error in a ruling handed down by the court, there is an **obligation** to reopen the proceedings on the said matter. It is not simply a right granted the litigants to protect their interests, but rather an obligation that devolves upon the judge with a view to ensuring that he does his utmost to arrive at a satisfactory judgment.

> A judge who hands down a decision, and his conscience bothers him, saying that he is mistaken, should not seek to justify his decision with supporting evidence because he is too embarrassed to retract, but should inform both sides that he is retracting, so that a truly just judgment can be issued.
>
> *Shulhan Arukh*, HM 17:8

Indeed, this is the theoretical basis for the law, cited above, that when there is a suspicion that the ruling handed down is erroneous, the obligation to initiate a reopening of the legal proceedings devolves on the judge himself.

In the following responsum, R. Joel Teitelbaum, a twentieth-century authority, addresses the question of whether a dissenting judge is obliged to try and bring the case to a re-hearing, since he believes the majority erred:

> The holy Torah said, "Follow the majority," and in every court of three judges, if two of the three maintain that they handed down a proper decision that fully accorded with the dictates of the law, the opinion of the [other] one does not override that of the two. And moreover, the view of most of the decisors is that they can force the third judge to sign on to the ruling even though he stands and screams at the top of his lungs that the judgment is not, according to the holy Torah, truthful.
>
> Indeed it is true that certainly, if it becomes clear that they erred in a manner that would require a nullification of the decision… their ruling is not valid. But such a clarification can only be made by a court that has heard both sides, or if the whole court received their claims in writing. But as to what this one arbitrator has written, it is clear that just as it is forbidden to decide a case on the basis of the claim of only one side, so too it is impossible to nullify a ruling on the basis of the claims and argumentation of an arbitrator chosen by one side. Hence any argumentation that he writes … to other rabbis on the matter is superfluous, for no court can nullify a ruling under these circumstances. Thus, there is no way to rectify the matter other than for the court to meet again and examine all of the proceedings connected with the case.
>
> *Responsa Divrei Yoel*, HM 149

Indeed, this obligation devolves not only on the judge in question, but also on a third party who is not involved in the legal proceedings, but is able to point to an error in a ruling that has been issued. Jewish law requires such an individual to bring the error to the judge's attention so that he can reopen the legal proceedings on the ruling.[24]

To account for the fact that the obligation to seek a reopening of such a case devolves upon third parties who have no direct connection to the matter, some scholars have based the obligation on the law of returning lost articles (*hashavat aveida*). The meaning of this biblical precept was significantly broadened by its talmudic interpretation, which took it to require the prevention of potential damage to someone else's property. The Rashbash, a fifteenth-century North African halakhic authority, argues that pointing out a mistake in a court ruling falls under the rubric of returning lost articles, for it protects the party who was falsely obligated by the ruling.

> It is a commandment and an obligation, arising from the obligation to return a lost object ... that he [the litigant] should not meet his demise without justice having been done.
>
> *Responsa Rashbash*, #529

In practice, by basing this law on the obligation to return a lost object, the legal authorities made all members of the community indirectly responsible for ensuring the veracity of court rulings, and to a certain degree made them too, and not only the judges, party to the ruling handed down. This connection, created in the context of private law, calls to mind an apparent parallel to a phenomenon in the area of contemporary administrative law, namely, the broadening of the right to stand before the court (*locus standi*), which has gained momentum over the past few decades. Originally, the *locus standi* doctrine established that only a party directly harmed by an act of the government could petition the court against it. By contrast, those seeking to broaden the scope of the principle so that anyone may petition the court against an inappropriate administrative action, base their stance on the assumption that an injustice perpetrated by the government affects all members of a society, hence any citizen should be permitted to petition the court about it. Indeed, Jewish law goes one step further and grants this right not only with respect to matters pertaining to the public at large, but also with respect to matters pertaining only to individuals. The grounds for this extension are, again, the principle of mutual responsibility, and the attendant obligation devolving on members of the community to defend the interests of other members.

In this respect, the reopening of legal proceedings on the basis of an erroneous judgment differs from the reopening of legal proceedings on the basis of new evidence or new legal arguments. Whereas the initiative for seeking to reopen the case on the strength of newly-discovered evidence or arguments must be taken by the interested party, that is, one of the

24 *Responsa Rosh*, 99:6; *Responsa Rashbash*, #529.

litigants, this is not so when there is apprehension that the decision is erroneous. In the latter case, it need not be a litigant who takes the initiative to have the erroneous decision overturned, but rather, any individual, whether within the court or outside it, can do so. The reason for this is that as long as the decision stands, the court is responsible for the perpetuation of an injustice, or at least the perpetuation of a suspected injustice. The suspicion must therefore be investigated, in order to determine whether or not an error has been made.

The obligation to hand down truly just rulings is expressed in another feature of Jewish law. Although it sets down that a student is obligated to honor his teacher, and is even forbidden to render a legal decision in the presence of his teacher, it also establishes that if a student discerns a mistake in a ruling handed down by his teacher, not only is he permitted to tender proof of the mistake, but he is **obliged** to do so. There is, however, no contradiction between the law mandating respect for one's teacher and the law mandating that a student must speak out about his teacher's erroneous ruling, but rather, a hierarchy of values: respect for the Torah, that is, for the law, takes precedence over respect for one's teacher. In the case of civil law, the imperative to speak up when one is aware of an erroneous ruling is also grounded in another prohibition, namely, the prohibition against extracting money unlawfully from one who is exempt from payment, "and all this falls under the rule of 'keep thee far from a false matter.'"[25]

## 4 Finality, truth, and judicial religious obligation

The laws discussed above, which are designed to ensure that a truly just ruling is handed down, are, as we have already discerned, rooted in meta-legal considerations having to do with the role of the judge. The fact that a ruling is never absolutely final, that it can be reconsidered on the basis of new evidence, new legal arguments, or error, reflects the theological underpinnings of the Jewish legal process.

Indeed, the explanation for the fact that the approach to the question of finality of judgment in Jewish law differs so markedly from that found in other legal systems lies in the fact that Jewish law is a religious legal system.[26] The religious context within which Jewish law must be understood constitutes the basis for its commitment to the value of pursuing truth. The truth reflected in a judicial ruling is not just that of the judge, but that of God Himself. The obligation to issue a truthful ruling is not simply a legal duty, but also—indeed, primarily—a religious obligation. In fulfilling his judicial function, the judge is not merely serving as a referee in a dispute

25 *Responsa Sheeilat Yaavetz*, 1:5.

26 This point is disputed in H. Ben-Menahem, "Talmudic law: a jurisprudential perspective," *Cambridge History of Judaism*, vol. 4, The Late Roman-Rabbinic Period (Cambridge: 2006), 877–97, esp. 878–82.

between two individuals, but fulfilling a divine precept as well. Thus the judicial commitment to thorough examination of any alleged deficiencies in a ruling handed down by the court, even after it has been issued, is very deep. It must be acknowledged that from a logical standpoint, the fact that Jewish law is a religious legal system does not necessitate a commitment to the issuance of satisfactory (truly just) rulings to the point where it countenances, or even demands, the continual reopening of cases that have been decided. It might, indeed, be argued that the religious nature of the system actually entails that rulings issued by its courts have a unique validity and objectivity, particularly insofar as the source of their authority is divine and not just political.

Although the 'no finality' policy does not necessarily follow from the religious nature of Jewish law, many scholars nonetheless see this feature as the explanation for the rejection of *res judicata*. Silberg, for instance, argues for the connection between the religious profile of Jewish law and the judge's strict obligation and responsibility to render as truthful a ruling as possible:

> The ruling of the secular judge is not similar to the ruling of the religious judge. Before the secular judge, there is no **absolute** legal truth. He maintains the law in the way that he understands it, even if it is only circumstantial and an estimation. When he makes a mistake, either his ruling is overturned by a higher court, or it stands. His heart does not have to ache if others who are wiser than he determined that he erred in his interpretation of the law. In contrast, the religious judge is obligated to ensure that his ruling is **completely true**, without doubt or hesitation regarding his interpretation.... He must be in a state of fear and trembling that his ruling might deviate even to the slightest degree from the strict truth.[27]

It is important to distinguish, however, between the religious–legal obligation of the judge to issue truly just rulings, which, we have argued, generates a willingness to reconsider rulings even after they have been handed down, and Jewish law's pluralistic orientation, on which a variety of legal opinions about a given issue are recognized as legitimate on the strength of the principle that "both views are the words of the living God."[28] While Jewish law does, indeed, identify one view from the spectrum of proffered interpretations as 'the law' that is to be observed in practice, it is important to keep in mind that, as already noted, Jewish law has no hierarchy, no highest instance, no court of appeals. In short, rulings are never incontrovertible. As a result, arguments as to the law arise frequently. The inherent controvertibility of halakhic rulings, however, is

27 H.C. [High Court of Justice] 130/66, *Segev v. Rabbinical Court*, 21(2) PD 505, 548 (emphasis in original).

28 bEruvin 13b.

beyond the scope of the discussion here; it is explored elsewhere in this volume. Our remarks on the judge's obligation—when there is suspicion that a decision was erroneous—to reopen the deliberations, refer only to the judicial process.

Concerning this religious obligation, Maimonides writes as follows:

> At all times a judge should think of himself as if a sword were suspended over his head and Gehenna gaping under him. He should know whom he is judging and before Whom he is judging, and Who will call him to account if he deviates from the line of truth, as it is written: "God stands in the congregation of God, in the midst of the judges He judges" (Ps. 82:1); and it is also written: "Consider what you do; for you judge not for man, but for the Lord" (2 Chron. 19:6).
>
> *Code*, Laws concerning the Sanhedrin 23:8

The punishment for error is severe. In the next paragraph (23:9), Maimonides states, in accordance with the talmudic law, that God will exact the judge's life if he errs:

> A judge who does not render an absolutely true judgment causes the Divine Presence to depart from Israel. If he unlawfully expropriates money from one and gives it to another, the Holy One, blessed be He, will exact his life from him, as it is said: "And the Lord will despoil of life those that despoil them" (Prov. 22:23).

Maimonides asserts that God will exact the life of one who "unlawfully expropriates money from one and gives it to another." That is, this is the fate that awaits a judge who does not issue a truly just ruling in a monetary case. Note that the gravity of the sanction imposed by God—taking the judge's life—is not commensurate with the act of infringing the monetary rights of one of the parties. The sanction God metes out appears to be far harsher than what is warranted by the judge's misdeed. This is, perhaps, an indication that the damage caused by an erroneous judgment goes beyond the consequences suffered by the litigant denied the redress due him, and extends to the metaphysical realm: withdrawal of the Divine Presence and perversion of the sacred value of seeking truthful judgment.

At times, the judge may also bear financial liability for damages caused by his erroneous ruling, even if it was inadvertent. In some cases, an erroneous judgment, once implemented, may bring about an irreversible situation, in which case the judge may bear responsibility for compensating the party who was unlawfully injured as a result of the judgment. In the language of the Talmud: "What he did is done and he must pay from his own property."[29]

29 bSanhedrin 33a. This responsibility does not arise in the case of every erroneous ruling, but only within certain well-defined parameters. See Maimonides, *Code*, Laws concerning the Sanhedrin 6:3; *Shulhan Arukh*, HM 25:3.

It is important to note that in many legal systems, judges are granted immunity from liability for any damage that might result from erroneous rulings they hand down. This immunity applies both with respect to criminal liability and tort liability, even when the perversion of justice was malicious or showed bad faith.[30] A classic statement of this idea is the following: "It is a principle of our law that no action will lie against the judge of one of the superior courts for a judicial act, though it be alleged to have been done maliciously and corruptly."[31] One of the primary considerations in favor of this policy is that it gives the judge the confidence to express his true view without hesitation and apprehension lest he be wrong. If the judge can expect to be sanctioned for errors in his rulings, his decisions may be so timid as to seriously compromise the judicial acuity he can achieve.

To ensure that the judge will do his work faithfully and will not be deterred by the sanctions ensuing from erroneous rulings, Jewish law offers the judge incentives to issue appropriate and truly just rulings. Alongside the prohibition against being deterred from handing down a correct ruling due to timidity, and the sanctions imposed for erroneous rulings, Jewish law sets down a religious obligation, fulfillment of which brings with it a religious reward, to engage in the act of judging. Just as Jewish law repudiates erroneous judgments, it also repudiates refusal to judge. Thus the incentive given to the judge is not immunity from liability for the consequences of his errors, but the momentous value ascribed to sustaining a just legal system. The judge who is faithful to the law in his decisions is worthy of the highest praise. As Maimonides puts it:

> Every judge who, even for a single hour, renders absolutely true judgments, is as if he had set the world in order and caused the Divine Presence to dwell in Israel, as it is said, "God stands in the congregation of God" (Ps. 82:1).
>
> *Code*, Laws concerning the Sanhedrin 23:9

It thus appears that the issue of finality of judgment embodies one of the fundamental legal problems: the inexorable tension between two values—that of true justice, and that of pragmatism. The first militates toward broadening to the greatest possible extent the right to reopen a case that

30 Needless to say, in the case of malicious wrongdoing by a judge, he bears criminal liability. See., e.g., *Responsa Rashba*, 4, #204.

31 *Fray v. Blackburn* (1863) 3 B & S 576, 122 E.R. 217. A related question is whether the state should be liable to pay compensation for damage caused by an erroneous ruling. Here there is a difference between common law jurisdictions, which exempt the state from such responsibility, and civil law jurisdictions, which impose it. See M. Cappelletti, "Who watches the watchmen? A comparative study of judicial responsibility," 31 *Am. J. Comp. L.* (1983), 1, 7–15.

has already been decided, the second impels us to limit it. Where a legal system stands vis-à-vis this dilemma reflects the broader ideology and cultural context within which it functions. In the case of Jewish law, it is profoundly influenced by the religious significance ascribed to the act of judgment. This may well account for the fact that in Jewish law *res judicata* is not enshrined as a fundamental principle, but relegated to the procedural margins of the law.

## 5 Finality of judgment and the institution of the court of appeals

Above, we explored the underlying reasons for the absence of the institution of the court of appeals in Jewish law. The court's essentially unlimited capacity to correct mistakes in judgment rendered superfluous creation of a higher instance that would serve as a court of appeals. Such an institution is necessary in a system that accepts—in principle—the doctrine of finality of judgment, but nonetheless wishes to offer some recourse to a litigant who feels he has been harmed by a ruling of the court. In such a case, the aggrieved party is given an additional opportunity, usually a one-time chance, to turn to a higher court. In a system where litigants can repeatedly question a ruling that has been handed down, however, applying to a court of higher instance is essentially meaningless. Since the ruling can always be questioned, the judicial hierarchy, being finite, can never suffice to engender finality. In other words, a legal system that leaves decisions open for ongoing reconsideration within the context of the court that judged the case has no need for a process that handles questions about a judgment by sending the matter to a higher court. As we said, the classic sources of Jewish law make no provision for any judicial institution for appeals, and challenges to rulings—whatever the grounds, including legal error–are dealt with by reopening the case.[32]

This situation changed during the British Mandate that ruled Palestine in the first half of the twentieth century (1919–1948). The Mandatory government pressured the Chief Rabbinate to establish a rabbinical court of appeals, which it viewed as a necessary element of any modern and developed legal system. This demand was not easily accepted by the rabbinical establishment in Israel, and the debate it engendered was stormy indeed. Ultimately, however, it was decided to accept the British demand, and in 1921 a rabbinical court of appeals was established. The appeals court was later incorporated into the rabbinical judicial institutions of the State of Israel.[33]

32 On the rare instances where courts of appeal were established by Jewish communities, see S. Assaf, *The Courts and Their Procedures after the Finalization of the Talmud* (Hebrew), (Jerusalem: 1924).

33 See Assaf, ibid., 74; Elon, n. 12 above, 2: 2824.

This new reality invites further discussion of the question of the existence of a doctrine of finality of judgment in Jewish law. As we have seen, the appeals system originated in the context of legal systems that endorse the *res judicata* doctrine. This generates a conundrum: should someone who had a matter adjudicated by a rabbinical court, and wishes to bring new evidence or raise a new legal argument, turn to a court of appeals, or to the court that judged the case? Furthermore, what about someone who, having turned to the court of appeals—which, ruling against him yet again, upheld the lower court's ruling—is convinced that the ruling is erroneous? Can he ask the court of appeals to reconsider the case once more, even though the matter has already been adjudicated twice?

Let us now turn to an examination of how the rabbinical courts in the State of Israel preserve the non-finality of judgment principle within the context of a hierarchical legal system encompassing a court of appeals. We will see that the rabbinical court regulations do, in fact, preserve the core value of non-finality of judgment, even if certain specific changes with respect to its realization had to be introduced.[34]

With regard to the presentation of new evidence for the purpose of having the court reconsider a ruling already handed down, the regulations governing proceedings in Israel's rabbinical courts preserve the accepted practice in Jewish law—litigants may present new evidence to the court that judged the case, not the court of appeals. This is stated in section 129 of the *Regulations for Proceedings in Rabbinical Courts in Israel, 1993–5753*:

> A litigant has the right at any time to request a new hearing from the court that judged his case, on the basis of factual claims or new evidence of which he was not aware at the time of the previous hearing.

The emphasis on "any time" is important, as the right granted pertains even after the legal proceedings have come to a close. At the same time, the rule restricts this right to the presentation of evidence that was not previously known about. As we saw above, this limitation is anchored in the sources of Jewish law. Sub-section 2 of the rule even requires that the party seeking to present new evidence "must submit a written request specifying the claims or new evidence, and the reason he did not adduce them at the previous proceeding."

What does the language of section 129 tell us about the possibility of raising new legal arguments? Although it establishes that a litigant has the right to request that the case be reopened only "on the basis of factual arguments or new evidence," it seems that the intention here was not to deny a litigant the right to have the case reopened on the basis of legal arguments. And indeed, the Tel Aviv Rabbinical Court decided thus in a 1965 case. At the beginning of the hearing, the defendant entered a

34 For the full text of the regulations, see Appendix.

preliminary plea that a ruling against the plaintiff had already been handed down by a certain rabbi, and the two parties had accepted his decision. The plaintiff argued that at the time of the hearing before the said rabbi, he was not represented by an attorney, and did not know how to present his arguments himself. The Tel Aviv Rabbinical Court, in accepting the plaintiff's argument, ruled as follows:

> According to the law, since the plaintiff says that he has additional arguments that could refute the judgment ... the defendant must answer the claims that have been presented to the court in order to clarify the plaintiff's claims.[35]

It is important to emphasize that the justification for this ruling was not the fact that at the first proceeding, the plaintiff was not represented by counsel. In Jewish law, representation by professional counsel is not a necessary condition for a properly-conducted hearing. Rather, the justification for the decision was that the court was sincerely convinced that the plaintiff had new arguments that had not been considered.

Moving on to the question of whether new legal proceedings are to be opened on the basis of a legal error in the court's decision, here we find that the rabbinical court *Regulations* reflect a more complex position. Section 128 of the *Regulations for Proceedings in Rabbinical Courts in Israel, 1993–5753* states:

> If the court suspects that it erred in its judgment, it can invite the parties for further clarification. In the meantime, the court can suspend execution of the judgment pending the clarification.

We see, therefore, that with respect to presenting new evidence or new legal arguments, the *Regulations for Proceedings in Rabbinical Courts in Israel* preserve the principle that litigants can request a reopening of the proceedings. On the other hand, the *Regulations* specify that a claim that there was an error in a judgment handed down by the court can only be brought as an appeal before the Supreme Rabbinical Court.

Hence, in this regard, that is, with respect to reconsideration of a judgment by the court that issued the original decision, the regulations governing rabbinical court procedures do not preserve the classic stance of Jewish law. A litigant who wishes to point out an error in judgment is unable to do so in the court that handed down the ruling in the case, and instead must turn to the court of higher instance, namely, the Supreme Rabbinical Court. It would seem, however, that if one of the litigants feels that the ruling on the appeal is incorrect, there is no bar to his returning to the court (viz., the Supreme Rabbinical Court) to request a reconsideration

35 3301/717 (5725) [1964] PDR 6, 317–18.

of the judgment. For at this point—when there is no higher instance to which to submit an appeal of the higher court's decision—the traditional halakhic principle that the court that hears a case must reconsider its decision as many times as are needed to dispel any concerns it might be erroneous, once again comes into play.

In contrast to the situation vis-à-vis aggrieved litigants' seeking reconsideration of a judgment, the court that ruled on the matter can, according to the provisions of the *Regulations for Proceedings in Rabbinical Courts in Israel, 1993–5753,* itself initiate such a reconsideration if it has concerns that its ruling was erroneous. This is consistent with the traditional position of Jewish law on the non-finality of judgment. But the court can renew consideration of a case on the grounds that its decision was in error only as long as the matter has not been brought before the Supreme Rabbinical Court. Clearly, allowing the court that rendered the decision in question to reopen its deliberations after the case has been taken up by the higher instance would undermine the organizational framework within which both courts operate. When, however, the first court only wishes to point out an error in a ruling handed down by the higher court, and the latter admits that it did, in fact, err, its decision is obviously void, and the case is reopened.

Before concluding, it is important to draw attention to a law that might appear to conflict with our account of the halakhic attitude to finality of judgment. I refer to the rule, established by the Sages, that resolving disputes by way of compromise arrived at through arbitration, is to be preferred to dispute-resolution through the courts, which render their decisions strictly in accordance with the law. Maimonides codifies this rule as follows: "It is a religious obligation to first say to the litigants, Do you want a judgment or a compromise? If they want a compromise, then arbitrate a compromise. A court that always brings about a compromise is to be praised."[36] This might be taken to imply that arriving at the truth is not the uppermost value, and the halakha manifests a preference for a functional solution that is agreed upon by both parties. But this is by no means an accurate understanding of the admonition to seek out compromise solutions. When the sides to a dispute choose arbitration, they do not bring their legal question to the table at all, and thus obviate the need for a ruling. Compromise, far from reflecting an alternative legal desideratum, an alternative halakhic value, bypasses the legal realm altogether. Nevertheless, it can be argued that the preference for conflict resolution on the basis of compromise reflects the same deep concern about rendering mistaken rulings and thereby subverting the law that is manifest is the legal process proper.[37]

36 Maimonides, *Code,* Laws concerning the Sanhedrin 22:4.

37 See Berachyahu Lifshitz, "Compromise" (Hebrew), in *Kovetz Mishpatei Aretz* (Hebrew), (2002), 137.

## Appendix *Regulations for Proceedings in Rabbinical Courts in Israel, 1993–5753*

### Chapter 14 Annulment of a Judgment and Re-Hearing a Case

128. New Hearings at the Initiative of the Court
If the court suspects that it erred in its judgment, it can invite the parties for further clarification. In the meantime, the court can suspend execution of the judgment pending the clarification.

129. New Hearings at the Request of a Litigant
i A litigant has the right at any time to request a new hearing from the court that judged his case, on the basis of factual claims or new evidence of which he was not aware at the time of the previous hearing.
ii The party making the request must submit a written request specifying the claims or new evidence, and the reason he did not adduce them at the previous hearing.

130. Consideration of the Request
i The court will consider the request without hearing arguments from either side, and will decide whether to reject it, or to invite the parties to a hearing regarding the request.
ii If the court decides to invite the parties to a hearing regarding the request, it can suspend execution of the judgment pending the clarification.

131. The Judgment
After the clarification has been conducted, as specified in this chapter, the court will either affirm the judgment, or nullify it and issue a new judgment.

### Chapter 15 Appeal

132. Appeal of a Judgment or Decision
i Any judgment or decision handed down by a district rabbinical court that decisively decides the matter in a manner that precludes issuance of further judgments can be appealed to the Supreme Rabbinical Court.
ii Temporary or interim judgments cannot be appealed unless the Supreme Rabbinical Court has granted permission to appeal.
iii The Supreme Rabbinical Court is permitted, under special circumstances, to allow an appeal for reasons not listed here.

133. Appeal by Permission
i A request for permission to appeal must include a copy of the judgment or decision being appealed, the grounds for the appeal, and [in the case of an interim judgment] the arguments why the appeal should not be heard after the final judgment has been issued.

ii The time-limit for filing a request, as indicated, is ten days from the day the judgment or decision that is the subject of the appeal was handed down. If the litigant did not receive advance notice regarding the time the judgment or decision would be handed down, the ten day period will begin from the time that he was informed that the judgment or decision had been handed down.

iii Regarding requests for permission to appeal, to lengthen the period for submitting an appeal, or for advancing or postponing a hearing date, the court or the president of the Supreme Rabbinical Court or one of the judges on the bench of the Supreme Rabbinical Court who is authorized to do so, will make a decision on the basis of the written material, without hearing arguments from the litigants.

iv If it is decided to grant permission to appeal, as indicated, the said request will serve as the statement of appeal, notice of which will be given the litigants.

v Within two weeks of the day notice is given to the appellant, he must complete everything required for submitting an appeal, as detailed below.

134. Conditions for Appeal
The Supreme Rabbinical Court is permitted, at its discretion, to make submission of an appeal conditional on the deposit of appropriate guarantees.

135. Grounds for Appeal
Appeals must be based on the following grounds only:
a An error in law.
b A manifest error in the exercise of [the Court's] discretion or in establishing the facts.
c A defect in the conduct of the hearing that influenced the outcome of the hearing.

136. Material that was Not Provided to the Court that Issued the Judgment
Appeals cannot be based on circumstances that arose after the hearing had concluded, or on evidence or facts that were not brought before the court that issued the judgment.

137. Waiver of the Right of Appeal
A judgment that was issued on the basis of an arbitration document cannot be appealed if it was noted in the document that both sides waive the right of appeal, or if both sides declared before the court that they waive the right of appeal. If only one side waived the right of appeal as indicated, he cannot appeal unless the opposing side appeals.

138. Time-Period for Submitting an Appeal
i For all litigants, the period within which an appeal can be submitted is thirty days from the day the judgment was handed down.

ii If the litigant did not receive notice in advance regarding the time at which the judgment would be handed down, the thirty day period will begin from the time he was informed that the judgment had been handed down.

139. Extension for Filing an Appeal
Under special circumstances, the Supreme Rabbinical Court may decide to accept an appeal that is submitted after the stated time period, after giving each litigant the opportunity to express his opinion thereon.

140. Method for Submitting an Appeal
An appeal is submitted by conveying a statement of appeal to the secretary of the regional court that judged the case, or to the secretary of the Supreme Rabbinical Court.

141. Statement of Appeal
Every statement of appeal must include the following items:
a The name of the appellant and his address, identity number, and telephone number.
b The name of the respondent and his address, identity number, and telephone number–if they can be ascertained.
c The court that issued the judgment or decision that is the subject of the appeal.
d The date it was issued or received.
e The grounds for the appeal.
f The appellant's petition.

142. Provision of the Reasons for the Judgment
If an appeal was submitted regarding a judgment that was issued without its underlying reasons, the Supreme Rabbinical Court is permitted, even before the beginning of the deliberations on hearing the appeal, to instruct the district rabbinical court to provide an account of its reasons within a time-period that it establishes. It is also authorized to suspend execution of the judgment until this account is provided. The litigants may by agreement waive provision of the court's reasoning.

143. Copies
i The statement of appeal must be submitted with four copies for the court, and an additional number of copies corresponding to the number of respondents.
ii Four copies of the judgment or decision that is the subject of the appeal must be attached to the statement of appeal, one of which must be certified by the court's secretariat.

144. Response to the Appeal
The secretariat of the Supreme Rabbinical Court will send a copy of the statement of appeal and the attached documents to the respondents. Each respondent has fifteen days from the day he receives the statement of appeal to submit a response.

145. Counter-Appeal

i The respondent may submit a counter-appeal within fifteen days of receiving the copy of the statement of appeal. After this time, he can submit a counter-appeal only in accordance with the conditions stated in section 139.

ii All the directives governing appeals set down in this chapter apply equally to counter-appeals, except for the submission of copies of the judgment that is being appealed.

146. Execution of the Judgment and Suspension Thereof

i The appeal does not suspend execution of the judgment unless this was stipulated in the original judgment or ordered by the court that issued the judgment.

ii If the court that issued the judgment decided not to suspend its execution or if it did not render a decision within three days of the submission of a request to suspend execution of the judgment, and the matter has been established to the satisfaction of the president of the Supreme Rabbinical Court–the party found liable may submit a request to suspend execution of the judgment to the Supreme Rabbinical Court.

iii The court that decides to suspend execution of the judgment may make the suspension conditional on the fulfillment of provisions, including the deposit of guarantees by the party requesting the suspension.

147. Hearing the Arguments of the Litigants in an Appeal

i On the date that has been set for deliberating the appeal, the appellant will present the claims on which his appeal is based. The court may immediately reject the appeal without the respondent being required to respond to it. If the court does not immediately reject the appeal, they will proceed as indicated in section 150.

ii The Supreme Rabbinical Court may decide an appeal solely on the basis of the written material in the file, if all of the parties to the appeal agree to this. Nevertheless, even under these circumstances, the court may decide at any time to have the litigants present their claims orally.

148. Written Summaries

The court may instruct the litigants to summarize in writing their arguments regarding either the entire case or a specific question set by the court, whether in addition to or in place of oral arguments, whether the oral arguments have begun or not.

149. Hearing from Counsel

In an appeal, counsel may argue in place of his client, and the litigant himself need not be heard or present in the court, unless instructed otherwise by the court.

150. Procedure for Hearing an Appeal
The court will first hear the appellant and then the respondent. The court may, as it sees fit, allow the appellant to answer a specific point or points raised by the respondent.

151. Non-appearance of Litigants
   i If the litigants, having been summoned according to the law, do not appear at a meeting that was set to clarify the appeal, the court may, as it sees fit, postpone the deliberation to another day or cancel the appeal.
   ii If the appellant appears, but the respondent, having been summoned according to the law, does not appear, and it is not clear that there is sufficient cause for his absence–the court may, as it sees fit, consider the appeal in the absence of the respondent or postpone the deliberation to another day.
   iii If the respondent appears, but the appellant, having been summoned according to the law, does not appear, and it has not been clarified that there is sufficient cause for his absence–the court may, as it sees fit, postpone the deliberation to another day, consider the appeal in the absence of the appellant, or cancel the appeal.

152. Bringing Witnesses and Evidence
No testimony or evidence is to be presented to the Supreme Rabbinical Court unless the Supreme Rabbinical Court so decided because of extenuating circumstances.

153. The Judgment
The court may reject or accept an appeal. It may change a previous judgment, cancel it, or issue a new judgment in its place. It may also return the case to the court that originally judged it, or to the same court but with a different composition, or to a different district court, for further clarification, to gather evidence, or to more fully articulate the rationale for the judgment.

# Self-help

# 6 Self-help



## 1 Introduction

> It was stated: R. Judah said, One may not take the law into his own hands; R. Nahman said, One may take the law into his own hands.
>
> bBaba Kama 27b

Every legal system addresses the issue of self-help. The universality of self-help rests on the recognition that there are occasions when recourse to the courts cannot be expected. These occasions will vary from one society to another. The concept of self-help demarcates the sphere within which the individual is free to act on his own behalf, distinguishing it from the sphere within which one has a legal obligation to resort to the courts. This chapter will explore the classic talmudic source for the doctrine of self-help, and rulings on self-help by the post-talmudic authorities. As will become apparent, whereas Jewish law initially took a rather liberal approach to self-help, over time it came to uphold a more restricted view.

All societies recognize that their members have, to one degree or other, various rights. These rights can be realized by enlisting the aid of societal agencies—the police, the courts, and so on—or by direct action on the part of the individual in question, without recourse to legal intervention. The latter action is known as 'self-help.' We can distinguish two contexts in which this sort of action might conceivably be taken: the civil law context, and the criminal law context. With regard to civil, that is, monetary, matters, one might act unilaterally to protect his interests, to recover his belongings from someone who has taken them unlawfully, collect a debt, levy a distraint, and so on. In the criminal context, one might punish an offender to avenge a wrong, or act in self-defense to protect his person and property. But although the scope of self-help may extend to both these areas, it is not clear that it does. We must therefore begin by exploring the scope of self-help in Jewish law.

## 1.1 Scope of self-help

Is self-help indeed appropriate in both the criminal and the civil law contexts? Contemporary western law answers this question unequivocally in the negative: a criminally-injured party has no right to punish an offender, though he may have some standing to be heard at the sentencing stage of the legal process, or at parole hearings. Punishment is meted out by the collective, by society as a whole, not by the individual. Since the victim has no right to punish the offender who has wronged him, it follows that he may not act to vindicate a non-existent right. Hence in contemporary western law, self-help is relevant only in the civil law context.

Jewish law, too, relates differently to self-help actions in civil and criminal matters, though it makes no conceptual distinction between the two realms. Biblical law, for example, permits the individual to avenge the murder of a relative, see Numbers 35.

Is individual action more acceptable in criminal or in civil law? The answer to this question turns on several considerations. Is it just and reasonable to expect an injured party to forbear direct action and sue his opponent in court? Consider self-defense to prevent damage to property. It is, perhaps, reasonable to restrain the injured party from using force and instruct him to turn to the courts to redress his losses. But would the same expectation be reasonable if he is exposed to physical danger? Should we instruct him to submit to violence and then sue for the loss of a limb? Conversely, if we argue that private action in self-defense is not permitted, does this mean that self-help to assert monetary rights is forbidden a fortiori?

A hybrid position is also conceivable: recourse to self-help may be efficacious from the victim's perspective, and may even be legally acceptable, but the action itself might nonetheless constitute a felony. This obviously generates tension between the civil and criminal spheres. The forcible recovery of goods by their rightful owner illustrates this tension. While the action itself is recognized by the law, and the goods are left in the possession of the rightful owner, he may still bear criminal liability for assault or trespass committed during his recovery of the goods. Such inconsistency between the various branches of the law is found in legal systems that do not, as a matter of principle, recognize the individual's right to self-help, and permit self-help only in special cases.

This chapter focuses on self-help in civil law.[1]

### 1.2 Dilemma of self-help

Arguments for and against granting the right to self-help can be put forward.

The strongest argument in favor of self-help is that there are undoubtedly instances where immediate action may prevent irreparable monetary loss, loss that financial compensation awarded later will not make good. Furthermore, private action is often faster, cheaper, and more efficient than litigation, and may act as a deterrent against offenders who count on protracted legal proceedings.

The arguments against self-help are weightier. Englard summarizes them as follows:

> All legal systems are somewhat suspicious of and unsympathetic to this remedy. Its disadvantages are obvious. The litigant cannot properly assess the extent of his rights, and use of force may be met by opposition, leading to a breach of peace, so that the more violent party gains the upper hand regardless of his legal position. This remedy originated in societies where lack of a strong central government left considerable latitude for individual action. In the absence of such an authority, the individual could only rely on his own resources to assert his rights. Historically, ineffective governments strove to restrict self-help. In thirteenth century England, a time when the country was

1 Certain aspects of self-help in the criminal context are addressed in Chapter Seven below, "Law of the pursuer."

> ravaged by feudal wars, self-help was totally banned. With the emergence of stronger central government, opposition to self-help diminished, as the authorities gained confidence in their ability to confine private action to reasonable limits.... No wonder, therefore, that most systems allow for private action only within clearly defined limits.[2]

The main argument against allowing self-help is fear of breach of the peace. It is likely that individual action will involve the use of force which, if resisted, will lead to chaos and anarchy. The tendency to restrict the individual's right to self-help thus reflects concerns about the public good.

The relationship between recognition of self-help and the presence of a strong central authority may be reflected in the talmudic sources. As we will see, the legality of self-help is debated by the Amoraim, and R. Nahman, the chief exponent of self-help, was himself an active judge with extensive power to exercise his authority.

What is the general attitude of Jewish law to these problems? Preserving public order is indeed a significant consideration in Jewish law, and various laws and enactments take the public interest, in the broad sense, into account. The following mishnaic law is an example:

> These things were enacted in the interest of peace ... the cistern near the aqueduct is to be filled first—in the interest of peace. [Removing wild] animals, birds, or fish from traps is considered theft—in the interest of peace.
>
> mGitin 5:8

The market overt enactment (*takanat hashuk*) is another example of legal intervention to promote the public interest. Ordinarily, an owner retains title to goods until he transfers it. The market overt enactment governs the sale of stolen goods to an innocent third party. It sets out an exception to this general rule: the original owner may recover his goods, but must refund the purchase price to the unwitting purchaser of the stolen goods. This enactment gives precedence, not to individual's property rights, but to the public interest in ensuring that commercial activity can be conducted unimpeded.

Despite these examples, however, the general tendency of Jewish law is to keep legislation of this sort to a minimum, and give precedence to the individual interest over the public interest. A good illustration is the case of partially illegal contracts, that is, contracts made for legitimate purposes, but containing illegal clauses, such as clauses that contravene tax laws or

2 I. Englard, "Self-help" (Hebrew), in G. Tedeschi (ed.), *Law of Civil Wrongs: The General Part* (Hebrew), (Jerusalem: 1969), 533–34.

currency regulations. In English law, such contracts are void and cannot serve as the basis for any claim. In the words of Lord Mansfield:

> The objection, that a contract is immoral or illegal as between plaintiff and defendant, sounds at all times very ill in the mouth of the defendant. It is not for his sake, however, that the objection is ever allowed; but it is founded in general principles of policy, which the defendant has the advantage of, contrary to the real justice, as between him and the plaintiff, by accident, if I may so say. The principle of public policy is this: *ex dolo malo non oritur actio*. No court will lend its aid to a man who founds his cause of action upon an immoral or illegal act.[3]

The policy of English law is to void any benefit derived from an illegal action. Jewish law, on the other hand, upholds the interests of the individual even when this is not in the public interest, and thus—apart from the illegal clause—recognizes the contract, which can serve as the basis for claims against the parties involved.

More generally, the institution of self-help is useful in explicating the halakhic approach to the dilemma of individual rights versus the public interest. Relative to other legal systems, Jewish law tends to sustain the individual's right to self-help, despite the possibility that this will be detrimental to the public interest. This tendency may reflect a fundamental trust in the individual, the assumption being that he would not take the law into his own hands unless this was justified, and that, even then, he would act with restraint, using the minimal force necessary to defend his rights.

A less idealistic explanation for this disparity between Jewish law and western law has also been suggested:

> There is no doubt that the purpose of law is to keep the peace and prevent individuals from taking the law into their own hands.... In this respect Jewish law represents a stage of partial public law, alongside the earlier system of direct individual action.[4]

Falk's claim that Jewish law has elements that are simply less developed than western law reflects acceptance of the western attitude to self-help, namely, that it is undesirable and to be avoided as far as possible. We contend, however, that Jewish law views self-help in a more positive light. Though Jewish law indeed limits the scope of self-help, this does not necessarily represent its general tendency. Due to practical constraints, any legal system will fall short of its ideals, but it can be argued that Jewish law aspires to grant the individual the right to self-help.

3 Holman v. Johnson 98 ER 1120, 1121 (1775).
4 Zeev Falk, *Legal Values and Judaism* (Hebrew), (Jerusalem: 1980), 14, 67.

### 1.2 Jurisprudential basis of self-help

There are two main schools of thought regarding the jurisprudential basis of the right to self-help in Jewish law. Some halakhic authorities argue that the right of ownership includes the right to recover property usurped by another. Since such recovery of misappropriated property does not take place within the framework of the judicial process, it is not constrained by the rule that one may not adjudicate his own case.[5] Others understand self-help as a power delegated by the court to the individual: the individual may act as if he were the court. On this understanding, self-help is regarded as an exception to the rule that a sole judge may not adjudicate, as stated by R. Jacob b. Asher (Tur):

> Even though one person may not render judgment [by himself], he may take the law into his own hands.
>
> *Tur*, HM 4

This view is implicit in comments by various Early Authorities:

> One may take the law into his own hands.... therefore if his adversary complained about him and brought the matter before the court, and the court investigated, and found that he had acted in accordance with the law, and rendered a true judgment for himself, then his judgment is not reversed.
>
> Maimonides, *Code*, Laws concerning the Sanhedrin 2:12

Note, however, that this law appears in the *Code* among the laws governing the conduct of judges.

In the same vein, R. Joseph Colon writes:

> It is not considered an instance of "one may take the law into his own hands" unless he acted as a quasi-judge, for instance, by distraining in place of a debt, or by meting out corporal punishment ... to enforce payment.
>
> *Responsa Maharik*, #161

However, this view is problematic. The main function of courts is to settle disputes with finality. The authority to do so was clearly never delegated to individuals, since the losing side could always then turn to the court. Rather, the individual who takes the law into his own hands is accountable to the court, which will determine whether his action was justified.

It is doubtful whether R. Joseph Colon intended to provide a theoretical characterization of self-help. Rather, he seems to provide a practical

5 See Y. Dinari, "Self-Help in Jewish law" (Hebrew), 4 *Dine Israel* (1973), 91–107.

definition of the scope of self-help—that is, of the principle "one may take the law into his own hands," namely, it covers actions that are usually carried out by the court or with its authorization. Similarly, Maimonides' description of the individual's action—"[he] rendered a true judgment for himself"—in judicial terms may be no more than a figure of speech, and not intended to imply a conceptual identification of the two institutions.

Some Later Authorities, however, explicitly state that an individual who has recourse to self-help is acting in a judicial capacity.[6]

A novel approach to the concept of self-help has been put forward by a contemporary scholar, Shalom Albeck, who has written extensively on the status and authority of courts in talmudic law. He maintains that talmudic law does not grant courts any special authority to adjudicate over and above that granted to individuals. On this view, every individual has the authority to administer justice:

> For by law, the authority of permanently appointed judges has no basis in the halakha, and the fundamental laws concerning judges, and the foundations of judicial authority, do not apply only to them, but to everyone in Israel, and are the purview of all members of the nation equally.[7]

From this perspective, the individual's right to adjudicate for himself is self-evident; he is not granted this right by the courts. Rather, the courts' right to adjudicate is an extension of the right enjoyed by every individual.

## 2 The talmudic *sugya*, bBaba Kama 27b–28a

The main talmudic source for self-help is bBaba Kama 27b–28a. The *sugya* begins by describing a case of assault and battery about which the Amora R. Nahman was consulted.

### 2.1 Talmudic examples

#### i The shared cistern

> There was a water cistern owned by two partners, from which each of them would draw water on alternate days. One came and drew water on a day that was not his. The other said to him, This is my day. The first took no notice of him. The other hit him with the handle of his spade. [R. Nahman said to R. Hisda]: [He is entitled to hit him even] a hundred times with the handle of his spade.
>
> bBaba Kama 27b

6 Shakh, *Tekafo Kohen*, §103; R. Tzvi Hirsh Kalischer, *Moznaim Lamishpat*, §93.
7 S. Albeck, *Law Courts in Talmudic Times* (Hebrew), (Ramat Gan: 1987), 14.

The Talmud proceeds to analyze the case to identify the principle underlying the doctrine of self-help. First, can it be concluded from R. Nahman's ruling that self-help is legal?

> Even those who say that one may not take the law into his own hands would, when an irreparable loss is involved, say that one may take the law into his own hands. For we learned: R. Judah said, One may not take the law into his own hands; R. Nahman said: One may take the law into his own hands.

The question of whether one may take the law into his own hands is the subject of an Amoraic dispute. The *sugya* delineates the scope of the dispute. In a situation where an irreparable loss will be incurred if someone waits and sues his adversary in court, everyone agrees that one may have recourse to self-help. There is only controversy over the case where no irreparable loss is incurred, that is, where, if the injured party refrains from resorting to self-help, and instead turns to the court, he will incur no loss by doing so. In the latter case, R. Judah says that one is not permitted to resort to self-help ("for since no irreparable loss is pending, let him go before the judge"), whereas R. Nahman says he is permitted to resort to self-help ("for since he acts in accordance with the law, he need not exert himself [to go to court]").

The Talmud does not regard the case of the shared cistern as the paradigm case of self-help, since it has a special feature—irreparable loss. The Talmud proceeds to examine a number of baraitot, each of which recounts an act of self-help, to ascertain whether the law is in accordance with the view of R. Judah or in accordance with the view of R. Nahman.

### ii The forceful intruder

> Ben Bag Bag says: When recovering your possessions, do not enter your fellow's courtyard without his permission, lest he take you to be a thief; rather break his teeth and tell him, 'I am taking that which is mine.'

This baraita seems to support the view of R. Nahman.

### iii The aggressive ox

> An ox climbed on the back of another ox and was about to kill it. If the owner of the ox on the bottom came and pulled his own animal away, and the ox that was on top fell and died, [the owner] is exempt. Is this so only with regard to a 'prone-to-do-damage' ox, where no loss is involved? No, it is so with regard to an innocuous ox, where irreparable loss is involved. But if so, read the final clause '[if the owner of the ox

> on the bottom] pushed off the ox that was on top, and it [fell and] died, [the owner] is liable.' If it was an innocuous ox, why is he liable? Because he should have pulled his own away, but he did not pull his own away.

This passage consists of two parts: the baraita, and its analysis by the Talmud. The baraita itself needs no explanation. However, to understand the Talmud's reasoning, a principle of biblical tort law set out in Exodus 21:35–36 must be taken note of: the owner of an ox that is a first-time offender pays for only half the damage caused by his animal. A first-time offender is termed an "innocuous" animal (*tam*). If the ox has already attacked three times, however, its owner is liable for the entire amount of damage incurred. Such an animal is termed "prone to do damage" (*muad*) in Exodus 21.

The Talmud concludes that this baraita cannot be used in support of either R. Judah or R. Nahman, because the status of the attacking ox is not mentioned. If it was prone to do damage, then no loss was involved, since full damages could be recovered in court. This would support the opinion of R. Nahman. If it was innocuous, then half the damage would have to be sustained as a loss, in which case the baraita would not contradict the view of R. Judah. All that can be stated with certainty is that recourse to self-help is legally justified if such an action averts an irrecoverable loss, as noted above.

Discussion of the baraita does, however, advance our understanding of self-help, since it introduces the 'reasonable force' principle. Given that self-help is permissible where there will be irreparable loss, what is the import of the distinction between pulling out one's own animal and pushing off the attacking animal? The Talmud introduces this distinction in order to limit self-help to the use of reasonable force. An individual acting to safeguard his interests may use only the force needed to neutralize the threat, and no more.

### iv The obstructed courtyard

> If someone filled his fellow's courtyard with jars of wine and jars of oil, the owner of the courtyard may break them as he goes in and out.

This is a case of trespass, where the person who stored his jars in the other party's courtyard did so without permission; his deed obstructed the courtyard owner's ability to pass through and use the courtyard. The law set down in the baraita is that the owner may remove the obstruction even by breaking the jars. This baraita, then, supports R. Nahman's position vis-à-vis self-help: one may take the law into his own hands.

To align this baraita more closely with the stance of R. Judah, the Talmud adds a qualification. R. Nahman b. Isaac stipulates that breaking the jars is only permissible if the courtyard owner has to leave home (and therefore pass through the courtyard) in order to go to court to lodge a complaint against the obstruction. Does the baraita condone the use of unlimited force? It might be argued that breaking the jars constitutes excessive force, since the owner could simply have rearranged the jars so that they did not obstruct his path, without breaking them. And indeed, the *Tosafot* raised this query, answering that having to constantly rearrange the jars would be an unreasonable imposition on the courtyard owner, and he was under no obligation to take the trouble to prevent the loss by rearranging the jars. However, note that the Talmud implies that the owner may break only those jars that obstruct him "as he goes in and out."

These three baraitot (the intruder, the ox, the courtyard) were adduced by the Talmud in support of R. Nahman's position that one may resort to self-help even where there is no irreparable loss, and though R. Judah was able to meet the challenge, his reply is not persuasive: these three baraitot are clearly in accordance with R. Nahman's position.

The Talmud also adduces several other baraitot, but the Early Authorities are not in agreement as to whether they were intended to support the view of R. Judah, contra R. Nahman, or whether were invoked to counter both views, that is, whether they were intended to cast doubt on the legitimacy of self-help under any circumstances. Let us consider one such baraita:

## v The relocated road

> Someone had a public road crossing his field ... he took possession of it and allocated a road for the public on the side. What he has allocated has been allocated [i.e., is now public] and what he repossessed is not his [but remains public]. And should you say that one may take the law into his own hands, he could take a stick and guard over his property.... for R. Judah said, A path that has [long] been in the possession of the public cannot be interfered with.

Were self-help legal, the owner would have been able to close the first road, whose users are, after all, trespassing. This ruling contradicts the view of R. Nahman if no loss is involved, or the views of both R. Nahman and R. Judah if loss is involved. Whether there was or was not a loss is debated by the commentators. However, the Talmud informs us that the case in question is an exceptional one, inasmuch as in this type of case, a different rule—namely, the rule that 'A path that has [long] been in the possession of the public cannot be interfered with'— takes precedence over the usual rule. The upshot is that the ruling in the case of the relocated road cannot be adduced in support of either R. Nahman's position or R. Judah's.

To recapitulate, the structure of the *sugya* is as follows: a case is presented (the shared cistern); R. Nahman's ruling is reported; a controversy between the Amoraic Sages R. Nahman and R. Judah over the general legitimacy of self-help is recounted; the scope of the controversy is delineated (there is only controversy over cases where no irreparable loss will be incurred); after which the Talmud adduces a series of cases where self-help might be relevant, in an effort to infer from them which opinion is correct, R. Nahman's or R. Judah's. The diversity of the adduced cases is characteristic of the Talmud's casuistic reasoning. The Talmud delineates the boundaries of the concept under discussion by examining qualifications to and limitations on a number of only loosely-related cases. Indeed, as we will see, the element common to all the cases discussed by the Talmud is the need to resort to force or even inflict damage. Self-help, according to the *sugya,* is an action, involving force or causing damage, undertaken by an individual to realize a right that has been appropriated by someone else.

All in all, the Talmud discusses eight paradigmatic cases of self-help. For a comprehensive discussion of these cases and an exposition of the underlying principles, see Appendix 2.

We can conclude that the Talmud recognizes, in general, the legitimacy of self-help. However, the rulings in the talmudic examples to some extent defer to R. Judah's opinion that there is a right to self-help only where one would otherwise suffer an irreparable loss.

## 2.2 Post-talmudic rulings

The Talmud does not unequivocally state that the law is decided in accordance with the view of R. Nahman, that is, in favor of self-help even in the absence of a monetary loss, but some post-talmudic authorities, such as R. Hananel, see a clear tendency in this direction. Furthermore, a rule in bKetubot 13a stipulates that the views of R. Nahman on matters of civil law are binding, since he was a practicing judge. Consequently, the majority of post-talmudic authorities accept the R. Nahman's position that self-help is permitted even when no monetary loss is at stake. A minority of authorities support the view of R. Judah. Let us review them first.

### i *The Book of Sheiltot*

The *Book of Sheiltot* (Queries) is the first extant work written after the redaction of the Talmud. Its author, R. Aha, lived in Shabha, Babylon, in the first half of the eighth century. The book consists of approximately two hundred sermons presented in the form of questions and answers.

The following passage appears in the second sermon:

> One who has a claim against his fellow must not take violent action against him. Rather, he needs to go to the judge, who will decide for them in accordance with Torah law.... for the world rests upon truth and law, as was taught in the Mishnah.[8]

8 The passage goes on to cite mAvot 1:18: "Rabban Shimon b. Gamaliel says: 'The world is sustained by three things: by law, by truth, and by peace.'"

The Talmud, we saw, maintains that self-help, and the use of force, is permitted if an irreparable loss would be incurred by waiting and going to court. R. Aha makes no mention of this. He also ignores the opinion of R. Nahman, whose other rulings on points of monetary law he recognizes as binding. Apparently, R. Aha opposed recourse to self-help under any circumstances. Yet it is hardly conceivable that R. Aha ruled contrary to established halakhic principles.

A number of solutions to this problem have been proposed. For example, in his *Haamek Sheeila* commentary on the *Book of Sheiltot*, the nineteenth century halakhist R. Naftali Z. Berlin (Netziv) suggests that R. Aha refers to a case where the party in question lacks evidence that would be admissible in court, and consequently was not allowed to take the law into his own hands. In other words, according to the Netziv, one can resort to self-help only regarding a property-right that can be proven in court, should the party in question later be sued on account of his having inflicted damage while taking the law into his own hands.

However, the context of R. Aha's dictum should be taken into account. If we keep in mind that the *Book of Sheiltot* is a collection of sermons, it is not surprising that the author does not exhort his audience to engage in acts of violence, but rather advises them to follow the pious, who choose to forbear their legal rights out of moral considerations. Advice of this kind is common even in strictly legal works, which sometimes recommend supererogatory conduct: conduct beyond that which is required by the law, conduct that is desirable, but not obligatory.[9] Hence R. Aha's position as to the law, or his stance regarding the Amoraic controversy between R. Nahman and R. Judah, cannot be inferred with certainty.

### ii *Halakhot Gedolot*

*Halakhot Gedolot* is a collection of laws authored by R. Shimon Kaiara of Basra, Babylonia, in the eighth century. His stand on self-help is manifest in his version of the 'forceful intruder' case:

> Ben Bag Bag says: When recovering your possessions do not enter your fellow's courtyard without his permission, lest he take you to be a thief; rather, break his teeth with the law and tell him, 'I am taking that which is mine.'

Comparing this version with the talmudic version quoted above reveals that R. Shimon Kaiara has made an important insertion— "with the law"— which softens the violent image evoked by Ben Bag Bag, reading it as a metaphor meaning, 'sue him and vanquish him in court.' The source of the inserted phrase is the continuation of the talmudic *sugya*, where an attempt

9 See Chapter Eight below, "Equity."

is made to reconcile the baraita with R. Judah's view. Ben Bag Bag's dictum was quoted in support of R. Nahman's view. The Talmud responds on R. Judah's behalf by adducing a dictum of R. Yanai: "What does 'break his teeth' mean? [It means] with the law."

As it stands, this passage of *Halakhot Gedolot* seems to support R. Judah's view, though without saying so explicitly. This would suggest that the halakhic authorities in post-talmudic Babylonia rejected self-help. However, as quoted by the Tosafist R. Moses of Coucy in his *Sefer Hamitzvot Hagadol* (*Semag*), the opinion of *Halakhot Gedolot* is just the opposite:

> And the law is in accordance with the view of R. Nahman in matters of civil law, and this was the decision of Alfasi and *Halakhot Gedolot*.
>
> *Semag*, Positive Precept 93

Moreover, R. Meir Hakohen of Rothenburg, the author of *Hagahot Maimoniot*, a commentary on Maimonides' *Mishne Torah*, also cites *Halakhot Gedolot* as concurring with R. Nahman. It seems probable that the halakhic authorities of Franco-Germany had a different tradition as to the view of R. Shimon Kaiara: these scholars may have been in possession of a version of *Halakhot Gedolot* in which the problematic phrase was not added.

### iii Rabbenu Efraim

Rabbenu Efraim of El-Kala, a student of Alfasi, is the only authority in the early post-Geonic period who expressly rules in accordance with the view of R. Judah, that is, against self-help where waiting and taking up the issue in court would not result in a monetary loss.

> This is not a civil law matter, since it does not determine who is liable and who is exempt [from paying].... Rather, it is a disagreement over that which is permissible and that which is forbidden. For R. Nahman contended that one may take the law into his own hands, but R. Judah contended that one is forbidden to take the law into his own hands where he incurs no loss by waiting to take the matter to the court.... And the law is in accordance with the view of R. Judah.
>
> *Commentary on Alfasi*, Baba Kama ch. 3, letter 1 (Vilna edition, page 12b)

Rabbenu Efraim argues his decision as follows. First, he addresses the rule that in civil (viz., monetary) matters, the law is decided in accordance with the view of R. Nahman, stating that "this is not a civil law matter." He classifies self-help as falling under the rubric of ritual law (*isur veheter*), the laws governing that which is permissible and that which is forbidden. Since controversies on points of ritual law are not subject to the said decision-making rule, we are free to decide the law in accordance with whichever of the two views we wish. He then proceeds to argue for R. Judah's view, and against R. Nahman's.

Rabbenu Efraim's argument is not convincing, since the legitimacy of self-help involves more than just the permissibility of taking action *ab initio*. Indeed, another issue—and perhaps the main issue—at stake here, does have monetary implications, namely, the issue of whether one who has recourse to self-help must compensate the other party for any damage ensuing from the actions taken in self-help. The Rosh rules, for instance, that "one may take the law into his own hands and is exempt from paying for ensuing damages to his fellow."[10] Furthermore, the Talmud itself adduces cases in which the question of liability is explicitly raised, for instance, the baraita of the 'aggressive ox.'

There is a tradition that under the influence of Alfasi, Rabbenu Efraim changed his mind, and decided the law in accordance with R. Nahman's view:

> ... in accordance with the view of R. Nahman and not in accordance with the view of R. Judah.... and this was the decision of the *Halakhot Gedolot*, and of R. Hananel and also of Alfasi, who debated this point with Rabbenu Efraim until he conceded to him.
>
> *Hagahot Maimoniot*, Maimonides, *Code*, Laws concerning the Sanhedrin, ch. 2, note 5

This passage led to a controversy among later scholars. Who conceded to whom? The text, though ambiguous, seems to imply that it was Rabbenu Efraim who was won over by Alfasi's persuasive arguments. In general, while there is reason to think, in light of the above quotations from *The Book of Sheiltot*, *Halakhot Gedolot* and Rabbenu Efraim, that a few of the early post-talmudic authorities did rule in accordance with R. Judah's view that recourse to self-help is illegitimate,[11] it is by no means clear that this is so.

In any event, the majority of the Early Authorities ruled in accordance with R. Nahman's view, in line with the rule that in matters of civil law, the law is in accordance with R. Nahman's view. These decisors include Rabbenu Hananel, Alfasi, Maimonides and the Rosh. Consider once again Maimonides' expansive and unequivocal statement of the law of self-help:

> One may take the law into his own hands if he has the power to do so. Since he is acting fully in accordance with the law, he is not obliged to exert himself and bring the matter before the courts, even though he would sustain no monetary loss if he were to put off taking action and [instead] bring the matter before the court. Therefore if his adversary

10 *Piskei Harosh*, Baba Kama, ch. 3, sec. 3.

11 This claim is argued for in Dinari, n. 5 above.

> complained about him and brought the matter before the court, and the court investigated, and found that he had acted in accordance with the law, and rendered a true judgment for himself, then his judgment is not reversed.
>
> *Code*, Laws concerning the Sanhedrin 2:12

This law is the *Code*'s main statement of the legality of self-help, though Maimonides also adduces the specific talmudic examples of self-help in the appropriate sections of the *Code*.

R. Jacob b. Asher (Tur), writing in the fourteenth century, takes the following position on self-help:

> Even though one person may not render judgment [by himself], he may take the law into his own hands. This means, if he sees his belongings in the hands of someone who robbed him, he may take them back from the one who robbed him. And if the said party resists and protests, he may beat him till he lets him take back his possessions.... Even if he would lose nothing by waiting until he can bring him to justice, but he does not want to exert himself to bring him to justice, even so, since it is clear to him that he is right, and justice is on his side, he is permitted to save his own property, even by the use of force, if he cannot do it by some other means.
>
> *Tur*, HM 4

In the wake of the rulings by Maimonides and the Tur, the *Shulhan Arukh* ruled similarly. These opinions will be discussed in the following sections.

## 3 Self-help in tort law

### 3.1 Introduction

We have seen that self-help is defined as an act taken by an individual against someone else to prevent a monetary loss without resorting to court action. In the context of tort law, self-help is an action intended to remedy damage, for example, taking back goods from the robber who stole them. Such an action performed at the time of malfeasance must be distinguished from an action carried out at a subsequent time. The former is an act of self-defense, and seeks to forestall the damaging act, or its completion, whereas the latter aims at re-establishing the *status quo ante*. From a legal and equitable perspective, these two types of action differ significantly. Defense, or prevention of injury, is obviously justified; it would be preposterous to expect anyone to let the offender proceed undisturbed and then to file a suit against him in court. Indeed, this kind of action is regarded by most contemporary legal systems as self-defense, and recognized as the inalienable right of every individual. Such action is not deemed to fall under the rubric of self-help. On the other hand, acts that typically take place after the damage has been done, such as seizing property, and seek to restore the *status quo ante* without involving the courts, are considered to be the classic instances of self-help. Yet arguably, acts of self-defense can also be regarded as taking the law into one's own hands, since these too are instances where an individual uses force against someone else under circumstances involving loss that is not necessarily irreparable afterwards—monetary compensation may be a sufficient remedy—and may be recoverable by court action.

The talmudic *sugya* we have examined understands self-help, that is, taking the law into one's own hands, in this wider sense, that is, as encompassing not only the classic cases of self-help, but also self-defense at the time the harmful act is actually being carried out. However, its principal focus is tort law. As we have seen, according to Jewish law, in certain situations, it is permissible for the victim to resort to force while engaging in self-help.

The basic rule governing self-help can be stated as follows: one may take the steps necessary to protect one's property from damage (as in the case of the aggressive ox), and one may also act to redress the injury or damage sustained, even by means not permitted in ordinary circumstances, provided that only reasonable force is employed (as in the case of the obstructed courtyard). Acts of self-help are subject to judicial review. If such an action is found to be unjustified—for example, if the person who had been in possession of an object was indeed entitled to have it, and the individual who resorted to self-help was not—then the individual who carried it out is liable to pay damages to the party against whom he acted. However, the burden of proof is on the party injured by the act of self-help, and the outcome of the act of self-help is deemed legal until proven otherwise.

It should be noted that it is not always easy to categorize cases of self-help as unequivocally falling under the category of 'self-defense while harm is being committed' or 'restoration of the *status quo ante*.' Which category a given case falls under may depend on the specific circumstances of the incident. The incident depicted in the baraita of the shared cistern, for example, may be a one-time event, where the partner whose right to water is being usurped can intervene to prevent imminent harm, or it may be a case where the arrangement of alternate days for each partner has been eroding, and the goal of the self-help is to exert pressure on the non-compliant partner so that he will honor the arrangement, thereby restoring the *status quo ante*.

In upholding the legitimacy of self-help, Jewish law differs from most contemporary western legal systems. While the latter recognize cases in which the individual may take the law into his own hands, these are the exception rather than the rule. In Jewish law, the opposite is true: the general rule is that self-help is permitted, and the exceptions are specified.

In addition to the two goals of self-help mentioned above—prevention of harm and restoration of the *status quo ante*—a further goal of self-help in the tort law context is to obtain restitution for injury or damage, usually by levying a distraint in lieu of the damages sustained, with no attempt to restore the *status quo ante*. This type of action is problematic in Jewish law, which hesitates to make the offender's property subject to restitution.

Let us now turn to a detailed analysis of how self-help plays out with respect to the three motivations for recourse to self-help in tort law: abatement of nuisances; restoring the *status quo ante*; and levying a distraint.

### 3.2 Abatement of nuisances

In Jewish law, the rubric of 'self-help' encompasses protective actions undertaken when harm is imminent or while harm is being inflicted. The best example is the baraita of the aggressive ox, discussed above.

> An ox climbed on the back of another ox and was about to kill it. If the owner of the ox on the bottom came and pulled his own animal away, and the ox that was on top fell and died, [the owner] is exempt.
>
> bBaba Kama 28a

The Talmud cites this case to support R. Nahman's opinion that self-help is permitted even when no monetary loss is involved. However, the case itself is one where there is indeed an imminent risk of loss. Specifically, it is a case where an aggressor is engaged in doing damage, and the owner of the property must take immediate action to repel the aggressor and save his property. The ruling implies that one may defend his property against attack or damage, and may use force and cause damage to the aggressor, without incurring any liability to compensate the aggressor for the damages caused. These implications are articulated in the halakhic literature. For instance, R. Menahem Hameiri asserts:

> If anybody uses force against that which belongs to his fellow, and the attacked party is there and sees the attack ... he may take the law into his own hands to repel [the attacker] so as to make him desist. He may even beat him several times ... until he repels him.
>
> *Beit Habehira*, bBaba Kama 27b

#### i Abatement of nuisances in the responsa literature

Incidents in which individuals are called upon to defend their property are frequently encountered in the responsa literature, which presents actual decisions on queries submitted to various rabbinical authorities.[12] We will examine two such responsa. The first was written by R. Yair Bacharach in seventeenth-century Germany.

> A learned man had a shop in front of the entrance to his house [where he sold] all kinds of legumes and grains. His neighbor's chickens kept scurrying to the shop and eating the grain. Even though the owner chased them away several times, they kept returning. A number of times he told the chickens' owner to watch them ... but he was indifferent. And then one time when the chickens returned and ate the grain, the shopkeeper struck a blow at them and killed one of them, one of the best egg-layers and brooders ... and they came before the court.
>
> *Responsa Havat Yair*, #168

The shopkeeper justified his action by invoking the dictum "one may take the law into his own hands." Nevertheless, he lost his case and had to pay for the dead hen. In his opinion, R. Bacharach notes that the "one may take the law into his own hands" rule applies "only against someone who seeks to inflict harm voluntarily and intentionally." If those circumstances exist, R. Bacharach asserts, then one may defend himself and his property, "but that is not the case here, where his fellow's animal is harming him without its owner's volition or understanding."

This is significant: the responsist has set down a new rule, which limits the right to defend oneself against the infliction of damage.

This determination clearly contradicts the ruling of the baraita of the aggressive ox, which allowed the attacked ox's owner to defend his ox against the attacking ox. R. Bacharach himself cites this baraita as contrary to his view, saying that the contradiction warrants further study, but he nevertheless concludes the responsum with the declaration: "in any event, the law, as I have rendered it, is the true law." His reasoning may have been that the baraita permits the handling of one's own animal, but not the intentional infliction of harm on someone else's. The shopkeeper attacked the neighbor's animals, which is analogous to pushing off the attacking ox, which was forbidden by the baraita.

Let us now turn to another responsum on nuisance abatement. The nineteenth century decisor R. Shalom Schwadron of Brzezany (Maharsham) was asked to give a ruling about a case where, after having repeatedly warned his neighbor to keep his animals away, someone scattered poison in a field to keep the animals from harming his crop.[13] Relying on R. Yair

12 See B. Lifshitz, "The legal status of the responsa literature," in H. Ben-Menahem and N. Hecht (eds.), *Authority, Process and Method: Studies in Jewish Law* (Amsterdam: 1998), 59–100.

13 *Responsa Maharsham*, #140.

Bacharach's ruling on the hungry chickens, R. Shalom Schwadron does not rule that the poisoning was permissible. In both the case of the chickens and that of the poisoning, the action was taken within the harmed individual's own domain, and the neighbor's animals entered without permission, presumably at their own peril. Nevertheless, after deploring cruelty to animals, which is also a transgression, R. Shalom Schwadron says: "It is not possible for me to be lenient, as there were other means [available to achieve the desired end]." Even for the legitimate purpose of protecting one's property, recourse to force exceeding that which is necessary cannot be condoned.

### 3.3 Restoring the *status quo ante*

The classic case of self-help, as noted above, is an act carried out after harm has been inflicted, the aim of which is to restore the situation that existed prior to the damage. The most commonly-encountered instance of such self-help involves recovery of property, either moveable or immoveable, that someone else is holding unlawfully.

#### i Seizure of movable property

Let us return to the baraita of the forceful intruder in Baba Kama.

> Ben Bag Bag says: When recovering your possessions, do not enter your fellow's courtyard without his permission, lest he take you to be a thief; rather break his teeth and tell him, 'I am taking that which is mine.'
>
> bBaba Kama 27b

This baraita clearly affirms the right to use force to recover belongings that are unlawfully held by someone else.

R. Jacob b. Asher's *Arbaa Turim* explicitly rules in line with the baraita:

> ... he may take the law into his own hands. This means, if he sees his belongings in the hands of someone who robbed him, he may take them back from the one who robbed him. And if the said party resists and protests, he may beat him till he lets him take back his possessions.
>
> *Tur*, HM 4

Maimonides, on the other hand, states the law governing self-help in a general way, and does not specify that it applies in the case of recovering misappropriated possessions. However, by virtue of being so broad and general, his formulation of the right to self-help certainly encompasses the right of distraint.

> One may take the law into his own hands if he has the power to do so. Since he is acting fully in accordance with the law, he is not obliged to exert himself and bring the matter before the courts.
>
> *Code*, Laws concerning the Sanhedrin 2:12

There are, however, other views, such as that put forward in the Meiri's commentary on Baba Kama:

> If anybody uses force against that which belongs to his fellow, and the attacked party is there and sees the attack … he may take the law into his own hands to repel [the attacker] so as to make him desist.… But if the forcible act is over—for example, if they have already robbed him … it does not fall under this law, for the law applies only while the forcible act is ongoing.
>
> *Beit Habehira*, bBaba Kama 27b

R. Menahem Hameiri distinguishes between self-help at the time damage is being inflicted, and self-help after damage has been inflicted. He rules that self-help is permissible for the purpose of forestalling damage that is being inflicted, but once the damage has been done, the individual has no right to self-help to retrieve his misappropriated possessions. He thus restricts the right to have recourse to self-help, limiting it to self-defense and prevention of damage at the time it is being inflicted. That is, he explicitly distinguishes between defensive actions, and actions intended to restore the *status quo ante*. This distinction is also made, we saw, in contemporary western law. Yet this distinction diverges from the ruling in the baraita of the forceful intruder, which manifestly deals with restoration of the status quo after the misappropriation. Moreover, the Meiri seems to be contradicting what he wrote further on in the passage:

> Hence, one who sees his belongings in someone else's house and fears that this person intends to keep them permanently, may enter in that person's presence to recover his possessions by force … and tell him, 'I am taking that which is mine.'

Here, he is clearly speaking of restorative self-help after the misappropriation has already taken place.

The solution to the apparent contradiction is implicit in the phrase "fears that this person intends to keep them permanently." The Meiri argues that the baraita of the forceful intruder presents a case in which an individual's belongings came into someone else's hands lawfully. The owner may have given his belongings to the holder as a bailment, for safekeeping, or for any other reason, but now fears that the holder intends to claim they are his, and keep them. In this type of situation, the Meiri claims, the act of self-help does not restore the *status quo ante*, but rather, forestalls impending injury.

### ii Seizure of immovable property

Let us first recapitulate the talmudic ruling regarding seizure of property. Seizure of property is an act carried out by a property owner to regain property usurped from him. A distinction must be made between a usurper and a trespasser: a usurper denies the owner's rights, a trespasser does not. Accordingly, trespass will be dealt with separately.

The relevant talmudic passage is the baraita of the relocated road.

> Someone had a public road crossing his field ... he took possession of it and allocated a road for the public on the side. What he has allocated has been allocated [i.e., is now public] and what he repossessed is not his [but remains public]. And should you say that one may take the law into his own hands, he could take a stick and guard over his property.... for R. Judah said, A path that has [long] been in the possession of the public cannot be interfered with.

The Talmud's question is, why should the owner lose both allotments? Once he has given the public land for the replacement road, why must he also forfeit the land on which the original road was built? Should he not be entitled to "take a stick and guard over his property," that is, use force to keep the public from entering and using the original road? Such an action could be regarded as a preventative measure to forestall impending damage, but another reading of the case is more plausible. The road, though on the said individual's land, was used by the public, and could be regarded as in the public's possession. This being so, denial of usage would constitute seizure of the property, and amount to restoration of the *status quo ante.* Both from the counter-argument ("and should you say..."), and the reply that taking action against land in public possession is forbidden, it can be deduced that, as a rule, one is entitled to evict usurpers from one's property. Hence despite its ruling, the baraita of the relocated road cannot be adduced to argue against the right to self-help.

Yet this analysis is not universally accepted. R. Jacob Lorberbaum of Lissa cannot accept the permissibility of recourse to force in the self-help context.

> It thus appears ... that we must distinguish between land and movables. Regarding movables, where there is apprehension that loss may be incurred, the use of force is permissible ... but regarding land,

> where there is no apprehension about loss, the use of force is forbidden *ab initio.*
>
> *Netivot Hamishpat*, 4:3

R. Jacob of Lissa maintains that with respect to movables, where, by their very nature, loss is possible—due to breakage, for instance—an owner can resort to self-help to recover something that had been misappropriated. But with respect to land, where damage and loss are irrelevant, he maintains that the owner is not permitted to take the law into his own hands and seize that which is in his fellow's possession, but rather, must turn to the courts. This restrictive approach to self-help does not follow from the talmudic *sugya*, however, but is a forced reading motivated by the desire to restrict the scope of self-help.

### iii Action against trespassers

Trespass is the an act of entering and making use of someone else's property unlawfully, without contesting the owner's rights or title. Reference to trespass is made in the baraita of the obstructed courtyard, but there is a more explicit passage in bBaba Metzia:

> A certain man bought a vat of wine and had no place to put it. He asked a woman, Do you have a place for rent? She said, No. He went and betrothed her, and she gave him a place to store it. The man went home, wrote a bill of divorce and sent it to her. The woman went and hired porters, to be paid in wine, who carried the wine out and put it [the remainder] in the street. R. Huna the son of R. Joshua said: As he did, so was done to him; the fellow got what he deserved.
>
> bBaba Metzia 101b

The case of the deceitful wine-merchant is a clear case of self-help to evict a trespasser. The merchant gained access to the woman's premises under false pretenses, hence she can get rid of the wine even at its owner's expense. We can infer that one can act to evict a trespasser without involving the courts. It remains to be established whether this is a particular case of the general rule allowing self-help, or falls under a separate rule applicable solely to cases involving deceit.

Although the Talmud does not explicitly mention the "one may take the law into his own hands" rule, its relevance to the case is clear. This was noted by various Early Authorities and commentators, such as R. Eliezer b. Nathan (Raban), who states: "We can conclude that the law is thus, and in all similar cases one may take the law into his own hands, even where no loss is involved."[14]

14 *Even Haezer*, ad loc.

Maimonides rules:

> Regarding someone who placed his produce in his fellow's house without his knowledge, or misled him until he [was given permission] to place it there, and he left it there, and went off—the owner of the house may sell some of the produce to hire workers to take out the remainder, and discard it in the marketplace.
>
> *Code*, Laws concerning Hiring 7:7[15]

R. Jacob b. Asher's ruling is:

> Regarding someone who asked his fellow to rent him [space in] his house to place his produce there, but he did not want to, and he misled him until he [was given permission] to place it in the house—the owner of the house is permitted to take some of the produce to hire workers and discard the remainder in the marketplace ... for he can say, I do not want to rent to him, because he misled me.
>
> *Tur*, HM 319

This law can indeed be interpreted in a narrow sense, as addressing not trespass per se, but gaining entry by false pretenses, the consideration that justifies allowing self-help in this particular instance. However, Maimonides clearly understands the law in the wider, more general sense: the focus of his ruling is not the deception, but rather, the illegal act of trespass. This can be inferred from the fact that Maimonides identifies two conditions (placing the produce in the house without the homeowner's knowledge, and placing it there as the result of misleading him), either of which is sufficient to justify self-help. Maimonides, then, does not condition the permissibility of recourse to self-help on the presence of deceit. R. Jacob b. Asher, on the other hand, does just that, explicitly invoking the deception—"for he can say, I do not want to rent to him, because he misled me."

Other halakhic authorities add additional constraints on recourse to self-help in cases of trespass. Indeed, even Maimonides notes that: "[The homeowner manifests] the attribute of piety (*midat hahasidut*) by informing the court [that the produce has been removed from his house] and they will rent a place for it] with some of the produce, because it is like the return of lost property to its owner, even though he acted improperly."[16] Maimonides specifies that this is a moral admonition, not a legal obligation. But R. Asher b. Yehiel and R. Jacob b. Asher go further, asserting: "He must notify the trespasser, and if after having notified him, [the homeowner] was forced to take action, he is exempt."[17] R. Menahem Hameiri says, in a similar vein:

15 The *Shulhan Arukh* rules similarly.

16 Maimonides, *Code*, Laws concerning Hiring 7:7. On the attribute of piety, see Chapter Eight below, "Equity."

17 *Piskei Harosh*, Baba Metzia, ch. 8, sec. 26; *Tur*, HM 319.

"Not only that, but if [the trespasser] does not want to leave, the [homeowner] may sell some of the goods [the trespasser] stored there in order to hire workers to remove everything he had in the house and throw it onto the road, provided it can be assumed that the matter will come to the knowledge of the goods' owner [viz., the trespasser], so that he can come and salvage it."[18] Though he does not expressly state that the homeowner is obliged to notify the trespasser before acting, nevertheless, that is the thrust of the clause "if [the trespasser] does not want to leave," which implies that the trespasser must be informed of the homeowner's intention to evict him. Moreover, in stipulating that removal of the goods can only proceed if it can be assumed that the trespasser will be apprised of this development, the Meiri is further limiting the homeowner's right to have recourse to self-help against the trespasser. If we compare the Meiri's stance here with his remarks on the forceful intruder (section 3.3.i above), it is apparent that in both cases, he restricts the scope of permissible self-help.

R Yair Bacharach was asked to decide a case somewhat evocative of the 'deceitful wine-merchant' case:

> During the turmoil of the wars with the French, the villagers smuggled out their belongings to their relatives and acquaintances in the cities ... and among the city dwellers was a homeowner who had many such smuggled goods in his rooms, until they were almost full from one end to the other.... and he checked in the chests and bundles ... and he found a bundle, and inquired and investigated ... but could not ascertain whose it was.... Having expended effort on asking and inquiring to ascertain who the owner was, but being unable to ascertain this, he took the bundle and threw it into the courtyard.... And a few days later, the owner of the bundle came, and found that much of the contents of his bundle had been stolen, and a number of garments, pillows, and quilts had been ruined by the rain.... And the owner of the bundle sued the homeowner.
>
> *Responsa Havat Yair*, #165

Basing his decision on the case of the 'deceitful wine-merchant,' which he deemed a 'definitively articulated talmudic passage,' the local judge cleared the city dweller, though he suggested a compromise—namely, that the landlord would store the remaining items from the bundle for six months—which was accepted by the litigants. R. Yair Bacharach strongly criticized this decision, stating that if indeed the local judge exempted the homeowner from indemnifying the trespasser, he erred on a point of law (*toe bidvar mishna*), a judicial error that invalidates the ruling handed down.[19] In his opinion the case is not analogous to that of the 'deceitful

18 *Beit Habehira*, bBaba Metzia 101b.

19 See Chapter Four above, "Erroneous rulings," section 7.2, and Chapter Five above, "Finality of judgment," section 3.3.

wine-merchant,' in which entrance was gained under false pretenses. He points out that in the *sugya* of the wine-merchant, the woman did not place the vat where it was certain to be damaged. R. Yair Bacharach maintains that the city-dweller should have given the trespasser notice of his intention to remove the bundle, and in any event should not have moved the bundle to a place where its contents would be subject to damage, but should have sold some of the contents and used the proceeds to rent a place to store the remainder.

R. Yair Bacharach limits the scope of the 'deceitful wine-merchant' ruling to cases of deceit. Although other authorities share his opinion, his severe censure of the city judge is surprising. The latter's decision should not have been dismissed out of hand as in error on a point of law, given that it accords with the view of Maimonides and the *Shulhan Arukh*, both of whom rule that even in a case where there was no deceit, but rather, the trespasser placed his produce in his fellow's house without his knowledge, the homeowner may take action to remove the produce, and is exempt from liability. Furthermore, the Talmud and the post-talmudic authorities make it clear that the owner is not legally responsible for damage to the trespasser's goods. It is reasonable to suppose that the harsh circumstances of the case, namely, the turmoil caused by the war, influenced R. Yair Bacharach's decision to limit the right to self-help in this particular instance. This sensitivity to exceptional circumstances is often encountered in responsa, which do not seek to render a ruling that will apply to all cases, but to decide only the case at hand. When appropriate, the responsist will deviate from the opinion of earlier authorities and adopt a creative interpretation of the law, in order to accommodate the unusual circumstances in question.

## 3.4 Conclusion

We can conclude that there is wide scope for self-help in the realm of tort law. One may have recourse to self-help to prevent ongoing damage, but it is principally invoked to restore the *status quo ante.* One may use force even to the extent of injuring the other party. Some authorities, however, limit recourse to self-help. For instance , R. Menahem Hameiri, who prohibits self-help post-factum, limits self-help to cases that are akin to self-defense, and R. Jacob of Lissa denies the right to self-help where land is concerned. Still others, for example, R. Yair Bacharach, restrict recourse to self-help to cases of deceitful intent. These limitations, however, are limitations on the circumstances in which self-help can be resorted to. Moreover, it must be kept in mind that these restrictive rulings are minority views. The general principle that "one may take the law into his own hands," however, is universally endorsed by the halakhic authorities. Overall, Jewish law provides considerable scope for recourse to self-help. In this, it differs markedly from contemporary western legal systems, which uphold the opposed position, namely, that the individual is forbidden to act on his own to realize his rights, except in a small number of exceptional situations.[20]

## 4 Self-help in collecting debts

Thus far, we have examined two areas where self-help comes into play: abatement of nuisances and restoration of the *status quo ante*, for instance, by taking back a misappropriated object. In the next section, we will consider the question of self-help to obtain restitution for injury or damage, usually by levying a distraint in lieu of the damages sustained, when it is not possible to restore the *status quo ante*. The intuitive rationale for self-help is intimately connected with the harmful act, seeking to either preempt it or 'undo' it. But where the act can neither be preempted nor undone—as, for example, when a stolen possession has been sold or destroyed—how relevant is self-help? Self-help is a suitable means for achieving abatement of nuisances and restoration of the *status quo ante*, but its suitability for attaining restitution is more tenuous, since the harm in question is irreversible.

May one distrain the offender's property to compensate oneself for a loss caused by the offender? Where a misappropriated object, for instance, does not exist any longer, its owner's claim becomes a monetary one, and his rights are those of a creditor. It is an established principle of Jewish law that a creditor may not enter the debtor's premises, and is limited in his right to levy distraints. It is to this issue that we now turn.

### 4.1 Introduction

Whereas the foregoing discussion dealt with tort law, we are now in the realm of contract law, which governs the relationship between borrower and lender, a realm fundamentally different from that of tort law. The Torah lays down detailed laws pertaining to borrowing and lending in general, and recovery of debts and seizure of pledges in particular.

> If thou lend money to any of My people, to the poor among you, do not act toward them as a creditor; exact no interest from them. If you take your neighbor's garment in pledge, you must return it to him before the sun sets.
>
> Exodus 22:24–25

> When you make a loan of any sort to your neighbor, you shall not go into his house to seize his pledge. You shall stand outside, and the one

20 Other scholars have taken a different view of Jewish law's attitude to self-help, taking it to be far more circumscribed. Dinari, e.g., contends that in light of the various qualifications to the principle that recourse to self-help is permissible, the disparity between Jewish law and western law vis-à-vis self-help is basically cosmetic, see Dinari, n. 5 above, 91.

> to whom you made the loan shall bring the pledge out to you. If he is a needy man, you shall not go to sleep in his pledge.
>
> Deuteronomy 24:10–12

Protection of the debtor is clearly the paramount consideration. Thus the creditor's right to resort to self-help against debtors cannot be taken for granted. The extent of the self-help to which a creditor is entitled must be investigated.

### 4.2 Taking a pledge without a court order

> One who lent money to his fellow must not take a pledge from him, except by court order, and he may not enter the debtor's house to seize a pledge, as it is said, "you shall stand outside" (Deut. 24:11).
>
> mBaba Metzia 9:13

The Mishnah, in adducing the biblical injunction "you shall stand outside" to prohibit the taking of a pledge without a court order, is in essence ruling out self-help in this context. A creditor cannot act on his own, but must turn to the courts to take a pledge from a debtor as security for a loan. There are some halakhic authorities who maintain that even seizing a pledge outside the debtor's house is forbidden by Rabbinic enactment. But since, as we saw, the general tendency of Jewish law is to endorse self-help, we can expect to find that this Mishnah is usually interpreted by the halakhic authorities in a manner that limits its applicability.

Such a restrictive interpretation is offered by Rabbenu Tam. He suggests that only the seizure of a pledge given as a security is forbidden. For the purpose of collecting the debt itself, however, the creditor may enter the debtor's house and seize his belongings as a distraint. Doing so does not contravene the biblical prohibition "you shall not go into his house," Rabbenu Tam argues, which covers only collection of the collateral pledged by the debtor. Collection of the debt itself, however, falls under the rubric of self-help, and hence is permissible. He thus makes a distinction between taking a pledge before the payment is due, as a security to ensure that the debt will be paid, and levying a distraint after a default. The latter is permissible without recourse to the courts.[21]

Although Rabbenu Tam's reading of the law is not forced, and does not distort the plain meaning of either the biblical or the mishnaic law, it is nevertheless rejected by most of the halakhic authorities, who prohibit any private action by the creditor against the debtor.

The twentieth-century scholar Asher Gulak has argued that the mishnaic injunction against taking a debtor's pledge was not upheld in practice, and creditors did indeed seize pledges on their own, without first turning to the court, in line with the long-standing popular tradition of taking

21 *Sefer Hayashar*, sec. 602 (Schlesinger edition).

pledges. Moreover, he argues that this was fully in accord with the biblical law, which, he stresses, prohibits the creditor from entering the debtor's home, but not from taking the pledge: "you shall not go into his house to seize his pledge. You shall stand outside, and the one to whom you made the loan shall bring the pledge out to you" (Deut. 24:10–11).[22]

Gulak substantiates this claim by adducing passages from the Babylonian and Jerusalem Talmuds. One such passage is the following:

> A creditor who comes to take a pledge must not enter the debtor's house to take the pledge, but must stand outside, and the latter enters and brings it out to him.
>
> bBaba Metzia 113b

According to Gulak, this passage proves that the creditor takes the pledge on his own. But Gulak's reading is not necessarily correct. First, there is no reason not to interpret the talmudic passage as implying that the creditor has obtained the court's permission, in line with the mishnaic stipulation quoted above. Second, there is no indication that the creditor intends to take the pledge by force, without having attained the debtor's consent. The passage in question specifies that while it is permissible for a creditor to demand that the debtor bring him the pledge, it is unacceptable for him to invade the debtor's space and forcibly remove the pledge. Though Gulak also adduces other passages from the Rabbinic literature that describe seizure of pledges, they by no means prove unequivocally that individual action of this kind is deemed permissible *ab initio*.

### 4.3 Collecting a debt not originating in a loan

The Mishnah quoted above, mBaba Metzia 9:13, regulates the relationship between debtor and creditor when the debt originates in a loan, but not when the debt arises out of unpaid wages or rental arrears. This distinction is set forth in the following baraita.

> One is not permitted to enter the home [of a borrower], but one is permitted to enter in order to collect wages for porterage, wages for driving donkeys, rent for a room at the inn …
>
> bBaba Metzia 115a

The baraita deals specifically with a debt originating in unpaid wages or rent, stating that the prohibition against entering the debtor's home does not apply in these cases. It remains to be ascertained whether the cases mentioned in the baraita are merely examples of obligations that do not originate in loans, or whether they are the only cases to which the rule

22 A. Gulak, *History of Jewish Law: Talmudic Period* (Hebrew), vol. 1, Law of Obligation and its Guaranties (Jerusalem: 1939), 128.

applies. Rashi understands this law broadly, as applying to "any debt that is not a loan." Rabbenu Tam, who interprets the aforementioned Mishnah (mBaba Metzia 9:13) literally, restricting its applicability, concurs with Rashi, adding "and a vendor may enter the home of a buyer, just like one who collects rent."[23] Here, as in the distinction between seizure of pledge and levying a distraint, Rabbenu Tam interprets the biblical prohibition in a manner that minimizes its scope, or to put it differently, in a manner that maximizes the space for permissible recourse to self-help.

R. Isaac b. Sheshet Perfet (Ribash) takes a similar stance:

> [Since one may take the law into his own hands,] the creditor may seize anything in the debtor's possession or in his home, as long as the debt did not originate in a loan. But if it was a loan, he certainly must not enter [the debtor's] home or seize any of his possessions.
>
> *Responsa Ribash*, #396

This approach, which seeks to restrict the biblical prohibition to cases of monetary loans only, was not universally accepted.

Indeed, many authorities prohibit self-help to collect any debt, regardless of how it was incurred. These halakhic authorities contend that the right to self-help for the purpose of recovery extends only to recovery of goods unlawfully taken by another, and does not allow for the appropriation of either money or other property in lieu of the unlawfully-taken goods. This view thus favors an expansive reading of the mishnaic prohibition, and restricts the scope of self-help for recovery of misappropriated assets. It originated among the rabbinical authorities of thirteenth-century Franco-Germany, led by R. Meir of Rothenburg, the Maharam:

> Our rabbis of Speyer ruled, regarding the case of Reuben,[24] who was indebted to Shimon and did not pay back the debt, that Shimon may take and seize whatever belongings of Reuben he can find, because one may take the law into his own hands. And I wrote to them: Do not ascribe this inane view to R. Nahman, for we have learned in Baba Metzia, 'One who lent money to his fellow must not take a pledge from him.'... And what is said here, namely, that one may take the law into his own hands ... applies to [recovery of] the specific item alone, since because this particular item is his, he may seize it anywhere.
>
> *Responsa Maharam* (Prague edition), #950

That is, the Maharam, rejecting the view of the rabbis of Speyer, maintains that self-help is only permissible to recover one's own belongings, but not to distrain other property belonging to the debtor in place of a defaulted

23 *Sefer Hayashar*, sec. 354 (Schlesinger edition).

24 It is customary in the responsa literature to denote the litigants by the proper names of Jacob's sons.

loan. His opinion is supported by his students R. Mordekhai b. Hillel and R. Asher b. Yehiel.[25] R. Jacob b. Asher concurs:

> Even though one person may not render judgment [by himself], he may take the law into his own hands. This means, if he sees **his belongings** in the hands of someone who robbed him, he may take them back from the one who robbed him.... but he is not permitted to seize a pledge from him to secure a debt.
>
> *Tur*, HM 4

This decision is subsequently adopted by the *Shulhan Arukh*. However, this approach is obviously not in accord with the sources, and it is unclear what gave rise to it. The biblical injunction "you shall not go into his house," which is the basis for the view that limits the scope of self-help, refers specifically to the creditor-debtor relationship, and is so understood by the Mishnah and the Talmud. Moreover, the law's underlying rationale is the nature of the relationship between creditor and debtor, which is inherently imbalanced: the creditor has the upper hand.

It would seem that in Jewish law, as in western law, the tendency to restrict the scope of self-help reflects a desire to keep the peace and avoid distortion of justice due to unilateral high-handed action by aggressive individuals. The context most likely to lend itself to concern about inability to keep the peace would be that of levying a distraint.[26] It is also conceivable that the fact that entering a home to make a seizure is prohibited, and not merely deemed unseemly, was a factor in the emergence of a restrictive understanding of self-help. Of all the restrictions on the principle that "one may take the law into his own hands," the rule that self-help is permissible only to recover one's own article from someone holding it unlawfully is the most significant.

The following talmudic *sugya* sheds further light on the matter:

> Four hundred barrels of wine belonging to R. Huna had gone sour. He came before R. Judah ... and other Rabbis, and they said to him, You must examine your deeds [i.e., you must have done something to deserve this tribulation]. He said to them, Am I suspect in your eyes? They said to him, And is the Holy One, blessed be He, suspected of judging unjustly? ...We heard that you did not give your tenant farmer the vine twigs [that are his due]. He said to them, What was left for me when he [finished harvesting]?—he stole the whole lot! They said to him, So the saying goes, 'Stealing from a thief tastes of theft all the same.'
>
> bBerakhot 5b

25 See *Piskei Harosh*, Baba Kama, ch. 3, sec. 3.

26 R. Mordekhai b. Hillel refers to this explicitly, noting that were it permissible to enter and seize belongings, "no one would be able to survive, since everyone would say to his fellow, 'You stole my property,' hit him, and grab the [allegedly misappropriated] items" (*Mordekhai*, Baba Kama, ch. 3, sec. 30).

R. Huna withheld vine twigs from a tenant farmer who had stolen from him, yet the Sages considered him to have acted wrongly. This *sugya* is quoted by a number of decisors to show that levying a distraint is prohibited for any debt, even if it did not arise from a loan. The *Mordekhai*, for instance, makes this point it as follows:

> And it can be proven from the story in Berakhot … and R. Kalonymos queried, 'Yet was he not entitled to take it, since we uphold the principle that one may take the law into his own hands?' We must say [in reply] that one is permitted to take [back]—from any place one can retrieve it—the very possession that was taken from him, in line with what Ben Bag Bag said, 'he is taking that which is his.' But here he took [i.e., withheld] other vine twigs, not those that the tenant farmer had stolen.
>
> *Mordekhai*, Baba Kama, ch. 3, sec. 30

But is this case an appropriate one to adduce for the purpose of determining whether there is a right to distrain a debtor who has defaulted on a non-monetary-loan debt? Is the act described in this *sugya*, namely, R. Huna's withholding of wine twigs, really a case of self-help? It can be argued that the Sages' comments about the act do not address its legal status—lawful or unlawful—but rather, speak to its having failed to meet the standards expected of the pious, to go beyond that required by the law. The Sages felt that R. Huna, a role model and a learned scholar, should have gone out of his way to give his tenant-farmer all that he was entitled to, even though he claimed the latter had stolen far more from him than he was owed. Notice that the Sages invoke a popular saying rather than discussing the scope of the legal rule 'one may take the law into his own hands.' The way R. Huna conducted himself 'tastes of theft,' because regardless of the legal situation, and regardless of whether the thefts cancelled each other out, a public figure must not act in a way that could be considered high-handed or unfair. It should be noted that the concept of self-help is not mentioned in the *sugya*.

In summary, the biblical injunction against seizing a pledge is interpreted in two ways. Rabbenu Tam limits its scope to the seizure of a security, but allows self-help to realize the debt itself. Most of the halakhic authorities, however, expand the scope of the prohibition, so that it encompasses all private action against a debtor, and even debts that do not originate in a loan.[27]

27 The discussion in this chapter has revolved around the individual's right to have recourse to self-help. Whether self-help can be used by the community against an individual is also an interesting question. This issue is discussed in Quint and Hecht's *Jewish Jurisprudence*, 2:135–142, reproduced below in Appendix 3.

## Appendix 1 bBaba Kama 27b–28a*

It has indeed been stated: Rav Judah said: No one may take the law into his own hands to protect his interests, whereas R. Nahman said: One may take the law into his own hands to protect his interests. Where an irreparable loss is imminent, no one disputes the fact that he may take the law into his own hands to protect his interests: the difference of opinion is only with regard to cases where no irreparable loss is imminent. Rav Judah said: no one may take the law into his own hands to protect his interests, for since no irreparable loss is imminent, he can have recourse to the courts. R. Nahman said: one may take the law into his own hands to protect his interests, for since he acts in accordance with the law, why [must he] take the trouble [to turn to the courts]?

I

R. Kahana raised an objection: Ben Bag Bag says: do not enter your fellow's courtyard [stealthily] to take something that is yours without his permission, lest you seem like a thief to him. Rather, break his teeth and tell him, I am taking possession of that which is mine! They said to him [on behalf of Rav Judah]: **[28a]** It is true that Ben Bag Bag supports your view, but he is only one, and the Rabbis differ with him. R. Jannai said, 'Break his teeth' may also mean, [by way of the] courts. But if so, why 'and tell him'? Should it not read 'and they [viz., the courts] will tell him'? Again, [why] 'I am taking that which is mine'? Should it not read '[He] is taking that which is his'? This is indeed a difficulty.

II

Come and hear: An ox that climbed on top of another so as to kill it—if the owner of the ox that was underneath came and extricated his ox so that the ox that was on top fell down and died—he is exempt. Does not this ruling apply to a recidivate gorer, where no irreparable loss is imminent? No, it only applies to an innocuous animal, where irreparable loss is indeed imminent. But if so, read the next clause: If [the owner of the attacked ox] pushed the ox that was on top, and it died, he is liable. Now if this is said of an innocuous animal, why should he be liable? Because he could have extricated his ox from underneath, and did not so extricate it.

III

Come and hear: [Regarding] one who has filled his fellow's courtyard with pitchers of wine and pitchers of oil—the owner of the courtyard is entitled to break them when going out and break them when coming in. R. Nahman b. Isaac said: He is entitled to break them when going out [to lodge a

*This translation is based on the Soncino translation, and differs from that used in the body of the chapter.

complaint] in court and, to break them when coming back to fetch his documents [to present to the court].

IV

Come and hear: Whence is derived the ruling that in the case of a [Hebrew] bondsman whose term of service, previously extended by the boring of his ear, has ended, and whose master is anxious to release him, and in so doing injures him, [the master] is exempt [from compensating him]? We learn it from the words, "And ye shall take no ransom for him that is … come again …" (Num. 35:32), implying that we should not order compensation for someone who has 'come again' [i.e., extended his service]. But here, what are we dealing with? A case where the servant seeks to commit theft. But how is it that up to that time he did not commit any theft and only at that point seeks to commit theft!? Up to that time he had the fear of his master upon him, whereas now fear of his master is no longer upon him. R. Nahman b. Isaac said: [The case is one of] a bondsman whose master assigned him a Canaanite maidservant as a wife: till the close of the term [of his service] this arrangement was lawful, whereas now [i.e., from that point on] it is forbidden.

V

Come and hear: "If someone places a pitcher in the public domain and someone else comes and stumbles over it and breaks it, he is exempt" (mBaba Kama 3a). The reason is that he stumbled over it, but in a case where it is broken directly, he is liable. R. Zebid said in the name of Rava: That is the law even in the case of one who breaks it directly, for the Sages' phrase "and stumbles" was inserted merely because of the next clause, which reads, "if he was injured by it, the owner of the barrel bears liability for the damage to him," which, of course, applies only to a case of stumbling, but not to an act of [direct] breakage, for in that case he would be injuring himself. It was therefore on this account that [the words] "and stumbles" were inserted in the opening clause.

VI

Come and hear: "Then thou shalt cut off her hand" (Deut. 25:12) means only a monetary fine. Does this ruling not apply even in a case she was unable to save [her husband] by any other means? No, it applies only to the case where she was able to save [him] by some other means. But in a case where she was unable to save him by any other means, she is exempt. But if so, should not the next clause have been: "And putteth forth her hand" (Deut. 25:11) excludes an officer of the court [from liability for any injury he might cause while carrying out court orders]? Could not the distinction be made by continuing: 'by some other means'–that is, if she was able to save him by some other means, but if she was unable to save him by any other means, she was exempt? So too, 'by some other means' [might mean]—that is, if she was able to save him by some other means, but if she was unable to save him by any other means, taking matters into her own hands acquired the force of acts performed by officers of the court, and she is exempt.

VII

Come and hear: "In the case of a public road that passes through someone's field, and he appropriates the road but gives the public another at the side [of his field], what he has given, he has given, but [the old road] did not thereby become his" (bBaba Batra 99b) Now, if you maintain that one may take the law into his own hands to protect his interests, why should he not sit there with a whip? R. Zebid said in the name of Rava: This is a decree to prevent someone from giving them [the public] a roundabout path [in place of an established road]. R. Mesharsheya said: it is said regarding someone who indeed gave them a roundabout path. R. Ashi said: Any road at the side constitutes a roundabout path, for though closer for some, it is further away for others. But if so, why does [the old road] not thereby become his? Why can he not say [to the authorities]: 'Take back yours [the old road] and return mine to me'? Because of Rav Judah's ruling, for Rav Judah said: A path once taken possession of by the public may not be obstructed.

VIII

Come and hear: If an owner leaves the corners of the field on one side of the field, whereas the poor arrive at another side and glean there, both sides are subject to the law of leaving corners (*peia*). Now, if you say that one may take the law into his own hands to protect his interests, why should both sides be subject to the law of leaving corners? Why should the owner not sit there with a whip? Rava said: What is the meaning of 'both sides are subject to the law of leaving corners' ? Its meaning is that they are both exempt from tithing, as has been taught: "If someone, after having renounced ownership of his vineyard, rises early the next morning and harvests the grapes, he is liable for *peret*,[1] *olelot*,[2] 'the forgotten crop' (*shikheha*)[3] and *peia*,[4] but exempt from the tithe."

1 Grapes that fall off during the harvest, which are to be left for the poor, as mandated by Leviticus 19:10.

2 Small single bunches that are to be left as gleanings for the poor, as mandated by Leviticus 19:10 and Deuteronomy 24:21.

3 Produce forgotten in the field, which is to be left for the poor, as mandated by Deuteronomy 24:19.

4 Produce in the corners of the field, which is to be left for the poor as mandated by Leviticus 19:9.

## Appendix 2 E.B. Quint and N.S. Hecht, *Jewish Jurisprudence* 2:91–106, "The manner in which a person may engage in self-help"

CHAPTER FOUR

THE MANNER IN WHICH A PERSON MAY ENGAGE IN SELF-HELP

Introduction

The Jewish legal system is structured on the assumption that most disputes will be adjudicated in the courts described in the previous chapters. There are, however, situations where a claimant may protect his[1] interests without resorting to the courts. This chapter describes those situations where one may resort to self-help and may even employ force to protect his rights.[2] Throughout this chapter, for simplicity's sake, the person employing self-help is designated as the plaintiff, and the person against whom self-help is being used is designated as the defendant.

This chapter deals with self-help situations where the chattel or money in controversy is taken from the holder without a final court judgment. In addition, it discusses analogous issues, such as requiring litigants to post security to insure payment after trial or attaching a party's property before judgment to assure satisfaction of a final judgment. It should be emphasized that, even in those cases where one has the right to employ self-help, it is generally preferable to bring the case to court, since a plaintiff who employs self-help may be liable for damages if he does not act in the precise manner prescribed by law. By obtaining a court judgment, an individual can avoid the numerous legal pitfalls which are associated with the use of self-help.

A. TALMUDIC BACKGROUND

*1. Cases Involving an Irreparable Injury*

The primary source for the principle of permitting a person to take the law into his own hands is found in a case in T. Baba Kamma and in the eight reported cases immediately following it.[3] In the principal case, A and B jointly owned an irrigation well, with each party having the exclusive right to use the well on alternate days. On a day when only A had the right to use the well, A discovered B drawing water from the well. A asked B to cease and, when B refused, A struck him with a hoe handle, forcing B to cease. B brought an action against A to recover damages for the assault.

1 Women are also included in the law of self-help. See Kovetz haPoskim (1969), p. 64.
2 Certain aspects of self-help are also discussed in Volume 1, Chapter One, pp. 104–114.
3 T. Baba Kamma 27b.

When the case came before R. Hisda,[4] he sent an inquiry to R. Nahman[5] to ascertain the rule of law to apply in the case. R. Nahman replied that, in this type of case, A could have struck B one hundred blows without being liable for the assault. (B's cause of action was accordingly dismissed.) R. Nahman further stated that, although there is a difference of opinion whether a person may employ self-help if he will not suffer irreparable injury by waiting to have his controversy resolved in court, all authorities agree that he may use self-help where he will suffer irreparable loss by waiting to have his claim adjudicated. Rashi[6] therefore explains that the case which came before R. Hisda involved irreparable loss to A, either because all of the well water might be consumed or because A might not be able to prove how much water B had used.

The holding of this case may be broken down into four points. In turn, these points will be refined by the eight cases which follow the principal case in the Talmud. Accordingly, as those eight cases are analyzed, the main points will be reformulated continually. The following four points emerge from the principal case:

POINT I: Where there is irreparable loss, one may deliberately employ self-help in the first instance and need not wait for a judicial determination of one's rights. This is a positive principle of law that may be invoked by plaintiff in the first instance. It does not represent a *post facto* acquiescence in his action. It should also be noted that this case only decides that self-help may be employed where there will be an irreparable loss if one waits for a judicial determination. It does not address the issue of whether self-help may be used where no irreparable loss would be entailed by waiting for a judicial determination of the dispute.

POINT II: The person taking the law into his own hands may use physical force to obtain his ends. He may use so much force as is necessary, but no more. He will not be liable for injury caused by such force.

POINT III: The person employing self-help must have a clear and recognizable right to the possession of the personality over which he is employing self-help. Such a possessory right may, of course, be separate from any ownership rights. In the principal case B had ownership rights in the well, but A had the right of exclusive use on that particular day. Other analogous cases easily come to mind. A pledgee, for example, has the right to possession of the item pledged, but does not own the pledge. Similarly, a bailee has the exclusive right to possession of the bailment, but does not own the chattel.

POINT IV: Self-help is subject to judicial review. Self-help terminates the original dispute between the parties and there is therefore no need for further court adjudication of the original controversy. However, the one

4 R. Hisda, Babylonian Amora (217–309).
5 R. Nahman, Babylonian Amora (3rd–4th cent.).
6 Rashi (1040–1105) on T. Baba Kamma 27b, introductory words: *b'mokom d'ika.*

against whom self-help was employed may institute suit against the one employing self-help to determine if the use of self-help was legal under the circumstances. Thus in the principal case, had the court found that A erroneously used self-help, he would have been liable to B for the assault.

### 2. *Cases Not Involving An Irreparable Injury*

While all agree that self-help can be employed where the plaintiff may suffer an irreparable injury, there is a difference of opinion between R. Nahman[7] and R. Judah[8] in cases where the delay occasioned by instituting suit will not cause the plaintiff to suffer an irreparable loss. R. Judah holds that where there is no irreparable injury entailed by waiting to go to court, the plaintiff may assert his rights only through a judicial proceeding. R. Nahman holds that even in these cases the plaintiff may employ self-help.

Eli Quint[9] explains that their dispute is predicted on the fact that R. Judah does not believe that the bother and expense of a lawsuit is an irreparable loss, whereas R. Nahman holds that the loss of time and money resulting from a lawsuit is as much of an irreparable injury as the loss of a chattel. This perceptive observation helps to explain why the Talmud frames their dispute in terms of vexation, by having R. Nahman state that the plaintiff should not have to be bothered in retrieving what is legally his. R. Judah holds that if there is no irreparable injury to the chattel, then the plaintiff must undertake the trouble of going to court, while R. Nahman holds that he need not be bothered. The Talmud[10] then cites eight cases to ascertain whether the law is in accord with R. Judah or R. Nahman. These cases will be referred to as Case 1, Case 2, etc.

Case 1 is cited as an objection to the view of R. Judah. It involved a ruling by Ben Bag Bag[11] that plaintiff should not stealthfully enter onto defendant's premises to recover that which rightfully belongs to him, lest he be viewed as a thief. Rather, he should openly enter upon defendant's premises and use any necessary force to recover his chattel. As explained by Tosafoth,[12] this case does not involve irreparable loss since the plaintiff is not permitted to sneak onto defendant's property. He adds that if irreparable loss were involved, because of the claimant being forced to go to court, then plaintiff could even enter defendant's property stealthfully. In the case of irreparable loss, plaintiff should not be given the limited choice of either suffering an irreparable loss or attempting to use force which he might not be capable of employing. It is seen from Ben Bag Bag's ruling that the plaintiff may use force even in cases where there is no

7 See note 5 *supra*.
8 R. Judah, Babylonian Amora (3rd cent.).
9 As transmitted to his son, co-author Emanuel Quint.
10 T. Baba Kamma 27b–28a.
11 Ben Bag Bag, Tanna (2nd cent.).
12 Tosafoth (12th–13th cent.) on T. Baba Kamma 27b, introductory words: *elah shavoor.*

irreparable loss by waiting to go to court, which apparently contradicts the position of R. Judah. The Talmud replies on R. Judah's behalf that Ben Bag Bag's ruling may only be that of an individual, rather than reflecting the majority view. This is, however, a forced answer, and the fact remains that Ben Bag Bag's ruling agrees with R. Nahman. The rule of law stated by Ben Bag Bag first appears in the Tosefta,[13] where he is quoted as saying that one should not steal his own property from the house of another because he would appear to be a thief, nor should one steal his own property from the house of the thief who stole it since he would also appear to be a thief. Rather, the owner should use force openly and seize his chattel from the other person.

Commenting on the Tosefta, Hasdai David[14] points out that two situations are mentioned. First, even where the defendant originally obtained possession rightfully (through a bailment, for example), plaintiff may, if he has a clear right to recover possession, use appropriate force. Second, even where defendant had obtained possession of the plaintiff's chattel by illegal means, the plaintiff should not resort to theft to recover it. Hasdai David adds that the example of recovering one's chattel in the Tosefta is a case where no irreparable loss will be involved by waiting to go to court. Yet the plaintiff may take the law into his own hands and may even use force. Minhas Birkurim[15] adds the interesting comment that the reason Ben Bag Bag rules that one should not retake his chattel by theft is because he would then have undergone the experience of stealing. This reflects a teaching appearing in another tractate of the Talmud,[16] that one should not steal an object, even if it is rightfully his, since he will thereby have experienced the act of stealing.

Zvi Hirsh Chayes[17] concludes that the answer given on behalf of R. Judah, that Ben Bag Bag may represent a minority view, is not tenable, since the Tosefta does not cite anyone as disputing Ben Bag Bag. He points out that, according to Samuel,[18] if a teaching mentions the name of the author of a rule of law and does not state that the author's view is disputed, then the teaching should be given the weight of an anonymous teaching, which is always accepted as the prevailing rule.

Rashba[19]also explains that only those attempting to defend R. Judah's view suggest that the majority view may dispute Ben Bag Bag; in reality, however, no one disputes Ben Bag Bag. Rashba proves this contention by citing the alternate answer which is given in the Talmud to support R. Judah's position. The alternate answer is that when Ben Bag Bag says that

13 Tosefta, T. Baba Kamma, Chapter 10, 38 (Zuckermandel ed., Jerusalem, 1970).
14 Hasdai David (1719–1792) on Tosefta; T. Baba Kamma, Chapter 10, 16.
15 Minhas Bikurim (1705–1771) on Tosefta; T. Baba Kamma, Chapter 10, 16.
16 T. Berakoth 5b.
17 Zvi Hirsh Chajes (1805–1855) on T. Baba Kamma 28a.
18 Samuel, Babylonian Amora (180–257).
19 Rashba (1245–1310) on T. Baba Kamma 28a.

force may be employed, he actually means forcing the defendant to appear in court. If Ben Bag Bag merely holds that a plaintiff may only recover his property by taking the defendant to court, then there would not be a majority view which differs from this view, since the first answer which is given on behalf of R. Judah is that the majority holds that, when there is no irreparable injury, plaintiff must go to court. Both the first and second explanations would be the same, and there would be no necessity for the second explanation. Thus, there is no majority disputing Ben Bag Bag.

Briefly summarizing the foregoing, Case 1 clearly holds, in accordance with R. Nahman, that a plaintiff may take the law into his own hands to retrieve personalty which is unquestionably his, even where no irreparable loss would be caused by waiting to go to court. In so doing, he may employ force.

Case 2[20] also refutes the view of R. Judah. Plaintiff saw defendant's ox leap upon plaintiff's ox, and plaintiff's ox was in danger of being killed. Plaintiff quickly pulled his ox out from underneath and, as a result, defendant's ox fell down and was killed. Defendant sued to recover the value of his ox. Judgment was rendered on behalf of plaintiff, who had used self-help.

In using this case to refute R. Judah's view, the questioner assumes that Case 2 deals with a situation where defendant's animal is a "forewarned" ox.[21] In such a case, defendant would be liable to plaintiff for the full value of the loss sustained; thus plaintiff would suffer no loss by waiting to go to court, since he would collect full damages. This would support the view of R. Nahman that plaintiff can save his property without having to resort to the alternative of litigation to collect damages.

The Talmud answers on behalf of R. Judah that the defendant's animal in the case was an "innocuous" ox, not a forewarned one. Since, in such a case, the owner of the ox is only liable for one-half of the damage caused to plaintiff's property, plaintiff would suffer an irreparable loss by going to court. Accordingly, plaintiff was entitled to take the law into his own hands to save his animal. The Talmud then objects to this answer by referring to the second half of the opinion in Case 2, which states that if plaintiff had pushed defendant's ox off his ox, rather than pulling his ox out from beneath defendant's ox, then plaintiff would be liable to defendant for the injury to defendant's ox. If, as stated on behalf of R. Judah, Case 2 deals with an ox which is not forewarned, then there should be no difference whether plaintiff pulled his ox or pushed defendant's ox off. In either case plaintiff would suffer irreparable loss if he waited to recover damages in court rather than acting immediately, because he would only be entitled to recover one-half of his damages. The Talmud answers this

20 See note 10 *supra*.

21 See Rambam (1135–1204), Laws of Damage by Chattels, Chapter 5; see also Volume 1, Chapter One, p. 42.

objection by explaining that plaintiff normally would have caused a lesser injury to defendant's ox by pulling his ox out from beneath defendant's ox rather than by pushing the defendant's ox off, and that, when resorting to self-help, plaintiff must minimize damage caused to defendant.

Jacob Zvi Yolles[22] comments that the Talmud could have answered that, even if defendant's ox was a forewarned ox, the loss to plaintiff would still be irreparable, since a damage award by a court of law would not fully compensate plaintiff. There are certain intangibles, such as the training given an animal, for which the court does not grant compensation. If this view were to be followed, then almost every case would involve irreparable loss to the plaintiff, since there is almost always some intangible quality related to one's ownership of a specific article which cannot be measured in monetary terms.

According to R. Nahman, Case 2 concerns a situation involving defendant's forewarned ox, and thus no irreparable injury is involved. The reason why plaintiff is nevertheless liable when he pushes defendant's ox off, but is not liable when he pulls his ox out, is that the plaintiff is under an obligation to minimize the damage to defendant. Thus, according to both R. Nahman and R. Judah, in any situation where a plaintiff is entitled to take the law into his own hands, he must do it in a way that will minimize the damage caused to defendant; otherwise he will be liable for damages.

POINT II may now be restated as follows: A plaintiff taking the law into his own hands may use physical force to obtain his ends. He may use only as much force as is necessary. If he uses force, then he must minimize the damage caused thereby. If he does not attempt to minimize the damage, then he will be liable for the damage caused.

In Case 3,[23] the defendant owned many jars filled with wine and oil, which he stored on plaintiff's property without permission. The vessels were placed in such a manner that plaintiff was not able to leave or enter his house. Plaintiff smashed some of defendant's jars when leaving and re-entering his house, and defendant sued to recover for damage caused by plaintiff. It was held that plaintiff was not liable, and that he had an absolute right to smash defendant's vessels upon leaving and re-entering his house. While there might be irreparable loss if plaintiff could not leave his premises, this case does not seem to involve irreparable loss in his not being able to re-enter his house. Plaintiff could summon defendant to court and obtain an order directing defendant to remove his jars of wine and oil. This holding of Case 3, that plaintiff is not liable to defendant even when re-entering his premises, seems to indicate that a plaintiff can take the law into his own hands even in cases which do not involve irreparable injury. This case then seems to refute R. Judah's view. On behalf of

22 Jacob Zvi Yolles (d. 1825) on T. Baba Kamma 28a.
23 See note 10 *supra*.

R. Judah, R. Nahman b. Yitzhak[24] answers that this case holds that plaintiff may break defendant's jars only on leaving the premises to go to court to obtain an order directing defendant to remove the jars. In this case, plaintiff was found not liable for breaking the jars upon re-entering the premises only because he was returning home to obtain evidence required by the court to prove that he owned the premises. Were plaintiff not able to re-enter his house to obtain evidence of ownership, defendant's contention that the property was his might have been accepted and plaintiff might have suffered an irreparable loss. The irreparable loss that plaintiff would have suffered in this case falls into the same category as the irreparable loss that can result when one has to wait for a judicial decision.

As explained on behalf of R. Judah, this case deals with the right to possession of realty rather that personalty. Thus, even in cases involving realty, there are rare situations where a plaintiff might be entitled to engage in self-help because he is about to suffer an irreparable loss. However, according to R. Nahman's view, this case involves the personal right of the plaintiff to move about freely in his own home, and the case holds that self-help may be employed although no irreparable loss would be entailed by waiting to go to court. It is shown below[25] that the law follows R. Nahman and that the law is extended to cases involving personal freedom of movement, but it is not extended to cases involving the possession of realty.

Tosafoth[26] asks, why was plaintiff not required to move defendant's jars aside by lifting and placing them one upon the other to clear a path for himself? Why was he found free of liability when he smashed defendant's jars since according to the holding of Case 2 plaintiff should have been required to minimize the damage? Tosafoth answers that a person engaging in self-help must minimize damage to the other party only when it will not place an additional burden on him. Thus, in Case 2, plaintiff is liable because he could just as easily have pulled out his own ox as he could have pushed defendant's ox off. In Case 3, however, it would have been more burdensome for plaintiff to lift defendant's filled jars and to place them one upon the other than to break the jars in order to clear a path when he left and re-entered his premises. Accordingly, in this case, plaintiff is not liable for damages.

As explained by N'Mukai Yosef,[27] Case 3 deals with a situation where defendant completely filled plaintiff's premises with his jars, leaving plaintiff with no means of leaving or entering his home. If, however, plaintiff's premises were not completely filled and he could find a way to pass through, then he would be liable to defendant for any damage. This

24 See note 5 *supra*.
25 See notes 56–73 *infra* and accompanying text.
26 Tosafoth (12th–13th cent.) on T. Baba Kamma 28a, introductory words: *meshaber v'yotzeh*.
27 N'Mukai Yosef (early 15th cent.) on Alfasi, T. Baba Kamma 28a.

is so despite defendant's trespass on plaintiff's property; although plaintiff would, of course, have an action against defendant for trespass.

Rambam[28] writes that the law applies even when defendant received permission to place his jars on plaintiff's property because plaintiff did not accept the responsibility of caring for them. Rabad[29] comments that Rambam's holding refers to a case where plaintiff did not give defendant permission to fill the premises, because if plaintiff had given such permission, then he would have been liable for breaking defendant's jars. Rambam adds that, if the plaintiff purposely broke the defendant's jars, then he would be liable to defendant, although defendant placed them on plaintiff's property without permission. Maharshal[30] asks, if defendant received permission to place his jars on plaintiff's property, then why should the plaintiff not be required to move the jars out of the way instead of being able to break them? He answers that, in granting permission to place the jars on plaintiff's property, it is implicitly understood that defendant will not fill plaintiff's property with jars in such a manner as to interfere with plaintiff's ability to leave and enter his home.

Case 3 thus further modifies points II and III so that they may now be restated as follows:

POINT II: A plaintiff taking the law into his own hands may use physical force to obtain his ends. He may use only as much force as is necessary. If he uses force, then he must minimize the damage caused thereby, as long as the minimization does not entail additional bother. If it would require extra bother for the plaintiff to minimize damages, then he is not liable for the damage caused.

POINT III: The person employing self-help must have a clear and recognizable right either to the possession of the personalty over which he is employing self-help, or to freedom of movement which is being restricted.

Case 4[31] involves a Hebrew servant[32] whose term of servitude had ended.[33] When the servant refused to leave his master's premises, the master forcibly evicted him and, in so doing, injured him. The servant sued for personal injuries, and a verdict was rendered in favor of the master on the basis of a hermeneutic interpretation of a Torah verse.[34] It would appear that this case refutes the holding of R. Judah, since there would be no irreparable injury to the former master if he sought a court order to evict the former servant; yet the master was allowed to use self-help to evict him forcibly. In defense of R. Judah, it is answered that as long

28 Rambam (1135–1204), Laws concerning Wounding and Damaging, Chapter 6, ¶ 5.

29 Rabad (1125–1198) on Rambam, Laws Concerning Wounding and Damaging, Chapter 6, ¶ 5.

30 Maharshal (1510–1574), Yam Shel Shlomo, T. Baba Kamma, Chapter 3, 2.

31 See note 10 *supra*.

32 See Exodus 21:2–6 and Leviticus 25:10

33 See Rambam (1135–1204), Laws Concerning Slaves, Chapter 2, ¶2.

34 Numbers 35: 32.

as the master-servant relationship existed, the servant feared his master, but upon termination of that relationship the former servant no longer feared his former master. The former master, fearful that the former servant would steal something if he were permitted to remain in his home, acted forcibly to evict him immediately. Thus this case actually involves an act to prevent an irreparable loss. This case extends the principle of self-help to cases involving the right of peaceful enjoyment of one's property free from the fear of trespassers. Accordingly, Point III may now be restated in the following manner:

POINT III: The person employing self-help must have a clear and recognizable right to the possession of the personalty over which he is employing self-help. He may also use self-help if his right to freedom of movement on his property is being restricted, or if his right to peaceful enjoyment of his property is being disturbed by trespassers.

In Case 5,[35] defendant placed jars in a public thoroughfare. Plaintiff, while walking along the street, tripped over one of the jars and broke it. Defendant sued to recover the value of the jar. As reported in the Mishna,[36] the holding in the case is that plaintiff is not liable. The commentators explain that this case involves a situation where defendant placed his jars across the thoroughfare, interfering with passers-by. According to Rashi,[37] the situation involves an irreparable injury, since plaintiff was denied free movement in the street. According to Tosafoth,[38] however, this case is also one not involving an irreparable injury, since plaintiff could use another street to walk to his destination. Moreover, even those who hold that there is irreparable injury in Case 3 would admit that plaintiff in this case would not suffer an irreparable loss by having to take a circuitous route to his destination.

The holding in this case is that plaintiff is not liable for breaking defendant's jar when he tripped over it. The inference to be drawn from this holding is that, if plaintiff had used self-help and intentionally smashed defendant's jar, instead of accidentally breaking it when tripping over it, then he would have been liable for employing self-help.[39] According to Rashi, who holds that Case 5 involves an irreparable injury, this inference would bring into question the entire doctrine of self-help, since it seems to infer that self-help is not permitted in a case where an irreparable injury is involved. According to Tosafoth, however, this case seems to refute only R. Nahman, who holds that self-help may be employed even when there is no danger of an irreparable injury. Hananel[40] similarly holds that this case is raised as an objection only to the view of R. Nahman, since it does

35 See note 10 *supra*
36 Mishna, T. Baba Kamma, Chapter 3, Mishna 1.
37 Rashi (1040–1135) on T. Baba Kamma 28a, introductory words: *ha shavra chayav.*
38 Tosafoth (12th–13 cent.) on T. Baba Kamma 28a, introductory words: *ta'ama d'niskol.*
39 See Rambam (1135–1204), Laws of Damage by Chattels, Chapter 13,115.
40 Hananel (990–1055) on T. Baba Kamma 28a.

not involve an irreparable injury. In like fashion, Yafeh Ainayim[41] cites Pre Migadim[42] as agreeing with Tosafoth on the strength of a passage in the Jerusalem Talmud,[43] where this case is held to be analogous to Case 2, which does not involve an irreparable injury (except as explained on behalf of R. Judah).

In replying to the apparent refutation of R. Nahman, R. Zvid[44] states in the name of Rava,[45] that the inference (that plaintiff would be liable if he had intentionally broken the jars) is not warranted. In fact, plaintiff would be free from liability even if he deliberately smashed the vessel on the public street. The reason why the Mishna, in stating the rule, uses the words "if he trips" is not to limit the non-liability of plaintiff to accidental damage. Rather, for reasons of parallelism, the Mishna wants to employ the same term in the first part of the rule that it must employ when it discusses the second part of the rule. Specifically, if plaintiff is injured by "tripping" over the jar, then the defendant is liable for plaintiff's personal injury; however, if plaintiff intentionally breaks the jar, then he assumes the risk and defendant is not liable for plaintiff's personal injuries, even though plaintiff has the right to employ self-help by intentionally breaking defendant's jars.

The answer given by R. Zvid in the name of Rava is not the law.[46] In employing self-help, plaintiff does not have the right to break defendant's jar intentionally. However, from Case 5 we do derive an additional principle in the law of self-help. Even where a person is permitted to take the law into his own hands, he assumes the risk of injury to himself and may not recover compensation for injuries incurred. As just indicated, this principle is derived from the second part of the Mishnaic case regarding plaintiff's counterclaim for personal injury. If plaintiff's conduct was accidental, he could recover; if it was intentional, he could not.

POINT II may now be restated as follows: The person taking the law into his own hands may use physical force to obtain his objective and will not be liable for damages caused by his action if he employs as much force as necessary. If he uses force, he must minimize the damage caused to the other party, if the minimization does not entail extra bother. The one who employs self-help assumes the risk of consequential injuries and will not be compensated for them.

Case 6[47] arose from a situation in which plaintiff's husband and defendant were engaged in a physical struggle. Plaintiff, in attempting to rescue her husband from physical harm, grabbed defendant in an embarrassing manner. Defendant sued to recover damages for indecent

41 Yafeh Ainayim (1820–1886), on T. Baba Kamma 28a.
42 Joseph b. Meir Teomim (1727–1792).
43 Jerusalem Talmud, T. Baba Kamma, Chapter 3, Halacha 1.
44 R. Zvid, Babylonian Amora (c. 330–385).
45 Rava, Babylonian Amora (299–352).
46 See note 28 *supra*.
47 See note 10 *supra*.

assault upon him, and the court rendered a judgment for defendant. It would appear from this decision that plaintiff could not take the law into her own hands even where an irreparable injury would result by waiting to bring the defendant to court. The irreparable injury would be the physical harm to plaintiff's husband. However, this apparent refutation of the doctrine of self-help is easily answered. In this case, plaintiff could have rescued her husband by pulling or pushing defendant away in another, less offensive manner, and since she did not conduct herself in this inoffensive way, she is liable.

In raising the objection to self-help from this case, it was apparent that the objection could readily be answered by stressing that plaintiff's liability would depend upon the availability of alternate methods of rescue. It must therefore be understood in the Case 6 situation that when the objection was raised, it was assumed that plaintiff would be liable even where rescue could not be effected by other means. This assumption was based on the supposition that a wife who rescues her husband in an embarrassing manner is always liable, in contrast to the privilege afforded a court officer to conduct a rescue in the same embarrassing manner with exemption from liability. It was thought that the privileged exception on behalf of a court officer is an exclusive one, and that the wife would be liable even if she could not rescue her husband in any other way. From this case, we therefore see that this is not so. Where the plaintiff cannot effect the rescue by any other means, she stands in a privileged position similar to that of a court official, and is not liable.

POINT I may now be restated as follows: a person may employ self-help in the first instance and need not wait for a judicial determination of his rights. The one employing self-help stands in a quasi-official position.

In Case 7,[48] a public road ran through a field owned by plaintiff. He sought to eliminate this road and to replace it with another at the side of his field. In an action brought against plaintiff, it was held that both the old and the new roads were now public thoroughfares. This holding seems to refute the general doctrine that self-help may be employed where plaintiff will suffer an irreparable injury by waiting to sue in court. As explained by Tosafoth,[49] the refutation assumes that the old road should have reverted to plaintiff, but that it did not revert to him in this case because it would not have been possible for him to bring every potential passer-by into court. But, if a person may employ self-help, then plaintiff should have been permitted to stand at the entrance to the old road and forcibly bar passers-by. The refutation is answered by pointing out that both roads are now public for different reasons, which are not remedy related. The rule is that the new road, once dedicated to the public interest, cannot be retaken by the donor; and the old road cannot be appropriated since the change would

48 See note 10 *supra*.
49 Tosafoth (12th–13th cent.) on T. Baba Kamma 28a, introductory word: *v'linkot*.

inconvenience those users who find the old road closer or more direct. If not for this inconvenience to some users of the old road, plaintiff would have been permitted to employ self-help and forcibly bar the public from using the road on his property. This explanation of Case 7 discloses that self-help may be employed against a group as well as against individuals.

Point I may now be restated as follows: A person may employ self-help in the first instance and need not wait for a judicial determination of his rights, and the one employing self-help stands in a quasi-official position. Self-help may be employed against an individual or a group.

In Case 8,[50] plaintiff left one end of his field for the poor people to reap in order to fulfill his Torah obligation regarding the law of *pe'ah* (that the poor and strangers must be permitted to harvest one end of the field).[51] The poor, however, reaped at another end of the field. Plaintiff brought an action seeking a determination that only the second area where the poor were now reaping should be set aside for them as their edge of the field, and that the first end which originally had been set aside for them should revert to him. The court ruled that both ends of the field were now subject to the law of *pe'ah.* This case again brings into question the entire doctrine of self-help. If the plaintiff could employ self-help, then why could he not evict the poor from the first end of the field, which had originally been set aside for them, when the poor sought to use the second end of the field for their reaping? Moreover, this case clearly involves an irreparable injury to plaintiff, whose field would become subject to *pe'ah* at both ends. Rava[52] explains that the ruling that both ends of the field have the law of *pe'ah* does not mean that the poor can reap at either end of the field. The ruling should be understood as embracing two issues. As it relates to the rights of the poor, they can reap at the second end only, and therefore that part of the field is subject to the law of *pe'ah.* As to that part of the ruling which states that the first end has the law of *pe'ah,* this refers to another issue, namely, that the first end retains the law of *pe'ah* in regard to retaining its exemption from tithes since it became exempt when it was originally set aside for the poor.[53] It is thus clear that plaintiff could forcibly evict the poor from the first end of the field that he had originally designated for them, which again demonstrates that self-help may be employed against a group.

### 3. *Four Points Emerging from the Talmudic Cases*

From an analysis of the principal case and the succeeding eight cases reported in the Talmud, four conceptual points concerning the doctrine of self-help emerge.

50 See note 10 *supra.*
51 See Leviticus 19 : 9 and 23 : 22.
52 See note 45 *supra.*
53 See Rambam (1135–1204), Laws of Gifts to the Poor, Chapter 1.

POINT I: A person may employ self-help in the first instance against another individual or a group, and need not wait for a judicial determination of his rights. When one employs self-help he obtains absolute title or right to possession of the property seized as if the seizure had been pursuant to a court order. The one employing self-help stands in a quasi-official position.

POINT II: The person taking the law into his own hands may use physical force to obtain his objective, but may employ only as much force as necessary. In resorting to self-help, he must minimize the damage caused to the other party, provided that this does not entail extra bother. If he does not minimize damages where he should, then he will be liable for any damage caused. The one employing self-help assumes the risk of injury and will not be compensated for injuries thereby occasioned.

POINT III: The one employing self-help must have a clear and recognizable right to the possession of the personalty over which he is employing self-help, or he must have the right to freedom of ingress or egress upon his property which is being restricted, or he must have the right to peaceful enjoyment of his property which is being disturbed. It is clear that self-help may be employed when one's personal safety or the safety of others is involved.

POINT IV: Self-help is subject to judicial review. While self-help is an end in itself in that it terminates the controversy between the parties, determines the right to possession and/or the ownership of the personalty, and eliminates court adjudication of the controversy, the one against whom self-help was employed may institute suit against the one employing self-help to determine if the self-help was legal.

## Appendix 3 E.B. Quint and N.S. Hecht, *Jewish Jurisprudence* 2:135–142, "Self-help where a community is a party"

### B. POST-TALMUDIC DEVELOPMENT

#### 6. *Self-Help Where a Community is a Party*

##### a. Commercial Cases

Thus far, the discussion has revolved around the right of an individual to employ self-help. The balance of this chapter focuses upon the right of a group or of a city to use self-help against an individual, that is, whether a community may seize a person's money or property without a prior court determination. The most common type of self-help employed by a community is the seizure of property or money for the payment of taxes when there is a dispute between the community and the taxpayer over his tax assessment.

Ramo,[1] in his Darkai Moshe, developed some of the principles and sources governing this area of the law. Initially, Ramo cites a responsum by Asheri,[2] which holds that if the elders of a community or the majority of a community know that an individual possesses something which belongs to the community, then they may take the object from him by employing self-help.

In his responsum, Asheri states the following:

> ... Since no witness will appear on behalf of the community due to the fact that they are interested parties and thus disqualified, the community may seize the object without any witnesses on their behalf. This can be derived from T. Moed Katan[3] where R. Joseph[4] says that a scholar of the academy may take the law into his own hands in a case in which he is certain. Rashi[5] explains that if he is certain as to the law, he may judge and forcibly seize from his debtor and may impose a ban regarding the controversy. It appears to me by an inference from the minor to the major that if the matter is clear to the majority of the inhabitants of a city or to the elders of a city, then they may forcibly seize the object.

The novelty involved here is not that a community may employ self- help, for its legal position is certainly not inferior to that of an individual. Rather, it is that self-help may be employed when the community does not have a

1 Ramo (1520–1572), Darkai Moshe on Tur Hoshen haMishpat, Chapter 4.
2 Asheri (1250–1327), Responsum, Chapter 6, ¶25.
3 T. Moed Katan 17a.
4 R. Joseph, Babylonian Amora (3rd–4th cent.).
5 See note 148 *supra.*

claim that can be proved in court. This might occur either because the members of the community are ineligible to testify on the basis of interest, since they will derive a benefit from their testimony if the community is successful, or because no one in the community wants to undertake the burden of instituting a lawsuit on behalf of the community.

Ramo thereafter cites Mordecai,[6] who comments on Case 7[7] (the attempt by plaintiff to eliminate a public road which runs through his field), as it is reported in T. Baba Bathra.[8] Mordecai states that he heard in the name of Eliezer of Metz[9] that a community has the power to require the posting of security by an individual before the community will appear in court.

Elijah of Vilna[10] also cites Case 7, as it is reported in T. Baba Bathra, to support the rule that a community may employ self-help even though certain requirements, such as having a claim that is provable in court, are not met. In the Talmudic discussion of Case 7 (which held that when the owner of a field through which a public road runs dedicates a second road to public use in order to eliminate the first road, both roads become public roads), R. Eliezer[11] states that members of a community may choose to travel over whichever road they please. Rashbam[12] explains that this is true although no permission was granted by the owner of the property, since a community has more rights than an individual. This may be seen from the rule that an individual, whose easement over his neighbor's field was blocked, may only retrieve his easement through a court action or through the consent of the owner. However, a community is not required to go to court, since no one in the community might trouble himself to take the property owner to court to enforce the community's rights. The community therefore may reassert its easement without the necessity of a court order and without the owner's permission.

### b. Tax Cases

Ramo[13] cites another passage in Mordecai,[14] where Mordecai discusses the Mishna in T. Baba Bathra[15] which states that under certain circumstances a tree may not be maintained on private property within twenty-five cubits of a town. If the town was in existence first, then the tree is to be cut down and the owner will not be compensated. The reason why the tree should

6 See note 10 *supra*.
7 Mordecai (1240–1298) on T. Baba Bathra, Chapter 6, Law 569.
8 T. Baba Bathra 100a.
9 Eliezer of Metz (1115–1198).
10 Bi'oor haGra (1720–1797) on Shulhan Aruch Hoshen haMishpat, Chapter 4, ¶116.
11 R. Eliezer b. Hyrcanus, Tanna (end 1st–beg. 2nd cent.).
12 Rashbam (1080–1174) on T. Baba Bathra 110a.
13 Ramo (1520–1572), Darkai Moshe on Tur Hoshen haMishpat, Chapter 4.
14 Mordecai (1240–1298) on T. Baba Bathra, Chapter 2, Law 522.
15 Mishna, T. Baba Bathra, Chapter 2, Mishna 7.

first be cut down and then compensation awarded is that a community is made up of many individuals, each one of whom feels that someone else will protect the communal interest. If the tree is cut down first, however, the owner will surely bring a lawsuit to recover the value of his property. Mordecai states that this law serves as a basis for the practice in many communities with regard to an individual who has a dispute with the community regarding tax matters. The taxing authorities may first enforce collection of the tax and thereafter, upon request of the taxpayer, a court will decide whether the tax collector's action was legal or not. The community, by the act of the tax collector, thereby becomes the holder of the money and the burden of proof is placed on the individual to retrieve the money. If this were not the practice, the community would suffer because each member of the community would rely on others to litigate the matter with the person disputing the tax assessment and no one would sue. Many people would therefore take advantage of this and would not pay their taxes. For this reason, Mordecai says, the owner of the old road in Case 7 may not use self-help against the public. He then quotes Meir of Rotenberg[16] as holding that this is the law and that a passage in T. Baba Metzia[17] is the source of the law. In that Talmudic discussion, regarding usurious transactions, R. Papa[18] and Rava[19] refer to a case in which some members of the academy paid taxes for certain people and then put these individuals to work for them. It was explained in the name of R. Shesheth[20] that the warrant for these people lies in the king's record room, the king having ordered that if a person does not pay his taxes, then he must work for the one who paid his tax for him. Mordecai adds that since the warrants for these taxes lie in the king's record room, the king is deemed to be already in possession of these taxes and the burden of proof is on the one claiming exemption from the tax. Accordingly, Mordecai concludes that the community should follow its usual practice, whether the collectors will swear at the ensuing trial that the tax is due or whether the taxpayer will swear that the tax is not due. However, the community is under an obligation to litigate the matter if the taxpayer so desires. It cannot claim immunity from litigation, since a community has no special privilege to seize property illegally from an individual.

### c. Presumptions in Favor of a Community

Terumath Hadeshen[21] discusses a case that was submitted to him, in which the king had levied a special wartime tax assessment on two communities.

16 Meir of Rotenberg (1215–1293), Responsum 49 (Cremono edition).
17 T. Baba Mezia 73b.
18 R. Papa, Babylonian Amora (ca. 300–375).
19 Rava, Babylonian Amora (299–352).
20 R. Shesheth, Babylonian Amora (late 3rd–early 4th cent.).
21 Terumath haDeshen (1390–1460), Responsum 341.

The first community sought to have its tax reduced because four substantial taxpayers had moved to the second community. The king ordered the first community to litigate the matter with the four taxpayers in a Jewish court. Terumath Hadeshen held that, in the circumstances of this case, the taxpayers would also have to pay their share of the first community's assessment. Ramo[22] gleans from the opinion a number of legal principles that are relevant to this chapter. In summarizing them, he finds that the community is presumed to be in the right against an individual and that it always has the upper hand. This, however, applies only in tax matters, and not in other types of disputes. Nevertheless, in all situations an individual must post security to pay for any judgment which the community may obtain against him before the community can be required to submit to the litigation. In all matters, including tax matters, if there is time to litigate the matter before the tax or obligation is due and the individual seeks a speedy trial, then the community should submit to a speedy trial.

Ramo cites Menahem of Merseburg[23] who writes that the presumption in favor of the community against an individual applies only in tax matters. Menahem further limits this ruling by stating that it only applies before the community has settled its obligations with the king. Furthermore, according to Menahem, if the individual claims that the community has a certain custom and the community disputes him, then the individual and the community stand on an equal footing as to this type of issue, since the theory of the individual's claim is based on the custom of the community. Ramo questions this last statement of Menahem because the position of an individual is never that of a community. Finally, he states in the name of Menahem, that if a sage claims an exemption from taxes because his sole occupation is the study of Torah, then the community does not have the benefit of any presumptions against him, and he is not even required to post security. Even where a sage is required to pay taxes, the community does not have the benefit of a presumption against the sage.[24] Elijah of Vilna[25] cites T. Baba Bathra[26] as the basis for the last statement. There it is taught that R. Judah[27] states: "Everyone, even orphans, must participate to repair breaches in the wall to defend the city, except scholars."

### d. Use of Gentile Courts by a Community

Ramo cites Maharik's[28] holding that the presumption in favor of a community operates only against an individual who is a member of that

22 See note 77 *supra*.
23 Menahem of Merseburg (1st half 14th cent.), p. 169.
24 Kovetz haPoskim (1969) p. 80.
25 Bi'oor haGra (1720–1797) on Shulhan Aruch Hoshen haMishpat, Chapter 4, ¶ 22.
26 T. Baba Bathra 8a.
27 R. Judah, Babylonian Amora (3rd cent.).
28 Maharik (1410–1480), Responsum 1.

community and only with regard to taxes. He also cites another responsum of Maharik[29] which enunciates a different view, that even if an individual is not part of the community, the latter has a presumption operating in its favor. In addition, Ramo cites Maharik[30] as ruling that Gershon Meor haGolah[31] decreed that it is permissible to employ gentiles to coerce an individual to pay taxes. This is also the view of Tur[32] who says that coercion at the hands of gentiles is permitted in situations involving taxes and charity. In another responsum,[33] Maharik indicates that, although resorting to coercion by gentiles is permissible, nevertheless it is prohibited to cause an individual other damages if the tax can be collected in another way.

Elijah of Vilna[34] cites T. Gittin[35] as the source for permitting legal acts to be done through the coercion of gentiles. The Mishna there states: "A divorce given under compulsion is valid if it is ordered by the Jewish court, but it is not valid if ordered by a gentile court; however, if the gentiles beat a man and say to him, 'Do what the Jews bid you,' it is valid."

### e. Legal Presumptions and Posting of Security

Having set forth his sources in his Darkai Moshe commentary, Ramo[36] subsequently states his conclusions in his emendations to Karo:

> ... and all the prior principles pertaining to self-help deal with situations involving one individual against another, but in a case where it is an individual against the community of which he is a member, the community may take the law into its own hands if they know that they have the law on their side. This statement applies although they cannot prove it in court, since they are ineligible to testify by being interested parties. In cases of disputes between them, the community is presumed to be in the right against the individual, and he must post security before they are required to litigate the matter with him. This presumption exists only in tax questions; nevertheless he must post security before they must go to court with him in regard to other matters. The foregoing applies if the individual is not a scholar. However, if he is a scholar whose sole occupation is the study of Torah and he disputes his tax assessment, then he does not have to post security, and they also do not have a presumption operating in their favor. It is permissible to coerce an individual through gentiles in tax

29 Maharik (1410–1480), Responsum 26.
30 Maharik (1410–1480), Responsum 17.
31 Gershon b. Judah (960–1028).
32 Tur (1270–1340), Hoshen haMishpat, Chapter 96.
33 Maharik (1410–1480), Responsum 27.
34 Bi'oor haGra (1720–1797) on Shulhan Aruch Hoshen haMishpat, Chapter 4, ¶ 23.
35 T. Gittin 88b.
36 Ramo (1520–1572), Shulhan Aruch Hoshen haMishpat, Chapter 4.

matters and to cause him a loss if they cannot exact payment of taxes in another manner.

When Ramo omits stating that the law of self-help applies in the case of a community against an individual if the individual is not a member of their community, he seems to be following the view expressed in Maharik's first responsum rather than that of his second responsum,[37] the responsa apparently being contradictory. Falk[38] indicates that Ramo did not specifically exclude the situation where the individual was not part of the community, since even in such a case it might have a presumption operating in its favor. Shach,[39] however, attempts to reconcile the apparently contradictory views of Maharik. The first responsum, where Maharik states that the community is favored over the individual if he is a member of the community, applies to self-help. The second responsum, where he states that the community is favored over an individual even where he is not a member of the community, does not apply to self-help. Instead, it addresses the presumption question in a lawsuit between a community and any individual. The community is always presumed to be in the right, and the individual has the burden of overcoming this presumption even when he is not a member of the community. Netivoth[40] cites the view of Shach.

It should be noted that there are other situations in which the community's legal position is superior to that of an individual. Thus, Piskai Teshuva[41] cites the holding of Shaar Mishpat,[42] that if the individual is also indebted to others, then the community's tax claim takes priority over the claims of other creditors. Falk[43] states that if there are various opinions containing different interpretations of the law, the community may choose that interpretation which favors it against the individual.

Aruch haShulhan,[44] in writing that an individual must post security for a judgment in cases in which he is involved with a community, explains that if no security were posted, then each member of the community would depend upon others to enforce collection of the judgment. Thus, the criterion is the unlikelihood that the judgment will be enforced. Accordingly, when two individuals are involved in a dispute, either party may demand that the other post security to insure collection of a judgment, since the jurisdiction of the rabbinic courts is limited in gentile countries and there may thus be little likelihood of enforcing a judgment.

37 See notes 220–221 *supra* and accompanying text.

38 Joshua Falk (1555–1614), Sma on Shulhan Aruch Hoshen haMishpat, Chapter 4,¶ 5.

39 Shach (1622–1663), on Shulhan Aruch Hoshen haMishpat, Chapter 4, ¶ 9.

40 Netivoth haMishpat (1760–1832), Hidushim on Shulhan Aruch Hoshen haMishpat, Chapter 4, ¶ 5.

41 Piskai Teshuva (1813–1868) on Shulhan Aruch Hoshen haMishpat, Chapter 4, ¶ 7.

42 Shaar Mishpat (19th cent.), Chapter 4, ¶ 3.

43 Joshua Falk (1555–1614), Sma on Shulhan Aruch Hoshen haMishpat, Chapter 4, ¶ 6.

44 Aruch haShulhan Hoshen haMishpat (1829–1908), Chapter 4, ¶ 4.

# 7 Law of the pursuer



## 1 Introduction

Self-defense is recognized today as a self-evident right, requiring no specific justification. Could someone under attack by another **not** be permitted to defend himself? As early as the first century BCE, Cicero argued that "self-preservation is a law by nature."[1] Nevertheless, there are complicated situations in which the right to self-defense is problematic. In particular, its applicability in cases that do not constitute self-defense in the full sense of the word can be questioned, for example, a farmer who

1 P. MacKendrick, *The Speeches of Cicero* (London: 1995), "The speech for Milo," 357.

shoots at youths stealing his apples, or someone who, upon witnessing an inebriated stranger threatening passers-by, wrestles him to the ground, injuring him in the process. A comprehensive treatment of the right to self-defense[2] should take into account such complications—*de minimis* attacks; disproportionality between the severity of the attack and the harm caused the attacker by the defender; self-defense by a third party; self-defense against an innocent aggressor (e.g., a psychotic aggressor); and so forth.

Self-defense permits the individual to commit what would otherwise be a crime in order to defend himself against an attack. The right of self-defense is a limitation on criminal liability, providing a defense that can be offered in response to a criminal charge, and resembling, in some ways, the defenses of compulsion[3] and necessity.[4] As we shall see below, however, the fact that the defender is **defending himself** against an unlawful attack by another makes self-defense a unique jurisprudential phenomenon.

Although the principle of self-defense is accepted by most legal systems, intense disputes have been and continue to be waged over its rationale.[5] Some, for example, base the principle on the right of one who is attacked to defend his liberty and bodily integrity; some base it on a moral preference for the innocent defender over the attacker seeking to harm him; and some base it on the public interest. Nor is there a consensus as to the nature of the exemption afforded the defender. Some see self-defense as an excuse, that is, an ex post facto exoneration afforded to the defender with respect to his crime of inflicting injury on the attacker; others (especially in modern times) have seen it as a justification, that is, a determination that the action taken by the defender was proper *ab initio*.[6] Explicating the nature of the right to self-defense and delineating its rationale are of more than just

2 If the right is extended to third parties as well, it is more accurately termed the right to 'private defense,' but we will continue to employ the usual term.

3 This defense can be asserted by one who is compelled to commit a crime, as where his life is threatened if he does not murder another.

4 This defense can be asserted by one who is compelled by objective circumstances to commit a crime in order to save his life, e.g., a shipwreck survivor clinging to a single plank who can retain the use of the plank and save his life only by loosening the grip of another survivor clinging to the same plank, causing him to drown.

5 See G.P. Fletcher, "Proportionality and the psychotic aggressor: a vignette in comparative criminal theory" 8 *Israel L. Rev.* 367 (1973); S. Kadish, "Respect for life and regard for rights in the criminal law," 64 *Calif. L. Rev.* 871 (1976); P. Montague, "Self-defense and choosing between lives," *Philosophical Studies* 40 (1981), 207–19; David Wasserman, "Justifying self-defense," *Philosophy and Public Affairs* 16 (1987), 356–78.

6 On the definition of 'excuse' and 'justification,' see H.L.A. Hart, *Punishment and Responsibility* (Oxford: 1968), 13–14: "In the case of 'justification' what is done is regarded as something which the law does not condemn, or even welcomes. But where killing … is excused, criminal responsibility is excluded on a different footing. What has been done is something which is deplored, but the psychological state of the agent when he did it exemplified one or more of a variety of conditions which are held to rule out the public condemnation and punishment of individuals. This is a requirement of fairness or of justice to individuals."

theoretical importance, as they help to clarify the limits of the dispensation to commit unlawful acts in the name of self-defense. But also, and perhaps primarily, understanding self-defense is of profound importance because it illuminates fundamental legal, social, and ethical questions, such as the extent of the individual's right to life and to autonomy, the measure of the individual's responsibility for the welfare of his fellows, the standards for triage where life is under threat, and so on.

The issue of self-defense is a venerable one in Jewish law, which from ancient times recognized the right of someone under attack to defend himself by injuring the attacker. The rubric under which the issue is discussed is the law of the 'pursuer' (*din rodef*)—one who pursues someone else with the intention of killing him. A well-known Rabbinic principle asserts: "If someone comes to kill you, preempt this by killing him."[7] Even early in the development of Jewish law, self-defense is regarded as a justification and not an excuse; that is, the defender is directed *ab initio* to kill the attacker, and not merely exempted from punishment after the fact. As the Rabbinic dictum implies, self-defense is not just condoned, but encouraged.

In this chapter, we will survey the classic analyses of self-defense in the halakhic sources, and attempt to trace the development of various theoretical approaches to self-defense. Because the Rabbis generally did not explicitly articulate the jurisprudential theories underlying their views, we will seek out the roots of the various positions upheld vis-à-vis self-defense by analyzing how they are applied. To this end, we will first examine an array of questions raised by the self-defense principle—questions not unique to Jewish law—as posed and elaborated on in other legal systems.

The discussion of self-defense in Jewish law has bearing on self-help, addressed in the previous chapter[8]; it also has bearing on the question of aborting a fetus that endangers its mother. But it is important to note the substantive differences between these areas, which are reflected in the terminology used in discussing them. **Self-defense** refers to defense against attack by committing (what would otherwise be) a crime against the attacker. In contrast, **self-help** refers to actions taken, outside the framework of a lawsuit, to realize a monetary right. Speaking very generally, self-defense falls under the category of criminal law, whereas self-help falls under civil law. But it is far from clear that the case of the apple thieves cited above would in fact be classified by Jewish law under the rubric of self-defense, though it is so classified in the general legal literature.

Aborting a fetus that endangers the mother is viewed by some halakhic authorities as falling under the category of self-defense. Others reject this

7 bSanhedrin 72a.
8 See Chapter Six above, "Self-help."

view, arguing that the fetus's growth is a natural event rather than a willful act on the part of the fetus. Those who take this position maintain that aborting the fetus to save the mother is permitted because the mother is fully a person, whereas the fetus is not, hence her life takes precedence. In any event, since the manifest features of self-defense are not present, abortion to some extent constitutes a sui generis category. The present chapter will address self-defense in the classic criminal law sense, namely, violent defense against physical attack.

The structure of the chapter is as follows. In the next section, as an introduction to our study of the halakhic understanding of self-defense, we present the primary justifications that other legal systems have offered for the principle of self-defense. Next we survey the biblical sources that constitute the basis for the approach taken by Jewish law, exploring their traditional interpretations. The main Tannaitic and Amoraic sources that address self-defense are then examined, with a view to articulating the rationales for self-defense that can be inferred from them. In the penultimate section, we explore the practical application of the right to self-defense, as reflected in the responsa literature.

## 2 Rationales for the right to self-defense

Three principal stages can be identified in the legal development of the principle of self-defense, as the history of English law clearly illustrates. During the first stage, in the early Middle Ages, the prevalent view was that anyone who committed a crime should be punished, even if he acted in self-defense. The justification was the need to strengthen the authority of the law and the government, and deter citizens from taking the law into their own hands, even where they were merely seeking to defend themselves. The government was regarded as having a monopoly on the use of force, and the exercise of force by a private citizen, even for self-protection, was unacceptable.

Later, toward the end of the Middle Ages, the law exempted from punishment anyone who committed an offense while acting in self-defense. The law did not regard such an action, though taken in self-defense, as something desirable, but as a crime whose perpetrator was nonetheless to be excused. It therefore mandated that a pardon be obtained from the crown; the pardon would rescind the penalty of death or imprisonment that was imposed on those who killed in self-defense, though not the concomitant monetary sanctions.

By the fourteenth century, such pardons became routine, but still did not extend to the monetary penalties imposed on the defendant. This changed in 1532, with the enactment of the statute 24 Henry VIII, c. 5, which ended the practice of confiscating the assets of one who had killed in self-defense; the statute represented an important step toward the recognition of self-defense as legally desirable.

The third stage, in which the law came to recognize that self-defense was not simply excusable or desirable, but fully justified, dates from the modern period, beginning around the eighteenth century. Today, self-defense, even though it entails actions that under other conditions would be considered serious crimes, is seen as something to be encouraged. The individual who defends himself need not seek a pardon for his action, and incurs no punishment.

Although the right of self-defense is now recognized by various legal systems, there is little clarity or agreement as to its scope and justification. A number of justifications, with significantly different implications vis-à-vis how the legal system in question deals with self-defense in practice, have been proposed. In essence, two main concerns underlie the various justifications—the interest of the individual, and the public interest. On the one hand, the principle of personal autonomy supports the right of every individual to the integrity of his body and his life, and to protect that integrity against one who endangers them. Where liberal theories that emphasize the place of the individual hold sway, this interest will likely be invoked as the basis for self-defense. On the other hand, the public interest, which requires the preservation of public order, deterrence of crime, and punishment of offenders, is also served by supporting the right of self-defense. Where a public interest agenda holds sway, self-defense will also be endorsed, but in this case, the emphasis will not be the right of the individual under attack to protect himself so much as the need to thwart an impending or ongoing crime by attacking its perpetrator. These two constraints—the preservation of personal autonomy and bodily integrity, on the one hand, and the preservation of public order and security, on the other—underlie the more specific justifications of self-defense that have been put forward in the legal literature. A review of these justifications will help us understand the various views within Jewish law regarding the law of the *rodef*.

### 2.1 The attacker's guilt

The classic justification for the right of self-defense in Anglo-American law is that when someone chooses to kill his fellow man, or declines to remove a danger he has created, he thereby relinquishes his right to life. It is not relinquished in an absolute sense—it is certainly forbidden to simply kill him other than in the context of self-defense or a death sentence imposed by the courts—but in any event it has been diminished, and hence, it is superseded by the right to life of the person being attacked. In other words, when we weigh the right to life of the attacker against the right to life of the victim, we favor the right of the innocent victim over that of the attacker, who is responsible for creating the situation.

This rationale yields several conclusions of practical import. First, there is no reason to grant the right to strike at the attacker to the victim only:

third parties should also be entitled to rescue the innocent victim by striking at the attacker. Second, inasmuch as the right to injure the attacker is based on his guilt, the injury inflicted on the attacker must be more or less proportional to the severity of his offense. For example, it is doubtful, on this approach, that a woman who is being subjected to verbal sexual harassment is permitted to defend herself by inflicting serious injury on the harasser.

The principal drawback of this approach is its inability to explain the right to defend oneself against attack by a non-guilty attacker (assuming there is a right to self-defense in such cases). Consider, for example, someone in the midst of a psychotic episode who takes a gun and tries to kill a bystander. Even if he succeeds, he is unlikely to be punished, for the law regards him as lacking responsibility for his actions—that is, he bears no guilt. The fact that many legal systems decline to punish acts of self-defense even when committed against blameless attackers[9] suggests that the attacker's guilt is not an adequate rationale for the self-defense principle: it does not account for instances when we deem self-defense justified even absent blameworthy acts of aggression.

## 2.2 The victim's autonomy

A different justification for the right of self-defense is based on the principle of personal autonomy.[10] Everyone has the right to life, bodily integrity (physical inviolability), and property, and it follows that everyone has the right to defend himself against anyone who threatens his life, bodily integrity or property (though only where the authorities charged with preventing the threatened attack cannot do so effectively). This notion is expressed in the adage 'right should never give way to wrong.' On this approach, the right to defend oneself even at the cost of injuring the attacker arises from the unlawful invasion of those realms over which the victim has autonomy.

This justification can explain the right to defend oneself even against a blameless attacker. The attacker undergoing a psychotic episode may not be responsible for the act he seeks to perpetrate, but the act remains an unlawful violation of the victim's autonomy, hence the victim has the right to defend himself against the attack and thwart its perpetration.

This rationale has two main drawbacks. First, it may erode the requirement of proportionality. If the rationale is, indeed, preventing invasion of the individual's autonomy, the criterion for the appropriateness

9 See American Law Institute, Model Penal Code, Proposed Official Draft (Philadelphia: 1962), §3.11(1); Law Commission (no. 218), Legislating the Criminal Code–Offences against the Person and General Principles (London: 1993), 27(3); German Criminal Code, sec. 32.

10 See G.P. Fletcher, *Rethinking Criminal Law* (Boston, Toronto: 1978), 770.

of the response may be set on the basis of what is needed to avert the attacker's action, rather than on the basis of the attack's severity. In a much-discussed German case from the 1920s, a group of boys broke into an orchard and stole apples. The owner, trying to stop the theft, shot at the boys to frighten them away, seriously wounding one of them. The trial court acquitted the orchard owner and the decision was affirmed by the German Supreme Court.[11] Critics of the decision argue that it makes no sense to permit life-threatening gunfire merely to ward off an offense as trivial as the theft of a few apples. But even if the need for proportionality can be sustained—on the argument that even the defense of one's personal autonomy must remain within reasonable limits—the autonomy rationale is still conducive to expansion of the right to defend oneself and to injure an attacker in the process, even in the face of a relatively mild attack.

The second drawback of this rationale is revealed when a third party seeks to intervene and injure the attacker in order to rescue the victim. If the victim's right to self-defense is grounded in his right to autonomy, it is unclear by what right a third party, not himself threatened, is permitted to commit a crime and attack the attacker. Nevertheless, most if not all contemporary legal systems permit a third party to defend someone under attack, even at the cost of injuring the attacker.

### 2.3 Preservation of public order

Another interest that may be invoked to justify self-defense is preservation of the public order. On this approach, self-defense is justified not because it serves the victim's interest, but because it is in the interest of society. Had there been a police presence in the vicinity of the attack, it would certainly have exercised force to prevent the attacker from committing the crime. In the absence of any police presence, the victim defending himself is justified because he is, in effect, functioning as a 'private' police officer, de facto serving as the long arm of the law. His action averts the offense, restores public order, and even deters potential offenders, who will now have to be apprehensive about a ubiquitous 'private' police presence.

It is important to note that some legal systems recognize, in addition to self-defense, another limitation on criminal liability: no penalty is imposed where force is exercised for the purpose of preventing someone from committing a crime.[12] Both in spirit and in content, this provision has much in common with the self-defense limitation.

11 Sept 20, 1920, 55 *Entscheidungen des Reichsgerichts in Strafsachen* [RGSt] 82. (F.R.G).

12 With respect to American law, see *American Jurisprudence*, 2nd ed. (Rochester and San Francisco: 1999),vol. 40, 649. For English law, see *Criminal Law Act, 1967*, §3: "A person may use such force as is reasonable in the circumstances in the prevention of crime, or in effecting or assisting in the lawful arrest of offenders or suspected offenders or of persons unlawfully at large." See also C. Harlow, "Self-defense: public right or private privilege?" *Crim. L. Rev.* (1974), 528.

Inasmuch as it is the entire community's interest, and not just the interest of the victim, preservation of public order accounts nicely for the fact that third parties also have the right to defend someone being attacked. Moreover, the value of preserving public order may also serve to justify the infliction of injury on someone threatening to attack other public interests. On the other hand, this justification has the same drawback as the first justification considered above (namely, the attacker's blameworthiness): it fails to account for the right of self-defense against a blameless attacker. It is difficult to regard such an attacker as a threat to public law and order, as evidenced by the fact that we do not subject him to punishment. Hence if preservation of public order is our justification for the right to self-defense, it is unclear whether it extends to such situations.

### 2.4 The lesser evil

All the above approaches to justifying the right to self-defense are unable to account for every case where self-defense seems warranted. A different approach forgoes the search for a single justification that can account for the right of self defense in every case. It maintains that acts of self-defense are, in fact, undesirable and best avoided, as they involve violence and the infliction of serious injury or death on another human being. Their justification lies not in their propriety per se, but in their being a lesser evil, on balance—that is, when the interests of all relevant parties (the victim, the attacker, the community, and so on) are taken into account—than the alternative of forgoing self-defense.[13] The victim does not have to explain why the act he resorted to in self-defense was not a crime; rather, he must explain why the crime he committed was, all things considered, a lesser evil than the crime the attacker was about to be commit, which was averted by the act of self-defense.

The advantage of this approach is its great flexibility. Not bound to a single rationale, it can take into consideration a wide range of interests and thus justify self-defense in a wide range of situations. But flexibility is also the principal drawback of this integrative approach, as it can readily be stretched to the point of utter vacuity. In other words, the 'lesser evil' justification can be distorted to cover virtually any situation. It is difficult to predict in advance the situations in which self-defense will be taken by the courts to justify self-defense, given that so many different sets of interests can be invoked. And despite the best efforts of legal theorists to identify a conceptual basis for the 'lesser evil' doctrine that can provide a consistent criterion that sets clear boundaries for the right to self-defense, no such basis can be articulated.

13 See P.H. Robinson, *Criminal Law Defenses* (St. Paul MN: 1984), 2:71.

## 3 Self-defense in biblical law

The law of the *rodef* (pursuer) is treated extensively in the Mishnah and other Tannaitic sources. As we have seen throughout this volume, the Sages are wont to anchor the legal principles they propound in biblical sources. They suggest that the Bible itself contains passages that serve as a legal source for the law. In this section, we will briefly examine these passages, and assess the extent to which they provide a grounding for the right to self-defense.

### 3.1 Rape of a betrothed maiden

A passage in Deuteronomy deals with the punishment imposed on a betrothed maiden who is discovered having sexual relations with someone other than the man to whom she is betrothed, which is considered adultery by biblical law. A distinction is made between two situations: if the maiden is caught in an urban area, it can be assumed she has willingly gone along with the man involved, for had she wanted to resist, she could have cried out for help. She did not do so, and thus deserves punishment. But if she is apprehended in an open field, she is not presumed to have gone along willingly, for she might well have cried out for help and not been heard:

> But if the man find the damsel that is betrothed in the field, and the man take hold of her, and lie with her; then only the man that lay with her shall die. But unto the damsel thou shalt do nothing; there is in the damsel no sin worthy of death; for as when a man riseth against his neighbor, and slayeth him, even so is this matter. For he found her in the field; the betrothed damsel cried, and there was no one to save her.
>
> Deuteronomy 22:25–27

Here the Torah sets down the principle that punishment must not be imposed in the absence of culpability. With this principle in mind, the Sages reinterpreted the biblical distinction between city and field in a more substantive way: the question is not whether the place where she was found is rural or urban, but whether or not she could have called for help:

> If there was someone who could have saved her, whether in the city or in the field, then she is liable; if there was no one who could save her, whether in the city or in the field, she is exempt.
>
> Sifre Deuteronomy, Ki Teitze, 243 (Finkelstein edition, p. 273)

In any case, according to the Sages, it is clear that the Torah assumes that if indeed there is someone who can rescue the girl, he is obligated to do so. The Torah does not specify, however, the measures the rescuer is permitted to take to save the girl being raped. Sifre goes on to interpret the passage to mean that it is permitted to rescue the girl[14] even at the cost of the rapist's life:

> This teaches that in all cases in the Torah, those who [commit crimes] under duress are exempt, and [victims] can be rescued by [taking] their [the attackers'] lives.

The argument for the rescuer's right to kill the rapist is based on an analogy drawn by the Torah itself. Scripture emphasizes the rape victim's innocence by comparing her to a murder victim: "for as when a man riseth against his neighbor, and slayeth him, even so is this matter." Apparently, the Sages extended the analogy, which originally compared the rape victim's innocence to the murder victim's innocence, applying it to the rescue of the rape victim. Just as the rescue of someone under murderous attack almost certainly entails inflicting a mortal blow on the murderer, so too, the Sages conclude, rescuing a victim of rape will likely entail striking at the rapist, even at the cost of taking his life.

Two points should be noted. The rescuer here is a third party. The premise is that the maiden does not have the strength to save herself, and can at most call for help from others. It follows that the right to self-defense is granted not only to the victim, but to third parties as well. Secondly, it appears that the Torah affirms that in some cases—which must, of course, be defined—it is permitted to inflict on the attacker an injury more severe than that he intended to inflict on the victim. Although the attacker meant to rape the victim, the Sages maintain that in order to save her, it is permitted even to kill the attacker.

### 3.2 The stealth burglar

Elsewhere, in setting out the laws of theft, the Torah adds the following provision:

> If a thief be found breaking in, and be smitten so that he dieth, there shall be no bloodguiltiness for him [lit., he has no blood]. If the sun be risen upon him, there shall be bloodguiltiness for him—he shall make restitution; if he have nothing, then he shall be sold for his theft.
>
> Exodus 22:1–2

There is some ambiguity in these verses, but it is clear that a distinction is being drawn between two types of situations: those where it is permissible

14 This dispensation does not apply to all rapes, but only where the sexual act, even were it consensual, would nonetheless be forbidden as adultery or incest. We will discuss this point in section 4.2 below.

to kill a burglar, and those where it is forbidden to do so. It seems that in the first verse, the Torah asserts that it is permissible to kill a burglar found as he is tunneling under a wall, presumably so as to break into the house secretly, under cover of darkness. The intent of the phrase "there is no bloodguiltiness" seems clear: one who kills such a burglar does not incur the punishment of death that is meted out to those who commit murder. The second verse forbids the killing of a burglar on whom "the sun be risen," that is, who is caught in the light of day. The Sages explain the difference between the two cases in terms of the likelihood the burglar will physically attack the homeowner, escalating the incident from a burglary to a murder. A burglar who breaks in secretly, at night, is suspected of being willing to kill the homeowner if necessary (that is, if he has to do so in order to perpetrate the theft without being apprehended); killing the burglar is therefore permissible. The Mishnah indeed rules: "[The thief] who breaks in clandestinely is judged in terms of what his end will be."[15]

The Talmud explains the Mishnah's statement as follows:

> Rava said: What is the rationale of the 'he who breaks in clandestinely' law? Because it is a presumption that no one remains passive [lit., stands] where his property is concerned; therefore this one [the thief] will certainly say, 'If I go there, he [the homeowner] will confront me and not let me [do as I wish]; but if he does so, I will kill him.' Hence the Torah decreed, "If someone comes to kill you, preempt this by killing him."
>
> bSanhedrin 72a

A stealth burglar is thus viewed as determined to carry out his nefarious plan no matter what, even by taking the homeowner's life. On the other hand, a burglar who operates during the day is considered less dangerous, and unlikely to hurt the homeowner; accordingly, he is not to be killed. The Sages offer two explanations for the fact that the daytime burglar is deemed less dangerous. Onkelos translates the phrase "if the sun be risen upon him" as "if the eye of a witness has fallen on him," that is, if the burglar is caught in the open. In Onkelos' view, the burglar is not to be killed if he is apprehended in a public space. His reasoning may be that under those circumstances, there is no concern that the burglar will commit murder. A second Rabbinic explanation sees the shining of the sun as a metaphor for the degree of danger posed by the burglar's actions.

> Is it only on him that the sun has shone? Has it not shone on the entire world? Rather, just as the sun [represents] peace in the world, so, too,

15 mSanhedrin 8:6.

> if it is known that this burglar comes in peace [viz., intends no violent harm] and [the homeowner nevertheless] kills him, he [the homeowner] is liable.
>
> Mekhilta de-Rabbi Ishmael, masekhta de-nezikin, 13 (Horowitz edition, p. 293)

According to the Rabbinic interpretation, then, these verses inform us that killing the stealth burglar is prohibited unless there is a risk of mortal harm to the homeowner.

There is a disagreement among the medieval commentators as to the import of the clause "there shall be no bloodguiltiness for him." The literal meaning of the Hebrew is 'he has no blood,' a highly ambiguous locution.[16] Disagreement as to its meaning has direct bearing on the question of the legal basis for the right to self-defense. Who is the subject of the clause—the burglar or the homeowner? Rashi, in his commentary on the Pentateuch, offers the following interpretation: "'There shall be no bloodguiltiness for him'—this is not murder, for he is as if dead *ab initio*." He rephrases this idea in his commentary on the Talmud: "'There shall be no bloodguiltiness'—that is, he is to you like one who lacks blood and soul, and it is permitted to kill him."[17]

According to Rashi, then, the words "There shall be no bloodguiltiness for him," the literal meaning of which, as we said, is 'he has no blood,' refer to the **burglar**; they mean that he will in any event be subject to the punishment of death by the court for the murder he can be expected to commit, so there is no reason to punish the homeowner for killing him. Since the attacking thief is in any case going to die after murdering the homeowner and being convicted in court, it is preferable to kill him now, even without a judicial proceeding, and thereby save the homeowner's life. In effect, according to Rashi, killing the burglar is justified because it is a kind of anticipatory punishment that is beneficial in preventing unnecessary bloodshed (the homeowner's murder).

Rashi's understanding of the verse contrasts sharply with the interpretation offered by R. Abraham ibn Ezra: "And the meaning of 'there shall be no bloodguiltiness for him' is that his killer is not guilty of bloodshed." According to Ibn Ezra, the phrase refers to the **homeowner** defending himself; it means that one who kills a stealth burglar is not considered a murderer and not subject to the punishment of death that a court would impose for murder. In other words, self-defense is permissible.

16 To translate these words is, therefore, ipso facto to interpret them, as is borne out by any survey of Bible translations. For example, the KJV reads: "there shall no blood be shed for him," while the Douay-Rheims Bible reads "he that slew him shall not be guilty of blood."

17 bSanhedrin 72a s.v. *mai taama*.

### 3.3 The wife who attacks her husband's adversary

Yet another biblical passage sets down a law pertaining to an action that can be classed as self-defense; this passage, too, is obscure, and the commentators disagree regarding the situation it addresses. The case involves a violent conflict between two men:

> When men strive together one with another, and the wife of the one draweth near to deliver her husband out of the hand of he who smiteth him, and putteth forth her hand, and taketh him by the genitals; then thou shalt cut off her hand, show her no pity.
>
> Deuteronomy 25:11–12

The meaning of these verses is unclear. They can be understood as addressed to the courts: as imposing a duty on the courts to punish anyone who injures his fellow's genitals. Alternatively, they can be understood as addressed to the victim of such an attack, directing him to save himself from injury—that is, defend himself—by preemptively injuring his attacker (in this case, the wife). Thus viewed, the law falls under the rubric of self-defense.

According to the Sifre, the Sages take the law propounded in the verses to grant the right to self-defense: the wife attacks her husband's antagonist in an illicit manner—seizing his genitals—and Scripture allows him to respond by defending himself and injuring her. R. Judah, however, regards the verses as addressed to the court that punishes the wife:

> "You shall cut off her hand"—this teaches that you are obligated to save her by her hand. How do we know that if you cannot save her by her hand you should save her by her life? As it is written, "show her no pity."
>
> R. Judah says: Scripture here says "show her no pity" and elsewhere (Deut. 19:21) says "show no pity"; just as there it refers to monetary compensation, so too here it refers to monetary compensation.[18]
>
> Sifre Deuteronomy, Ki Teitze, 293 (Finkelstein edition, p. 312)

The Sages, who interpret the verses as addressing the issue of self-defense, read it as granting a dispensation to injure the wife in order to thwart her

18 The biblical text speaks of cutting off the woman's hand. There are several instances where biblical law specifies that one who causes physical injury to another is to be punished by physical injury to himself. Leviticus 24:19–20, e.g., declares: "If anyone maims his fellow, as he has done so shall it be done to him: fracture for fracture, eye for eye, tooth for tooth. The injury he inflicted on another shall be inflicted on him." As is well known, the Rabbis inferred from this that the defendant should be subjected to a monetary rather than a corporal penalty: "eye for eye—[this means an equivalent sum of] money" (bBaba Kama 83b).

attack. The addition of "show her no pity" expands the dispensation to include killing the assailant if that is necessary. (The meaning of the obscure phrase "save her by her hand" will be addressed below). On R. Judah's interpretation, "show her no pity" is addressed to the judges presiding over a proceeding determining the assailant's punishment, directing them to punish her in a manner proportionate to the injury she inflicted.[19]

The interpretation that deems the wife an attacker invites a question: why is she not considered a **rescuer**, given that her attack is motivated by the desire to save her husband, as the biblical verse expressly states. One possible explanation is that the violent conflict between the two men did not really endanger either of them, and thus the wife's action did not constitute legitimate self-defense. Alternatively, it might be argued that an implicit premise underlying this passage is that the right to self defense is granted only to the victim, and not to a third party. The wife's action is thus considered an unlawful attack rather than an instance of self-defense.

The Babylonian Talmud, in bBaba Kama 28a, addresses this matter, explaining that the situation is one in which the wife could have used non-violent defensive measures, but nonetheless chose to physically attack her husband's adversary. The Talmud explains her punishment as follows: "Regarding which circumstances was this stated? Regarding the case where there was some other means at her disposal to save [him], for had she been unable to save [him] by other means, her resort to force [lit., her hand] would be tantamount to that of an agent of the court, and she would be exempt." This formulation, incidentally, clearly reflects the notion that one who has recourse to self-defense is free of liability because in effect he functions as the long arm of the law: "her hand would be tantamount to that of an agent of the court." The 'preservation of public order' justification for the right to self-defense is reflected in this formulation.

Overall, the Bible seems to recognize the right to self-defense even at the cost of injury to the attacker. This is the clear implication of the 'stealth burglar' case, and seems to be suggested by the 'betrothed maiden' and 'wife who attacks her husband's adversary' cases. But the pertinent biblical passages do not elaborate on the nature and limits of this right. The Rabbinic sources take up these issues, expanding the discussion considerably.

## 4 Self-defense in the Mishnah and the Talmud

### 4.1 Biblical prooftexts for the law of the pursuer

We begin our inquiry into the Rabbinic approaches to the law of the pursuer by examining the talmudic debate over which of the three scriptural passages discussed above it is grounded in, or to put it differently,

19 This interpretation is also implied by the discussion in bBaba Kama 28a.

which passage constitutes the prooftext for the law. Although the 'stealth burglar' passage is the clearest and least ambiguous of the three, the Rabbis preferred to rely on the other passages.

The Mishnah rules that one is to rescue the victim by taking the pursuer's life.[20] The Talmud asks: "Whence do we know that he who pursues his fellow to slay him may be saved by [taking] his life?"[21] It goes on to answer:

> It is inferred by a fortiori reasoning from the betrothed maiden. If, regarding a betrothed maiden, whom [the attacker] only seeks to dishonor, the Torah decreed that she may be saved by [taking] the life of the attacker, how much more so does this hold for one who pursues his fellow to slay him!
>
> But can punishment be inflicted on the strength of a fortiori reasoning [alone, where there is no explicit biblical source]?[22]
>
> The School of Rabbi [Judah the Prince] taught, It is derived by analogy: "for as when a man riseth against his neighbor, and slayeth him, even so is this matter" (Deut. 22:26). But what do we learn from [this analogy with] a murderer? It is invoked to shed light, and is itself illuminated. The [case of the] murderer is compared to [the case of] a betrothed maiden; just as a betrothed maiden can be saved [from dishonor] by [taking the attacker's] life, so in the case of a murderer, he can be saved by [taking] his life.
>
> And whence do we know this of a betrothed maiden? As the School of R. Ishmael taught. For the School of R. Ishmael taught: "and there was no one to save her" (Deut. 22:27); but if there is someone who can rescue her, he must save her by any means possible.
>
> bSanhedrin 73a

According to this passage, the Talmud sees the verse about the betrothed maiden as the legal source for the law of the pursuer. It infers the right to strike at the rapist from the words "and there was no one to save her": that is, it is proper to rescue the girl by any means necessary, including killing the rapist. And from the right to strike at the rapist, the Talmud infers a corresponding right to strike at someone who seeks to murder his fellow.

20 mSanhedrin 8:7.

21 On another reading, the verse is understood as asking, "Whence do we know that he who pursues ... may be saved [**from sin**] by [taking] his life?"

22 Use of the term "punishment" here is surprising. How is the killing of the pursuer to be viewed? Is it a form of anticipatory punishment, or simply the only possible means of saving the victim? R. Jacob Ettlinger formulated this quandary as follows: "[The query] 'Can punishment be inflicted as result of a fortiori reasoning?' is somewhat problematic, for there is no doubt that the issue at hand [the permissibility of killing the attacker] is raised not with respect to punishment, but because the Torah emphasizes rescue of the victim" (*Arukh Laner*, bSanhedrin 73a).

Maimonides approached the question very differently. Here, we will sketch his general approach to the law of the pursuer, leaving the details for later in the chapter.

> 6 ... But as to one who pursues his fellow to slay him ... it is the obligation of every Israelite to rescue the pursued one from the pursuer, even by [taking] the pursuer's life.
>
> 7 ... If the one being pursued can be saved by [injuring] one of the pursuer's limbs, for instance by striking him with an arrow or a stone or a sword and cutting off his hand or breaking his leg or blinding his eye, this should be done. If, however, it is impossible to make a precise strike, and he can be rescued only by killing the pursuer, then he is to be killed even though he has not yet killed anyone, as it is said, "you shall cut off her hand; show her no pity" (Deut. 25:12).
>
> 8 [Concerning this rule] there is no difference between the private parts (cf. Deut. 25:11) and any other part of the body [injury to which] may endanger life, or between a man and a woman. The intent of the aforementioned scriptural passage is that if anyone intends to strike his fellow a death-blow, the pursuee should be saved at the cost of the pursuer's hand. And if this is impossible [i.e., if they cannot target a blow precisely], he is saved even by [taking] the pursuer's life, for Scripture says, "show her no pity."
>
> 9 That we have no pity on the life of the pursuer is, moreover, a negative commandment.....
>
> 10 The rule is the same whether one is pursuing another to kill him, or pursuing a betrothed maiden to rape her, as it is said, "for as when a man riseth against his neighbor, and slayeth him, even so is this matter" (Deut. 22:26). And Scripture also says, "though the betrothed girl cried out for help, there was no one to save her" (22:27), but if there is someone who can rescue her, he must save her by any means possible, even by killing the pursuer.
>
> *Code*, Laws concerning Murder and the Preservation of Life 1:6–10

According to Maimonides, the source for the law of the pursuer is the passage about the wife who attacks her husband's adversary (7). That verse, in his view, instructs us that it is permitted to injure her, even to take her life, in order to avert the damage she is about to inflict. The dispensation to kill a rapist is inferred only at the second stage of the analysis (10), where it is derived via an analogy with the case of the murderer—the opposite of the sequence in the Talmud.[23] It appears, therefore, that

23 Maimonides reiterates this line of thinking in the *Book of Precepts*, positive commandment 247; negative commandment 293.

Maimonides endorsed the first opinion in the Sifre,[24] which interprets the law of the wife who attacks her husband's adversary as granting the right to self-defense: the attacked man is entitled to defend himself against the woman attacking him. The Babylonian Talmud, on the other hand, takes the case of the betrothed maiden to be the primary source for the law of the pursuer, extrapolating from it to the case of murder by way of analogy.

It is not clear why Maimonides favored the Sages' interpretation (that is, the first view) in the Sifre over that of the Talmud. He may have been troubled by the Talmud's question, "But can punishment be inflicted on the strength of a fortiori reasoning [alone, where there is no explicit biblical source]?" The question, we saw, rests on the conception that the law of the pursuer reflects a kind of anticipatory punishment. If Maimonides sees the law of the pursuer, not as reflecting anticipatory punishment, but strictly as a matter of rescuing the victim—a thesis we will demonstrate later in this chapter—he would favor the analysis adduced in the Sifre over that proffered by the Babylonian Talmud.

## 4.2 Mishnaic "law of the pursuer"

The right to self-defense finds its clearest and most explicit statement in a Mishnah in tractate Sanhedrin, a Mishnah that raises new exegetical difficulties.

> The following are saved by [taking] their lives: he who pursues his fellow to slay him, [or pursues] a male [for sexual relations], [or pursues] a betrothed maiden [to rape her.]
>
> But he who pursues an animal [to engage in bestiality], or who desecrates the Sabbath, or commits idolatry, is not be saved by [taking] his life.
>
> mSanhedrin 8:7

The offenses enumerated in the Mishnah—murder, sodomy, sexual relations with a betrothed maiden, bestiality, desecration of the Sabbath, and idolatry—are all capital offenses. Nevertheless, the Mishnah distinguishes between the first group of offenses, which are to be averted even at the cost of the perpetrator's life, and the second group, where pre-emptive killing of the perpetrator is forbidden. The offenses in the first group involve harm to a fellow human being—murder or rape. They are offenses committed by one person against another. Those in the second group—bestiality, Sabbath desecration, and idolatry—involve, not harm to a person, but offenses against God. It thus appears that a necessary condition for any dispensation to strike at someone who is about to commit an offense is that there be apprehension that someone will be injured,

24 See section 3.3 above.

injury that can be avoided by the defensive action. In the view of this Mishnah, simply averting the offense itself is not enough to justify the use of mortal force against the offender. In other words, **rescuing the victim would seem to be the main thrust of the law of the pursuer**. When the attacker is committing a capital crime and there is a danger that someone else will be seriously harmed, both the victim and third parties are permitted to kill the attacker.

Analysis of this Mishnah reveals a concept of self-defense quite different from that current today. The Mishnah appears to imply that the right of self-defense does not depend solely on the anticipated injury to the victim, but also on the severity of the offense being perpetrated. On the one hand, it is clear that the right is granted only on account of the danger threatening the victim, and not just because of the serious offense the perpetrator is about to commit. The second part of the Mishnah expressly sets down that intending to commit an offense that is 'between man and God'—as opposed to an offense against another human being—no matter how severe, does not justify striking at the perpetrator in order to forestall it. Maimonides discusses this in his *Guide for the Perplexed*, where he explains that the law of the pursuer applies only to two offenses:

> This law—I mean the prescription to kill him who wishes to accomplish an act of disobedience before he performs it—is only applicable to two kinds of acts: *If one pursues his fellow man in order to kill him, and if one pursues someone in order to expose the latter's nakedness*. For these are acts of wrongdoing that cannot be repaired once they have been accomplished. As for the other *transgressions* that are punished with *death by order of a court of law*, such as *idolatry* and the profanation of the *Sabbath*, they do not constitute an act of wrongdoing with regard to someone else, but concern only thoughts; and therefore the transgressor is not killed because of his wish, but only if he commits the transgression.
>
> *Guide for the Perplexed* III:40 (Pines translation)

On the other hand, the criterion governing the applicability of the right to injure the pursuer is not solely a matter of the severity of the potential injury to the victim, but also the severity of the impending offense, as indicated by the distinction, implied by the Mishnah, between attempted rape of a betrothed maiden and of an unbetrothed maiden. The betrothed maiden has the status of a married woman, and raping her is considered adultery (the technical definition of which is intercourse between a married woman and someone other than her husband). This offense is punished more severely—it incurs the death penalty—than rape of an unbetrothed woman, which is not deemed adultery, and not punishable by death—even though the harm to the victim in both cases is the same. It is thus evident from the Mishnah that preventing the pursuer from sinning is a factor taken into account in setting the boundaries of the right to self-defense.

### i Minority views regarding mSanhedrin 8:7

Some Tannaim disagree with the Mishnah's determination that the right to self-defense is conditioned on two distinct elements; in effect, they extend the law of the pursuer beyond self-defense proper and see its thrust as prevention of the offense. On their view, preventing certain offenses 'between man and God' warrants preemptively striking at the perpetrator. Let us consider two such opinions: that of R. Shimon b. Yohai and that of his son, R. Eleazar. The former is presented in a baraita cited by the Talmud:

> It has been taught: R. Shimon b. Yohai said: An idolater may be ... saved by [taking] his life. This is deduced by a fortiori reasoning: If the dishonoring of a human being [viz, a betrothed maiden] must be averted even at the cost of [the violator's life], how much more so the dishonoring of the Most-High![25]
>
> bSanhedrin 74a

The Tosefta cites a similar opinion in the name of another Sage: "R. Eleazar b. Zadok says: One who commits idolatry is to be saved by [taking] his life."[26]

Both these Tannaim broaden the right of self-defense beyond the bounds of transgressions 'between man and his fellow man'—offenses involving injury to another person. On their view, idolatry, one of the most serious transgressions 'between man and God,' also warrants preemption by striking at the perpetrator. There is no doubt that the rationale for R. Shimon b. Yohai's teaching differs from that expressed in the Mishnah.

R. Shimon b. Yohai's son, R. Eleazar, broadens the dispensation to preemptively strike at the pursuer to encompass an additional transgression:

> It has been taught: R. Eleazar, son of R. Shimon said: He who desecrates the Sabbath may be saved ... by [taking] his life.
>
> bSanhedrin 74a

It is evident that in the opinion of R. Shimon b. Yohai and his son, R. Eleazar, the thrust of the law of the pursuer is prevention of serious offenses, perhaps so as to save the transgressor from sinning, and not necessarily the rescue of those in imminent danger of being harmed.

25 The language R. Shimon b. Yohai uses to explain his position—"how much more so the dishonoring of the Most-High"—suggests that his primary concern is not the spiritual welfare of the attacker, that is, saving the pursuer from committing a transgression, but rather, enhancing the glory of God. This explains why he does not extend the dispensation to other transgressions of 'between man and God' precepts, such as desecration of the Sabbath, but limits it to idolatry, which is universally prohibited.

26 tSanhedrin 11:11 (Zuckermandel edition).

Accordingly, it applies even where there is no clear victim or no victim at all. Their opinions call to mind, to some extent, the English doctrine mentioned above[27] that permits the use of force to prevent commission of a crime and thereby preserve public order. But R. Shimon b. Yohai and his son go further than the English rule, permitting—in the context of especially serious, capital offenses—not just the use of force, but the taking of the perpetrator's life.

### ii Textual analysis of the mishnaic law

Juxtaposing the text of the Mishnah to the words of R. Shimon b. Yohai and his son R. Eleazar highlights the fundamental question pertaining to the laws of self-defense: are they based on the desideratum of rescuing the victim or that of preventing the offense?

The question is raised by the dissenting Tannaitic views, but can be discerned even in the wording of the Mishnah itself. The Mishnah's focus, we saw, is rescuing the victim: the right of self defense obtains when there is a human victim, but not in connection with an offense that is 'between man and God,' where there is no right to preemptively strike the attacker to avert commission of the offense. Nevertheless, examination of the language of the mishnaic law reveals that the putative focus on rescuing the victim is not quite so unequivocal.

The Mishnah speaks of those "who are saved by [taking] their lives." This could certainly mean that the person saved is the one who is being pursued: the preemptive attack on the pursuer saves the one who is being pursued. If so, the right to self-defense is based on the desideratum of rescuing the victim. But given the ambiguity, which exists in the original Hebrew, of the pronoun "their," it has another possible meaning. Perhaps the person saved is the pursuer, who, by being killed, is kept from transgressing—he is 'saved' from sinning. If this is the case, the right to self-defense is based on the desideratum of preventing transgression.

Though our earlier analysis of the mishnaic law interpreted it as focusing on **rescue of the victim**, a closer look at its language points to a reading on which the thrust of the law is that **the attacker is to be saved** from the transgression he is about to commit. First, the phrase "the following are saved by [taking] their lives" implies that the one saved is the attacker, not the victim, for the words "are saved" and "their lives" appear to have the same referent: the attacker is saved "by" his life, that is, by taking his life, viz., by killing him. This reading is, syntactically speaking, far more natural than the reading on which the rescuee is the party being pursued, which requires us to take the words "the following" as referring to the victim(s), a reading that is utterly forced and implausible, and "their lives" as referring to the pursuer(s).

27 See section 2.3 above.

The conclusion that the rescuee is actually the pursuer is supported by the continuation of the sentence: the Mishnah does not say 'the following are saved by [taking] their lives: he who is **pursued by** his fellow who is intent on slaying him; or is **pursued by** a male [for sexual relations], or a betrothed maiden **pursued** by [one intent on rape].' It speaks of the **pursuer,** not the one being pursued ("The following are saved by [taking] their lives: he who pursues his neighbor. . . ."). This certainly seems to show that the pursuer, not the victim, is the one who is rescued.

Moreover, as we noted above, the second half of the Mishnah speaks of offenses 'between man and God,' where there is no dispensation to strike at the perpetrator preemptively. The Mishnah concludes with the words "is not be saved by [taking] his life." Here, there is no victim at all, so it is quite clear that the person who is not to be "saved by [taking] his life" can only be the attacker. And if the person whom the second part of the Mishnah says is not to be saved is the attacker, we can infer that the one who **is** to be saved, in the first part of the Mishnah, is likewise the attacker.

And in fact, Rashi interprets the Mishnah in precisely this way:

> "The following must be saved"—from sin. "By [taking] their lives"—any person is permitted to kill them in order to save them from sin.

The *Tosafot* support Rashi's view by adducing the linguistic structure of the Mishnah, as we just did:

> The meaning of the phrase "saved by their life" is that the pursued party is saved by [taking] the life of the pursuer. But it is impossible to give this interpretation in the case of one who pursues an animal and so on. Therefore it seems more reasonable to interpret it as saying that the person is saved from sin by [the taking of] his life.
>
> *Tosafot* ad loc. s.v. *lehatzilo benafsho*

This is not to say, of course, that Rashi regards saving the attacker from sin as sufficient to ground the right of self-defense. It is clear that the element of rescuing the victim must also be present, and there is no right to preemptively attack someone about to commit an offense between man and God. Rashi himself emphasizes this:

> It is not permitted to save him by [taking] his life unless it is a case of sexual transgression [adultery or incest] involving shame and dishonor to the pursued, such as [where someone intent on rape pursues] a male or a betrothed maiden.
>
> bSanhedrin 73a s.v. *aval harodef*

A more precise statement of Rashi's position, then, would be that rescuing the attacker from sin is the purpose of the law of the pursuer, but the element of saving the victim is a necessary condition for the dispensation to strike at the pursuer.

In sum, the Mishnah incorporates two different justifications for the right to strike a pursuer preemptively in self-defense, which it seems to view as cumulative requirements. One justification is rescue of the victim; it is this justification that underlies the Mishnah's distinction between offenses against another person, where the right to self-defense may be invoked, and offenses against God. The second justification is preventing sin, in effect saving the pursuer; it is this justification that underlies the distinction between different classes of attacks on the basis of the seriousness of the transgression involved as opposed to the harm that would be caused to the victim. This justification also underlies the phraseology "are saved by [taking] their lives," which alludes to saving the attacker from the sin he is about to commit.

The following sources, presented here without disambiguating renderings of the problematic Hebrew phrase "by his (her, their) life" (*benafsho*) in square brackets, highlight the ambiguity as to the core justification for the dispensation to strike out preemptively:

> Just as a betrothed maiden can be saved by his life, so in the case of a murderer, he can be saved by his life.
>
> bSanhedrin 73a

> Our Rabbis taught: He who pursues his neighbor to slay him, or [pursues] a male [for sexual relations], or [pursues] a betrothed maiden, or [pursues] relations that render him liable to the punishment of death imposed by the court, or [pursues] relations that render him liable to divine extirpation (*karet*)—these are saved by their lives.
>
> bSanhedrin 73a

> "You shall cut off her hand"—this teaches that you are obligated to save her by her hand. How do we know that if you cannot save her by her hand you should save her by her life? As it is written, "show her no pity."
>
> Sifre Deuteronomy, Ki Teitze, 293 (Finkelstein edition, p. 312)

## 4.3 Tannaitic and Amoraic limitations on the law of the pursuer

We will now examine various qualifications and limitations discussed by the Rabbis with regard to the law of the pursuer and its application in practice, some of which shed light on the law's theoretical underpinnings. As we will see, the discussion focuses on three main issues: saving the victim's life; saving the pursuer from transgression; and anticipatory punishment for the offense.

### i Proportionality and minimizing harm

The classic case of self-defense is where someone intent on murdering his fellow is preemptively killed. There is complete proportionality between the actions of the pursuer and the defender. At times, however, such proportionality is compromised in one of two ways. First, the pursuer may be intent on causing harm short of death, such as rape, or, even less severe, property damage. In such cases, is there a dispensation to kill the pursuer? Second, the defender may have recourse to several effective means of defense, some lethal and others less so. For example, someone attacked by a would-be murderer may, in some circumstances, be able to thwart the murder by injuring rather than killing the pursuer. Is the victim obliged to employ the least dangerous means of defense available to him, or is he permitted, in the face of danger to his life, to use, reflexively, whatever means of defense he has? There are, then, two questions to be considered: (1) Is it permissible to inflict on the pursuer an injury more severe than that which the pursuer intends to inflict on the victim? (2) Is there an obligation to minimize, as much as possible, the injury to the pursuer?

These questions are manifestly related to that of the justification for the law of the pursuer. If, for instance, the thrust of the law is to save the pursuer from transgression, it would be reasonable to seek to harm him no more than necessary to preempt the transgression. This would also appear to be the case if the thrust of the law is rescuing the victim, a goal that justifies striking at the pursuer, but not harming him any more than is necessary to rescue the victim. If, however, the thrust of the law is anticipatory punishment, a case might be made for exonerating a defender who inflicts a measure of harm equivalent to the punishment the pursuer would have incurred had the offense been carried out—even if the pursuer's attack could have been prevented by some lesser action. We say a case **might** be made, because that conclusion does not necessarily follow: even if the thrust of the law of the pursuer is anticipatory punishment, it could be argued that as long as the offense has not yet in fact been committed, defensive–punitive actions should be no more severe than the minimum needed.

The justification for the law of the pursuer also has bearing on the first question: can the attacker be subjected to injury more severe than that he seeks to inflict (for instance, can a would-be rapist be preemptively killed)? Here, the differences between the various justifications are more salient. The anticipatory punishment approach will not permit inflicting harm more severe than the penalty prescribed by the law for the offense the attacker sought to commit, for instance, whereas the approach based on rescuing the victim will likely permit whatever acts are needed to prevent the attack, however severe the injury they cause. We leave open for now the question of what restrictions, if any, would be imposed on the approach that sees saving the pursuer from transgression as the thrust of self-defense.

The Tannaim and Amoraim addressed these questions separately. Following their lead, we will do so as well, beginning with the question of minimizing harm to the pursuer. Against the backdrop of the Mishnah's determination that it is permitted to kill the pursuer, the Tosefta raises the issue of neutralizing the attack by lesser means:

> One who pursues his fellow [to slay him] is saved by [taking] his life. In what way is he saved by his life? He cuts off one of his limbs, and if he [still] cannot withstand him [i.e., withstand the pursuer's attack], he kills him.
>
> tSanhedrin 11:1 (Zuckermandel edition)

The victim, then, must try to limit, to the extent possible, the injury to the pursuer, and injure him only to the extent necessary to prevent continuation of the attack.

The Babylonian Talmud cites a baraita that takes a similar position, but adds an important point not mentioned in the Tosefta:

> It has been taught: R. Jonathan the son of Saul said: A pursuer who was pursuing his fellow to slay him, and could have been saved by [the maiming of] one of his limbs, but the pursuee did not save him thus [but instead killed the pursuer]—[the pursuee] is put to death for this.
>
> bSanhedrin 74a

The point added is that injuring the attacker more than the minimum necessary to stop him is not only forbidden, it may even be murder, and may render the victim/defender himself subject to the punishment of death by the court. The pursuer's deeds do not automatically divest him of his right to live. The baraita rejects the line of thinking that, by his actions, the pursuer loses the right to life, and one who kills him in self-defense should not be subject to the punishment of death by the court. This additional provision is clearly inconsistent with the idea that the thrust of the law is anticipatory punishment.

The provision set out in the baraita was, however, accepted as law by Maimonides, who rules:

> 7 … If the one being pursued can be saved by [injuring] one of the pursuer's limbs, for instance by striking him with an arrow or a stone or a sword and cutting off his hand or breaking his leg or blinding his eye, this should be done. If, however, it is impossible to make a precise strike, and he can be rescued only by killing the pursuer, then he is to be killed….
>
> 13 If he could have saved [the victim] by [the maiming of] one of [the pursuer's] limbs, but did not take the trouble to do so, but saved

> [the victim] by the life of the pursuer, and killed him—he is deemed a shedder of blood, and he incurs the punishment of death. He may not, however, be put to death by the court.
>
> *Code*, Laws concerning Murder and the Preservation of Life 1:7, 13

Maimonides' concluding words, however, add a new twist: "He may not, however, be put to death by the court." He so rules even though R. Jonathan b. Saul suggested nothing of the sort, but clearly implied that one who kills a pursuer who could have been stopped by the infliction of injury alone, is deemed a murderer and subject to the punishment of death imposed by the court. And, indeed, criticism of this stance was soon voiced. R. Jacob b. Asher, for instance, comments as follows:

> Maimonides wrote: "If he could have saved [the victim] by [the maiming of] one of [the pursuer's] limbs, but did not take the trouble to do so, but saved [the victim] by the life of the pursuer, and killed him—he is deemed a shedder of blood, and he incurs the punishment of death. He may not, however, be put to death by the court." But I do not know why, if he deserves death, the court does not put him to death.
>
> *Tur*, HM 425

Several explanations for Maimonides' ruling can be suggested. First, it would be difficult to convict such a person of murder, especially given the stringent requirements of Jewish criminal law. It would be difficult to demonstrate his criminal intent, as he can argue in his defense that under the stressful circumstances in which he found himself, he was convinced there was no way to rescue himself or the victim other than by killing the attacker. Moreover, it is hard to imagine that it would have been possible, in the said circumstances, to satisfy the forewarning condition (to be discussed below), whereby someone intent on killing his fellow must have been formally cautioned by witnesses to the events that were unfolding that he would be perpetrating a capital crime. Without such forewarning, the court cannot impose the punishment of death.

Second, Maimonides may have felt that putting such a person to death would be unjust, since he intended only to save himself or his fellow from mortal danger. He may have used excessive force in doing so, but it would be unjust to convict him of murder on that account.

Both these points are raised by R. Joseph Caro in commenting on the *Tur*'s remarks regarding Maimonides' position:

> It may be said that Maimonides' rationale is that since [the victim/defender] was authorized to have recourse to the action, it would be unlawful for the court to execute him. Moreover, the difficulty [raised by the *Tur*] is in any case irrelevant, since there had been no forewarning,

and he had not acknowledged [being forewarned], since he intended only to rescue the victim.

*Beit Yosef*, *Tur*, HM 425

The Tannaim also considered the question of whether a pursuer may be subjected to injury more severe than the injury he meant to inflict on the victim. We have already seen that, according to the Mishnah, not every act of rape justifies killing the rapist; it is justified only if the rape is also an act of adultery, as in the case of the betrothed maiden. This suggests an intermediate position, which does not regard rape and its consequences as in itself justifying killing the pursuer, but at the same time does not restrict the right of self-defense (even to the point of killing the pursuer), to cases where the pursuer is intent on murder.

At least one Tanna, however, disputes the mishnaic view, and, to an extent, questions the very legitimacy of killing the rapist to prevent the rape. R. Judah, whose view is cited in the Tosefta, does not absolutely deny the right to kill the rapist, but maintains that the rape itself is not the factor that justifies taking this step:

> R. Judah says: If she says 'leave him be'—he is not saved by [taking] his life [Why, then, is he saved by taking his life if she does not say 'leave him be'?] Because were he let alone, he would ultimately commit a capital crime.

tSanhedrin 11:1 (Zuckermandel edition)

The Babylonian Talmud sharpens the dispute between R. Judah and the mishnaic Sages. It explains that they disagree regarding a case where the sexual relations were indeed non-consensual, but the victim did not resist for fear of jeopardizing her life: she preferred being raped to being murdered. The Talmud sees this situation as a test case for a fundamental principle.

> Regarding which case do they [R. Judah and the Sages] differ? Rava said: When she is distressed about the dishonor [lit., the stain], yet lets him [rape her], so that he will not slay her. The Rabbis maintain, The Merciful One was distressed about the dishonor, and she too is distressed about it [hence her pursuer may be slain]. But R. Judah [maintains]: The Merciful One's decree that he should be slain pertains to a case where she is prepared to give her own life [rather than be violated]; but this one does not intend to give her life [i.e., she will not resist the rape].

bSanhedrin 73b

The Sages thus believe that the rape itself constitutes adequate reason to rescue the victim even at the cost of killing the rapist. Accordingly, even when it is clear that the rapist is not jeopardizing the victim's life (since, fearing for her life, she does not resist), she may be rescued by killing him. R. Judah, in contrast, believes that the dispensation to kill the rapist is based on the concern that the rape will deteriorate into murder. Hence he argues that if there is good reason to think that this will not happen, it is forbidden to rescue the victim by killing the rapist.

Thus R. Judah upholds the requirement that there be strict proportionality between the injury the pursuer intends to inflict and the injury that may be inflicted on him to avert the attack. Killing the pursuer is permitted only if he is likely to inflict a parallel injury—death—but not if he is likely to inflict only non-mortal injury. The Sages, on the other hand, allow the life of the pursuer to be taken not only to save life, but also to prevent rape.

### ii Is there a preferred means of killing the pursuer?

An interesting issue arises in relation to situations where the defender has available several courses of action, all likely to bring about the same result: rescue of the person being attacked at the cost of killing the pursuer. The question is whether there is a preferred means of accomplishing the latter. Exploring this question may provide insight as to whether Jewish law takes rescue of the victim, or anticipatory punishment of the pursuer, to be the legal basis for the dispensation to kill the pursuer preemptively.

In explicating the 'stealth burglar' passage (Exod. 22:1–2), the Mekhilta of R. Shimon b. Yohai[28] concludes from the non-specific wording of the biblical verse—"and be smitten so that he dieth"—that "so that he dieth" means "by any means." In other words, the burglar, who puts the homeowner's life in jeopardy, can be killed in any effective way. To the author of this Midrash, that is, the Mekhilta of R. Shimon b. Yohai, this seems to call for little if any discussion: it is almost self-evident. But in bSanhedrin 72b, the Babylonian Talmud ponders why there is a need for a special biblical source for the rule that a pursuer may be killed by any possible means, and it cannot simply be deduced from the laws governing murderers.[29]

According to the law, although it is preferable for a convicted murderer to be put to death by the sword, if this proves impossible, any method of execution is acceptable ex post facto. Why, then, the Talmud wonders, does the Midrash feel the need to derive its dispensation through exegesis of the phrase "so that he dieth," when it could have grounded it in a simple analogy between the death of the pursuer and that of a murderer convicted

28 Epstein-Melamed edition, pp. 191–93.

29 In Jewish law, four main modes of capital punishment are imposed by the court: stoning, burning, strangulation, and the sword. The Rabbis ranked capital offenses in order of seriousness on the basis of the severity of the mode of death prescribed for them. Murderers are executed by the sword.

by the court? To assess the aptness of the analogy, the Talmud proceeds to engage in exegetical analysis of Numbers 35:21, the biblical prooftext for the law of the murderer.

For our purposes, the details of the argument are less important than the fact that the Talmud contemplates an analogy between the case of the murderer, who is judged and sentenced by the court, and that of the pursuer, who has not yet committed an offense. It seems to suggest that the Talmud takes anticipatory punishment to be the legal basis for the law of the pursuer.

The claim that the case of the pursuer is comparable to that of the murderer could have a significant practical implication. R. Menahem Hameiri, for instance, asserts:

> Inasmuch as we adjudge him [the pursuer] to be one who pursues his fellow to slay him, it is proper for the killer [of the pursuer] to try to kill him with a sword. But if he is not able to kill him with a sword, or he does not have a sword at hand, he may kill him any way he can … as we have explained in connection with the [law of the] murderer.
>
> *Beit Habehira*, bSanhedrin 72b

By contrast, Maimonides implies that the rescuer is permitted *ab initio* to kill the pursuer any way he can; he need not make an effort to kill him specifically by the sword:

> One who breaks in, whether by day or by night—there shall be no bloodguiltiness for him. And if the owner of the house or someone else kills him, they are exempt. Everyone is permitted to kill him … by any means whereby they can put him to death.…
>
> *Code,* Laws concerning Theft 9:7

Maimonides thus seems to disregard the inference that can be drawn from the talmudic passage discussed above, namely, that, where possible, the pursuer is to be killed by the sword. He may reject the idea that killing the pursuer constitutes a sort of anticipatory punishment, and regard it solely as a means of rescuing the victim. If so, it stands to reason that he would favor the Mekhilta's laconic formulation over the Talmud's hermeneutical analysis.

### iii Third parties

Frequently, it will be a third party, rather than the victim himself, who strikes at the pursuer. In such cases, we must ask whether a third party should be permitted to defend the victim at the cost of injuring the attacker. And if it is permitted, is such conduct to be viewed as excusable, justified, or obligatory?

As we saw above, it is by no means self-evident that the right to self-defense should be extended to third parties. The position taken on this issue may reflect the rationale on which the right is deemed to be based. For example, if the right to self-defense is grounded in the desideratum of preserving public order, this favors extending the right to a third party, but the desideratum of protecting personal autonomy would likely be taken to support limiting the right to the victim himself.

The Sages based extension of the right of self-defense to third parties on biblical verses. We saw that the 'stealth burglar' passage speaks of killing the burglar in non-specific language—"and be smitten so that he dieth." Just as the Sages took the non-specific language to imply that **any means** of injuring the pursuer was legitimate, they likewise took it to imply that **anyone** was permitted to injure him. The Mekhilta de-Rabbi Shimon b. Yohai explains: "'and be smitten'—by anyone."

The Talmud points out that this extension is not self-evident:

> "'And be smitten so that he dieth'—by anyone" is necessary: for one might think that only the homeowner may be presumed not to remain passive [lit., stand] where his property is concerned, but not a stranger. [Scripture] therefore teaches us that he is regarded as a pursuer, whom even a stranger may kill.
>
> bSanhedrin 72b

Rashi ad loc. explains:

> "The homeowner"—it is he who is permitted to kill [the burglar], for the burglar is certain that [the homeowner] will not remain passive where his property is concerned, and whom the burglar accordingly contemplates killing [if he must do so to steal the property].
>
> "But not a stranger"—for this thief contemplates killing only the homeowner.
>
> "[Scripture] therefore teaches us"—that because he contemplates killing an Israelite, he is a pursuer and the homeowner may be saved by [taking] [the burglar's] life.

In other words, it might have made sense to narrow the right to strike at the burglar and grant it only to the homeowner himself, inasmuch as only he is actually in mortal danger. The burglar initially plans to take property, not life, but he recognizes that the homeowner will confront him, for there is a presumption that "no one remains passive where his property is concerned"; his willingness to undertake the burglary, the Talmud argues, implies willingness to kill the homeowner, who will attempt to prevent him from stealing his property. But even though the homeowner is the only one who is in mortal danger, the Torah nevertheless uses non-specific wording ("and be smitten so that he dieth") to emphasize that the right to strike at the burglar is granted to all.

The Sages go even further, suggesting that self-defense is not only a right given to third parties, but an obligation imposed on them. Whereas this is not explicit in the Mishnah, which states only: "The following are saved... by [taking] their lives...", the baraita cited by the Talmud in juxtaposition to the Mishnah makes the matter much clearer, for it considers the source of the law of the pursuer. The baraita attempts to ground the law of the pursuer and the right of self-defense in the obligation not to stand by—to remain passive—when one's fellow is in jeopardy. The biblical dictum, "Neither shalt thou stand idly by the blood of your neighbor" (Lev. 19:16) is not merely an ethical exhortation, but sets down an obligation to assist one who finds himself in danger:

> Our Rabbis taught: Whence do we know that he who pursues his fellow to slay him" can be saved by [taking] his life? Scripture teaches, "Neither shalt thou stand idly by the blood of your neighbor" (Lev. 19:16).
>
> bSanhedrin 73a

Later, however, the Talmud rejects the attempt to ground the obligation to rescue someone being pursued in the biblical obligation not to "stand idly by," for the latter obligation does not speak to the propriety of injuring the attacker. According to the Talmud, the verse obligates one to take concrete steps to save his fellow, but does not authorize him to injure anyone, even a pursuer. The Talmud proceeds to anchor the third party's obligation to rescue someone being pursued in a different biblical source, the law of the "betrothed maiden," as we saw above. It is nonetheless noteworthy that the baraita appears to assume that third parties are obliged to rescue a pursuee, and not merely granted the assurance that doing so will generate no liability for injury to the pursuer. Though the attempt to derive the law of the pursuer from the "Neither shalt thou stand idly by" law fails, the notion that rescuing the victim is obligatory has not been rejected. Maimonides, we saw, takes attacking the pursuer to be an obligation, not just a right:

> But as to one who pursues his fellow to slay him ... it is the obligation of every Israelite to rescue the pursued one from the pursuer, even by [taking] the pursuer's life.
>
> *Code*, Laws concerning Murder and the Preservation of Life 1:6

Though the obligation to rescue someone being pursued is imposed on third parties, there may arise complicated situations where the impending danger to the victim is not clear-cut. In such situations, the rescuer must use his own judgment as to the nature of the danger. This may explain why in the case of the 'stealth burglar,' Maimonides does not impose on third parties an obligation to rescue someone under attack.

> If a thief enters by breaking in, by day or by night [cf. Exod. 22:1], there shall be no bloodguiltiness for him [lit., he has no blood], and if the homeowner or anyone else kills him, they are exempt, and all are permitted to kill him.
>
> *Code*, Laws concerning Theft 9:7

Here, therefore, the rescuer is authorized to use his own judgment as to whether or not to strike at the burglar.

That self-defense, including the right to preemptively injure the pursuer, is obligatory on third parties does not necessarily follow from any of the justifications for self-defense discussed above—saving the victim from attack, saving the aggressor from sin, inflicting anticipatory punishment—but does not conflict with any of them, either. It thus appears that the fact that under Jewish law there is an **obligation** to defend someone being attacked ("Neither shalt thou stand idly by") is not directly connected to the legal basis for the law of the pursuer, but rather, follows from the values of social solidarity and mutual responsibility that Jewish law attempts to foster within Jewish society.

### iv The forewarning requirement

As a threshold condition for inflicting punishment pursuant to the Torah, Jewish law requires that the perpetrator be formally forewarned. Maimonides describes the forewarning process as follows:

> How is he forewarned? He is told, 'Desist, or refrain, from doing it, for this is a transgression that will render you liable to the punishment of death imposed by the court, or flogging.' If he desists, he is exempt. And so too, if he remains silent, or nods his head, he is exempt. And even if he says, 'I know that it is so,' he is exempt, unless he surrenders himself to death, saying, 'Despite that I shall do it,' after which he is put to death. And he must commit [the transgression] immediately after the forewarning, that is, within an utterance. But if the time that elapses is longer than an utterance, another forewarning is necessary.
>
> *Code*, Laws concerning the Sanhedrin 12:2

In contrast to legal systems that uphold the "ignorance of the law is no excuse" rule, Jewish law does not punish someone who was unaware that he was committing an offense or what punishment would be incurred. It makes imposition of punishment conditional on the defendant's having been apprised of these facts prior to carrying out the offense.[30]

30 This is not to say that one who commits an offense without full *mens rea* or commits it out of negligence, is altogether blameless. In the case of homicide he may be subject to banishment to a city of exile, and for other offenses he may be subject to the obligation to

To understand the nature of the forewarning requirement, it is important to distinguish—though the sources do not do so explicitly—between a **forewarning** (*hatraa*) not to commit an offense and an **admonition** (*azhara*) not to do so. Admonition involves informing someone that the action he is about to perform is an offense and that it incurs a particular punishment. Forewarning, as the halakha defines it, has an additional element: the perpetrator's declaration that though he is aware of the significance of his actions, he chooses to proceed with carrying out the offense. To punish an offender, it does not suffice for him to have been admonished, he had to have been forewarned. In effect, the forewarning process is intended to single out refractory offenders, who break the law as a matter of principle rather than out of a desire to advance some interest or other. The Rabbis term this sort of offender an "insolent offender" (*avaryan lehakhis*)—one who sins to cause anger. The only offender who is punished, then, is one who in effect declares that he answers to this description.[31] The question that arises vis-à-vis the law of the pursuer is whether the permissibility of self-defense should be conditioned on criminal intent on the pursuer's part, and if so, whether the forewarning requirement should apply in this context. How we answer this question will reflect our position on the primary justification for self-defense. If we maintain that the justification is the basic right to personal autonomy, which includes physical integrity, this right may be invoked even against a negligent assailant, and perhaps even against an assailant who is entirely innocent. They too illicitly violate the victim's autonomy, and he therefore has the right to defend himself against them, even at the cost of injuring them. On this approach, there is a right to self-defense even absent criminal intent on the attacker's part. On the other hand, if the right to self-defense is grounded in the blameworthiness of the pursuer, who by his own actions forfeits his right to live, it stands to reason that the right must be conditional on the presence of criminal intent.

The same holds vis-à-vis the other justifications for self-defense put forward in the halakhic literature. If saving the pursuer from sinning is taken to be the justification, will there be any basis for permitting an assault on a pursuer who lacks criminal intent, and therefore is not, from the

bring a guilt offering at the Temple in Jerusalem. Scholars are divided over the question of whether these religious consequences have any implications for our understanding of Jewish criminal law.

31 The forewarning requirement appears to be a rigorous procedural element that results in many criminal actions going unpunished. The strictness of the condition, it would seem, is likely to undermine the legal system's capacity to penalize crime, paralyze efforts to fight crime, and call into question the efficacy of Jewish criminal law in general. Scholars have suggested, however, that the admonition requirement reflects one of the **theoretical** principles of Jewish criminal law: punishment is conditional on the offender's being unequivocally guilty of the crime. **The law to be put into practice**, however, is interpreted leniently, allowing for punishment without forewarning.

perspective of the law, transgressing at all, or is at most transgressing inadvertently? Similarly, if the law of the pursuer is seen as grounded in anticipatory punishment, there is no basis for imposing anticipatory punishment on one who, were he to carry out the action, would not be punishable by death. But if the thrust of the law is rescuing the victim—that is, if its justification is the right to life, bodily integrity, and property, and the ensuing right not to be attacked—the victim may well be permitted to defend himself even where his attacker means no harm. In that case, however, we will still have to clarify why we give precedence to the victim's life over the pursuer's, since they are equally blameless.

Two Tannaitic sources within the *sugya* in the Babylonian Talmud—bSanhedrin 72a–74a—explicitly address the relationship between the law of the pursuer and the warning/admonition requirement. A close reading of the relevant sources shows that apparently minor differences between them reflect substantive conceptual differences. The Talmud was also aware of this, reinterpreting them to render them consistent with its view. We will examine each one separately and then see how they are incorporated into the talmudic *sugya* in bSanhedrin 72b.

A Regarding a pursuer who was pursuing his fellow to slay him: [one who observes the incident] says to him, 'Behold, he is an Israelite, and a party to the Covenant, and the Torah said: "Whoso sheddeth man's blood, by man shall his blood be shed" (Gen. 9:6), that is, the Torah said to save the blood of the pursued by the blood of the pursuer.'

B Regarding a pursuer who was pursuing his fellow to slay him: [one who observes the incident] said to him, 'Behold, he is an Israelite, and a party to the Covenant, and the Torah said: "Whoso sheddeth man's blood, by man shall his blood be shed" (Gen. 9:6), that is, the Torah said to save the blood of the pursued by the blood of the pursuer.' If he [the pursuer] said: 'I know that it is so'—he is exempt; if he said, 'Despite that, I shall do it,' he is liable.

The passages illustrate the difference between admonition and forewarning, a difference that undoubtedly reflects different views as to the justification for the law of the pursuer. According to the first source, the pursuer must be **admonished** of what he can expect following the rescue operation, which is imminent. The rescuer must be sure that the pursuer knows he is committing a transgression, and can expect to be killed; he is giving the pursuer a chance to retreat. In effect, the purpose of the procedure is to verify the pursuer's blameworthiness, on which the permissibility of striking at him is conditioned. It is apparent that this passage reflects the notion that the pursuer should be saved from transgression; hence, if the rescuer is to be permitted to attack him, it is necessary to first establish the pursuer's blameworthiness.

In contrast, the second passage mandates the full **forewarning** procedure. Note that once the pursuer says, 'I know that it is so,' there is no doubt that he is blameworthy, even if he does not add, 'Despite that, I shall do it,' but this is not sufficient to render the preemptive attack permissible, according to this source. It is evident that the second source sees a preemptive attack on the pursuer as parallel to court-imposed punishment, and it therefore makes recourse to self-defense subject to the forewarning requirement. It is apparent, therefore, that the second source construes self-defense as a kind of anticipatory punishment of the offender.

How does the Talmud deal with the apparent contradiction between the two sources? It interprets the second source as referring to a specific and unique type of situation (*ukimta*):

> [It refers only to the case where] they are standing on two opposite sides of the river, so that he cannot save him. [In these circumstances], what can be done? He must be brought before the court. But [for punishment by] the court, forewarning is necessary.

The Talmud distinguishes between two situations. When it is possible to physically stop the pursuer and thwart his intention, it is permitted to strike at him even without forewarning. But when he cannot be stopped—for instance, when he is on the opposite side of the river, and all that can be done is to keep track of his actions and later testify about them in court—then he should be duly forewarned so he can be punished in accordance with the law.

There is no doubt that the Talmud's underlying interpretive motivation is to reject the idea that the law of the pursuer is based on the principle of anticipatory punishment; accordingly, it endeavors to draw a sharp distinction between the forewarning requirement, which is related to the penal process, and the law of the pursuer. To this end, it prefers to interpret source (B) as speaking of a judicial proceeding and not an instance of private self-defense.[32]

Before concluding our discussion of forewarning, let us consider another relevant passage in the *sugya* that suggests several interpretive directions. The passage discusses the legal explication of the biblical verses that address the stealth burglar (Exod. 22:1–2). The Sages understood these verses as referring specifically to a burglar tunneling under the wall of a house. They raise the question of a burglar who breaks into a house some other way:

32 Note that this conclusion is supported by literary evidence as well. Source (B) uses the terms "exempt" and "liable," which are typically used is handing down a judgment in court. Were the point at issue the permissibility of striking at the pursuer in self-defense, formulating the law in terms of "permitted" and "forbidden" would have been more appropriate.

> Our Rabbis taught: [If the thief is seized] "breaking in [lit., while tunneling]": from this I know that [the burglar may be killed] only in cases of tunneling. [Whence do we know that the burglar may be killed if seized] on the roof, in the courtyard, or in an enclosure [attached to the house]? Therefore Scripture teaches, "if a thief be found," implying, wherever he is seized as a thief. If so, why does the verse state "breaking in [lit., while tunneling]"? Because most burglars enter by tunneling.
>
> Another baraita taught: [If the thief is seized] "breaking in [lit., while tunneling]": from this I know that [the burglar may be killed] only in cases of tunneling. [Whence do we know that the burglar may be killed if seized] on the roof, in the courtyard, or in an enclosure [attached to the house]? Therefore Scripture teaches, "if a thief be found," implying, wherever he is seized as a thief. If so, why does the verse state "breaking in [lit., while tunneling]"? Because this tunneling is his forewarning.
>
> bSanhedrin 72b

The first source explains the biblical verse in line with its simple meaning: because break-ins via tunneling are commonplace, the Torah uses tunneling to represent the broader concept of a burglar who endangers a homeowner. According to the explanation in the second paragraph, however, the Torah adduces tunneling to emphasize an additional rule: namely, that there is no need to explicitly forewarn a burglar who breaks in via a tunnel, for the very fact that he is tunneling under the house demonstrates his full awareness of his deed. Rashi explains this clause as follows:

> "This is his forewarning"—He needs no further forewarning and may be killed at once, for inasmuch as he undertook the effort and devoted himself to tunneling, he did so with the knowledge, 'if [the homeowner] confronts me, I will kill him'; and the Torah says that since he is a pursuer, no forewarning is necessary, but he is saved by [taking] his life.

The second source can be interpreted in two ways, with an important legal difference between them. It may mean that there is no need to forewarn a pursuer, as **the act of pursuing in itself makes it permissible to kill the pursuer as a preventative measure, with no need for forewarning**. But it could be argued that the paragraph reflects the very opposite reasoning: because the tunneling burglar's actions demonstrate his intentions beyond any doubt, he is an **exception to the general rule that killing a pursuer is conditional on the pursuer's having been forewarned**. In the case of a tunneling burglar, and only in this case, there is no need for prior warning, but in all other cases of pursuit, where the pursuer's criminal intent is in doubt, forewarning is required.

From the continuation of his remarks, it appears that Rashi understands the paragraph in the latter sense:

> But if [the burglar] entered someone's courtyard or rooftop through the door, he may not kill him until witnesses have forewarned him, 'we see what you are doing and will kill you,' and he accepts the forewarning and says, 'I know, and despite that I shall do it; if you block me, I will kill you.' But without forewarning—[he may] not [be killed], for perhaps he has not come with a mind to kill but only because he happened upon the entrance, and if he is confronted, he will leave.

The burglar entering via a tunnel, where forewarning is not mandated, is an exception, but in other cases where a burglar breaks into a dwelling, if a preemptive attack on him is to be permissible, the burglar must be forewarned and must accept the forewarning.

Maimonides, on the other hand, appears to understand the paragraph in the first sense: "If he was admonished but still pursues the other person, then even though he has not accepted the forewarning, he is to be killed, since he is continuing to pursue him."[33]

It thus appears that whereas Rashi takes self-defense on the strength of the law of the pursuer to be a kind of anticipatory punishment of the pursuer, making forewarning necessary except when the nature of the pursuit itself implies forewarning (namely, the case of the stealth burglar), Maimonides rejects this approach.

### v Minors

Borderline cases that frequently come up in the literature on self-defense involve situations in which the pursuer acts blamelessly or at least cannot be regarded as having criminal intent. The halakhic literature on pursuers who are minors, that is, under the age of criminal responsibility, is quite extensive.[34]

On the one hand, if we take the view that the right to self-defense is grounded in the pursuer's blameworthiness, we cannot ensure rescue of the victim, as the aggressor would apparently be deemed blameless and bear no criminal responsibility. If, for example, a child playing with a gun begins to sprays bullets in every direction, someone standing nearby would not be permitted, on this approach, to save his own life or the lives of other bystanders, by inflicting potentially lethal injury on the child. On

33 *Code*, Laws concerning Murder and the Preservation of Life 1:7.

34 There is also much literature on fetuses that endanger their mothers. As noted in the introduction to this chapter, however, the unique features of the case of the fetus distinguish it from the classic case of a pursuer.

the other hand, the view that grounds the right to self-defense solely in the victim's right to life and bodily integrity must be able to explain why, in the said circumstances, the life of the victim takes precedence over that of the (blameless) pursuer. There can also be an intermediate position that distinguishes between a minor who is not legally responsible and punishable for his conduct, but nonetheless understands what he is doing and knows that it is wrong, and an infant who does not yet have that minimal understanding of his behavior. In the former case, the pursuer is legally innocent but morally blameworthy; in the latter, he is neither legally nor morally culpable.

The ruling in the *sugya* in the Babylonian Talmud is terse and unambiguous:

> R. Huna said: A minor in pursuit may be saved by [taking] his life. He thus maintains: No forewarning is necessary for a pursuer, whether he is an adult or a minor.
>
> bSanhedrin 72b

It seems, then, that R. Huna draws no connection between the right to strike at the pursuer and the idea of anticipatory punishment, for even if the minor pursuer understands his act and its consequences, he will not be punished for killing the pursued party. If R. Huna takes all minors to be covered by his ruling, it follows that on his view, the law of the pursuer is not grounded in the pursuer's blameworthiness.

Some hint as to R. Huna's view vis-à-vis the definition of a 'minor' can be gleaned from the ensuing talmudic discussion. When a pregnant woman's life is endangered during childbirth, the fetus may be killed to save the mother's life. Once its head has emerged from the womb, however, it may not be killed, since at that point it is considered to have been born and to be an autonomous life. The Talmud asks why, given R. Huna's view that even a minor may be killed in self-defense, this newborn child is not considered a pursuer who can be killed. Its reply is that the case of the fetus is different, for here, it is "heaven" that is pursuing the mother. This statement is generally understood to mean that the birth of the fetus is a natural event, not a human act. Clearly, then, R. Huna does not include all minors within the scope of his ruling. Nevertheless, the scope of the ruling is unclear.

The Early Authorities put forward various interpretations of R. Huna's ruling. Maimonides—who, as we have seen, rejects the forewarning requirement in the context of the pursuer—accepts R. Huna's ruling at face value: "But as to one who pursues his fellow to slay him, even if the pursuer is a minor, it is the obligation of every Israelite to rescue the pursued one from the pursuer, even by [taking] the pursuer's life."[35]

35 *Code*, Laws concerning Murder and the Preservation of Life 1:6.

Maimonides' words here are fully consistent with his view that killing the pursuer is warranted given that the thrust of self-defense is rescuing the victim; whether the pursuer is punishable or not makes no difference. The principle was formulated by R. Meir Abulafia, in his explanation of R. Huna's rule: "And even though a minor is not punishable, he is killed not because of his own liability, but to save the other party."[36]

It remains unclear, however, why the victim's life should take precedence over that of the (minor) pursuer, who is not considered blameworthy and does not even understand the meaning of his actions. But the difficulty posed by this rule is far greater for Rashi, who ascribes much more weight to the pursuer's blameworthiness. Rashi takes the killing of the pursuer to be an act of saving him—from transgression—and therefore, other than in exceptional cases, as we just saw, invokes the forewarning requirement in the context of the pursuer. How, then, can Rashi account for the ruling that permits the killing of a pursuer who is a minor?

Although Rashi does not raise the question explicitly, he addresses it indirectly, in offering the following gloss on R. Huna's rule: "'A minor in pursuit'—[in pursuit of] another minor with intent to kill him." This might be taken to imply that killing a minor to save someone whom the minor threatens is permissible only when the minor is threatening another minor, but not an adult. This represents a very significant narrowing of the applicability of R. Huna's rule. It is not entirely clear why this limitation is justified or why any weight should be given to the age of the target of the threat. It may be that Rashi seeks to narrow R. Huna's ruling because he takes the justification for attacking the pursuer to be grounded in his blameworthiness and the fact that he will, in any event, be sentenced to death by the court, neither of which applies in the case of minors.

It is also possible that Rashi did not intend to restrict R. Huna's ruling to the case of a minor in pursuit of another minor. It may be that he sought merely to describe what he thought to be the most likely scenario vis-à-vis pursuit by a minor. Both in the talmudic era, and in Rashi's day, pursuit with murderous intent would ordinarily have involved hand-to-hand combat. An adult could usually defend himself against a minor by means other than killing the minor. Even so, R. Huna's ruling appears to be inconsistent with the view that the law of the pursuer is grounded in anticipatory punishment.

The nineteenth century decisor R. Joseph Saul Nathanson explained Rashi's view as follows:

> In my humble opinion, there is something new here. For it seems very dubious, inasmuch as a minor is deemed to lack thought[37]... and if so,

36 *Yad Rama*, bSanhedrin 72b s.v. *amar rav huna*.

37 I.e., the mental capacity needed to perform actions with legal effect; see L. Moscovitz, "The actions of a minor are a nullity"? Some observations on the legal capacity of minors in Rabbinic law," 17 *Jewish Law Annual* (2007), 63–120.

> how can he be saved by [taking] his life? He may not intend to kill, he may simply be playing, and how can we kill him, given this doubt? ... But in my humble opinion, the decision is that a **third party** should not touch the minor, but that the victim himself, because he is afraid for his life, is permitted to save himself by [taking] the life of the pursuer ... but a third party may not kill him. But in my humble opinion, this is so when the victim is an adult, who knows how to save himself, but when he, too, is a minor and does not know how to save himself, then we are commanded to stand in for him and save him.
>
> *Responsa Shoel Umeshiv*, 4th ed., 2, #50

According to R. Nathanson, Rashi maintains that a minor pursuer may not be killed, for we cannot be certain there is criminal intent underlying his actions. Only the victim himself may harm the pursuer in this situation, and a third party may not intervene, for in the case of a non-blameworthy pursuer, the right to self-defense is given only to the victim. The case where the minor is threatening the life of another minor is an exception. Here, a third party may intervene to protect the victim even at the cost of mortally injuring the aggressor, for the minor victim is presumed to be unable to defend himself.

Whatever its merits, this explanation certainly highlights the gap between Rashi's approach, which focuses on the pursuer's guilt, and R. Huna's ruling, which permits striking at a minor pursuing another in order to kill him.

## 5 Self-defense in the responsa literature

Like other areas of law, the "law of the pursuer" must be examined not only from the perspective of the theoretical law as set out in the Mishnah and talmudic literature, but also from the perspective of legal practice, that is, the responsa literature. Yet, in the responsa literature there is virtually no treatment of the law of the pursuer, at least not in the its classic formulation, which we have explored above. Though often mentioned in passing in other contexts, it is rarely referred to in what would seem to be the most appropriate context, namely, the laws governing criminal offenses.[38]

38 One medieval context in which the law of the pursuer was invoked was that of how best to deal with the problem of informers. An 'informer' (*moser*) is a member of the Jewish community who provides information to the Gentile authorities regarding another member of the community, thereby leading them to move against the latter or his property, often ending with the informed-on individual enduring great suffering and death. Jewish law took a very severe view of the informer's actions, which injured not only the individual informed on, but also the autonomy of the Jewish community and the delicate fabric of its life. Things reached the point that, on occasion, it was permitted to strike at an informer and kill him in order to avert his deeds. The dispensation to do so was based on the law of the pursuer, as the informer is regarded as jeopardizing the lives of others

During the twentieth century, the bloodshed and strife that accompanied the Zionist settlement of the land of Israel, and have continued to beset the State of Israel, often gave rise to questions regarding injury to terrorists and their supporters in the course of military operations in response to terror. Against this background, the contemporary halakhic authorities invoked the law of the pursuer; see Appendix 2.

There is indeed an explanation for the absence of responsa on matters connected to the law of the pursuer. Cases to which this law might be relevant would ordinarily involve either a victim or a third party who has killed a pursuer, and defends his act by invoking the law of the pursuer. As such, they fall under the ambit of criminal law. However, for reasons both internal and external, medieval and later Jewish courts have not, in general, adjudicated criminal law cases.[39] This is well illustrated by a responsum written by R. Jacob Reischer:

> Question: Concerning a lad in tears over [an incident in which he was] traveling with another lad, and they began to fight with each other, and the [other] lad took out a knife, intending to kill [his companion], who arose and killed [the wielder of the knife]. He now wants to repent for his action, but do we say [it is a case of] "If someone comes to kill you, preempt this by killing him"?
>
> Answer: In our day, we do not have the power to apply these laws, the laws governing capital cases. Nevertheless, I will not refrain from expressing what appears, in my humble opinion, to be the view of the Torah, as a matter of theoretical analysis, though not to be applied in practice.
>
> *Responsa Shvut Yaakov*, 2, #187

The question posed to R. Reischer was **not** whether the killer should be found liable by a rabbinical court, or how he should be punished, but whether he had a religious obligation to repent for his deed. The questioner thus did not regard the incident as calling for criminal adjudication, and R. Reischer affirmed that view, stating that "in our day [i.e., since the

and, at times, the life of the community overall. Implementing the law of the informer, however, required taking account of factors beyond the usual considerations of the criminal law. These additional considerations pertained primarily to the relationship of the Jewish community to the governmental authorities, and the community's interest in preserving its autonomy. Every act of informing was considered an attack on that autonomy that could have far-reaching consequences for the life of the community as a whole. Because of those exceptional considerations, the law of the informer is not discussed in this chapter.

39 A survey of these factors is beyond the scope of this discussion, but see A. Enker, "Aspects of interaction between Torah law, the king's law, and Noahide law in Jewish criminal law," 12 *Cardozo L. Rev.* (1991), 1137; M. Elon, *Principles of Jewish Law* (Jerusalem: 1975), 29.

destruction of the Temple[40]], we do not have the power to apply these laws." Later in the responsum, R. Reischer concludes that the young man's actions entail a measure of culpability, since he could have defended himself without killing his attacker (by "saving himself through one of his limbs"); moreover, he too may have been partly to blame for starting the fight. Accordingly, he did have to repent even though he had acted in self-defense. But it is clear in any event that both the question and the answer take it for granted that the criminal law issues that would seem to be raised by the lad's conduct are **not** a matter for halakhic deliberation, despite the not unreasonable expectation that analysis of the case should focus on whether the accused is guilty or innocent of murder.

### 5.1 Remanding criminals to the Gentile authorities

To deal with criminal activity in their midst, Jewish communities often had to avail themselves of the enforcement agencies of the Gentile regimes under which they lived—that is, to turn criminals over to the Gentile justice system. Doing so was by no means simple or taken for granted. For one thing, it subjected the offender to considerable danger—economic, personal, and sometimes mortal—for the Gentile authorities had their own rules for dealing with criminals. Moreover, it entailed a sort of collaboration with an alien legal system, and the submission of legal questions for its determination, something Jewish law strongly discourages.

In this context, R. Haim Or Zarua, a leading thirteenth century halakhic authority, concluded that these concerns did not require Jews to avoid asking the Gentile justice authorities, when necessary, to deal with potentially violent criminals. In support of this view, he adduces the law of the pursuer:

> Since this assailant will certainly strike, anyone is permitted to tell the [Gentile] judge to have him apprehended, even if he will thereby lose all his property.... Accordingly, it appears that anyone known to regularly commit battery has the status of one who may be informed on. But if he merely happened to commit battery once and regrets it, and it is clear to all that he will not commit this bad deed again, then it is certainly forbidden to kill him or cause him to lose his property....
>
> We need not say that only the victim himself may complain to the Gentiles; rather, it is a duty incumbent on everyone to tell the [Gentile] judge: 'A has struck B, and remains angry, do what is needed so that he will not continue to do this.' And if as a result the judge mistreats him and confiscates all his assets, the person who told the judge

40 By law, capital cases are to be adjudicated by the Sanhedrin convened in the Temple's Hall of Hewn Stone.

> [about it] is exempt; for were this not so, no one would rescue his fellow from an attacker. The situation is analogous to one who is pursuing a pursuer and, in so doing, damages the property of a third party. Certainly, if he can rescue his fellow with one of [the assailant's] limbs, he ought to do so … but is it not better to tell the judge and cause him to be deprived of his property, than cause him to lose one of his limbs?
>
> If the assailant is someone who regularly and frequently batters others and has done so a second and a third time, and continues to do as he pleases, and his actions clearly demonstrate his intention to assault anyone who does not do his bidding, it is a precept of the highest order for any Jew to tell the judges and ruling authorities, and ask them to stop him. And if that results in their mistreating him and confiscating all his property, the one who told [the authorities about him] has committed no offense.
>
> *Responsa R. Haim Or Zarua*, #142

R. Haim Or Zarua's adducing of the law of the pursuer in this context has interesting implications for the scope of the authorization to remand a criminal.

The dispensation to turn the criminal over to the government, being based on the law of the pursuer, is limited to situations in which there is a clear danger to human life. It does not cover crimes against property, which do not pose a danger to human life,[41] or crimes committed by those who pose little danger of reoffending, as their crimes appear to be one-time slip-ups, especially if they have expressed remorse.

Grounding this rule in the law of the pursuer has two additional implications. The first pertains to the class of those permitted to remand the criminal to the Gentile authorities. As we have seen, the law of the pursuer extends the right of self-defense to third parties, and R. Haim Or Zarua accordingly sets down that "it is a duty incumbent on everyone to tell the [Gentile] judge." That is, the right to remand a violent individual to the Gentile authorities—a halakhically irregular step—is extended to everyone. In contemporary legal terminology, we would say that, with regard to handing over a violent criminal to the authorities to be brought before a Gentile court, the halakha, on the strength of the law of the pursuer, grants standing to every member of the community.

The second consequence pertains to liability for damages that may be suffered by the criminal in being remanded to the Gentile authorities. R. Haim Or Zarua rules that if the Gentile authorities treat the said criminal harshly and confiscate all his property, the person who turned him over to

41 It is important to note that this does not mean that those who commit such crimes may never be turned over to the government; doing so, however, requires other legal justifications.

the authorities will bear no responsibility for compensating him. This determination is based on a provision of the law of the pursuer that we have not examined: a third party who strikes at the pursuer bears no liability for damages caused in the course of the defensive action, whether to the pursuer himself or to someone else. The purpose of the exemption from liability is to ensure that people are not deterred from involvement in rescue attempts by fear of liability for damages. In the words of Maimonides, "this rule is not strict law, but it is an enactment made so that one should not refrain from rescuing [his fellow] or tarry to think it over while in pursuit."[42] R. Haim Or Zarua applied this exemption to the case of someone remanding a violent criminal to the authorities.

We see, then, that the influence of the law of the pursuer both narrows and broadens the dispensation to remand violent criminals to the Gentile authorities. It narrows the dispensation by limiting it to very dangerous crimes and criminals; it broadens the scope of the dispensation by extending it to everyone in the community, and granting an exemption from liability for consequential damages to anyone who utilizes the dispensation.

### 5.2 The law of the pursuer and civil cases

Although in the halakhic literature on matters of criminal law, we do not find extensive discussion of the practical import of the law of the pursuer, there is substantially more such discussion in the area of private law that regulates rights in property, where the application of the law of the pursuer in actual practice is indeed addressed. The case we will examine deals with an act that was, according to one side, the act of a pursuer, that is, an act that threatened the pursuee's life; it was further claimed that the victims could be rescued only by harming, not the pursuer's life, but his assets and property rights.[43] The case was brought before R. Samuel di Modena (Maharashdam), a sixteenth century halakhic authority.

A group of Jewish merchants had set out to sea, and their ship was commandeered by pirates. The authorities captured some of the pirates, and said they would not be released unless the captives were freed and their goods were restored to them. The pirates were willing to free the captives, but claimed they no longer had the goods in their possession. Almost all the captive Jews declared their willingness to forgo the return of their merchandise as long as they themselves were freed, but one captive, R. Yehiel, refused to be released without his silken goods, thereby blocking the deal that would have released the whole group. The other captives wrote to the Maharashdam, asking him to require

42 *Code*, Laws concerning Wounding and Damaging 8:14.

43 Since the threat was to human life, not only to property, this falls under the rubric of the law of the pursuer rather than that of self-help.

R. Yehiel to give up his property and allow the release of the captives to go forward:

> There was an incident in which R. Joseph son of Solomon Simkhes, may his rock and redeemer protect him, was in a certain fishing vessel with other Jewish merchants ... and they were taken captive along with all they had, including the merchandise; this included silken goods belonging to R. Yehiel Shaki. The Merciful One, may He be blessed, had mercy on them and, through the intervention of our exalted majesty the king, some of the captors were arrested by the authorities from Venice, and are being held until the captive Jews and their goods are released. The Gentile captors would have been willing to release the Jews in order to redeem their uncircumcised cronies, but they insisted that the silk and other merchandise they had taken was no longer *in esse*, since each had taken his share and there was no way to restore it. The captives—the aforementioned R. Joseph and his associates—want to be freed even if they receive not a penny of their property, for they see it cannot be restored. But R. Yehiel Shaki is blocking the deal, not wanting the pirates held by the authorities to be released without giving him back his silks. This has caused the aforementioned R. Joseph and his fellow captives to cry out due to the torment of their captivity, pleading 'will it be good in God's eyes if we die on account of R. Yehiel's silk?' And they ask whether the aforementioned R. Yehiel is obligated to relinquish his claim, so that the authorities will release the uncircumcised [pirates], so that the captors free the Jews, or do we say that R. Yehiel is not obligated to do so, for why should he lose his property?
>
> *Responsa Maharashdam*, HM #344

The Maharashdam concluded that while one need not forgo his property to save someone else, the situation here was different: R. Yehiel's property was not merely an instrument by which the other captives could be saved, but was, in effect, the cause of their continued captivity. And since the captivity was endangering the lives of the captives, the law of the pursuer applied to R. Yehiel's property, and it could be forfeited to save the victim, that is, the other captives. The practical import of the law was that R. Yehiel was obligated to give up his property and allow the deal to free the captives to go forward.

The Maharashdam based his ruling on the following talmudic passage and interpretations thereof by various halakhic authorities:

> A certain man managed to get his donkey onto a ferryboat before those on the boat had disembarked. The boat was about to sink, so someone came and pushed that man's donkey into the river, and it drowned. When the case was brought before Rabbah, he declared him exempt.

> Said Abbaye to him: Was that person not rescuing himself by means of another man's money? He said to him: this one was from the outset a pursuer.
>
> bBaba Kama 117b

According to this *sugya*, a donkey that is endangering the lives of others may be cast into the river on the strength of the law of the pursuer. The donkey lacks culpability and bears no criminal responsibility. Characterizing the donkey as a pursuer severs the connection between the law of the pursuer and questions of blameworthiness and criminal responsibility, grounding it exclusively in the victim's right to life, bodily integrity, and property. Rashi's interpretation of Rabbah's ruling—"the owner of the donkey is a pursuer, intent on killing people"—is significant in this context, for he characterizes the donkey's **owner**, and not the donkey itself, as the pursuer. Rashi seems to be seeking a way to base the right to self-defense through preemptive attack on some element of blameworthiness, and therefore construes the donkey's human owner, rather than the donkey itself, as the pursuer.

Maimonides extends the talmudic ruling:

> If a ship seems likely to break apart from the weight of its load, and one of those on board goes and lightens the load by throwing some [of the cargo] into the sea, he is exempt, because it is as if the load is pursuing the passengers to kill them. And he fulfilled an important religious precept in throwing it overboard and saving the passengers.
>
> *Code*, Laws concerning Wounding and Damaging 8:15

Maimonides thus likens the case of the cargo weighing down the ship to that of the donkey weighing down the ferry; accordingly, he rules that the cargo should be thrown into the sea, and he who throws it overboard incurs no liability for damages.

R. Abraham b. David (Rabad), a contemporary and critic of Maimonides, strongly disputed this extension of the talmudic ruling. He distinguishes between the cases and rules that the cost of the property tossed into the sea is to be shared by all the ship's passengers, who must compensate the owner. In the case of the donkey on the ferry, the donkey (or its owners) can be identified as the specific factor creating the risk that the ferry will sink. By contrast, in the case of the overloaded ship, it is the combined weight of all the passengers and cargo that bears down on the ship, and it is impossible to single out one specific entity that is at fault. Hence the responsibility for the danger, and the cost of throwing the cargo overboard, must be shared by all the passengers.[44]

44 *Hasagot Haraavad* ad loc.

As to the case before him, the Maharashdam comments that both Maimonides and the Rabad would agree it was R. Yehiel and his silk that jeopardized the captives, for only R. Yehiel's stubbornness was preventing implementation of the deal that would free them. He therefore concludes:

> It is known who causes [the danger] ... hence all would concur that it is proper to compel R. Yehiel to relinquish his claim and release the uncircumcised ones [the pirates], so that they will free the captives, and he will not be their pursuer.

It is noteworthy that the Maharashdam required R. Yehiel not only to abandon his merchandise to secure the captives' release, but also to bear the entire financial burden of doing so; he could have, but did not, spread the burden among all the captives. It seems likely that the Maharashdam's ruling is rooted in his characterization of R. Yehiel as a pursuer endangering his fellows, inasmuch as he is unwilling to give up his property to allow the deal to free his fellow captives to go forward. If he is a pursuer, it is proper for him to bear the financial consequences of his actions. Despite the fact that R. Yehiel is himself a victim, the Maharashdam considers him a pursuer. His stubbornness, given the negligible chance of recovering the assets, and the high probability the captives will be released if the claim is relinquished, renders him a pursuer.

## 6 Concluding remarks

This chapter has examined the manner in which Jewish law approaches the right to self-defense: the dispensation to take the law into one's own hands for the purpose of preventing the commission of a serious crime. We looked at the conceptual frameworks invoked for discussing this issue in the general legal literature, and then surveyed the main themes and principles adduced for this purpose in the classic sources of Jewish law. We saw that the right to self-defense goes back to the earliest stages of Jewish law; it is of broad scope; and extends to third parties. Moreover, self-defense is best characterized not only as a right, but equally importantly, as an obligation. At the same time, the sources reflect several different understandings of the legal basis for self-defense. Some see it as a kind of anticipatory punishment of the offender; some see it as a means of preventing transgression, or to put it differently, a means of saving the would-be offender from carrying out a malevolent intention; and some see it as an expression of the victim's right not to have his life, person or property violated. In this context, we examined various talmudic *sugyot*, and also discovered systematic differences in approach between several medieval commentators.

The rabbinical sources, especially the talmudic, constitute a complex mosaic, emphasizing first one aspect and then another of the law of the pursuer. At times the law's main thrust and underlying justification appears to be saving the victim, at times, prevention of transgression, and at times anticipatory punishment. So in the final analysis, what is the legal foundation for the law of the pursuer in Jewish law? In light of the many and varied talmudic opinions, how are we to understand the right to self-defense? Some scholars maintain that the various sources represent different historical stages in the doctrine's development within Jewish law; they see a transition from a punitive and preventative notion to a concept based squarely on rescuing the victim. Others have tried to harmonize the sources into an integrated and consistent picture encompassing the various justifications. We cannot resolve the matter here, and must content ourselves with noting that the wealth of sources we have discussed, and the conflicting tendencies they reflect, attest to the complexity of the question of the extent to which a private individual should be permitted to preempt an offense against him by committing an offense against the would-be perpetrator. The sources do concur, however, in maintaining that a dispensation to commit such a preemptive crime should, in fact, be granted, though they do not agree on either the justification for this dispensation, or its scope and limits.

We saw that the various justifications for the right to self-defense draw on different theories of society: some centered on the individual, others emphasizing the community; some emphasizing the inner dimension—conscience and morality—and others the external and material aspect of life. The simultaneous presence of these justifications in the sources of Jewish law is not surprising, as Jewish law indeed incorporates a spectrum of stances on social and existential questions. We can, for instance, identify a number of laws grounded in the notion of individual liberty, including some explored in other chapters of this volume: the injunctions against slavery and measures enacted to limit its scope; the right of a worker to breach an employment contract and quit a job at midday[45]; the right and obligation to disobey a verdict regarded as incorrect[46]; and many others. From this perspective, the Rabbinic adage, "If someone comes to kill you, preempt this by killing him," is likely to be interpreted as establishing **the right of the individual** to defend himself against threats to his welfare. On the other hand, there are many laws that stress public and communal responsibility. Among these laws are the obligations to sustain the poor and promote social welfare[47]; the limits placed by the halakha, in certain circumstances, on freely competitive markets, for the purpose of protecting weaker merchants[48]; and similar laws. In the context of the right to self-defense, this approach will likely emphasize **the duty, incumbent**

45 See Chapter Twelve below, "Employee and Independent Contractor."
46 See Chapter Four above, "Erroneous Rulings."
47 See Chapter Nine below, "Charity and Distributive Justice."
48 See Chapter Fourteen below, "Free Market Competition."

**on all,** to come to the aid of the victim at the expense of the pursuer, especially when the latter bears responsibility for the attack. The unresolved tensions between the different halakhic sources that address the question of self-defense thus reflect broader and more general tensions within Jewish law.

## Appendix 1 The law of the pursuer during the Holocaust in Europe

The horrific situations faced by Jews as the Nazis sought their annihilation during the Second World War gave rise to unusual halakhic and legal quandaries, some of which were the subject of responsa, questions addressed to and answered by halakhic authorities. One such responsum, invoking the law of the pursuer, was posed to R. Shimon Efrati:

> Regarding a question that makes one's hair stand on end, as follows: An entire community of Jews were in a concealed bunker, hiding from the torment of the enemy, may its memory be erased, so that they would not be found by the vile accursed ones, may their memory be erased. It was clear that if they were found, they would be killed. It happened that while those evil ones carried out searches to find these unfortunates, a baby, who was among the hidden, began to cry, and there was no way to quiet him. Had his voice had been heard outside, they would all have been caught and killed. The question arose whether it would be permissible to insert a pillow into the baby's mouth to quiet him. This act posed a risk that the baby would be suffocated. After a while, someone went over and put the pillow in the baby's mouth. And after the accursed wicked ones were past [that spot], they went to remove the pillow and saw, to their dismay, that the baby had suffocated.
>
> The question, then, is whether it was permitted to put the pillow [in the baby's mouth] to save the others, or it was not permitted, and whether the man who did it, albeit inadvertently, is required to do penance for his sin.
>
> *Responsa Migei Hahariga*, #1

This question presents the polar case for the law of the pursuer: a minor, unaware of his actions, much less responsible for them, is endangering the lives of others. It is important to note that even in this difficult, out-of-the-ordinary situation, the question is posed only after-the-fact, following commission of the act; and even here, it is not the criminal nature of the act that is under review (viz., whether or not the killer of the baby should be punished), but its religious significance for the person who carried it out—must he do penance for killing the baby?

R. Efrati considers the question from several perspectives; we, of course, will focus on that of the law of the pursuer. The responsist wants to regard the infant as one who, by his cries, pursues the other occupants of the bunker and puts their lives in jeopardy, and may, accordingly, be killed. This determination, however, is neither simple nor self-evident. Above, we mentioned the talmudic dictum that a fetus which has emerged from its mother's womb and is endangering her should not be killed, for "she is being pursued by heaven," that is, she is endangered, not by the actions of the fetus, but by natural causes, hence the fetus may not be killed. This seems, on the face of it, to be the situation here. The infant's cries are the normal actions of every normal baby, and why should we not say here as well that those hiding in the bunker are being pursued 'by heaven,' not by the baby?

But R. Efrati tries to distinguish between the cases, focusing the inquiry on the outcome likely in each. Just as we must ask ourselves whether killing the pursuer will, in fact, save the person being pursued (if the answer is no, the pursuer must not be killed), we must also ask whether refraining from killing the pursuer will leave the pursuer alive. In most cases, it is clear that not killing the pursuer will, in fact, leave him alive. The situation, then, is one where two lives hang in the balance. The pursuer's life must be weighed against the life of the pursuee, and unless it is a case of 'pursued by heaven,' where the human pursuer does not create the danger, the life of the pursuee takes precedence. That is the usual situation. But in the exceptional case where the **pursuer** will be killed in any event—even if we do not kill him to defend the pursuee—then it is clear that the life of the pursuee takes preference and the pursuer should be killed, even if he does not create the danger himself, but it is produced 'by heaven.'

In the case at hand, R. Efrati argues, we are confronted by two options: (1) to kill the baby, thereby increasing the chances that the bunker's other occupants will be saved, or (2) not to kill the baby and thereby jeopardize the lives of everyone in the bunker, including the baby himself, since if the Nazis find the bunker, they will in all likelihood kill all its occupants, including the baby. Under these circumstances, there is no real chance that the baby can be saved, and therefore, R. Efrati concludes, it is permitted to kill him even though his act of 'pursuit' is involuntary.

This unusual state of affairs led R. Efrati to conclude further that killing the baby, though permitted, was not required:

> In such a situation, one who is pursued and who does not want to kill the pursuer and is thus killed by him "shall be called holy" (Isa. 4:3), and fulfills [the verse] "and I shall be sanctified amidst the children of Israel" (Lev. 22:32). Accordingly, those people (and there were such cases in my family, may God avenge their blood), who did not want to save their lives by suffocating a Jewish child, thereby sanctified the name of God. But one who did do it need have no pangs of conscience, for he acted in accordance with the law in order to save Jewish lives.

## Appendix 2 The law of the pursuer and anti-terror operations

The halakhic analysis of the law of the pursuer took a dramatic turn during the twentieth century, coming to be a routine aspect of daily life in the land of Israel, and subsequently, the State of Israel. Operations against terrorists, and especially against the wider circles in which they moved, often raised moral and legal dilemmas; and halakhic decisors rendered opinions on the proper way to conduct such operations. The law of the pursuer was one of the central elements considered in this context. Here, we will present portions of one well-known treatment of the subject, which focused on the Kibiya operation.

On October 13, 1953, Arab assailants from the vicinity of Kibiya—an Arab village in Samaria—threw a grenade into a Jewish house in the immigrant settlement of Yehud. A mother and her two children were killed as they slept. The incident, which came in the wake of a string of murderous attacks in the region, led to a retaliatory operation by the Israel Defense Forces. On October 14, Israeli forces attacked Kibiya, which was situated a fair distance from the cease-fire line. More than fifty residents of the village were killed, and forty houses were destroyed. The operation provoked world-wide outrage. Israel's explanation failed to satisfy the international community, and the United Nations Security Council strongly reprimanded Israel. Much was written about the incident in the press and by ethicists. R. Saul Yisraeli discussed the halakhic issues arising from the incident in a responsum.[1]

The central question he grapples with is the status of anti-terrorist military operations likely to cause injuries to residents of the communities within which the terrorists reside. He begins by considering the possibility of justifying such actions as punishment for prior attacks. He concludes that the Arab population's support for terror operations against the Jewish state could not justify punitive actions that involved the taking of human lives: "in practice, there is no adequate basis for permitting an operation against a community that does not fulfill its obligation to remove the murderers from its midst, as long as they can allege that this is due to fear or compulsion and so forth."

He next considers deterrence:

> The population of the Arab border villages knowingly provides cover for the murderous gangs, enabling them to carry out their deeds without fear of punishment. Since it is clear that these gangs can be regarded not only as murderers, on account of their past actions, but also as pursuers, on account of their predilections [to act thus] vis-à-vis the future, the population that assists them, providing them all

1 *Amud Hayemini*, #16.

> manner of support, falls under the category of those who assist a pursuer to commit acts of murder.... It is clear that their providing this assistance broadens the base for [the gangs'] future activities, so that the number of attacks will grow as a result of this support provided by the populace. It is necessary, therefore, to clarify the law with respect to one who assists a pursuer, providing him cover so he can carry out his murderous activities unimpeded.
>
> *Amud Hayemini*, #16

According to R. Yisraeli, applying the law of the pursuer to a population that supports terror raises two key legal questions: (1) Does the law of the pursuer also apply to someone who assists the pursuer indirectly; that is, is the victim permitted to strike at those who support the pursuer who is trying to kill him? The premise is that the Arab residents of the villages in question encourage the terrorists and provide them with the logistical support and infrastructure they need in order to carry out their attacks, but do not themselves engage directly in terrorist activities. (2) Does the law of the pursuer also apply in the case of someone compelled against his will to endanger the lives of others? This question is mainly about the children in the said Arab villages, who may be part of the society that supports the terrorists, but certainly do not themselves do so as a matter of conscious choice.

The complexity of the first question stems from the fact that according to Jewish law, one who abets a murder is not subject to the punishment of death imposed by the court as is the murderer himself. Hence it is not clear that the victim should be permitted to kill someone assisting the pursuer. After analyzing the legal sources relevant to the law of the pursuer, R. Yisraeli concludes that the desideratum of saving the victim's life provides sufficient justification for killing one who assists the pursuer.

More problematic in R. Yisraeli's view is the prospect that military actions against terrorists might also injure children. It would be preferable, of course, to give innocent parties advance warning of the impending counter-terror operation and allow them to leave, but doing so would undoubtedly cause the operation to fail. In effect, the terrorists, by hiding among the villagers, with children in their midst, turn the entire population, children included, into a shield against military action, thereby causing them to be regarded as helping the terrorists hide and prepare for their next attack. Does the fact that terrorists use the populace—adults and children alike—as a human shield justify attacking it? In R. Yisraeli's opinion, the matter is by no means clear:

> At first glance, it seems plain that if we forbid the action, the children wind up helping the pursuer, serving as instruments by means of which the pursuer can carry out his malevolent plan; and thus they too are like pursuers, as explained above, for one who assists a pursuer

> and causes murder [indirectly] is considered a pursuer himself. But [here] that assistance is not conscious: they do not provide it, but rather, it is the pursuer who draws support from them. This is like the case of a pursuer who hides behind someone else against that person's will, where even though that person is the mechanism by which the pursuer conceals himself, it would seem that in any event that person should not be injured, since he does not want to [shield the pursuer].

R. Yisraeli analyzes the dispute between Maimonides and the Rabad, discussed above, regarding the case of the cargo weighing down the ship and threatening to sink it. According to R. Yisraeli, they disagree as to the fundamental question of whether the law of the pursuer applies to a factor that endangers human life, but does not do so consciously or voluntarily:

> We can say that our case too hinges on this difference of opinion. According to Maimonides, even these children fall under the law of the pursuer, even though they are acting under compulsion ... but according to the Rabad, who maintains that one who is compelled to pursue does not fall under the law of the pursuer, it follows that these children do not fall under the law of the pursuer.

But in attending to the distinction between the cargo, which directly creates the danger for the ship's passengers, and the children, who do not directly create the danger but simply prevent a strike at the terrorists, R. Yisraeli reaches a different conclusion. He argues that the sources allow for applying the law of the pursuer to one who assists a pursuer, and some halakhic authorities allow for its application to one who unwillingly creates a danger that jeopardizes the lives of others. Nowhere, however, is the law of the pursuer applied where both conditions are fulfilled. He concludes that the law of the pursuer cannot justify military operations against terrorists that entail injury to children in whose homes the terrorists are hiding out. The operations may be needed for self-defense, but there has been no demonstration that the lives of the terror victims take precedence over the lives of the children compelled to serve as human shields.

Notwithstanding the foregoing, R. Yisraeli notes that the law of the pursuer is not the proper legal prism through which to analyze the status of retaliatory operations against terrorists. By its nature, the law of the pursuer is pertinent to civil and criminal law; retaliatory operations, in contrast, are an element of a sovereign state's battle against its enemies. The appropriate legal context, therefore, is the law of warfare, not the law of the pursuer. And where there is a state of war, different rules apply with regard to injuring enemy soldiers and the enemy population:

> Thus far we have considered the matter from the perspective of everyday life. But there is another way to approach the subject, namely,

> to see it as an act of war. For the law permits war against Gentiles, and [where war is concerned], the prohibition against injury to human life is of necessity set aside. Moreover, in war there is no obligation to draw fine distinctions between one life and another. Even though it is forbidden, after conquering an enemy city, to kill its women and children ... it is clear that the prohibition applies only after the city is conquered and subdued; but during the course of the war, while the city is besieged and so forth, there is no obligation—indeed, it is impossible—to be meticulous about this. Thus we must clarify whether an operation of the sort in question can be considered warfare.

In effect, R. Yisraeli is distinguishing between the dilemmas raised by political sovereignty from those addressed in the classic analyses of the law of the pursuer. The law of the pursuer can be adduced as a relevant halakhic category vis-à-vis cases ordinarily covered by the criminal law, but R. Yisraeli doubts its contemporary applicability in the context of laws governing the conduct of sovereign states. He takes war to be a situation applying only to entities with political sovereignty, and characterized by sui generis rules. Decisions pertaining to wartime dilemmas, therefore, must rest on considerations very different from those that define the parameters of pursuer situations.[2]

Whether or not the law of the pursuer is a suitable category under which to consider the IDF's retaliatory actions against terrorists and the villages that harbor them, sovereign life in the State of Israel has raised other questions, numerous and varied, that have renewed and reinvigorated the law of the pursuer, which had been dormant for centuries. These questions rendered the law relevant and of considerable pragmatic import. When halakhic decisors are called upon to consider such questions as security service interrogation of captured terrorists, 'targeted assassination,' and the treatment of terrorists regarding as 'ticking bombs' and their abettors, they look to the law of the *rodef* for guidance on the boundaries between the forbidden and the permitted.

2 In that, as we saw, its focus is preservation of the individual's life and physical integrity (and according to some views, his religious integrity), the law of the pursuer differs from both the law of the informer and the laws of war, the object of which is preservation of the community and its way of life.

# List of halakhic authorities and scholars

R. Aaron b. Joseph Halevi (Spain c. 1235–c. 1303), Talmud commentator, decisor

R. Abdallah Abraham Joseph Somekh (Baghdad, 1813–1889), responsist

R. Abraham b. David (Rabad; Raavad), (France, c. 1120–c.1198), Talmud commentator, responsist, critic of Maimonides

R. Abraham b. Solomon Akra (Italy, late 16th c.), author of *Meharerei Nemeirim*

R. Abraham ibn Ezra (Spain, 1089–1165), Bible commentator, poet, philosopher, grammarian, astronomer.

R. Abraham Isaac Kook (Greiva [Courland] 1865–Jerusalem 1935), influential religious thinker and responsist, first Ashkenazic chief rabbi in the land of Israel

R. Abraham Isaiah Karelitz (Hazon Ish), (Kosova 1878–Bnei Brak 1953), leading haredi decisor

R. Aha of Shabha (Babylonia, 8th c.), one of the greatest scholars of the Geonic period, author of the *Sheiltot*, the first post-talmudic halakhic work

Arukh Hashulhan see R. Yehiel Mikhel Epstein

R. Aryeh Grossnass (1912–1996)

R. Arye Leib Heller (Galicia, 1745–1813), author of *Ketzot Hahoshen*, a seminal commentary on *Shulhan Arukh*, HM

R. Asher b. Yehiel (Asheri, Rosh), (Germany 1250–Toledo 1327), eminent decisor, responsist, and Talmud commentator, authored *Piskei Harosh*, a widely-used summary of talmudic rulings

Asher Gulak (Dankira, Latvia 1881–land of Israel 1940), one of the founders of modern academic study of Jewish law, professor of Jewish law at the Hebrew University

Bah see R. Joel Sirkes

Beit Yosef see R. Joseph Caro

R. Bezalel Ashkenazi (Egypt c. 1520–Jerusalem c. 1592), author of *Shita Mekubetzet*, an anthology of commentaries on the Talmud

R. Chaim Ozer Grodzinski (Ivye [Belorussia] 1863–Vilna 1940), preeminent decisor, responsist, leader of the ultra-Orthodox community, one of the founders of Agudath Yisrael

R. David b. Samuel Halevi (Taz), (Ludmir 1586–Lemberg 1667), author of *Turei Zahav* commentary on the *Shulhan Arukh*

R. David ibn Avi Zimra (Radbaz), (Spain 1479–Safed 1573), Talmud commentator, chief rabbi in Egypt for decades, prolific responsist

R. David Pardo (Venice 1719–Jerusalem 1792), author of *Hasdei David* commentary on the Tosefta

R. David Tzvi Hoffman (Verbo [Slovakia] 1843–Berlin 1921), scholar, commentator, leader of German Orthodoxy

Rabbenu Efraim of El-Kala [North Africa], a student of Alfasi

R. Efraim b. Aaron Navon (Constantinople 1677–1735), decisor and responsist, author of *Mahane Efraim*

R. Eliezer b. Joel Halevi of Bonn (Rabia, Raavya), (Germany, c. 1140–c. 1220), Tosafist, liturgical poet

R. Eliezer b. Nathan (Raban; Raavan), (Germany, 1090–1170), Tosafist, liturgical poet
R. Eliezer Waldenburg (Jerusalem, 1915–2006), influential responsist and decisor, authority on bio-medical halakhic issues
R. Elijah b. Haim (Raanah), (Turkey, 1530–1610), responsist
R. Elijah b. Solomon of Vilna (Gra, Vilna Gaon), (Vilna, 1720–1797), acclaimed halakhic leader, one of the greatest eighteenth century halakhic minds, commentator of encyclopedic breadth, opponent of Hasidism
Ephraim Elimelech Urbach (Poland 1912–Israel 1991), scholar of rabbinical literature and history of the talmudic and medieval periods
R. Ezekiel Landau (Opatow 1713–Prague 1793), author of *Responsa Noda Biyehuda*, leading decisor, chief rabbi of Prague
Rabbenu Gershom b. Judah (Light of the Exile), (Metz 960–c. Mayence 1028), one of the founding halakhic authorities in Ashkenaz, enacted important communal ordinances, authored responsa, commentaries, and liturgical poetry
R. Hai b. Sherira Gaon (Babylonia, 939–1038), Talmud commentator, last head of the Pumbedita academy, decisor, responsist, and influential shaper of halakhic thinking
R. Haim b. Isaac Alfandari (the Younger), (Constantinople, mid 17th c.–Jerusalem 18th c.), kabbalist
R. Haim b. Menahem Algazi (Turkey, c. 1640–c. 1710), author of *Bnei Hayai*, novellae on the *Shulhan Arukh*
R. Haim Benveniste (Turkey, 1603–1673), author of *Shiurei Kneset Hagedola*, an anthology of halakhic rulings
R. Haim David Halevi (Jerusalem 1924–Israel 1998), Sefardic chief rabbi of Tel Aviv-Jaffa from the 1970s to the 1990s
Haim H. Cohn (Lubeck 1911–Jerusalem 2002), Israel Supreme Court justice, scholar of Jewish law
R. Haim Halberstamm of Sanz (Tarnogrod 1793–Sanz 1876), decisor, responsist, hasidic rebbe
R. Haim Hezekiah Medini (Jerusalem 1832–Hebron 1904), author of *Sdei Hemed*, a comprehensive halakhic encyclopedia, served as rabbi in the Crimea for decades, and later, as rabbi of Hebron
R. Haim Joseph David Azoulay (Hida), (Jerusalem 1724–Livorno 1806), decisor, kabbalist, historian, bibliographer
R. Haim Or Zarua (Germany, 13th c.), son of R. Isaac of Vienna (Riaz); student of the Maharam of Rothenburg, responsist
R. Haim Palagi of Smyrna (Smyrna, 1788–1869), prominent decisor
Rabbenu Hananel b. Hushiel (Kairouan [North Africa], died c. 1056), Talmud commentator
Hatam Sofer — see R. Moses Sofer
Hazon Ish — see R. Abraham Isaiah Karelitz
Hida — see R. Haim Joseph David Azoulay
ibn Migash — see R. Joseph ibn Migash
R. Immanuel Jakobovits (Koenigsberg 1921–England 1999), a pioneer in the field of Jewish biomedical ethics and chief rabbi of the United Kingdom from 1967–1991
Don Isaac Abarbanel (variant: Abrabanel), (Lisbon 1437–Italy 1508), Bible commentator, philosopher, royal financier

R. Isaac Alfasi (Rif), (El-Kala [North Africa] 1013–Lucena 1103), one of the first codifiers, and author of *Sefer Hahalakhot*, a classic compendium of the Babylonian Talmud's rulings

R. Isaac Arama (Spain c. 1420–Italy 1494), Bible commentator, philosopher, homilist

R. Isaac b. Abraham (the Younger) (Ritzba) (France, d. 1209), brother of the famed Rash of Sens (R. Samson b. Abraham), Tosafist, headed the yeshiva at Dampierre after R. Isaac the Elder's death

R. Isaac b. Asher (Riva), (Germany c.1055–c. 1130), one of Rashi's preeminent students, first Tosafist in Germany

R. Isaac b. Moses of Vienna (Riaz, Or Zarua), (Germany, c. 1180–c. 1260), author of the *Or Zarua*

R. Isaac b. Samuel of Dampierre (France, 12th c.), known as Ri (the Elder), great-grandson of Rashi, and one of the most prolific Tosafists

R. Isaac b. Sheshet Perfet (Ribash), (Spain 1326–Algiers 1408), prolific and influential responsist

R. Isaac of Corbeil (France 1210–1280), eminent Tosafist and codifier, author of *Sefer Mitzvot Katan*

R. Isaac the Elder see R. Isaac b. Samuel of Dampierre

R. Isaac Jacob Weiss (Hungary 1902–Jerusalem 1989), responsist, head of Eda Haredit rabbinical court in Jerusalem

R. Isaac Judah Schmelkes (Galicia, 1828–1905), headed rabbinate in Brzezany, Przemysl, and Lemberg, author of *Responsa Beit Yitzhak.*

R. Isaac Liebes (d. New York 2000)

R. Isaiah Horowitz (Shela), (Prague c. 1565–Tiberias 1630), mystic, homilist

R. Israel Isserlein (Trumat Hadeshen), (Regensburg 1390–Wiener-Neustadt 1460), leading decisor of 15th c. Ashkenaz, responsist

R. Israel Meir Kagan of Radin (Chofetz Chaim), (Zhetel [Dvorets] 1838–Radin 1933), known by the name of his seminal work on the laws of defamation, author of the *Mishna Brura*, a commentary on the Orah Haim section of the *Shulhan Arukh*

R. Issachar Ber Eilenburg (Poznan 1550–Austerlitz 1623), Talmud commentator

R. Jacob b. Asher (Tur, Baal Haturim), (Germany 1269–Spain 1343). Fled Germany with his father, the Rosh, settling in Spain; author of the seminal four-part code *Arbaa Turim*

R. Jacob b. Moses Lorberbaum of Lissa (Poland, c. 1762–1832), author of numerous works, including *Netivot Hamishpat* commentary on the Hoshen Mishpat section of the *Shulhan Arukh*

R. Jacob Emden (Yaavetz), (Altona, 1697–1796), commentator and responsist, critic of claims regarding the Zohar's provenance, anti-Sabbatean polemicist

R. Jacob Ettlinger (Karlsruhe 1798–Altona 1871), commentator, responsist, leader of German Orthodoxy

R. Jacob Joshua Falk (Pnei Yehoshua), (Cracow 1680–Offenbach 1756), Talmud commentator, opponent of Sabbateanism

R. Jacob of Marvège (France, late 12th–13th c.)

R. Jacob of Orleans (d. England 1189), Tosafist and student of Rabbenu Tam; killed at the coronation of Richard I (the Lionhearted)

R. Jacob Reischer (Bachofen), (Prague c. 1670–Metz c. 1736), responsist

R. Jacob Tam (Rabbenu Tam), (France, 1100–1171), grandson of Rashi and brother of the Rashbam, leading Tosafist, decisor, and poet

R. Joel Sirkes (Bah), (Lublin 1561–Cracow 1640), author of the *Bayit Hadash* commentary on the *Tur*, responsist
R. Joel Teitelbaum (Sighet 1887–New York 1979), Satmarer Rebbe, responsist
R. Joseph b. Solomon Colon (Maharik), (France 1420–Padua 1480), responsist
R. Joseph B. Soloveitchik (Pruzhany 1905–Boston 1993), talmudic scholar and philosopher, leader of American modern Orthodoxy
R. Joseph Babad (Tarnopol c. 1800–Safed 1874), author of *Minhat Hinukh*
R. Joseph Caro (Spain 1488–Safed 1575), preeminent codifier, author of the *Shulhan Arukh* and *Beit Yosef*, responsist
R. Joseph di Trani (Maharit), (Safed 1568–Constantinople 1639), responsist and leader of communities in Egypt and Turkey
R. Joseph Habiba (Nimukei Yosef), (Spain, early 15th c.), Talmud commentator
R. Joseph ibn Migash (Spain 1077–1141), Alfasi's student and successor as head of the Lucena yeshiva, Talmud commentator, responsist
R. Joseph Saul Nathanson (Brzezany 1810–Lemberg 1875), prominent decisor and communal leader, chief rabbi of Lemberg, prolific responsist
R. Joshua Boaz (b. Spain, d. Italy, 1557), author of *Shiltei Hagiborim* commentary on Alfasi's *Sefer Hahalakhot*
R. Joshua Falk Katz (Lublin 1550–Lemberg 1614), author of the *Sefer Meirat Einayim* (*Sema*) commentary on the *Shulhan Arukh*, and the *Derisha* and the *Perisha*, twin commentaries on the *Tur*
R. Judah Ayash (b. Morocco–d. Jerusalem 1760), head of Algiers rabbinical court, decisor and responsist
R. Judah Gershuni (Poland 1908–Israel 2000)
R. Judah Loew b. Bezalel (Maharal) of Prague (Poznan c. 1525–Prague 1609), talmudist, philosopher, communal leader, homilist
R. Judah the Pious of Regensburg (Speyer 1150–Regensburg 1217), mystic, author of the ethical treatise *Sefer Hasidim*

| | |
|---|---|
| Maharal | see R. Judah Loew b. Bezalel |
| Maharam | see R. Meir of Rothenburg |
| Maharashdam | see R. Samuel di Modena |
| Maharit | see R. Joseph di Trani |
| Maharsha | see R. Samuel Halevi Edels |
| Maharshal | see R. Solomon Luria |
| Maharsham | see R. Shalom Mordekhai Schwadron |
| Maimonides | see R. Moses b. Maimon |

R. Masud Hai Rokeiah (Smyrna 1689–land of Israel 1749), halakhic leader of various Mediterranean communities, including Leghorn and Tripoli
R. Meir b. Todros Halevi Abulafia (Rama), (Burgos c. 1170–Toledo 1244), Talmud commentator, authority on the masoretic text of the Scriptures
R. Meir Eisenstadt, (1670 Poland–1744 Austria), author of *Responsa Panim Meirot*, Talmud commentator, rabbi of Eisenstadt and the famed "Seven Communities"
R. Meir Hakohen of Rothenburg (late 13th–early 14th c.) author of *Hagahot Maimoniot*, student of the Maharam of Rothenburg
R. Meir of Lublin (Lublin, 1558–c. 1618), responsist
R. Meir Posner (Poland c. 1728–Danzig 1807), decisor, author of *Beit Meir*
R. Meir of Rothenburg (Maharam), (Worms 1215–Ensisheim 1293), Tosafist, decisor, leader of 13th c. Ashkenaz; teacher of R. Asher b. Yehiel

R. Meir Simha Hakohen of Dvinsk (Lithuania 1843–1926), author of the *Meshekh Hokhma* commentary on the Pentateuch and the *Or Sameiah* commentary on Maimonides' *Mishne Torah*, Talmud commentator, philosopher

Meiri see R. Menahem b. Solomon Hameiri

Menachem Elon (b. Dusseldorf 1923), scholar, prominent advocate of the 'Mishpat Ivri' approach to the halakha, Israel Supreme Court justice

R. Menahem b. Solomon Hameiri (Meiri), (Provence, 1249–1316), Talmud commentator

R. Menahem Kasher (Poland 1895–US 1983)

R. Menahem Mendel Haim Landau of Strykow (Poland 1862–Otwock 1936)

R. Menahem Mendel Krochmal (Cracow 1600–Nikolsburg 1671), author of *Responsa Tzemah Tzedek*

R. Meshulam Rata (Roth), (Horodenka [Galicia] 1875–Israel 1962), rabbi of Czernowitz during the Holocaust years, responsist

R. Mordekhai b. Hillel of Nuremburg (Germany, 1250–1298), author of the *Mordekhai*, which supplemented Alfasi's *Sefer Hahalakhot* with rulings of Ashkenazic authorities, was martyred with his family in the Rindfleish massacres

R. Moses b. Jacob of Coucy (France, 13th c.), Tosafist, author of *Sefer Mitzvot Gadol* (*Semag*)

R. Moses b. Maimon (Rambam, Maimonides), (Cordoba, Spain 1138–Fostat, Egypt 1204), preeminent commentator, codifier, responsist, philosopher, communal leader and physician. His codification of the law, the *Mishne Torah*, also known as the *Yad Hahazaka*, is herein cited as the *Code*

R. Moses b. Nahman (Nahmanides) (Gerona 1194–land of Israel 1270), commentator on the Pentateuch and Talmud, responsist, kabbalist, communal leader

R. Moses Feinstein (Uzda [Belorussia] 1895–New York 1986), responsist, decisor, halakhic authority for North American Orthodoxy

R. Moses Halevi Mintz (Maharam Mintz),( Germany c. 1415–c. 1480), decisor and responsist

R. Moses Isserles (Rema), (Cracow, 1530–1572), authoritative glossator of the *Shulhan Arukh* for Ashkenazic Jewry, decisor and responsist

R. Moses Khalfon Hakohen (Djerba, 1874–1950), author of *Responsa Shoel Venishal*, chief rabbi of Djerba

R. Moses Margalit (Keidan [Lithuania] 1710–Brody [Galicia] 1781), author of *Pnei Moshe* commentary on the Jerusalem Talmud

R. Moses Sofer (Hatam Sofer), (Frankfurt 1762–Pressburg (Bratislava) 1839), leading decisor and responsist, led struggle against the Haskala and the incipient Reform movement

Moshe Silberg (Skaudvile [Lithuania] 1900–Jerusalem 1975), jurisprudential scholar, Israel Supreme Court justice

R. Naftali Z. Berlin (Netziv), (Mir 1817–Warsaw 1893), Bible commentator, responsist, headed the renowned Volozhin Yeshiva for decades

Nahmanides see R. Moses b. Nahman

R. Nathan b. Yehiel of Rome (Italy 1035–1110), authored the *Arukh*, a dictionary of talmudic terms

R. Nathan of Igra (Italy, died first half of the 16th c.), one of the leading Italian decisors, rabbinical court judge in Venice in 1531

Netziv see R. Naftali Z. Berlin

Nimukei Yosef see R. Joseph Habiba

R. Nissim b. Reuben Gerondi (=of Gerona) (Ran), (Spain 1310–c.1375), decisor, Talmud commentator, responsist, and philosopher

R. Nissim Solomon Algazi (Turkey c. 1610–Jerusalem c. 1683), leading opponent of Shabbetai Zvi

R. Ovadiah of Bartenura [Bertinoro], (Italy c. 1445–Jerusalem c. 1516), author of highly popular commentary on the Mishnah

R. Ovadiah Yosef (b. Baghdad 1920), decisor, prolific responsist, served as Rishon Lezion (chief rabbi of Israel's Sefardic/Mizrahi community) from 1973–1983, and remains its foremost spiritual and intellectual leader

Rabad see R. Abraham b. David
Raban see R. Eliezer b. Nathan
Rabbenu Tam see R. Jacob Tam
Rabia see R. Eliezer b. Joel Halevi
Radbaz see R. David ibn Avi Zimra
Rama see R. Meir b. Todros Halevi Abulafia
Rambam see R. Moses b. Maimon
Ramban see R. Moses b. Nahman
Ran see R. Nissim b. Reuben Gerondi
Rashba see R. Solomon b. Adret
Rashbam see R. Samuel b. Meir
Rashbash see R. Solomon b. Shimon Duran
Rashbatz see R. Shimon b. Tzemah Duran
Rashi see R. Solomon b. Isaac
Rema see R. Moses Isserles
Rif see R. Isaac Alfasi
Ritba see R. Yomtov of Seville
Rosh see R. Asher b. Yehiel

R. Saadia Gaon (Egypt 882–Sura, Babylonia 942), communal leader, biblical commentator, grammarian, and philosopher

R. Samuel b. Meir (Rashbam) of Ramerupt (France, 1085–c. 1174), Bible and Talmud commentator, Tosafist, grandson of Rashi, brother of Rabbenu Tam

R. Samuel b. Moses Kalai (Turkey, 16th c.), author of *Mishpetei Shmuel*

R. Samuel di Modena (Maharashdam), (Salonika, 1506–1589), halakhic authority throughout the Balkans and beyond, communal leader, prolific responsist

R. Samuel Halevi Edels (Maharsha), (Poznan 1555–Ostrog 1631), Talmud commentator, also wrote a commentary on the Talmud's Aggadic material

R. Saul Lieberman (Motol [Belorussia] 1898–Israel 1983), commentator on the Jerusalem Talmud and the Tosefta

R. Saul Yisraeli (Slutzk 1909–Israel 1995), decisor, author of *Amud Hayemini* on the issues arising from Israel's statehood

R. Shabtai Hakohen (Shakh), (Vilna 1621–Holleschau [Moravia] c. 1662), decisor, author of the *Siftei Kohen* commentary on the *Shulhan Arukh*

Shakh see R. Shabtai Hakohen

R. Shalom Mordekhai Schwadron of Brzezany (Maharsham), (Galicia, 1835–1911), eminent decisor and responsist

Shela see R. Isaiah Horowitz

R. Shimon b. Tzemah Duran (Rashbatz), (Majorca 1361–Algiers 1444), decisor, responsist, and communal leader

R. Shimon Efrati (Bessarabia 1908–Israel 1988), rabbi of Bendery, rabbi of Holocaust survivors in post-war Warsaw
R. Shimon Kaiara of Basra (Babylonia, 8th c.), author of *Halakhot Gedolot*
Shita Mekubetzet see R. Bezalel Ashkenazi
R. Shlomo Goren (Zambrow [Poland] 1917–Israel 1994), Ashkenazic chief rabbi of Israel from 1972 to 1983
R. Shneur Zalman of Liadi (Baal Hatanya), (Liozna [Belorussia] 1735–Piena [Belorussia] 1813), founder of Chabad hasidism
Shulhan Arukh see R. Joseph Caro
Simha Assaf (Osofsky), (Lyuban [Belorussia] 1888–Jerusalem 1953), scholar of rabbinical literature, esp. the Geonic period, Supreme Court justice
R. Solomon b. Adret (Rashba), (Barcelona, 1235–1310), Talmud commentator, responsist, leader of Spanish Jewry
R. Solomon b. Isaac (Rashi), (Troyes, 1040–1105), greatest of the Bible and Talmud commentators, communal leader, responsist
R. Solomon b. Shimon Duran (Rashbash), (Algiers, 1400–1467), responsist and philosopher
R. Solomon Efraim of Lunschitz (Leczyca [Poland] 1550–Prague 1619), Bible commentator and homilist, author of the *Kli Yakar* commentary on the Pentateuch
R. Solomon Kluger of Brody (Galicia, 1785–1869), prolific responsist and commentator, defended traditionalism against the Haskala
R. Solomon Luria (Maharshal), (Poland, 1510–1573), author of *Yam Shel Shlomo* commentary on the Talmud, decisor
R. Solomon Zalman Auerbach (Jerusalem, 1910–1995), decisor, wrote extensively on halakhic issues pertaining to agriculture, technology, and medicine; responsist
Trumat Hadeshen see R. Israel Isserlein
Tur see R. Jacob b. Asher
R. Tzvi Hirsh Kalischer (Lissa [Leszno] 1795–Thorn 1874), proto-Zionist thinker and activist, opponent of the Reform movement
R. Vidal of Tolosa (Spain, 1283–1369), author of *Magid Mishne* commentary on Maimonides' *Mishne Torah*
Vilna Gaon see R. Elijah b. Solomon of Vilna
R. Yair Haim Bacharach (Moravia 1638–Worms 1702), important decisor, author of *Responsa Havat Yair*, prolific writer
R. Yehiel Mikhel Epstein (Bobruisk 1829–Navarodok 1908), author of *Arukh Hashulhan*, codifier and decisor
R. Yekutiel Asher Enzil Zusmir (Mahariz Enzil) of Stryj and Przemysl (Poland, 19th c.)
R. Yekutiel Judah Teitelbaum of Sighet (1808–1883) (Yetev Lev), hasidic rebbe, great-grandfather of R. Joel Teitelbaum
R. Yomtov Lipmann Heller (Wallerstein 1579–Cracow 1654), commentator on the Mishnah, communal leader and rabbinical activist
R. Yomtov Lipmann Muhlhausen (Prague, 14–15th c.), scholar and polemicist
R. Yomtov of Seville (Ritba), (Spain, c. 1250–1330), one of the foremost Talmud commentators, responsist